CONTENTS

VOLUME III Inventions and Technological Things

EDITED BY RICHARD MENKE

KEYWORDS

1. Acoustics
2. Africa
3. Aniline Dyes
4. Arnold, Matthew
5. Automobile
6. Bell, Alexander Graham
7. Bicycle
8. Bose, Jagadish Chandra
9. Candle
10. Carlyle, Thomas
11. Crime
12. Crystal Palace
13. Dickens, Charles
14. Dyes
15. Edison, Thomas
16. Electric Lighting
17. Electricity
18. Eliot, George
19. Gas Lighting
20. Great Exhibition (1851)
21. Health
22. Hill, Rowland
23. Horseless Carriage
24. Ice Skating
25. Illumination
26. Imperialism
27. Industrial Revolution
28. Invention
29. Letters
30. Lighting
31. Linotype
32. Locomotive
33. Lombroso, Cesare
34. Machine Gun
35. Machinery
36. Matches
37. Maxim Gun
38. Meat
39. Mill, John Stuart
40. Miranda Pianista
41. Mobility
42. Optics
43. Patent
44. Phonograph
45. Phosphorus Matches
46. Photograph
47. Pianola
48. Player Piano
49. Pneumatic Tubes
50. Post Office
51. Postage Stamp
52. Postal Reform
53. Printing
54. Progress
55. Railway
56. Refrigeration
57. Roentgen Rays
58. Roofless Railway Carriage
59. Ruskin, John
60. Sewing Machine
61. Skating Rink
62. Steam Engine
63. Stereoscope
64. Technology

BIBLIOGRAPHY

Primary sources

Arnold, M., *Culture and Anarchy* [1869], in *The Complete Prose Works of Matthew Arnold*, ed. R.H. Super, 11 vols (Ann Arbor: University of Michigan Press, 1960–77), vol. 5, pp. 85–256.

Bennett, A.R., *On the Telephoning of Great Cities* (London: Whittaker, 1892).

Brewster, D., *The Stereoscope* (London: Murray, 1856).

[Carlyle, T.], ['Signs of the Times']. *Edinburgh Review*, 49 (June 1829), pp. 439–59.

Carpenter, W.B., 'On the Zoetrope and Its Antecedents', *The Student and Intellectual Observer of Science, Literature, and Art*, 1 (1868), 427–444, 2 (1869), pp. 24–31, 110–128.

Conder, F.R., 'The Best Friend of the Working Man', *Fraser's Magazine*, new series 19 (1879), pp. 225–237.

[Cunningham, H.], 'Horseless Carriages', *Edinburgh Review*, 183 (1896), pp. 408–427.

The Crystal Palace Exhibition Illustrated Catalogue, London (1851) (New York: Dover Publications, 1970).

Dickens, C., *Bleak House* [1852–53], ed. G. Ford and S. Monod (New York: Norton, 1977).

———, *The Letters of Charles Dickens*, Pilgrim edn, ed. M. House, G. Storey, K. Tillotson, et al. 12 vols (Oxford: Clarendon Press, 1965–2002).

———, 'A Preliminary Word', *Household Words*, 1 (30 March 1850), 1–2.

[Dickens, C., and R.H. Horne], 'The Great Exhibition and the Little One', *Household Words*, 3 (5 July 1851), pp. 356–60.

[Dickens, C., and W.H. Wills], 'Valentine's Day at the Post Office', *Household Words*, 1 (30 March 1850), pp. 6–12.

Donovan, C.H.W., *With Wilson in Matabeleland, or Sport and War in Zambesia* (London: Henry, 1894).

'Electric Lighting', *Cornhill Magazine*, 39 (1879), pp. 157–172.

Eliot, G., *Felix Holt: The Radical* [1866], ed. L. Mugglestone (London: Penguin, 1995).

'A Few Weeks from Home: The Electric Telegraph', *Chambers Edinburgh Journal*, 9 (25 July 1840), pp. 209–210.

Friswell, J.H., 'A Journey Underground', *Once a Week* (20 Sept. 1862), pp. 361–363.

Garvey, M.A., *The Silent Revolution, or the Future Effects of Steam and Electricity upon the Conditions of Mankind* (London: Cash, 1852).

Griffith, M., 'An Electric Eye: The Marvellous Discovery of an Eastern Professor Which Distances the Röntgen Rays As They Distance Photography', *Pearson's Magazine* (December 1896), pp. 749–756.

Harrison, J., 'Food Committee', *Journal of the Society of Arts*, 22 (28 Nov. 1873), pp. 24–29.

Harwood, J.A., *Rinks and Rollers* (London: Routledge, [1876]).

Hill, R., *Postal Reform: Its Importance and Practicability* (London: Knight, 1837).

Holt, A., 'The Art of Type-Writing', *Cassell's Family Magazine* (1888), pp. 659–660.

'The Inventions Exhibition: The 'Miranda Pianista', *British Trade Journal* (1 May 1885), p. 297.

Jane, F.T., 'The Romance of Modern London, III: Round the Underground on an Engine', *English Illustrated Magazine*, 10 (1892/1893), pp. 787–792.

Knight, C., 'Illustrations of Cheapness: The Lucifer Match', *Household Words*, 1 (13 April 1850), pp. 54–57.

Knowles, J., 'Wireless Telegraphy and "Brain-waves"', *Nineteenth Century* (1899), pp. 857–864.

'The Latest Patent', *Answers* (29 August 1891), p. 249.

Lombroso, C., 'The Bicycle and Crime', *Pall Mall Magazine*, 20 (1900), pp. 310–316.

'The Maxim Machine Gun', *Chambers's Journal*, 64 (1887), pp. 190–191.

Mee, A., 'The Pleasure Telephone', *Strand Magazine* (1898), pp. 208–214.

Mill, J.S., *Principles of Political Economy* [1848], in *The Collected Works of John Stuart Mill*, ed. F.E.L. Priestley, et al., 33 vols (London: Routledge; Toronto: University of Toronto Press, 1965), vols 2–3.

[Morley, H.], 'Letter from a Highly Respectable Old Lady', *Household Words*, 1 (18 May 1850), pp. 186–187.

'Mr. Edison's Phonograph', *Times* (30 June 1888), p. 5.

Munro, J., 'Carriages Without Horses', *Cassell's Family Magazine* (1896), pp. 529–532.

———, 'From Candles to Gas', *Cassell's Family Magazine* (1880), pp. 225–228.

———, 'From Gas to Electricity', *Cassell's Family Magazine* (1880), pp. 282–284.

'The New Phonograph', *Cassell's Family Magazine* (1888), pp. 315–317.

'News of the Week', *The Spectator* (2 Oct. 1897), p. 1.

Parry, E.A., 'Mr. Twistleton's Type-Writer', *Cornhill Magazine*, 8 (1889), pp. 62–71.

Pepper, J.H., *The Boy's Playbook of Science* (London: Routledge, 1866).

Preece, W.H., 'The Phonograph', *Journal of the Society of Arts* (10 May 1878), pp. 534–538.

'Railway Politeness', *Punch* (1845), p. 10.

Railway Reform: Its Expediency and Practicability Considered (London: Pelham Richardson, 1843).

'Refrigeration and Preservation', *Cassell's Family Magazine* (1879), p. 189.

Ruskin, J., *The Cestus of Aglaia* [1865–66], in *The Complete Works of John Ruskin*, ed. E.T. Cook and A. Wedderburn, 39 vols (London: George Allen, 1903–12), vol. 19, pp. 41–159.

———, *The Stones of Venice* [1852–54], in *The Complete Works of John Ruskin*, ed. E.T. Cook and A. Wedderburn, 39 vols (London: George Allen, 1903–12), vols 9–11.

Salter, T.W., *Field's Chromatography; or, Treatise on Colours and Pigments As Used by Artists* (London: Winsor and Newton, 1869).

'Sewing Machines', *All the Year Round* (27 March 1869), pp. 394–397.

'A Shareholder' [pseud.], *The Linotype Composing Machine: A Retrospect and a Prospect* (London: Witherby, 1889).

'Skating Rinks and Rinkomania', *Cassell's Family Magazine* (1875), pp. 304–306.

'The Social Effect of Bicycling', *Spectator*, 76 (30 May 1896), pp. 769–770.

Somerville, A., *The Autobiography of a Working Man* (London: Gilpin, 1848).

Sterne, S., 'The Greathead Underground Electric Railway', *Forum*, 11 (1891), pp. 683–692.

Stoughton, J., *The Palace of Glass and the Gathering of the People: A Book for the Exhibition* (London: Religious Tracts Society, 1851).

'The Telephone', *Westminster Review*, 53 (1878), pp. 208–221.

'The Telephone: A Domestic Tragedy', *Temple Bar*, 107 (1896), pp. 106–110.

Tennyson, A., 'Locksley Hall' [1842], in *Tennyson's Poetry*, ed. R.W. Hill, Jr., 2nd edn (New York: Norton, 1999), pp. 115–21.

———, 'Ode for the Opening of the International Exhibition', *Fraser's Magazine*, 65 (1862), p. 803.

'The Third ClassTraveller's Petition', *Punch* (1845), p. 10.

Thorpe, T.E., T. Oliver, and G. Cunningham, *Report on the Use of Phosphorus in Manufacture of Lucifer Matches* (HMSO: London, 1899).

Timins, D.T., 'From Roofless Pen to Corridor Coach: The Evolution of the 3rd Class Carriage on the South Eastern Railway', *Railway Magazine*, 4 (1899), pp. 496–500.

Toynbee, A., *Lectures on the Industrial Revolution in England* (London: Rivingtons, 1884).

Trollope, A., 'The Young Women at the Telegraph Office' [extract], *Good Words* (1877), pp. 377–384.

Turner, E.B., 'Health on the Bicycle' *Contemporary Review*, 73 (1898), pp. 640–648.

Vincent, C.W., 'The Dangers of Electric Lighting', *Nineteenth Century*, 27 (January 1890), pp. 145–149.

Wallace, A.R., *The Wonderful Century: Its Successes and Failures* (London: Swann Sonnenschein, 1898).

'What Will Come of the Phonograph?' *Spectator* (30 June 1888), p. 9.

Wilde, O., 'The Soul of Man Under Socialism' [1891], in *The Artist as Critic: Critical Writings of Oscar Wilde*, ed. R. Ellman (Chicago: University of Chicago Press, 1982), pp. 255–89.

Wilson, G., 'The Electric Telegraph' [extract], *Edinburgh Review*, 90 (1849), pp. 459–463.

———, *What is Technology? An Inaugural Lecture Delivered in the University of Edinburgh on November 7, 1855* (Edinburgh: Sutherland and Knox; London: Simpkin, Marshall, 1855).

'Women on Wheels', *Cassell's Family Magazine* (1885), pp. 589–591.

'The World in a Hurry', *Sewing Machine Gazette and Journal of Domestic Appliances* (1 March 1881), p. 30.

Wynter, A., 'The Electric Telegraph', *Quarterly Review*, 95 (June 1854), pp. 118–164.

The Young Ladies' Treasure Book: A Complete Practical Cyclopedia of Practical Instruction and Direction for All Indoor and Outdoor Occupations and Amusements Suitable to Young Ladies (London: Ward, Lock, 1884).

Secondary sources

Adler, M.H., *The Writing Machine: A History of the Typewriter* (London: George Allen and Unwin, 1973).

Aftalion, F., *A History of the International Chemical Industry: From the 'Early Days' to 2000*, trans. O.T. Benfey, 2nd edn (Philadelphia: Chemistry Heritage, 2001).

Auerbach, J.A., *The Great Exhibition of 1851: A Nation on Display* (New Haven, CT: Yale University Press, 1999).

Bak, M.A., *Playful Visions: Optical Toys and the Emergence of Children's Media Culture* (Cambridge, MA: MIT Press, 2020).

Beauchamp, K., *History of Telegraphy: Its Technology and Application* (London: Institution of Electrical Engineers, 2001).

Bizup, J., *Manufacturing Culture: Vindications of Early Victorian Industry* (Charlottesville: University of Virginia Press, 2003).

Bowers, B. *Lengthening the Day: A History of Lighting Technology* (Oxford and New York: Oxford University Press, 1998).

Bowers, Q.D., *Encyclopedia of Automatic Musical Instruments* (Lanham, MD: Vestal, 1972).

Brandon, R., *Singer and the Sewing Machine: A Capitalist Romance* (London: Barrie and Jenkins, 1977).

Briggs, A., 'The Pleasure Telephone: A Chapter in the Prehistory of Media', in *The Social Impact of the Telephone*, ed. I. de Sola Pool (Cambridge, MA: MIT Press, 1977), pp. 40–65.

———, *Victorian Things* (Chicago: University of Chicago Press, 1988).

Brox., J. *Brilliant: The Evolution of Artificial Light* (Boston: Houghton Mifflin Harcourt, 2010).

Carter, I., *Railways and Culture in Britain: The Epitome of Modernity* (Manchester: Manchester University Press, 2001).

Clemm, S., '"Amidst the heterogeneous masses": Charles Dickens's *Household Words* and the Great Exhibition of 1851', *Nineteenth-Century Contexts* 27:3 (September 2005), pp. 207–30.

Cooper, A.J., *The World Below Zero: A History of Refrigeration in the UK* (Aylesbury: ACR Today and Battlepress, 1997).

Cooper, G.R. *The Sewing Machine: Its Invention and Development*, 2nd edn (Washington, DC: Smithsonian Institution, 1976).

Crary, J., *Techniques of the Observer: On Vision and Modernity in the Nineteenth Century* (Cambridge, MA: MIT Press, 1990).

Croome, D.F., and A.A. Jackson, *Rails Through the Clay: A History of London's Tube Railways*, 2nd edn (Harrow Weald: Capital Transport, 1993).

Darrah, W.C., *The World of Stereographs* (Gettysburg, PA: Darrah, 1977).

David, A.M., *Fashion Victims: The Dangers of Dress Past and Present* (London: Bloomsbury, 2015).

Davis, J.R., *The Great Exhibition* (Stroud: Sutton, 1999).

Ellis, J., *The Social History of the Machine Gun* (Baltimore: Johns Hopkins University Press, 1986[1975]).

Emsley, J., *The Shocking History of Phosphorus: A Biography of the Devil's Element* (London: Macmillan, 2000).

Freeman, M.J. *Railways and the Victorian Imagination* (New Haven, CT: Yale University Press, 1999).

Freidberg, S., *Fresh: A Perishable History* (Cambridge, MA: Harvard University Press, 2009).

Fryer, F., and C. Akerman (eds), *The Reform of the Post Office in the Victorian Era and Its Impact on Social and Economic Activity*, 2 vols (London: Royal Philatelic Society, 2000).

Galvan, J., *The Sympathetic Medium: Feminine Channeling, the Occult, and Communication Technologies, 1859–1919* (Ithaca, NY: Cornell University Press, 2010).

Garfield, S., *Mauve: How One Man Invented a Colour That Changed the World* (London: Faber and Faber, 2001).

Gelatt, R., *The Fabulous Phonograph, 1877–1977*, 2nd edn (London: Collier Macmillan, 1977).

Gitelman, L., *Scripts, Grooves, and Writing Machines: Representing Technology in the Edison Era* (Stanford, CA: Stanford University Press, 1999).

Godfrey, F.P., *An International History of the Sewing Machine* (London: Hale, 1982).

Gunning, T., 'The Cinema of Attractions: Early Film, Its Spectator, and the Avant Garde', in *Early Cinema: Space Frame Narrative*, ed. T. Elsaesser (London: British Film Institute, 1989), pp. 56–65.

Hadland, T., and H.-E. Lessing, *Bicycle Design: An Illustrated History* (Cambridge, MA: MIT Press, 2014).

Hecht, H., *Pre-Cinema History: An Encyclopaedia and Annotated Bibliography of the Moving Image Before 1896*, ed. A. Hecht (London: Bowker Saur/British Film Institute, 1993).

Herlihy, D.V., *Bicycle: The History* (New Haven, CT: Yale University Press, 2004).

Hilton, T., *John Ruskin*, 2 vols (New Haven, CT: Yale University Press, 1985–2000).

Hubbard, G., *Cooke and Wheatstone and the Invention of the Electric Telegraph* (London: Routledge, 1965).

Hughes, T.P, *American Genesis: A Century of Invention and Technological Enthusiasm, 1870–1970* (New York: Viking, 1989).

Huhtamo, E., and J. Parikka (eds), *Media Archaeology: Approaches, Applications, and Implications* (Berkeley and Los Angeles: University of California Press, 2011).

Hutchins, J., *Death Rattle: The British Soldier's Machine Gun 1870 to 2015* (Woking, Surrey: Tommy Atkins Media, 2016).

Jackson, A.A., *London's Metropolitan Railway* (Newton Abbot: David and Charles, 1986).

Jackson, T., *Chilled: How Refrigeration Changed the World, and Might Do So Again* (London: Bloomsbury Sigma, 2015).

Jennings, H., *Pandæmonium, 1660–1886: The Coming of the Machine as Seen by Contemporary Observers*, ed. M. Jennings and C. Madge (New York: Free Press, 1985).

Jepsen, T.C., *My Sisters Telegraphic: Women in the Telegraph Office, 1846–1950* (Athens: Ohio University Press, 2000).

Kahan, B., *Ottmar Mergenthaler: The Man and His Machine* (New Castle, DE: Oak Knoll Press, 2000).

Keep, C., 'The Cultural Work of the Typewriter-Girl', *Victorian Studies* 40 (1997), pp. 401–26.

Ketabgian, T., *The Lives of Machines: The Industrial Imaginary in Victorian Literature and Culture* (Ann Arbor: University of Michigan Press, 2011).

Kevles, B.H., *Naked to the Bone: Medical Imaging in the Twentieth Century* (New Brunswick, NJ: Rutgers University Press, 1997).

Kieve, J.L., *The Electric Telegraph: A Social and Economic History* (Newton Abbot: David and Charles, 1973).

Lang, W.R., *James Harrison, Pioneering Genius* (Newtown, Victoria: Neptune, 1982).

Lewis, J.E., 'Women Clerical Workers in the Late Nineteenth and Early Twentieth Centuries', in *The White-Blouse Revolution: Female Office Workers since 1870*, ed. G. Anderson (Manchester: Manchester University Press, 1988), pp. 27–47.

Linotype: The Film, dir. D. Wilson (OnPaperWings Productions, 2012).

Lowe, R., *The British Postage Stamps of the Nineteenth Century*, 2ndedn (London: National Postal Museum, 1979).

Luckhurst, R., *The Invention of Telepathy, 1870–1901* (Oxford: Oxford University Press, 2002).

Mackay, J., *British Stamps* (London: Longman, 1985).

Mannoni, L., *Great Art of Light and Shadow: Archaeology of the Cinema*, trans. R. Crangle (Exeter: University of Exeter Press, 2000).

Marks, P. *Bicycles, Bangs, and Bloomers: The New Woman in the Popular Press* (Lexington: University Press of Kentucky, 1990).

Marvin, C., *When Old Technologies Were New: Thinking about Electric Communication in the Late Nineteenth Century* (Oxford: Oxford University Press, 1988).

Marx, L., *The Machine in the Garden: Technology and the Pastoral Ideal in America* (Oxford: Oxford University Press, 1964).

Millard, A.J., *America on Record: A History of Recorded Sound*, 2nd edn (Cambridge: Cambridge University Press, 2005).

Mitchell, B.R., *British Historical Statistics* (Cambridge: Cambridge University Press, 1988).

Mossoff, A., 'The Rise and Fall of the First American Patent Thicket: The Sewing Machine War of the 1850s', *Arizona Law Review* 53 (2011), pp. 165–211.

Muir, D.N., *Postal Reform and the Penny Black: A New Appreciation* (London: National Postal Museum, 1990).

Nicholson, T.R., *The Birth of the British Motor Car, 1769–1897*, 3 vols (London: Macmillan, 1982).

Ord-Hume, W.J.G., *Clockwork Music: An Illustrated History of Mechanical Musical Instruments from the Musical Box to the Pianola, from Automaton Lady Virginal Players to Orchestrion* (London: Allen and Unwin; New York: Crown, 1973).

Osborne, R., *Vinyl: A History of the Analogue Record* (Farnham, Surrey: Ashgate, 2012).

Otter, C.*The Victorian Eye: A Political History of Light and Vision in Britain, 1800–1910* (Chicago: University of Chicago Press, 2008).

Parikka, J., *What Is Media Archaeology?* (Cambridge: Polity, 2012).

Perry, C.R., 'The British Experience 1876–1912: The Impact of the Telephone During the Years of Delay', in *The Social Impact of the Telephone*, ed. I. de Sola Pool (Cambridge, MA: MIT Press, 1977), pp. 69–96.

———, *The Victorian Post Office: The Growth of a Bureaucracy* (Woodbridge: Royal Historical Society Office, 1992).

Pike, D.L., *Subterranean Cities: The World Beneath Paris and London, 1800–1945* (Ithaca, NY: Cornell University Press, 2005).

Ransom, P.J.G., *The Victorian Railway and How It Evolved* (London: Heinemann, 1990).

Raw, L. *Striking a Light: The Bryant and May Matchwomen and Their Place in History* (London: Continuum, 2009).

Reblitz, A.A., *The Golden Age of Automatic Musical Instruments* (Woodsville, NH: Mechanical Music, 2001).

Robinson, H., *The British Post Office: A History* (Princeton, NJ: Princeton University Press, 1948).

Rochford, C., *Great Victorian Inventions: Novel Contrivances and Industrial Revolutions* (Stroud, Gloucestershire: Amberley, 2014).

Romano, F., *History of the Linotype Company* (Rochester, NY: RIT Press, 2014).

Schivelbusch, W., *The Railway Journey: Trains and Travel in the Nineteenth Century*, trans. A. Hollo (Oxford: Blackwell, 1980 [1978]).

Setright, L.J.K., *Drive On!: A Social History of the Motor Car* (London: Granta, 2003).

Shears, J. (ed.), *The Great Exhibition, 1851: A Sourcebook* (Manchester: Manchester University Press, 2017).

Simmons, J., and G. Biddle (eds), *The Oxford Companion to British Railway History from 1603 to the 1990s* (Oxford and New York: Oxford University Press, 1999).

Smith, A., *Machine Gun: The Story of the Men and the Weapon That Changed the Face of War* (London: Piatkus, 2002).

Smith, D.N., *The Railway and Its Passengers: A Social History* (Newton Abbot: David and Charles, 1988).

Stafford, B.M., and F. Terpak, *Devices of Wonder: From the World in a Box to Images on a Screen* (Los Angeles: Getty Research Institute, 2001).

Sterne, J., *The Audible Past: Cultural Origins of Sound Reproduction* (Durham, NC: Duke University Press, 2003).

Stone, H. (ed.), *The Uncollected Writings of Charles Dickens: Household Words 1850–59*, 2 vols (London: Allen Lane-Penguin, 1969; Bloomington: Indiana University Press, 1968).

Sussman, H.L., 'Machine Dreams: The Culture of Technology', *Victorian Literature and Culture*, 28:1 (Spring 2000), pp. 197–204.

———, *Victorians and the Machine: The Literary Response toTechnology* (Cambridge, MA: Harvard University Press, 1968).

———, *Victorian Technology: Invention, Innovation, and the Rise of the Machine* (Santa Barbara, CA: Praeger, 2009).

Swinney, G.N., 'George Wilson's Map of Technology: Giving Shape to the 'Industrial Arts' in Mid-Nineteenth-Century Edinburgh', *Journal of Scottish Historical Studies* 36:2 (2016), pp. 165–90.

Thompson, J.S., *The History of Compositing Machines* (Chicago: Inland Printer, 1904; rpt. New York: Garland, 1980).

Tracy, R., 'Lighthousekeeping: *Bleak House* and the Crystal Palace', *Dickens Studies Annual* 33 (2003), pp. 25–53.

Turner, J., and M. Zaidman, *The History of Roller Skating* (Lincoln, NE: National Museum of Roller Skating, 1997).

Van Dulken, S., *Inventing the 19th Century* (New York: New York University Press, 2001).

Volmer, C., *The Subterranean Railway: How the London Underground Was Built and How It Changed the City Forever*, rev. edn (London: Atlantic, 2012).

Volti, R., *Cars and Culture: The Life Story of a Technology* (Westport, CT: Greenwood, 2004).

Welch, W.L., and L.B.S. Burt, *From Tinfoil to Stereo: The Acoustic Years of the Recording Industry, 1877–1929* (Gainesville: University Press of Florida, 1994).

Welsh, D., *Underground Writing: The London Tube from George Gissing to Virginia Woolf* (Liverpool: Liverpool University Press, 2010).

Wenzlhuemer, R., *Connecting the Nineteenth-Century World: The Telegraph and Globalization* (Cambridge: Cambridge University Press, 2015).

Wershler-Henry, D.S., *The Iron Whim: A Fragmented History of Typewriting* (Ithaca, NY: Cornell University Press, 2007).

Winchester, S., *Exactly: How Precision Engineering Created the Modern World* (London: WilliamCollins, 2018).

Wing, P., *Stereoscopes: The First One Hundred Years* (Nashua, NH: Transition, 1996).

Young, P., *Globalization and the Great Exhibition: The Victorian New World Order* (Basingstoke: Palgrave Macmillan, 2009).

Zimmeck, M., 'Jobs for the Girls: The Expansion of Clerical Work for Women, 1850–1914', in *Unequal Opportunities: Women's Employment in England, 1800–1918*, ed. A.V. John (London: Blackwell, 1986), pp. 153–77.

INTRODUCTION TO VOLUME III

A machine age – Victorian writing about inventions and technological things

New contraptions and technological objects fascinated writers and their audiences in the nineteenth century. Indeed, the Victorians adored mechanical inventions – except when they abhorred them. Before the reign of Victoria even began, the influential sage and social critic Thomas Carlyle had already assailed the nineteenth century as an 'Age of Machinery, in every outward sense and inward sense of the word'.[1] In 'Signs of the Times' (1829), Carlyle takes machinery as the quintessential sign of a modernity in which 'nothing is now done directly, or by hand'. In this 'Mechanical Age',

> The shuttle drops from the fingers of the weaver, and falls into iron fingers that ply it faster. The sailor furls his sail, and lays down his oar, and bids a strong, unwearied servant, on vaporous wings, bear him through the waters. Men have crossed oceans by steam. . . . There is no end to machinery. Even the horse is stripped of his harness, and finds a fleet fire-horse yoked in his stead. Nay, we have an artist that hatches chickens by steam – the very brood-hen is to be superseded! For all earthly, and for some unearthly purposes, we have machines and mechanic furtherances; for mincing our cabbages; for casting us into magnetic sleep. We remove mountains, and make seas our smooth highway; nothing can resist us. We war with rude nature; and, by our resistless engines, come off always victorious, and loaded with spoils.[2]

Carlyle briefly concedes at least the potential benefit that machines might help satisfy human needs with less labour. But he spends most of the essay polemically extending the definition of machinery to encompass philanthropic movements, educational doctrines, political reforms and even religious institutions, all condemned as so many social and spiritual mechanisms. Machines stand for the turn to a 'pre-established apparatus' and 'cunningly devised implements' instead of to nature, individualism or dynamic growth and change.[3]

For Carlyle, mechanical ingenuity is not just the keynote of the era but an index to its besetting flaws and vices, its lazy turn to expedients for avoiding

DOI: 10.4324/9781315400303-1

intellectual and moral labour, not just reducing physical drudgery. Other Victorian writers echo and adapt Carlyle's judgements, elaborating an entire tradition of social critique centred on the machine. While Matthew Arnold's *Culture and Anarchy* (1869) attacks the verbal 'machinery' of political slogans and clichéd language, John Ruskin's chapter 'The Nature of Gothic' (from *The Stones of Venice* [1851–1853]) draws a damning contrast between the roughness and grotesquerie of Gothic architecture and the nineteenth-century's quest for mechanical perfection, seeing it as confirmation of the enslavement of modern workers before the regime of the machine.[4]

Amid a great era of industrialisation, the critical evaluation of machines and inventions could seem increasingly urgent and by no means merely metaphorical. Assessing the practical results of new technologies, the philosopher and economist John Stuart Mill, hardly a Luddite or a reactionary, puts the matter bluntly in his *Principles of Political Economy* (1848):

> Hitherto it is questionable if all the mechanical inventions yet made have lightened the day's toil of any human being. They have enabled a greater population to live the same life of drudgery and imprisonment, and an increased number of manufacturers and others to make fortunes. They have increased the comforts of the middle classes. But they have not yet begun to effect those great changes in human destiny, which it is in their nature and in their futurity to accomplish.[5]

Mill revised *Principles* several times over the following decades, but he never saw fit to alter this judgement. Such agreement among so many eminent Victorians, indeed among practically the entire traditional canon of Victorian prose writers, might seem to suggest a larger cultural consensus that inventions and technical things were the curse of the age or at best (as the even-handed Mill had it) a potential boon that remained unrealised.

Yet, even amid these powerful critiques, 'the Victorians loved machinery', as one of the great authorities on nineteenth-century writing about technology notes.[6] Indeed, Victorians could even identify with their machines, creating a rich technoculture in which machinery offered complex and competing models that could be applied to living things and emotions.[7] And as the texts included in this collection amply confirm, many literate Victorians were interested in reading and writing about mechanical devices and technologies. Inventions and technological objects had an unprecedented and obvious social significance at a time when coal-powered manufacturing, transport by rail and steamer and electrical communication networks were rapidly transforming work and leisure, the cities and the countryside, the physical geography of Great Britain and – less tangibly – the sense of how the nation and the world cohered and were interconnected. Furthermore, technological things frequently became objects of wonder, amusement, pleasure, curiosity or pride, not just to their developers and users but to those who saw or merely read about them. In one sense, the disparity between so many public intellectuals' attacks on machinery and the general interest in them is no mystery; as a relatively privileged class of writers sceptical of what they saw as Victorian Britain's unreflective norms and tendencies, cultural critics built their attacks around machines and inventions in part *because* they were objects of such social importance and interest. In the context of their criticism, machinery offered an all-purpose symbol that was also an increasingly ubiquitous reality, an efficient device for launching and expressing their critiques. Freighted and charged up – with power with electricity, with meaning – Victorian technological objects inspired not just uncertainty or ambivalence but a gamut of powerful and sometimes contradictory emotions.

Many Victorian critical animadversions on the machine tackle machinery in general, whereas much of the fascination and wonder at technology tends to focus on specific things. Indeed, this note of attraction and interest even shows up in the vegetable choppers and avian incubators with which the anti-mechanical Carlyle indulges his Dickens-like love of quirky lists and oddball details. However baleful machinery might be in the abstract, to write about the particulars of the latest or most surprising invention often means investing it with special interest and meaning.

The Tenth Muse

John Ruskin's reactions to trains and rail travel represent another version of these multifaceted responses. Ruskin deplored the loud, dirty railways that began to thunder their way between towns and through the countryside in the 1830s and 1840s. But as his modern biographer Tim Hilton notes, 'like everyone else of his generation', Ruskin also 'relished the minor adventure of an expedition by train', and he considered the railway 'a permanent part of modern life', calling for public ownership of the railway system and for the building of new rail lines to separate passenger service from the movement of freight.[8] Ruskin could even convey a rich sense of what Leo Marx calls 'the technological sublime', a feeling of awed wonder at the power and majesty of a technological thing.[9] As with Marx's examples from American writing of the era, the great technologies most apt to elicit such feelings in the nineteenth century are the steamboat and especially the railway. From the 1830s and the railway mania of the 1840s on, coal-powered engines rumbled through Great Britain, unleashing energies dug out the earth itself in the service of movement at unprecedented speeds. A network of tracks now sprawled across the landscape, the largest infrastructure project in British history to that date. This was technology on a scale that was immense, national and virtually geological; as Wolfgang Schivelbusch notes, the entire railway system functioned as a kind of interlocked mechanism with moving parts that fit together, so that it was almost as if the entire country had been overlaid with one vast machine.[10]

A rapturous moment from Ruskin's art writing, also cited by Hilton, captures the sublimity of a railway engine as Ruskin considers an issue that he says lies 'at the base of' all of his art and social criticism, 'namely, what may be the real dignity of mechanical Art itself?' – that is, how to assess the 'art' of creating not only Gothic cathedrals but also modern machines.[11] As with his critiques of polished modern architecture or cheap glass beads made to adorn Victorian ladies, Ruskin focuses on the workers behind the production of this sublime object of technology:

> I cannot express the amazed awe, the crushed humility, with which I sometimes watch a locomotive take its breath at a railway station, and think what work there is in its bars and wheels, and what manner of men they must be who dig brown iron-stone out of the ground, and forge it into That! What assemblage of accurate and mighty faculties in them; more than fleshly power over melting crag and coiling fire, fettered, and finessed at last into the precision of watchmaking; Titanian hammer-strokes beating, out of lava, these glittering cylinders and timely-respondent valves, and fine ribbed rods, which touch each other as a serpent writhes, in noiseless gliding, and omnipotence of grasp; infinitely complex anatomy of active steel, compared with which the skeleton of a living creature would seem, to a careless observer, clumsy and vile.
>
> But as I reach this point of reverence, the unreasonable thing is sure to give a shriek as of a thousand unanimous vultures, which leaves me shuddering in real physical pain for some half minute following.[12]

Awestruck, yet now repelled, Ruskin finds himself meditating on the 'nature of the Tenth Muse, who invented this gracious instrument'.[13] The unprecedented art of Victorian machinery demands a new muse among the ancient sisterhood, yet – even within this single sentence – Ruskin's sense of modern machinery's sublimity jostles against his irritation with the features that could make even this muse's greatest products exasperating and ludicrous. 'What are the æsthetic laws respecting iron cylinders; and would Titian have liked them rusty, or fresh cleaned with oil and rag?' he asks, at once mocking and baffled.[14]

As Ruskin's invocation of the Tenth Muse seems to recognise, what was new in the nineteenth century was not simply locomotives or electric telegraphy or photography – that is, not just this astonishing new invention or that impressive technological object. Rather, the Victorian era helped to invent a culture of invention itself. For one thing, in this regime of invention, new devices and technologies could more easily and routinely be developed, refined, promoted and put into use. But more broadly, the culture of invention could construe the march of new devices and technologies as signs and agents of human progress. Perhaps for the first time, the progress of technology could seem a practically autonomous force propelling society into the future that spread out before it.

It probably helped that the railway itself became a Victorian icon for this ramped up, communal, forward movement along the tracks ordained by history. Machines were useful things to think with. In the words of the restless young male speaker of Alfred Tennyson's poem 'Locksley Hall' (1842), 'Forward, forward let us range,/Let the great world spin for ever down the ringing grooves of change': the lines contain a famous misunderstanding of railway technology, but they aptly convey the sense of invention as collective advancement.[15] When in the opening page of *Felix Holt: The Radical* (1866) George Eliot imagines 'posterity . . . shot, like a bullet through a tube' on a pneumatic railway, she is simply modernising the image of history as high-tech transport – and heightening her readers' awareness of their own historical position as posterior to the imagined events of the novel, which is set in the time of the Great Reform Act of 1832 – that is, shortly before the coming of the railway.[16]

In reality, technological change was of course no independent, extrasocial force; the railway to the future depended on its various versions of surveyors, designers, navvies, stokers, ticket-sellers and drivers. Inventions are not developed in a vacuum, and technologies are not adopted simply because they exist. Rather, machines are part of what contemporary studies of technology often call an assemblage or a network, where scientific, social, industrial, economic, institutional and discursive agents and structures come together. More narrowly, we might note, for example, the general push to reform Britain's inefficient and expensive system for obtaining patents, a call taken up by Dickens and others. Parliament did indeed end up dramatically streamlining the patent process in the 1850s, with more reforms in subsequent decades. In 1851, the last full year of the old system, 455 English patents were awarded (patents that did not even cover the rest of the United Kingdom); half a century later, the United Kingdom was granting more than 13,000 patents every year.[17] Such legal and institutional reforms not only acknowledged the everyday importance of inventions, and the private right to own and exploit them, but also helped to make this culture of invention real.

A culture of invention

Other Victorian cultural innovations also helped to publicise the arrival of new machines and inventions and to normalise the process of their development and adoption. The 1851 Great Exhibition of the Works of Industry of All Nations was the first international exposition, bringing together a vast collection of items meant to exemplify culture, design and industry around the world – but in particular to highlight the products, resources and expertise of Great Britain and its colonies. The Great Exhibition took place in the Crystal Palace; specifically built for the occasion in London's Hyde Park, its wrought iron and plate glass made the structure a notable technological object in itself. The Great Exhibition ushered in a new era of expositions in North America and Europe, including the more specialised 1881 International Exposition of Electricity in Paris, where visitors could examine incandescent lights, dynamos and telephones, as a congress of electrical experts met to establish the modern system of units for measuring electrical current and charge. Invention had become an international pursuit, the sibling of the sciences, and a public amusement.

Dickens had been involved with the planning of the Great Exhibition of 1851, and in public he hailed the event as a mark of British achievement.[18] But privately he confessed that the experience of visiting the exhibition left him feeling 'used up': 'I don't say "there is nothing in it" – there's too much. . . . So many things bewildered me'.[19] Bewildered by 'so many things': in an apt play on words, Dickens suggests that he felt both confused by particular objects and overwhelmed by their sheer profusion. But international exhibitions and other special events were not the main day-to-day vehicle for charting the progress of invention and presenting the growing panoply of technological objects. Rather, it was printed writing that helped widely dispersed and heterogeneous audiences to apprehend a variety of technological objects and mechanical things as part of their world and to consider the advance of invention as part of modern life.

Dickens contributed to this enterprise, as well. Long interested in establishing and editing a journal, Dickens founded *Household Words* (1850–1859) and its successor *All the Year Round* (1859–1895) as up-to-date, respectable weekly reading for a general audience. In a 'Preliminary Word' to the first issue of *Household Words*, Dickens explains his intention for the journal to blend information with entertainment and wonder: 'To show to all, that in all familiar things, even in those which are repellant on the surface, there is Romance enough, if we will find it out'.[20] Those 'things' explicitly include contemporary 'inventions' and technological objects:

> The mightier inventions of this age are not, to our thinking, all material, but have a kind of souls in their stupendous bodies which may find expression in Household Words. The traveller whom we accompany on his railroad or his steamboat journey, may gain, we hope, some compensation for incidents which these later generations have outlived, in new associations with the Power that bears him onward; with the habitations and the ways of life of crowds of his fellow creatures among whom he passes like the wind; even with the towering chimneys he may see, spirting [*sic*] out fire and smoke upon the prospect. The swart giants, Slaves of the Lamp of Knowledge, have their thousand and one tales, no less than the Genii of the East.[21]

Modern transport again opens up the prospects of future growth and discovery. Only *Household Words* itself now functions as something like a Victorian-era, augmented-reality platform, bringing the traveller 'new associations' with steam power, with industrialism and with other human beings. The goal and even the language of this prefatory note to *Household Words* anticipate Dickens' proem to another great project of these years; in his preface to *Bleak House* (1852–1853), he declares that, in that novel, he has 'purposely dwelt on the romantic side of familiar things'.[22]

More concretely, Dickens' journals would implement this vision of the romance of invention via what he called 'process' articles, which infused excitement and imagination into descriptions of industrial or institutional activities, as well as via short histories of industries and objects and briefer 'chips' (short, factual articles written in advance and later used to fill out an issue).[23] Within these modes of writing, his journals considered technologies and industrial objects such as the steam plough, the telegraph, railway signals, power looms, the refining of gold, papermaking, playing cards, smelling salts and plate glass – to give just a sampling drawn from their early years. The present volume includes articles from *Household Words* about matches and about the transit of stamped and unstamped letters through the post office, pieces that suggest how the era's print media could assume and cultivate their readers' curiosity about such objects.

For Dickens and *Household Words* were not alone in addressing Victorian readers' interest in machines and in the applications of scientific and industrial know-how. A glance at the sources of the texts included in this collection confirms the widespread attention to inventions and technological things across a range of general and specialised periodicals, as well as in books and government reports. This attention only increased in the second half of the century, during what has been called the Second Industrial Revolution. In this period, the great innovations in steam-powered transport and manufacturing were joined by newer advances in chemistry and electricity, as well as by an emerging focus on technologies that promised to provide consumers and households with domestic convenience or entertainment. During these decades in particular, Victorian newspapers and magazines could make the incessant, steady advance of invention seem like a routine feature of modernity.

For instance, in a special section sometimes called 'The Gatherer: An Illustrated Record of Invention, Discovery, and Science' (or simply 'The Gatherer'), late-Victorian issues of *Cassell's Family Magazine* published brief pieces on new inventions, discoveries and technologies. Here aluminium cartes-de-visite might share a page with automated scarecrows or spectacles made to fit myopic horses. Quirky factoids, previews of possible future necessities, or opportunities for small but eye-catching illustrations (thanks to the continuing development of technologies for image reproduction), these articles offered a regular stimulus to monthly curiosity and mild wonder. Not only are these brief essays from *Cassell's* well represented in this collection, but they also have furnished the exclusive source for a recent book highlighting more than 200 quirky or prescient Victorian inventions – without any overlap with the texts chosen here.[24] On the pages of popular periodicals, courtesy of their mingling of topics and their mosaic format, the present state and future prospects of mechanical ingenuity take their place amid the other general interests of life. Notwithstanding the surprise that new inventions might evoke, with this regular space set aside for them in the columns of 'The Gathering' and other forums, their development could appear as constant and predictable as the coming issues of a printed magazine. Like periodicals themselves, by the end of the century, the progress of invention might seem to promise a steady stream of novel content along predetermined lines.

Writing technology

The Victorians rarely used the word *technology*. Appointed in 1855 as Great Britain's first Professor of Technology, George Wilson devoted his first lectures at Edinburgh University to explaining just what he was 'called upon to profess', under the assumption that the term would be unfamiliar to his listeners.[25] Originally used to denote a specialised genre of writing, a discourse or treatise about one of the useful arts, *technology* in Wilson's account now comes to denote such organised, practical knowledge itself – the principles that inform the applied or industrial arts, as opposed to the fine arts (painting, sculpture, music) or 'Useless Arts' (such as 'the Art of Conjuring' or 'cheating at cards', he suggests).[26] Wilson's broad conception of technology and his labours as a writer, professor and museum curator would influence the Victorians' wider ideas about the study of machines and the practical application of scientific and technical knowledge. A recent assessment of Wilson's work even argues for a 'resonance' between his understanding of technology 'as the intermeshing of human and non-human entities' and modern approaches in science and technology studies that center on the relationships between these same factors, including Bruno Latour's actor-network theory.[27]

Still, Wilson's notion of technology stops short of the modern sense in which we might today speak of the steam engine or bicycle or machine gun as 'technologies' – that is, *technology* not simply as applied knowledge but as the specific products of that knowledge, understood as a material component of human history and societies. This collection deals less with the history of technology in itself than with the ways that Victorians made technological things into a staple of print culture; in this sense, we might think of the obsolete definition of *technology*, as a particular kind of writing, as continuing to lead a shadow life. And in these pieces, we see not simply a parade of inventions but the invention of new ways of writing about and understanding technological objects. Thus, in the genres and textual spaces that Victorian print culture allotted to writing about inventions and about the material products of modern industry and ingenuity, we can perhaps see the modern sense of *technology*, as knowledge embodied in constructed things, coming into being.

The first cluster of texts in this collection highlights the meanings and emotions – not invariably excitement or wonder – that writers from across the period associated with technological advancement and the culture that supported it. It also illustrates the variety of modes and genres that contributed to writing about inventions, machines and technological objects – from autobiography and religious tracts to the occasional poem, technophilic prophecy and even comic spoof. The prophetic and fictional pieces here indicate that interest in real technological things could morph into the impulse to imagine strange or hypothetical ones, an inclination confirmed at the end of the century by Richard Marsh's weird fiction, as well as by H. G. Wells' scientific romances and utopias.

The other clusters proceed in wide thematic arcs, from the era's signature innovations in transport and textual communication, to technological objects that offered heat or light, and to those that promised new sights and sounds, including the photograph, telephone, phonograph and wireless. Such signature Victorian media were also communication devices, of course, although except for wireless telegraphy, they highlighted not the promise of newly mechanised or electrified textuality but the ability of new media to expand – perhaps to deceive – human capacities of hearing and vision. A final section collects brief accounts of a variety of technologies that promised sustenance, recreation, beauty, productivity or violent imperial conquest.

Many of the selections in this book are intended not simply to highlight the latest technology of the age but to draw attention to the particularities that made technologies part of Victorian material cultures, to emphasise what made them not simply ideas but things. To that end, for instance, selections on transport highlight not simply the railway in general but the third-class carriage and the London Underground, and those about photography focus on the stereoscopic photograph as a distinctive nineteenth-century medium. The volume contains a variety of kinds of texts as well. Some of the pieces selected were originally aimed at specialists, while others were intended for more general readership, including both adults and children. This collection includes texts written not only by journalists but also by designers, producers, promoters and users. The pieces here treat technological things in distinctive ways: as social infrastructure, as objects of individual consumption, as new forms of labour or leisure and as marvels or menaces within the culture that made them.

Today, our infatuation with contemporary gadgets often coexists with uneasiness and gloom or even technofatalism. Have our own most sophisticated technological objects become our most intimate observers, forever tracking our transits and recording our communications in order to deliver us as saleable data? Has the nineteenth century's great unleashing of fossil energy to power modern civilisation culminated in the ongoing planetary catastrophe of anthropogenic climate change and ecocide? Can newer technologies save us from what our embrace of older tech has wrought? Even among the late Victorians, we might find hints of a new technoscepticism that is more specific and perhaps better informed than Carlyle's wholesale denunciations of machinery.

That context of scepticism or pessimism gives a typically contrarian tinge to Oscar Wilde's endorsement of labour-saving inventions and technologies in his essay 'The Soul of Man Under Socialism' (1891). In a sense, Wilde is really returning to early Victorian faith in technological progress and extending the view of John Stuart Mill, who looked forward to a future period when the 'conquests made' by scientific discovery and invention would at last 'become the common property of the species, and the means of improving and elevating the universal lot'.[28] The problem, Wilde asserts, is not the machines themselves but the fact that they benefit individual owners rather than everyone. 'Up to the present, man has been, to a certain extent, the slave of machinery, and there is something tragic in the fact that as soon as man had invented a machine to do his work he began to starve', he laments.[29]

> The fact is, that civilization requires slaves. The Greeks were quite right there. Unless there are slaves to do the ugly, horrible, uninteresting work, culture and contemplation become almost impossible. Human slavery is wrong, insecure, and demoralising. On mechanical slavery, on the slavery of the machine, the future of the world depends.

Wilde anticipates a time when the collective benefits of technology will give inventors and scientists the 'delightful leisure in which to devise wonderful and marvellous things for their own joy and the joy of everyone else'.[30]

'Is this Utopian? A map of the world that does not include Utopia is not worth glancing at, for it leaves out the one country at which humanity is always landing'.[31] The famous line is seldom given its context: Wilde looks to invention as a shared expression of our utopian desires, to the march of technology as our communal transport to a better future via the sheer pleasure of invention. Against this backdrop, we might read even Victorian complaints and doubts about technological things as expressing not unreasoning technophobia but the disappointment of those half-formed hopes for general advancement. Victorian writing about inventions and technological things can offer more than assessments of the wonders or the horrors of the latest invention. Even amid the cruelties and injustices engendered by making matchsticks or weapons for wholesale murder in the colonies, writing about technological objects can offer glimpses of a world transformed, a world advancing thanks to human ingenuity and craft. At times, many of the texts reprinted here give us glances at the kinds of maps Wilde seems to envision.

Notes

1 [Thomas Carlyle], ['Signs of the Times'] *Edinburgh Review*, 49 (June 1829), 439–459, on p. 442.
2 Carlyle, 'Signs of the Times', p. 442.
3 Carlyle, 'Signs of the Times', p. 443.
4 Matthew Arnold, *Culture and Anarchy* [1869], in *The Complete Prose Works of Matthew Arnold*, ed. R. H. Super (Ann Arbor, MI: University of Michigan Press, 1960–1977), Vol. 5, pp. 85–256; John Ruskin, *The Stones of Venice* [1852–1854], in *The Complete Works of John Ruskin*, ed. E. T. Cook and Alexander Wedderburn (London: George Allen, 1903–1912), Vols. 9–11.
5 John Stuart Mill, *Principles of Political Economy* [1848], in *The Collected Works of John Stuart Mill*, ed. F. E. L. Priestley, et al. (London: Routledge; Toronto: University of Toronto Press, 1965), Vols. 2–3, in Vol. 3, pp. 756–757.
6 Herbert L. Sussman, 'Machine Dreams: The Culture of Technology', *Victorian Literature and Culture*, 28:1 (Spring 2000), pp. 197–204, on p. 197.
7 See Tamara Ketabgian, *The Lives of Machines: The Industrial Imaginary in Victorian Literature and Culture* (Ann Arbor, MI: University of Michigan Press, 2011).

8 Tim Hilton, *John Ruskin*, 2 vols. (New Haven, CT: Yale University Press, 1985–2000), Vol. 2, p. 82.
9 Leo Marx, *The Machine in the Garden: Technology and the Pastoral Ideal in America* (Oxford: Oxford University Press, 1964), p. 195.
10 Wolfgang Schivelbusch, *The Railway Journey: Trains and Travel in the Nineteenth Century*, trans. by Anselm Hollo (Oxford: Blackwell, 1980 [1978]).
11 John Ruskin, *The Cestus of Aglaia* [1865–1866], in *The Complete Works of John Ruskin*, ed. E. T. Cook and Alexander Wedderburn, 39 vols. (London: George Allen, 1903–1912), Vol. 19, pp. 41–159, on p. 60.
12 Ruskin, *The Cestus of Aglaia*, pp. 60–61.
13 Ruskin, *The Cestus of Aglaia*, p. 62.
14 Ruskin, *The Cestus of Aglaia*, p. 63.
15 Tennyson, Alfred, 'Locksley Hall' [1842], in *Tennyson's Poetry*, ed. Robert W. Hill, Jr., 2nd ed. (New York: Norton, 1999), pp. 115–121, lines 181–182.
16 George Eliot, *Felix Holt: The Radical* [1866], ed. Lynda Mugglestone (London: Penguin, 1995), p. 3.
17 B. R. Mitchell, *British Historical Statistics* (Cambridge: Cambridge University Press, 1988), pp. 438–439.
18 [Charles Dickens and Richard H. Horne], 'The Great Exhibition and the Little One', *Household Words*, 3 (5 July 1851), pp. 356–360. In this piece, Dickens jingoistically contrasts the material progress on display at the Great Exhibition with the supposed cultural stasis of China.

For a wider view of the journal's treatment of the exhibition, see Sabine Clemm, '"Amidst the heterogeneous masses": Charles Dickens's *Household Words* and the Great Exhibition of 1851', *Nineteenth-Century Contexts*, 27:3 (September 2005), pp. 207–230. Dickens' novel *Bleak House* (1852–1853) has sometimes been read as part of his response to the Great Exhibition; see Robert Tracy, 'Lighthousekeeping: *Bleak House* and the Crystal Palace', *Dickens Studies Annual*, 33 (2003), pp. 25–53.
19 Charles Dickens, *The Letters of Charles Dickens*, Pilgrim edition, ed. Madeline House, Graham Storey, Kathleen Tillotson, et al., 12 vols. (Oxford: Clarendon Press, 1965–2002), Vol. 6, p. 428.
20 [Charles Dickens], 'A Preliminary Word', *Household Words*, 1 (30 March 1850), pp. 1–2, on p. 1.
21 Dickens, 'A Preliminary Word', p. 1.
22 Charles Dickens, *Bleak House* [1852–1853], ed. George Ford and Sylvère Monod (New York: Norton, 1977), p. 4.
23 Harry Stone (ed.), *The Uncollected Writings of Charles Dickens: Household Words 1850–59*, 2 vols. (London: Allen Lane-Penguin, 1969; Bloomington, IN: Indiana University Press, 1968), Vol. 1, p. 53.
24 Caroline Rochford, *Great Victorian Inventions: Novel Contrivances and Industrial Revolutions* (Stroud, Gloucestershire: Amberley, 2014).
25 George Wilson, *What is Technology? An Inaugural Lecture Delivered in the University of Edinburgh on November 7, 1855* (Edinburgh: Sutherland and Knox; London: Simpkin, Marshall, 1855), p. 3.
26 Wilson, *What is Technology?*, p. 5.
27 Geoffrey N. Swinney, 'George Wilson's Map of Technology: Giving Shape to the 'Industrial Arts' in Mid-Nineteenth-Century Edinburgh', *Journal of Scottish Historical Studies*, 36:2 (2016), pp. 165–190, on p. 180.
28 Mill, *Principles of Political Economy*, Vol. 3, p. 757.
29 Oscar Wilde, 'The Soul of Man Under Socialism' [1891], in *The Artist as Critic: Critical Writings of Oscar Wilde*, ed. Richard Ellman (Chicago: University of Chicago Press, 1982), pp. 255–289, on p. 268.

30 Wilde, 'The Soul of Man Under Socialism', p. 269.
31 Wilde, 'The Soul of Man Under Socialism', pp. 269–270.

Works cited

Arnold, Matthew, *Culture and Anarchy* [1869], in *The Complete Prose Works of Matthew Arnold*, ed. R. H. Super, 11 vols (Ann Arbor: University of Michigan Press, 1960–77), vol. 5, pp. 85–256.

[Carlyle, Thomas], ['Signs of the Times']. *Edinburgh Review*, 49 (June 1829), pp. 439–59.

Clemm, Sabine, '"Amidst the heterogeneous masses": Charles Dickens's *Household Words* and the Great Exhibition of 1851', *Nineteenth-Century Contexts* 27:3 (September 2005), pp. 207–30.

Dickens, Charles, *Bleak House* [1852–53], ed. George Ford and Sylvère Monod (New York: Norton, 1977).

———, *The Letters of Charles Dickens*, Pilgrim ed., ed. Madeline House, Graham Storey, Kathleen Tillotson, et al. 12 vols (Oxford: Clarendon Press, 1965–2002).

———, 'A Preliminary Word', *Household Words*, 1 (30 March 1850), 1–2.

[Dickens, Charles, and Richard H. Horne], 'The Great Exhibition and the Little One', *Household Words*, 3 (5 July 1851), pp. 356–60.

Eliot, George, *Felix Holt: The Radical* [1866], ed. Lynda Mugglestone (London: Penguin, 1995).

Hilton, Tim, *John Ruskin*, 2 vols (New Haven: Yale University Press, 1985–2000).

Ketabgian, Tamara, *The Lives of Machines: The Industrial Imaginary in Victorian Literature and Culture* (Ann Arbor: University of Michigan Press, 2011).

Marx, Leo, *The Machine in the Garden: Technology and the Pastoral Ideal in America* (Oxford: Oxford University Press, 1964).

Mill, John Stuart, *Principles of Political Economy* [1848], in *The Collected Works of John Stuart Mill*, ed. F. E. L. Priestley, et al., 33 vols (London: Routledge; Toronto: University of Toronto Press, 1965), vols 2–3.

Mitchell, B. R., *British Historical Statistics* (Cambridge: Cambridge University Press, 1988).

Rochford, Caroline, *Great Victorian Inventions: Novel Contrivances and Industrial Revolutions* (Stroud, Gloucestershire: Amberley, 2014).

Ruskin, John, *The Cestus of Aglaia* [1865–66], in *The Complete Works of John Ruskin*, ed. E. T. Cook and Alexander Wedderburn, 39 vols (London: George Allen, 1903–12), vol. 19, pp. 41–159.

———, *The Stones of Venice* [1852–54], in of *The Complete Works of John Ruskin*, ed. E. T. Cook and Alexander Wedderburn, 39 vols (London: George Allen, 1903–12), vols 9–11.

Schivelbusch, Wolfgang, *The Railway Journey: Trains and Travel in the Nineteenth Century*, trans. Anselm Hollo (Oxford: Blackwell, 1980 [1978]).

Stone, Harry, ed., *The Uncollected Writings of Charles Dickens: Household Words 1850–59*, 2 vols (London: Allen Lane-Penguin, 1969; Bloomington: Indiana University Press, 1968).

Sussman, Herbert L., 'Machine Dreams: The Culture of Technology', *Victorian Literature and Culture*, 28:1 (Spring 2000), pp. 197–204.

Swinney, Geoffrey N., 'George Wilson's Map of Technology: Giving Shape to the 'Industrial Arts' in Mid-Nineteenth-Century Edinburgh', *Journal of Scottish Historical Studies* 36:2 (2016), pp. 165–90.

Tennyson, Alfred, 'Locksley Hall' [1842], in *Tennyson's Poetry*, ed. Robert W. Hill, Jr., 2nd edn (New York: Norton, 1999), pp. 115–21.

Tracy, Robert, 'Lighthousekeeping: *Bleak House* and the Crystal Palace', *Dickens Studies Annual* 33 (2003), pp. 25–53.

Wilde, Oscar, 'The Soul of Man Under Socialism' [1891], in *The Artist as Critic: Critical Writings of Oscar Wilde*, ed. Richard Ellman (Chicago: University of Chicago Press, 1982), pp. 255–89.

Wilson, George, *What is Technology? An Inaugural Lecture Delivered in the University of Edinburgh on November 7, 1855* (Edinburgh: Sutherland and Knox; London: Simpkin, Marshall, 1855).

PART 1

The march of invention

Alexander Somerville ['One Who Has Whistled at the Plough'], *The Autobiography of a Working Man* [extract] (London: Gilpin, 1848), pp. 358–361.

John Stoughton, *The Palace of Glass and the Gathering of the People: A Book for the Exhibition* [extract] (London: Religious Tracts Society, 1851), pp. 18–25.

Michael Angelo Garvey, *The Silent Revolution, or the Future Effects of Steam and Electricity upon the Conditions of Mankind* [extract] (London: Cash, 1852), pp. 1–13.

Alfred, Lord Tennyson, 'Ode for the Opening of the International Exhibition', *Fraser's Magazine*, 65 (1862), p. 803.

F. R. Conder, 'The Best Friend of the Working Man' [extract], *Fraser's Magazine*, new series 19 (1879), pp. 231–232.

'The World in a Hurry', *Sewing Machine Gazette and Journal of Domestic Appliances* (1 March 1881), p. 30.

'The Latest Patent', *Answers* (29 August 1891), p. 249.

A. R. Bennett, *On the Telephoning of Great Cities* [extract] (London: Whittaker, 1892), pp. 4–7.

Alfred Russel Wallace, *The Wonderful Century: Its Successes and Failures* [extract] (London: Swann Sonnenschein, 1898), pp. 1–3, 150–153.

Victorian writers often treated invention and the appearance of new technological objects as a story of human progress. For the radical working-class journalist and former soldier Alexander Somerville, a first view of the railway and locomotive engines in Manchester when he was a young man becomes intertwined with the prospects for political change just then opened up by the Great Reform Act of 1832; both new technology and political advancement would take us closer to the 'universal brotherhood' that Somerville, along with many other optimistic Victorians, believed was the ultimate destiny of the world. In an account by the non-conformist minister John Stoughton, the glories of art and industry on display at the 1851 Great Exhibition – as well as the Crystal Palace, the huge iron and glass structure that housed them – give us a sense of the power of the human mind, the aspirations of the human soul, and the still greater glory of the God who created them. The exhibition also inspires Michael Angelo Garvey's reflections on the sublime capabilities of the human mind and the great future of the human race.[1] In his capacity as Poet Laureate, Alfred, Lord Tennyson was charged with commemorating great events in the life of the nation, and his ode for a later London exhibition picks up these notes, as well as paying tribute to the late Prince Albert, the patron of the 1851 event; set to music, it was performed at the opening of the International Exhibition of 1862.

But the wonders of machinery and invention did not always seem so obvious, especially once the impact of sheer novelty or the spectacle of a public exhibition faded. Francis Conder, a civil engineer who worked on the railway, complains that ignorance and envy have prevented workers from understanding that the steam engine is actually a boon to the working class – never mind any brief, merely personal difficulties for the labourers whom the machines might replace. For a writer in the *Sewing Machine Gazette*, the proliferation of modern labour-saving machinery is both the sign and the agent of a world of increasing speed and hurry, whose ultimate logic is suicidal. Or, to take a different angle from such alarmed handwringing, perhaps the insatiable quest for invention and efficiency is simply comical, as a light piece from the penny newspaper *Answers* suggests, imagining a new machine that will automate the feeding, care and amusement of babies. Still, this cheerful vision of smoothly inhuman child-rearing also manages to convey a sense of unease just behind the farce.

Nevertheless, at the end of the century, even the call for a better British telephone system, and for new legislation to encourage it, could unleash electrical engineer Alfred Bennett's vision of universal telephone service as part of humanity's sacred destiny. Arguing that the nineteenth century has produced 13 out of the 20 greatest inventions since human beings first tamed fire, the evolutionist and devout spiritualist Alfred Russel Wallace worries only that the very ubiquity of the century's culture of invention has made those great achievements harder to appreciate and recognise.[2]

Notes

1 One of the major cultural events of its era, London's Great Exhibition of 1851 inspired an extensive amount of writing since even before it opened. For a look at how the Victorians wrote about and viewed the exhibition, see Jonathon Shears (ed.), *The Great Exhibition, 1851: A Sourcebook* (Manchester: Manchester University Press, 2017), as well as *The Crystal Palace Exhibition Illustrated Catalogue, London (1851)* (New York: Dover Publications, 1970). Important recent accounts of the exhibition include Jeffrey A. Auerbach, *The Great Exhibition of 1851: A Nation on Display* (New Haven, CT: Yale University Press, 1999); John R. Davis, *The Great Exhibition* (Stroud: Sutton, 1999); and Paul Young, *Globalization and the Great Exhibition: The Victorian New World Order* (Basingstoke: Palgrave Macmillan, 2009).

2 As the introduction to this volume notes, the Victorians did not have a unified term such as *technology* that covered both equipment or devices and the application of scientific knowledge for practical purposes. But many Victorians were fascinated by machinery and by advances in what were called the *useful arts* (that is, manufacture, craftsmanship or invention). Herbert L. Sussman's influential *Victorians and the Machine: The Literary Response to Technology* (Cambridge, MA: Harvard University Press, 1968) argues for a split in Victorian culture between literary technophobia and a rising culture of machinery and invention. More recent scholarship on Victorian print culture – including work by Sussman himself – has found closer relationships between imaginative literature and technology: Herbert L. Sussman, *Victorian Technology: Invention, Innovation, and the Rise of the Machine* (Santa Barbara, CA: Praeger, 2009); Tamara Ketabgian, *The Lives of Machines: The Industrial Imaginary in Victorian Literature and Culture* (Ann Arbor, MI: University of Michigan Press, 2011); Joseph Bizup, *Manufacturing Culture: Vindications of Early Victorian Industry* (Charlottesville, VA: University of Virginia Press, 2003).

For a fascinating collation of writing on machines from the English Restoration to the Victorians, see Humphrey Jennings, *Pandæmonium, 1660–1886: The Coming of the Machine as Seen by Contemporary Observers*, ed. Mary-Lou Jennings and Charles Madge (New York: Free Press, 1985).

Illustrated Victorian patent records have regularly provided material for anthologies of odd or impressive nineteenth-century inventions; the best of these is Stephen Van Dulken, *Inventing the 19th Century* (New York: New York University Press, 2001).

1

ALEXANDER SOMERVILLE, *THE AUTOBIOGRAPHY OF A WORKING MAN* [EXTRACT]

(London: Gilpin, 1848), pp. 358–361

Nothing occurred on my journey from London to Liverpool which I need remark upon, except that at Manchester I saw a railway, locomotive engines, and railway trains, for the first time. Upon the railway, not then out of the second year of its age, I proceeded to Liverpool. The opening of that railway is an epoch in the history of the world. In memory, I see my first whirl upon it, standing so prominently out among other recollections, that it seems like an epoch of my life. All sights which I had seen, in London or elsewhere – the beautiful, the grand, the wonderful – shrunk into comparative nothingness, when, after reaching Liverpool, I went into the country a week, in the neighbourhood of Prescot, and saw (each day I sought to see it, each hour of the day I could have stood to see it again) the white steam shooting through the landscape of trees, meadows, and villages, and the long train, loaded with merchandise, men and women, and human enterprise, rolling along under the steam. I had seen no sight like that; I have seen nothing to excel it since. In beauty and grandeur, the world has nothing beyond it. In wonder alone, the electric telegraph outstrips the railway; but they belong to the one family of wonders. I used to stand and look at it, and dream as I stood; and when I ventured to relate any of those dreams, people used to say that I was very dreamy indeed. Related now that sixteen years have passed, those thoughts would seem very sober realities.

The Reform Bill had just then passed into law. Some people saw no good in the Reform Bill, but much evil; some saw no good in the railways, but much evil; others saw no evil in either, yet not much good; the greater number saw boundless good in both. But many of those who saw boundless good in the Reform Bill, turned in the second, third, fourth, fifth, sixth, seventh, eighth, or ninth years of its existence, and did all they could, by fair means and unfair means, by their own votes, and by their influence over the votes of others, to oppose the principles of the Reform Bill, and the faithful adherents of it: they promoted the political principles opposed to it, and supported its opponents, because the boundless good which they expected to come out of it, did not come in the second, third, fourth, fifth, sixth, seventh, eighth, nor ninth years of its existence. The same order of minds who foresaw boundless good from the establishment of railways, and who

DOI: 10.4324/9781315400303-3

did not see it come in the shape, and within the time, that they expected it to come, would have put their backs to the locomotive engine, and would have prevented another train from starting, had they been strong enough.

To those who advocated the reform of 1832, it may be almost deemed a triumph, to have lived to see that it has done no harm. The opposition to it was not founded upon the probability of it doing no good, but on the certainty of its doing positive and irreparable mischief. He must be a bold reasoner, or a man too weak to reason, who says it has done no good. He must be a bolder or a weaker man, or one in whom both qualities are compounded, who says that the Reform Act has done evil. The first principle of magnitude – the greatest of all, indeed, solved by the establishment of the Manchester and Liverpool Railway, was this, that the *innovation* upon old customs was safe. The railways have proved that, and much more. The greatest principle established by our experience of the Reform Act, which gave Manchester two members for the first time, is, that *innovation* upon old customs, of admitting a large number of the population to share in the privileges of the constitution, is safe. The Reform Act has proved that, and much more.

And if the doors of the constitution were opened again, I have no fear but all the predictions of mischief to follow, would be like the predictions before the enactment of the Reform Bill; there would be no wrong, nor danger of wrong. Like the hopes formed of the Reform Bill by the sanguine, and those who do not accustom themselves to the use of reason, or who, being weak in the faculties which deal with *cause and effect*, cannot understand the operation of reason, there would be expectations formed only to be disappointed. No acts of parliament can make a population well clothed, well supplied with food, well lodged, and happy; but acts of parliament can remove the artificial hinderances to those desirable ends, and promote their accomplishment. Comfort and happiness depend on the self-exertions of those who seek them, and cannot be conferred by others. But so long as men are excluded from the political privileges of their birth-right as men, it is natural for them to think that they could make themselves more comfortable and happy, if they had the exercise of their natural rights.

The time when I first saw the railway uniting Liverpool and Manchester – spanning the bog where human foot could not tread – stands, as I have said, in memory, like an epoch of my life. I looked upon that most poetical and most practical of the grand achievements of human intellect, until people thought I stood and slept; and, when they heard the dream, they said it was very dreamy, indeed. I should fear to tell the dreams which I have now beside the electric telegraph, and on the railways, and within the regions of the god-like inventors and makers of machinery. There is a time coming when realities shall go beyond any dreams that have yet been told of those things. Nation exchanging with nation their products freely; thoughts exchanging themselves for thoughts, and never taking note of the geographical space they have to pass over, except to give the battery a little more of the electric spirit, if the distance which the thought has to go be many hundreds of miles; man holding free fellowship with man, without taking note of the social distance which used to separate them, except, perhaps, the lord (landed lord or cotton lord,) shall use a little more of the moral electricity, when conveying a thought to a working man, at the opposite end of the social pole, who used to be very far distant; that lord may put on a little more of the moral electricity, which shall then be discovered, to carry the instantaneous message of one feeling, one interest, one object, one hope of success from the lordly end, to the working man's end of the social world. Universal enfranchisement, railways, electric telegraphs, public schools (the greatest of the moral levers for elevating mankind named last – because last to be advocated, which should have been first); these are some of the elements of a moral faith, believing in the universal brotherhood of mankind, which I daily hold, and never doubt upon; which I believe will as certainly be realised, as I believe that *good*, and not *evil*, was the object of all creation, and is the end of all existence.

2

JOHN STOUGHTON, *THE PALACE OF GLASS AND THE GATHERING OF THE PEOPLE: A BOOK FOR THE EXHIBITION* [EXTRACT]

(London: Religious Tracts Society, 1851), pp. 18–25

The sight of these interesting objects is suggestive of important reflections. Imagining oneself left alone in the vast building – permitted to tread in silence the deserted halls – what musings might arise relative to themes awfully beautiful, which the giddy portion of the daily crowd within the walls have never entertained!

This repository of art, with all its varied contents, is the production of the human mind. Its constructive skill is singularly exhibited in the edifice itself; not such constructive skill as can be confounded with the instinct of the bird or bee, not a blind impulsive power; but a clear-eyed intelligence, which can survey, and consider, and contrive, and adapt, and fashion, according to the exigency of the case, in ways more various than art can classify. Of the power of human discovery, the detection of latent qualities in nature, a remarkable example is afforded in the history of the material out of which the building itself is chiefly wrought. – That the vitrification of sand and nitrium, noticed accidentally by the Phœnician mariners, according to the once generally received account by Pliny; or that some other occurrence at a much earlier period, as is now commonly believed, should have led men to perceive, in materials perfectly opaque, capabilities of transformation into a substance perfectly transparent; that out of dingy masses of mineral could be spread forth sheets of liquid diamonds, broad as the awning over the Coliseum at Rome; that it was possible to mould this brittle material, as if it were so much wax or clay; that, hard as rock, it might be blown into a bubble soft and light as a drop of water; that, white as the sunbeam, it could receive and retain all the dyes of the rainbow; constitute a series of marvels, forming but one out of a thousand chapters included in the annals of human discovery. The plastic power of the human mind is also here displayed in the almost infinitely diversified forms which, under its touch, the rude materials of nature have received. Timber and stone, cut into elegant shapes for useful purposes, or with astonishing truthfulness

DOI: 10.4324/9781315400303-4

made to resemble the most delicate expressions of animated nature, even to the feather of a bird and the petal of a flower! Earth moulded by hand or machinery, and metals wrought or cast in a thousand mimic fashions!

Nor should we omit to notice, in these objects of art, a deep desire to embody in material things the *beau idéal*, to rise above the dull purpose of mere utility and convenience, to give a touch of beauty to the commonest aids and implements of life, to lift art to a lofty sphere, and to surround it with a brilliant halo. Man is seen as the lover of artistic perfection, tasking his powers to conceive and execute what shall at least approach a standard too lofty for him yet to measure, but of the existence of which he has the consciousness, deep though dim. He may be said to fight a battle with the obstinate resistance of material nature, and though oft defeated, still struggles for the victory! The spiritual takes possession of the physical, as a foreign realm, which it seeks to subdue to its own purposes. The *distinct essence* of the soul is also asserted. Its attempt to rule over all around, and to enrich itself with the spoils of the conquered region, is not a contest with a co-ordinate and equal power, but it is the effort of a kingly nature so formed by God, created in his image, and inaugurated into regal office, at the beginning when the charge was given, 'Replenish the earth and subdue it'. The superiority of the mind over all material nature is thus unequivocally proclaimed.

And amidst all this, does he not catch glimpses of things purer, nobler, and more enduring than the things of earth? Does he not feel at times that there are objects existing somewhere, incomparably more beautiful than any work of art? Has he not raised within him a conception of invisible and spiritual realms more wonderful than the material? And is there not also to be recognised, in the ambition of the artist who strives to produce a work which his admirers vainly call immortal, a strong craving for some after-existence – a flinching from the thought, that death is to put an end to all – a wish, at least, to impress some characteristic idea of his own on some portion or particle of the great whole of things, so that he may live by representation if not in consciousness.

Yet, while such musings on the works of men open up to us deeps of power and beauty in the soul, they only reveal a small division of the vast world of human nature. We visit but a single province of the intellectual realm: we leave unexplored the vast domains enriched by the growths of literature and science; while the emotions, social affections, moral feelings, and religious capacities of the soul remain untouched. No account is here taken of conscience, and of the capability of knowing, loving, and serving his Maker, which form the highest distinction of man's nature. Yet even from our partial and limited view of the subject, we derive no slight conviction of the immortality of that nature to which such attributes as we have described belong. Great as may be the mystery of a future existence, most certainly the mysteries connected with the denial of this truth are greater still. It involves the supposition that what in nature, power, and capability is perfectly distinct from the material form in which it dwells, and by which it works, is to perish with it; – that the inmate is to die with the decay of his dwelling, the artist expire with the breaking of his implement; – that a being possessed of unbounded capacities of improvement is destined to advance only a few steps in his proper career, and then be arrested in his course for ever; – that a life of thought and feeling, which contains the germs of higher thoughts and feelings, awaiting, as essential to their full development, other influences than those which are shed on earth, is to be succeeded by eternal unconsciousness and oblivion; – and that a soul which finds in the present life a range too narrow for the full and vigorous scope of its nascent powers and feelings, is to be disappointed in its earnest longings and deep-seated hopes. It involves the supposition of a Divine design intimated, and then thrown aside – a Divine promise pledged and broken. The Great Architect would appear constructing a portico as if introductory to a magnificent temple, and then suddenly stopping short in the work, breaking it down, and scattering its beauty in the dust.

The construction of the Crystal Palace, with its contents, is a monument to the superiority of mind over matter; and that superiority indicates some great destiny hereafter. Immortality rises upon the eye of reason in the hazy distance: but confidence in relation to the future state must come from another quarter, through the exercise of faith. 'Life and immortality' are brought 'to light through the gospel'.

Nor can we properly terminate reflections of this order without going back to the source and origin of mind. If the material universe bears witness to the existence and character of a Great First Cause; if 'the invisible things of him from the creation of the world are clearly seen, being understood by the things that are made'; if 'the heavens declare the glory of God, and the firmament showeth his handiwork'; if the earth be full of his goodness; how much more does the soul of man, with all its capacities and powers, its intellect and genius, and, above all, its moral and religious susceptibilities, bear testimony to the being and attributes of the Creator. The marks of design in the mind of man, himself a designer, are more astonishing than those which we have in visible things. The power and beneficence of God, in giving us faculties of thought and susceptibilities of affection, appear with a plainness of expression even beyond what we discover in any of the material provisions for our comfort. While the whole universe is a volume in which God has, as it were, written down his thoughts, what page in it is so wonderful as the human mind? Whatever is great or beautiful in the imagination of man – whatever there is to admire in the works of his hands, fashioned according to the intellectual type within, must be traced up to the infinite source of intelligence, as its origin. Man has nothing which he has not received. What then must that unrevealed fount of beauty be, of which all the choice thoughts and beautiful imaginings of men from the beginning, however they have been expressed, are but as drops and spray!

3

MICHAEL ANGELO GARVEY, *THE SILENT REVOLUTION, OR THE FUTURE EFFECTS OF STEAM AND ELECTRICITY UPON THE CONDITIONS OF MANKIND* [EXTRACT]

(London: Cash, 1852), pp. 1–13

No one can contemplate the unexampled progress of science within the present century, without feeling that a new epoch has commenced in the history of our race. The divine powers of the human mind are extending their grasp and rising to a state of higher activity. Fields of knowledge undreamt of in the earlier ages of the world are successfully cultivated. The farthest regions of space are explored, and the secrets of their starry depths unfolded to men. The hidden forces of nature; the laws by which her phenomena are governed in their endless variety and succession; the economy of being; the structure and properties of matter; the relations of things and of ideas; the very mind itself: – all are undergoing a rigorous process of scientific investigation, from which result discoveries, that would be deemed miraculous, did not their number and frequency almost exhaust our faculty of wonder.

The great characteristic of this general intellectual movement is its practical tendency. The public in our day expects from its thinkers and experimentalists, not clever paradoxes, moving sentimentalisms, nor ingenious puzzles, but plain demonstrations of the best method of grappling with obstinate realities; discoveries of the means by which the powers of nature may be brought to subdue one another to the service of man in his ceaseless struggle with her material elements. Learning and skill are esteemed in proportion as they conduce to the well-being of society, and their value is measured by the extent of their application to the practical affairs of life. The genius of the age has responded to this expectancy. Philosophers have ceased to speculate in retirement upon unsubstantial and useless theories. Science is no longer a lifeless abstraction floating above the heads of the multitude. It has descended to earth. It mingles with men. It penetrates our mines. It enters our workshops. It speeds along with the iron courser of the rail. It tramples on the billows. It defies the tempest. It gives to man the sunbeam for a

DOI: 10.4324/9781315400303-5

pencil, and the lightning for a messenger. It lends to his feeble arm an irresistible might before which mountains crumble into dust; the barriers of kingdoms are removed, estuaries and straits are spanned with substantial road-ways, and the unstable waters, no less than the firm land, are subjected to his dominion. The talismans of Arabian fable never endowed their possessors with such power as that which science has bestowed upon mankind. It has placed at our command agencies, whose indefatigable energy, and adaptation to all human purposes, cast into shade even the genius of the ring or the lamp. What is there in all the recorded dreams of fancy more wonderful than the force of steam in its various applications? How stupendous in its power, and yet how manageable! A child may direct it. It would crush an army. A single touch puts in motion the majestic ship laden with the wealth of a nation. The rushing train, freighted with a thousand lives, or the complicated machinery that groans and whirls throughout the town-like factory, and a touch equally slight arrests the mighty power. In one place we see it wielding without effort a Nasmyth hammer of many tons weight, and forging the ponderous anchors destined to hold the floating castles of England against the fury of the hurricane. In another, polishing with an accuracy, beyond human skill, the delicate hairspring that is to trace and record the noiseless progress of time. Here it is employed upon massive blocks of iron, which it rolls out, cuts up, and moulds as the potter does the clay; and here it is spinning threads so fine that they almost elude the sight, and weaving them into airy textures that look like wreaths of morning mist. Unaffected by place, time or climate, incapable of fatigue, untouched by passions or infirmities, there stands the universal servant of man, ready to relieve him from all drudgery, and to supplement his limited ability in carrying out the intentions of his will. It matters not how difficult or various the services required, nor where they are to be performed. In the depths of the earth, or on the mountain top; in the open field, or in the crowded city; in the frozen north, or the burning tropics; whether they require the most gigantic strength, or the nicest care, this wondrous agent is suited to them all. It enables man, who is slow and weak compared with other terrestrial creatures, to pass from place to place with the speed of the eagle, carrying burdens in his flight that would crush the strong elephant to dust. By its means the force and dexterity of a million fingers are subjected to the control of one mind, and imbued with its intelligence. Under the transforming touch of this marvel-working power, the rudest substances assume forms of beauty and utility. The dark shapeless ore divides itself into multitudinous forms subservient to human purposes; it sparkles in the gorgeous service of the palace; it ministers to the humble comforts of the cottage; it gives instruments to the philosopher, and tools to the artisan; it furnishes man with means and appliances for executing his largest designs, and securing his conquest of the whole earth. The frail vesture of the cotton seed, that once rotted unnoticed where it fell, becomes clothing for nations, and when it has answered all possible purposes, and been reduced to the state of filthy worn-out rags which the very beggar on the high-way casts off with disgust, even these are taken up, and, by a magical process, transmuted into fair pages which are impressed with imperishable thoughts, multiplied with a rapidity like that of thought itself, and distributed throughout the world. Locomotion by steam is the complement of all its other applications; it has broken down the boundaries which time and space had set to human enterprise; it has emancipated the genius of our race from local restrictions, made the wonders wrought in any one place the common property of mankind, and combined the material interests of all nations. These are the miracles of steam, of the latent power in that impalpable vapour which has played before mankind since the creation, but which it was reserved for our age to control and subjugate. Science has taught us the spell by which the strong spirit of the mist is conjured from his dark abode in the mine, and compelled to execute our behests before he escape into the regions of air. The imponderable elements of nature are more powerful than her most obdurate substances. Xerxes tried in vain, with the strongest materials and the labour of myriads, to bridge the narrow Bosphorus; a single winter destroyed the vast structure: with us the most distant portions of the world are united by the invisible force that forms the summer cloud. But even the subtle influence of caloric, which thus animates the inert waters into titanic might, fails to excite our astonishment to so high a degree as electricity. If the one unites lands and transports material objects, the other seems destined to become the link of minds, the channel of intelligence and thought between all habitable parts of the globe. As yet, we can hardly venture to conjecture the form this mysterious power will assume, or the part it will perform in the future history of the world. Some general ideas are all we can fix upon as the basis of our speculations; but these are amongst the most astounding facts within the compass of human knowledge. They resemble the operations of a spiritual, rather than of a material agency, and the recondite manner in which they are effected entirely eludes our investigations. The electric telegraph is now a familiar object; we look upon it with a careless eye, we pass onward, and forget if we ever considered its miraculous properties. Yet, here we see realized more than the beautiful fiction of Strada; not between two minds alone does it establish a responsive sympathy, it creates a communion of thought between cities and kingdoms; it enables a man to utter his feelings, at the very instant they arise in his mind, to ears that listen for them at a distance of a thousand miles. What is this surprising and intangible power? What will it accomplish in its maturity, when it so far transcends all calculation in its infancy? One might think for ever, with increasing wonder, on the one supernatural fact, that without any perturbation of its parts perceptible to the finest organs, or appreciable by the most exquisite instruments, communications are transmitted along the wire, however great its length, with such inconceivable rapidity, that the moment of transit cannot be measured by the most nicely adjusted chronometers. There is no sensible lapse of time between the giving of the signal at one terminus, and its reception at the other, though the distance between them should be a thousand, ten thousand, or twenty thousand miles. Nay, if a wire were stretched round the whole earth, and the ends made to terminate in two dials placed immediately beneath the eye, the very instant the index that supplied the influence was moved, it would be replied to by that which received it after traversing twenty-five thousand miles of space; the movements would be to all intents and purposes simultaneous, and this result would be unaffected by the nature of the elements through which the conducting medium might pass. It would be still the same thought rivalling speed, whether the conductor were raised in the air or sunk in the earth, whether it passed over the loftiest mountain peaks, or lay at the bottom of the ocean with the world of waters rolling above. Whilst we look upon the electric wires as they stretch along by the great lines of railway, they appear perfectly quiescent. The weary little bird rests upon them in his flight, and clasps them in his tiny claws; yet along that motionless thread, and through that feeble grasp, there may be passing tidings of life or death, of ruin or prosperity – intelligence of the fall of kings and thrones, of battles lost and won, of events that change the destinies of millions, and plunge whole nations into mourning or intoxicate them with joy. A thousand fathoms beneath the keel of the war-ship, undisturbed by the tumult of the elements in which she reels and struggles; in the dark and silent abysses of ocean, where uncouth monsters make their retreat, and human vision has never penetrated; amidst objects strange to the eye of man, and scenes that have been secret since the beginning of time, there lies the wondrous ligature which connects the minds of nations, conveying manifold contributions to the sum of human wisdom and experience, from which man shall yet learn to still his mimic thunders, and to aspire after higher glories than those won by mutual slaughter, on the bloody waters, or the groaning field. Such are the new agencies whose influence upon the future condition of mankind we have to consider. But there is another power that incalculably transcends them, an agency to which steam and electricity and all other physical forces are merely means and instruments. It is that of the mind itself, the prime mover and director of them all, which defines their purposes, and controls their operations – that restless, indefatigable, and inscrutable principle to which even the human frame is but an apparatus of exquisitely adjusted organs – that intellectual power, which, as it feels, and thinks, and wills, impels man to action, designs his objects, directs his movements, and registers their results; which pushes its inquiries into every department of creation, and with the same insatiable thirst for knowledge scans the mightiest operations of nature, and scrutinizes her minutest processes; which surveys the past, anticipates the future, and ever and anon turns in upon itself to observe its own movements, and to conduct a marvellous analysis of which it is itself at once the subject, the instrument, and the performer – the immortal element in man's nature which tinges with the glow of its own etherial essence his feeble and delicate frame, investing him with sovereign dignity, and giving him power over all terrestrial things and beings.

To the study of this principle we must inevitably recur, if we would either trace with accuracy the progress of our race through the past, or indicate the probable course of its future destinies. It is the fountain of all human activity, and the final issues of all man's labour and discovery depend upon its character and tendencies. We propose to estimate these tendencies and to ascertain the conditions under which their development is either retarded or promoted, in order that we may be able to form some rational conjecture of the future of our species. This would be a difficult and uncertain task, if attempted from an abstract consideration only of the human faculties. There is, however, a sure and easy method of accomplishing that object. The path which man has already trodden from barbarism to civilisation, lies before us in authentic history, strewed with the memorials of his passions and his might. There we can calmly investigate his progress, note the difficulties and obstructions it has had to overcome, and deduce with certainty the principles that have given it its forward impulse, as well as the conditions under which that impulse has acted with greatest power and constancy. From the study of what man has accomplished, we shall rise with a fuller conception of what he is likely to accomplish, for the past is a dim mirror of the future, displaying in shadowy twilight the vague outline of that wondrous phantasmagoria in which he is the chief figure, and which is gradually rising into distinctness, as the great secular morning brightens into day. The principles of human action which have issued in the events of foregone history, are in their nature immutable, and will create the history of the times to come. The ages that have fled resemble those that are approaching, as the wilderness or partially reclaimed field resembles the highly cultivated garden. Their products are different, but the powers of the soil are the same, and all that art has done, has been to give those powers liberty of development. The same vital principles of life and growth that once clothed the desert with briars and thorns, now sustain the fragrant rose and the tree laden with golden fruit. In like manner the necessities, passions, and affections of our nature are constant in their operation, and from them spring all our actions; they are the very pabulum and support of human purposes and efforts. What we call social laws, or the principles upon which societies of men arise and are held together, are but the resultants of those innumerable minute impulses which are hourly and momentarily springing up in the breasts of individuals. To arrive at just conclusions, then, concerning the direction in which our race is moving, it will be necessary to consider this compound force by which it is impelled; this will imbue us with true notions of the subjective energy which has enabled mankind to attain its present degree of elevation; whilst, by tracing its previous course, the mind will acquire a corresponding momentum which will project it forward in the right line of conjecture as to the point at which that course will culminate, though its incidents remain hidden from us amongst the secrets of time.

4

ALFRED, LORD TENNYSON, 'ODE FOR THE OPENING OF THE INTERNATIONAL EXHIBITION'

Fraser's Magazine, 65 (1862), p. 803

Uplift a thousand voices full and sweet,
In this wide hall with earth's invention stor'd,
And praise th' invisible universal Lord,
Who lets once more in peace the nations meet,
Where Science, Art, and Labour have outpour'd
Their myriad horns of plenty at our feet.

O silent father of our Kings to be,
Mourn'd in this golden hour of jubilee,
For this, for all, we weep our thanks to thee!

The world-compelling plan was thine,
And, lo! the long laborious miles
Of Palace; lo! the giant aisles,
Rich in model and design;
Harvest-tool and husbandry,
Loom, and wheel, and engin'ry,
Secrets of the sullen mine,
Steel and gold, and corn and wine,
Fabric rough, or Fairy fine,
Sunny tokens of the Line,
Polar marvels, and a feast
Of wonder, out of West and East,
And shapes and hues of Art divine!
All of beauty, all of use
That one fair planet can produce,
Brought from under every star,
Blown from over every main,
And mixt, as life is mixt with pain,
The works of peace with works of war.
War himself must make alliance
With rough Labour and fine Science,
Else he would but strike in vain.

And is the goal so far away?
Far, how far, no man can say:
Let us have our dream to-day.

DOI: 10.4324/9781315400303-6

O ye, the wise who think, the wise who reign,
From growing Commerce loose her latest chain,
And let the fair, white-winged peacemaker fly
To happy havens under all the sky,
And mix the seasons and the golden hours,
Till each man find his own in all men's good,
And all men work in noble brotherhood,
Breaking their mailed fleets and armed towers,
And ruling by obeying nature's powers,
And gathering all the fruits of Peace and crown'd with all her flowers.

5

F. R. CONDER, 'THE BEST FRIEND OF THE WORKING MAN' [EXTRACT]

Fraser's Magazine, new series 19 (1879), pp. 231–232

If we say that every article of necessity or of luxury has been reduced in price by from one-half to nine-tenths by the services of the steam engine, we shall be far within the mark; and at the same time the wages of the labourer have been more than doubled, if measured in wheat, since 1820.

If it were possible, for a single day, to restore such a state of prices as would certainly now rule if we were deprived of the command of steam power, the distress produced would be overwhelming. And yet it is in spite of the steady and persistent opposition of the English working man that this prodigious change in his position has been effected. No great improvement has failed to encounter violent opposition. The greatest benefactors of the industrial classes have often been in peril of their lives for their inventive activity. The new machines have been broken, the masters who used them have been threatened, down to the moment at which we write, when the manufacture of pearl buttons is being driven from Birmingham to the United States by the declaration of the Operative Union of Pearl Button Makers against the use of steam in the service of their craft.

We may, therefore, well repeat the question, Have the working men of England ever formed a true estimate of the services rendered to their order by the steam engine? or, to put it more broadly, by the application of mechanical motive power? And by that question is intended, not matter of degree, but of kind. It is not how much good has been done, or can be done, by the use of the energy of heat, but has good or harm been thus done to the labourer? Is the steam engine a tyrant, or a slave, as far as the workman is concerned? Is it a competitor, or an invaluable appliance? What it really is no person of ordinary intelligence who takes the trouble patiently to inquire, can doubt. That it has been all along regarded under the false light of a competitor by the mass of the working people is, we fear, but too certain. That it is so regarded, even at the present moment, by some of them, we have above adduced evidence to show.

It cannot be denied that it is a matter of national importance that this great question should be put in its true light, and fully and unreservedly grasped by

DOI: 10.4324/9781315400303-7

those whom it so deeply concerns. Putting aside the motives – unfortunately too universal, though ignored by political economy – which dispose those who are ill provided with the world's goods to cast an evil eye on those who are better off; leaving out of sight the great moral force of envy; the chief cause that has tended to embitter the relations of capital, as it is called, to labour, has been the blindness of the labourer as to the services rendered to him by the accumulation of the outcome of labour. At present we confine this consideration to the one application of wealth in the production of steam machinery. While it is perfectly true that at the moment of the introduction of any new and improved method of production there may be a temporary confusion caused, and even a temporary distress occasioned to those who produce by the old and less efficient methods, there is no doubt that in every craft and every calling in which the services of mechanical power has [sic] been introduced, the workman has been elevated in consequence in the social scale. The burden has been taken from his shoulders; his weekly pay has been augmented; he has been raised from the condition of a servant into that of a master, and a master commanding the inexhaustible resources of an uncomplaining and untiring slave, a slave who consumes only coal and water, and who costs less for a day than a horse does for an hour.

6

'THE WORLD IN A HURRY'

Sewing Machine Gazette and Journal of Domestic Appliances (1 March 1881), p. 30

Everybody now knows that it is absurd to talk about, and still more so to sigh for, 'good old times'. The Laureate has declared that 'we are heirs of all the ages in the foremost files of time'. He is doubtless right. To-day is older than yesterday; and the further we look back the more of youthful national folly must we see. And yet there was a period when men and women were not always engaged in catching trains, in discounting their pleasures, in ante-dating bills of amusement, or in rejoicing over instalments of intelligence flashed across their bewildered eyes as a kind of heliographic abstract of the good or bad news awaiting them. It is proverbial that men in all ages have made haste to be rich; but there never was a period when the wheel of fortune, the whirligig of fashion, the red and black balls of speculation, and the teetotum of trade revolved with such rapidity as they do now. Falling stars, eccentric comets, and the secular acceleration of the moon possess no greater interest for advanced astronomers than do the means, appliances, and aids, material and moral, to the enjoyment of life, the prosecution of trade, and general aggrandisement, with intensified speed, for all orders of the community. 'Go-ahead!' is the motto of humanity, and steady progress has gone out of fashion. There was a time when wind and tide, waiting for no man, had matters very much their own way. A Nelson in pursuit of the enemy might be blown out of his course; and the navies of commerce or war cumbered the seas in a helpless way. But the giant Steam has accomplished more than he who wore the famous 'Seven-league Boots', dear to childhood; and a modern Puck, in the shape of Science, puts a girdle roundabout the earth in less than forty minutes. The electric telegraph, declining to follow the sun and keep company with the hours, outstrips time, and throws the best regulated chronometers into a state of agitation and doubt. Clocks are uniform in their records all over the land; space, distance, and locality have lost distinction; and events, as Hamlet's mother said of woes, tread upon each other's heels, so fast they follow. Schoolboys no longer creep like snails unwillingly to school, but are whirled thither by railway; and lovers who would write a ballad to their mistress's eyebrows must prepare themselves to do so while rattling along at sixty miles an hour. Observant students not only run and read, but ride and dine; nay more, they journey in their beds, going to sleep in Aberdeen and waking up in London, with nothing more than a faint memory of a nightmare in the form

DOI: 10.4324/9781315400303-8

of panting, puffing, snorting demons, with white, green, and red eyes, to disturb their minds. All the world is in a hurry, and people in the pursuit of pleasure or business, if not bustling from an arrival platform, are rushing, amidst the din of bells and the shouting of guards, into carriages on the departure side of the line!

Periodical literature comes out days in advance of its printed date, and Christmas books make their appearance long before the season of Advent. Almanacks for 'the ensuing year' may be bought in September, and 'Twelfth Night Characters' have scarcely disappeared before valentines gladden the hearts of amorous swains and delight the eyes of maidens in their teens. In such haste are they despatched that the Postmaster-General makes almost superfluous demands that they should be posted early; and the welcome 'Good morrow to St. Valentine!' has no sooner been uttered, than those who greeted the day prepare to speed the parting guest. Winter goods are 'sold off at less than cost price', that 'spring novelties' may be produced while yet the snowdrop is buried in the ground and frost holds the earth in bondage. These in turn give place to 'summer fashions' before the blossom is off the trees and the intrusive cuckoo arrives to occupy his place of usurpation. Fruits, fish, flowers, and vegetables are almost as plentiful out of the season as when they are legitimately 'in', and nothing is orderly but irregularity in the arrival of produce from the uttermost parts of the earth. Only the unforseen happens, and merchants seek to spring surprises upon our markets with greater earnestness and zeal than even characterises Mr. Gladstone's action in the political world. Steamboats are propelled at high pressure, and their skippers, in emulation of Mississippi captains, sit upon the safety valves of boilers; barges, wont to float lazily on the surface of the Thames, are tugged furiously along; and launches dart to and fro like fire-flies, endangering the outriggers, which have surpassed the tardy skiff and wherry as surely as express trains have taken the place of slow coaches. There are dress rehearsals of pantomimes before Boxing Day arrives, and private views of pictures in advance of the public exhibition of them. The husbandman not only strives to make two blades of grass grow where only one grew before, but deluges his land with patent manures, and adopts forcing processes that swift and sudden growth may reward his pains, and enable him to keep pace with rivals struggling to be first in gathering a harvest. Every possible effort is made to accelerate the speed of racehorses; and pedestrians walk and run thousands of miles continuously day and night. Swimmers are not content, like Leander or Byron, with crossing from Sestos to Abydos, but remain in the water for a week at a time, and make voyages to sea which would have frightened ancient Britons in their coracles, and taxed the skill of Roman navigators in their stoutest galleys. Journals are printed from endless rolls of paper, and produced by processes which secure almost simultaneous publication to hundreds of thousands; and a perfect Niagara of news is poured over the land without intermission. Photography may be carried on by night; and a system of continuous floating hotels bridges the Atlantic, and virtually provides a ferry to the Antipodes. Short cuts across continents by canals, and tunnels through mountain ranges tend to obliterate the lines of demarcation between nations, and practically bring closer together the members of the great family of man. Locomotion goes on by sea and land in the thickest fog, amidst the excitement of detonating signals, the clashing of monster gongs, and the sonorous roaring of gigantic horns; and garments are made by steam-driven machinery. People cannot stop to run up and down stairs, but take to lifts. The blackest night, equally with the brightest day, knows nothing of rest; 'haste, haste, haste, post haste!' is no longer an exceptional cry, but an incessant command. The telephone intensifies and extends the powers of hearing; the lightning has been tamed to obey domestic behests; the pneumatic tube sucks up communications and parcels with the voracity of an octopus; and a network of exquisitely sensitive nerves binds together the whole human race. Flashing signals enable armies at a distance to interchange intelligence with rapidity fleet as a glance of the mind; and the correspondence of business, friendship, and love is carried on by means of stenography. Reporters for the Press habitually transfix thought as it flies, with nimbler fingers than Gurney possessed in the zenith of his fame; and so eager are orators that their speeches should appear promptly in print, that they even have them set up in type before delivery, not to lose time in winning popular applause. State papers find their way into the public journals before they reach Parliament; and magazine articles are in the hands of reviewers before publication. In an astronomical sense the world may be moving in its orbit and on its axis as it has done from the days when 'the morning stars sang together for joy' to those of Galileo, and from his time to the present moment; but the peoples of civilisation who tread the great rotundity are rushing about in hot haste and moving on with ever-accelerated strides. No will-o'-the-wisp could rival their phantom-like swiftness of motion; and, watching the inordinate fondness for rapidity of action in process of development, a cynic, pausing for breath amidst the giddy whirl around him, might almost be pardoned for suggesting that, before long, death itself may come to be discounted by a world intent upon performing 'happy despatch' in emulation of the suicides of China and Japan.

7

'THE LATEST PATENT'

Answers (29 August 1891), p. 249

A most useful invention for nursery use, called a 'baby-washer', is announced, and the inventor describes his infant machine as follows:

> 'You simply insert the begrimed and treacle-coated infant in an orifice, which can be made any required size by turning a cogwheel with electric attachments.
>
> 'The child glides gently down a highly-polished plane. His lips are met at the terminus by an indiarubber tube, from which the infant can draw lacteal nourishment of the purest and most invigorating character, secured for the purpose at great expense, from a choice breed of the Alderney kine raised on the estate of her Majesty the Queen in the Isle of Wight.
>
> 'While in this compartment, which is formed of plate-glass mirrors, the perturbed spirits of the infant are soothed by its frantic efforts to demolish its own image, reflected in the glass, with a nickel-plated combined tooth-cutter, nail-knife, rattle, and tack-hammer, which is thrust into the baby's hand by an automaton monkey.
>
> 'Fatigued by its destructive efforts, the infant falls asleep, while the organ attachment plays softly the ravishing melody of "Put me in my little bed". Then it slips into the third compartment. Here the body is washed.
>
> 'Another small tube administers a dose of soothing syrup, and the infant glides from the machine, its nails pared and its hair combed, if it has any, ready for the habiliments rendered necessary by the fall of our first parents.'

DOI: 10.4324/9781315400303-9

8

A. R. BENNETT, *ON THE TELEPHONING OF GREAT CITIES* [EXTRACT]

(London: Whittaker, 1892), pp. 4–7

Every villa in the residential districts, every suburban shopkeeper, will be on the exchange, and the telephone will supersede in London, as it has already done elsewhere, the butcher's boy, the grocer's lad, and the baker's man – at least, so far as the daily calling for orders is concerned – and tend to make us more independent than we are at present of the domestic servant.

As the new generation grows – a generation familiarised from its cradle with the word 'telephone' and the idea of conversing at a distance with all and sundry, and consequently free from the prejudices and old-fashioned methods which have, in very many cases, deterred their fathers from availing themselves of the new agent – every young man starting in business will order a telephone connection at the same time that he orders his fuel, light, and water, just as a matter of course; and, if time is found at all for speculation on such a commonplace subject, it will be devoted to wondering how his steady-going progenitors did without it.

As an indication of how the telephone idea is taking root, I may mention that the builders of a new block of business offices in Manchester propose to put a permanent connection to the Mutual Telephone Company's Exchange into each suite of offices, paying the subscriptions themselves, and charging their tenants nothing extra. This is one of the first-fruits of cheap rates.

The possible demand being conceded, the question arises, 'Can it be met; and, if so, how?'

I answer that it can, and I propose to show how.

The establishment of an effective and popular telephone exchange in a large town, and one that can be added to and extended freely and economically, without pulling down what has already been done, involves the fulfilment of several indispensable conditions.

Firstly. – Speech must be loud and distinct, and privacy of communication complete; and a subscriber's line and apparatus must be adapted equally well to speaking to another across the street or to one five hundred miles away. There must, furthermore, be an absence of all disturbing sounds.

 DOI: 10.4324/9781315400303-10

Secondly. – The arrangements for connecting the subscribers together, subsequently disconnecting them, and, if required, immediately re-connecting them to others, must be so complete that eight or ten seconds should be the maximum time occupied within the compass of the largest town.

Thirdly. – The rates must be within the reach of even small householders and shopkeepers, and should not exceed £8 per annum.

Fourthly. – The general design must permit of the addition of new subscribers in every direction and to any extent, without interfering with the work already done.

All these conditions can be complied with. What is necessary to do to meet them can be broadly indicated under three headings.

(1) The universal use of metallic circuits, and the absence from the line of intermediate electro-magnets and other signalling devices, which tend to damp and deform the electrical vibrations which constitute telephonic speech.
(2) The provision of means by which certain and instantaneous communication can be established between subscriber and operator, and between one operator and another.
(3) The division of the town to be telephoned into districts or sections not exceeding a square mile in area, each of which is worked from a switch-room placed at or near its centre.

The fulfilment of these necessary conditions is easy, provided the undertakers, whomsoever they may be, are in possession of the right to open the streets of the town and lay their conductors in the same way as gas, water, electric light, and, in some instances, hydraulic and pneumatic power conductors are laid.

So long as the execution of any scheme is subject to the caprice or the blackmailing propensities of individual proprietors, a proper telephonic service, such as London, the first city of the world, ought to possess, will remain an aspiration and nothing more. It has always been a bugbear of telephonists in this country that they have to fix their wires, not where they want them, but where they are permitted to. A British telephone exchange system is consequently, generally speaking, the result of a constant endeavour to reconcile the desirable with the impacticable – a compromise rarely, if ever, satisfactory.

Legislative assistance, to the extent of placing the undertakers of telephone exchange systems on an equal footing with the ministers to other public wants is indispensable to the carrying out of a scheme designed, not only to meet the requirements of the moment, but those of a reasonable number of years to come.

I am not one of those who believe that there is no design in the conduct of the Universe – that railways and steamboats are because they happened to have happened, or because Newcomen, Trevithick, Watt, Stephenson, and Symington chanced to have ideas – that telegraphs are because Gauss and Weber, Cooke and Wheatstone, and Morse were scientific enthusiasts – that telephones are because Reiss, Varley, Bell, Edison, and Hughes were covetous of fame, fortune, or notoriety.

No! Railways and steamers, telegraphs and telephones, are means adopted by the Great Designer to meet the needs of growing populations – to render possible the feeding and clothing of the ever-increasing millions – to lay under contribution for their benefit the uttermost parts of the earth. They make the world larger by increasing its capacity for population, and, at the same time, smaller by quickening communication. The means at the command of our fathers a hundred years ago would not suffice to feed the populace of to-day. Famine and pestilence, without such beneficent provisions, would have kept back the multiplication of the human race; a certain stage would have been reached, but, without the new appliances, never passed. The process is still going on, and will not stop at telephones we may be sure. The future has greater wonders in store than any we have so far seen. Some are already casting intermittent scintillations of their brilliance before – just as telegraphs and telephones were talked of ages ago. It has been truly said that the dreams and fairy tales of one generation become the every-day commonplaces of the next.

Starting with the admission that the telephone is neither a fad nor a luxury, but a providential provision for man's use and benefit – a practical, earnest, matter-of-fact instrument, which has come to stay – we may likewise assume that it is not possible to stifle it, to relegate it to oblivion, or even to curtail its natural extension. Sooner or later it will be universally recognised that the general use of the telephone has to be provided for, and the legislative sanction I am now advocating will be granted in order that such an excellent servant may be turned to the best account.

9

ALFRED RUSSEL WALLACE, *THE WONDERFUL CENTURY: ITS SUCCESSES AND FAILURES* [EXTRACT]

(London: Swann Sonnenschein, 1898), pp. 1–3, 150–153

We men of the nineteenth century have not been slow to praise it. The wise and the foolish, the learned and the unlearned, the poet and the pressman, the rich and the poor, alike swell the chorus of admiration for the marvellous inventions and discoveries of our own age, and especially for those innumerable applications of science which now form part of our daily life, and which remind us every hour of our immense superiority over our comparatively ignorant forefathers.

But though in this respect (and in many others) we undoubtedly think very well of ourselves, yet, in the opinion of the present writer, our self-admiration does not rest upon an adequate appreciation of the facts. No one, so far as I am aware, has yet pointed out the altogether exceptional character of our advance in science and the arts, during the century which is now so near its close. In order to estimate its full importance and grandeur – more especially as regards man's increased power over nature, and the application of that power to the needs of his life to-day, with unlimited possibilities in the future – we must compare it, not with any preceding century, or even with the last millennium, but with the whole historical period – perhaps even with the whole period that has elapsed since the stone age.

Looking back through the long dark vista of human history, the one step in material progress that seems to be really comparable in importance with several of the steps we have just made, was, when Fire was first utilized, and became the servant and the friend, instead of being the master and the enemy of man. From that far distant epoch even down to our day, fire, in various forms and in ever-widening spheres of action, has not only ministered to the necessities and the enjoyments of man, but has been the greatest, the essential factor, in that continuous increase of his power over nature, which has undoubtedly been a chief means of the development of his intellect and a necessary condition of what we term civilization. Without fire there would have been neither a bronze nor an iron age, and without these there could have been no effective tools or weapons, with

DOI: 10.4324/9781315400303-11

all the long succession of mechanical discoveries and refinements that depended upon them. Without fire there could be no rudiment even of chemistry, and all that has arisen out of it. Without fire much of the earth's surface would be uninhabitable by man, and much of what is now wholesome food would be useless to him. Without fire he must always have remained ignorant of the larger part of the world of matter and of its mysterious forces. He might have lived in the warmer parts of the earth in a savage or even in a partially civilized condition, but he could never have risen to the full dignity of intellectual man, the interpreter and master of the forces of nature.

Having thus briefly indicated our standpoint, let us proceed to sketch in outline those great advances in science and the arts which are the glory of our century. In the course of our survey we shall find that the more important of these are not mere improvements upon, or developments of, anything that had been done before, but that they are entirely new departures, arising out of our increasing knowledge of and command over the forces of the universe. Many of these advances have already led to developments of the most startling kind, giving us such marvellous powers, and such extensions of our normal senses, as would have been incredible, and almost unthinkable even to our greatest men of science, a hundred years ago.

[. . .]

Having now completed our sketch of those practical discoveries and striking generalizations of science which have in so many respects changed the outward forms of our civilization, and will ever render memorable the century now so near its close, we are in a position to sum up its achievements, and compare them with what has gone before.

Taking first those inventions and practical applications of science which are perfectly new departures, and which have also so rapidly developed as to have profoundly affected many of our habits, and even our thoughts and our language, we find them to be thirteen in number.

1 Railways, which have revolutionized land-travel and the distribution of commodities.
2 Steam-navigation, which has done the same thing for ocean travel, and has besides led to the entire reconstruction of the navies of the world.
3 Electric Telegraphs, which have produced an even greater revolution in the communication of thought.
4 The Telephone, which transmits, or rather reproduces, the voice of the speaker at a distance.
5 Friction Matches, which have revolutionized the modes of obtaining fire.
6 Gas-lighting, which enormously improved outdoor and other illumination.
7 Electric-lighting, another advance, now threatening to supersede gas.
8 Photography, an art which is to the external forms of nature what printing is to thought.
9 The Phonograph, which preserves and reproduces sounds as photography preserves and reproduces forms.

10 The Röntgen Rays, which render many opaque objects transparent, and open up a new world to photography.
11 Spectrum Analysis, which so greatly extends our knowledge of the universe that by its assistance we are able to ascertain the relative heat and chemical constitution of the stars, and ascertain the existence, and measure the rate of motion, of stellar bodies which are entirely invisible.
12 The use of Anæsthetics, rendering the most severe surgical operations painless.
13 The use of Antiseptics in surgical operations, which has still further extended the means of saving life.

Now, if we ask what inventions comparable with these were made during the previous (eighteenth) century, it seems at first doubtful whether there were any. But we may perhaps admit the development of the steam-engine from the rude but still useful machine of Newcomen to the powerful and economical engines of Boulton and Watt. The principle, however, was known long before, and had been practically applied in the previous century by the Marquis of Worcester and by Savery; and the improvements made by Watt, though very important, had a very limited result. The engines made were almost wholly used in pumping the water out of deep mines, and the bulk of the population knew no more of them, nor derived any more direct benefit from them, than if they had not existed.

In the seventeenth century, the one great and far-reaching invention was that of the Telescope, which, in its immediate results of extending our knowledge of the universe and giving possibilities of future knowledge not yet exhausted, may rank with spectrum analysis in our own era. The Barometer and Thermometer are minor discoveries.

In the sixteenth century we have no invention of the first rank, but in the fifteenth we have Printing.

The Mariner's Compass was invented early in the fourteenth century, and was of great importance in rendering ocean navigation possible and thus facilitating the discovery of America.

Then, backward to the dawn of history, or rather to prehistoric times, we have the two great engines of knowledge and discovery – the Indian or Arabic numerals leading to arithmetic and algebra, and, more remote still, the invention of alphabetical writing.

Summing these up, we find only five inventions of the first rank in all preceding time – the telescope, the printing-press, the mariner's compass, Arabic numerals, and alphabetical writing, to which we may add the steam-engine and the barometer, making seven in all, as against thirteen in our single century.

PART 2

Transport

2.1

Third-class rail travel

DOI: 10.4324/9781315400303-13

2.1 Third-class rail travel

Railway Reform: Its Expediency and Practicability Considered [extract] (London: Pelham Richardson, 1843), pp. 2–3, 14–19.

'Railway Politeness' and 'The Third Class Traveller's Petition', *Punch* (1845), p. 10.

D. T. Timins, 'From Roofless Pen to Corridor Coach: The Evolution of the 3rd Class Carriage on the South Eastern Railway' [extract], *Railway Magazine*, 4 (1899), pp. 496–500.

The Wonderful Century (1898), Alfred Russel Wallace's vision of the era's great changes, sets off by celebrating its revolutions in transport, developments that seemed to bring the nation and the world physically closer for sociability, migration and tourism as well as for trade, exploitation and imperial control. The early part of the century brought the establishment of the canal system that was a crucial component of British industrialism, as well as the great roadworks of civil engineers such as Thomas Telford and John Loudon McAdam, but it was steam transport – the railway and steamship – that soon offered perhaps the signature technologies of the Victorian era. This volume's introduction and the preceding section, Part 1 'The march of invention', demonstrate how steam power provided a cornerstone of Victorian thinking about invention and how steam-powered travel could offer an image of a world speeding headlong into a limitless future of technological change.

These broad visions often center on abstract invocations of the steam engine or the railway, but matters could look quite different when it comes to particular technological things. For this reason, the selections included here focus on inventions as embodied by specific implementations of railway technology, by particular objects. Furthermore, they offer a reminder that the adoption of new technologies does not mean leaving old social divisions behind. The 'classes' of Victorian railway accommodation reiterated the class distinctions of Victorian society, from the plush furnishings and comparative privacy of a compartment in a first-class carriage to the discomforts of the third-class carriage of the 1830s and 1840s – typically, an open goods wagon lacking not only seats but also a roof.

While the writer of a pamphlet on railway reform deplores those conditions, the humorists of *Punch* turn them into poetry. With the Railway Regulation Act of 1844, Parliament helped dispatch the old third-class carriages, mandating that the railway companies establish a basic level of inexpensive service for third-class passengers on every route, in covered carriages with seats. At the end of the century, a writer for *Railway Magazine* looked back at the evolution of third-class rail travel on the South Eastern line through the 1870s, as the railways dealt with new challenges (heavy suburban traffic) and grudgingly began to meet the demands for more light, room and comfort on carriages, even for third-class travellers. Indeed, beginning in the 1870s, as third-class travel become more comfortable and more popular, many railways began ending second-class service altogether.

Victorian third-class rail travel thus became the ancestor of modern 'standard' railway accommodations in the United Kingdom.[1]

Note

1 The bibliography of sources on the Victorian railway is vast, but a list of some of the principal works offers a starting point for further reading, as well as conveying a sense of the variety of approaches to the topic: Ian Carter, *Railways and Culture in Britain: The Epitome of Modernity* (Manchester: Manchester University Press, 2001); Michael J. Freeman, *Railways and the Victorian Imagination* (New Haven, CT: Yale University Press, 1999); P. J. G. Ransom, *The Victorian Railway and How It Evolved* (London: Heinemann, 1990); Wolfgang Schivelbusch, *The Railway Journey: Trains and Travel in the Nineteenth Century*, trans. by Anselm Hollo (Oxford: Blackwell, 1980); David Norman Smith, *The Railway and Its Passengers: A Social History* (Newton Abbot: David and Charles, 1988). Jack Simmons and Gordon Biddle (eds.), *The Oxford Companion to British Railway History from 1603 to the 1990s* (Oxford and New York: Oxford University Press, 1999), a compendious general resource, includes hundreds of incisive encyclopedia-style entries with bibliographies.

10

RAILWAY REFORM: ITS EXPEDIENCY AND PRACTICABILITY CONSIDERED [EXTRACT]

(London: Pelham Richardson, 1843), pp. 2–3, 14–19

There are few subjects of more importance to us than that which relates to the facilities of transit – the conveyance of passengers and merchandize throughout the country at the maximum of speed and minimum of cost; and whilst we have gone on day by day extending by those mighty instruments of civilization – the Steam-engine and Railway – the means of accomplishing this good, we seem to have taken it as a matter of course that that good has been accomplished to its fullest extent.

The practical application of steam to the useful purposes of life, was a gigantic step in the progress of the arts and sciences, and may be justly said to have marked a new era in the history of mankind: few discoveries in physical truth have been attended with more important results, or promise in their future developement [sic] to produce such mighty changes over the face of the civilized globe. Nor is the versatility of its application less extraordinary than its power. 'Steam is but in its infancy', is a trite remark of daily occurrence, and the continual improvements which are taking place in the construction of the steam engine, – that mighty PROOF of the power of the human intellect, – and the diversified uses to which it is constantly being applied, attest the truth of the remark. If steam, then, is still in its infancy, what may not be expected from its mature age, when time shall have brought to perfection its varied powers and developed its mighty resources?

Amongst the varied purposes to which this power has been applied, that of locomotion in connexion with railways is by far the most important, and to that subject alone our present inquiries shall be directed. No application of any discovery in science, either in ancient or modern times, has, within the same period, produced such astonishing results as those which are witnessed daily and hourly, as displayed in the working of locomotives on railways. An inquiry, therefore, as to whether or not this power has been properly directed, cannot be out of place. From the first establishment of railways in this country down to the present time, the abuses attendant on their management have been a matter of constant complaint, and our object in investigating the subject shall be twofold:

DOI: 10.4324/9781315400303-14

1st. To institute an inquiry into the railway system, as it has been established, and is now carried on in this country.
2nd. To consider to what extent it could be modified – should it be found desirable – without injury to any party, and benefit to all.

Capital and skill have, within the last ten or twelve years, been directed with extraordinary energy to the improvement of inland transport, and this important instrument of national wealth and civilization has received a proportionate impulse. Effects are now witnessed which, had they been narrated twenty years since, would only have been admitted into the pages of fiction or volumes of romance. Who could have credited the possibility of a ponderous engine of iron, loaded with some hundreds of passengers, in a train of carriages of corresponding magnitude, and a large quantity of water and coke, taking flight from Manchester and arriving at Liverpool, a distance of more than 30 miles, in little more than an hour? And yet this is a matter of daily and almost hourly occurrence.

The rapidity of transport thus attained is not less wonderful than the weight transported. Its capabilities in this respect far transcend the exigencies even of the two greatest commercial marts in Great Britain: loads varying from 50 to 100 tons are transported at the rate of 25 miles an hour, and in one instance have we seen a load – we should rather say a cargo – of merchandize, to the amount of two hundred and thirty tons gross, transported from Liverpool to Manchester at the average rate of twelve miles per hour. The circumstances under which the steam engine is worked on a railway are not favourable to the economy of fuel; nevertheless, a pound of coke burned in a locomotive engine will evaporate five pints of water; in this evaporation they will exert a mechanical force sufficient to draw two tons weight on the railway a distance of one mile in two minutes. Four horses, working in a stage coach on a common road, are necessary to draw the same weight in six minutes.

A train of coaches weighing about 80 tons, and transporting about 240 passengers, has been taken from Liverpool to Birmingham, and back from Birmingham to Liverpool, the trip each way taking about 4¼ hours, stoppages included; the distance between the places by railway is 98 miles. This double journey of nearly 200 miles is effected by the mechanical force produced by the combustion of four tons of coke, the value of which is about five pounds. To carry the same number of passengers daily between the same places by stage coaches on a common road, would require 20 coaches and an establishment of 380 horses, whilst the journey in each direction would not be performed in less than twelve hours, stoppages included.

Such is the overwhelming power and economy of steam when duly directed.

[. . .]

This evidence is sufficient to shew the overwhelming power of a railway company, and the complete futility, unless under very peculiar circumstances, of any competition with it for the poorer any more than for the richer class of passengers. In regard, then, to the former class, Railway Directors have a twofold task to perform: – To commence by carrying third class passengers at such a low rate as to drive all opposition off the road; and when that is effectually done, and their opponents' stock in trade disposed of, the second part of their task commences, which is not less important than the first; which is, to prevent as far as possible any traveller availing himself of the third class carriages, and virtually compelling him to go by a second class. It will be remembered that, some years since, in consequence of the frightful number of appalling railway accidents, the legislature was obliged to interfere with the hitherto unlimited and irresponsible power possessed by railway companies, nor will it be forgotten the determined resistance which these bodies, individually and collectively, made to such interference; their opposition, however, was of no avail, and to the Board of Trade was confided the care of the lives and limbs of her majesty's subjects, the companies being bound to conform to its orders; and consequently an accident on a railway is now a matter of rare occurrence. It will likewise be remembered that the victims were almost without exception third class passengers, who were placed next the engine, without any carriage between them: – the frightful consequences of such a procedure are well known. The 'Times' took the matter up, and by bringing the whole force of public opinion to bear on it, this disgraceful and monstrous plan of intimidating the poorer classes of passengers was, in spite of all opposition, put an end to. There remains, however, ample means of compelling all travellers, with the exception of those who cannot possibly obtain the money, to forego the third class and travel by a higher. That object is attained in a variety of ways: by having but one train in the day, as on the Birmingham and Grand Junction; by starting at the most inconvenient hours, as on the Great Western, together with being detained a long time on the road, subject to every species of inattention and neglect: such are the general features of third class railway travelling. On some railways the porters are not permitted to assist 'waggon' passengers, as they are contemptuously called, with their luggage or in any other way which they might require. On no railway in the kingdom is the system of subjecting third class passengers to every possible discomfort, in order to compel them to travel by a higher class train, carried out to a greater extent than on the Great Western. The directors of this railway clung with great pertinacity to the plan of putting third class passengers next to the engine and tender, even after the danger of such a course of proceeding had been demonstrated to the satisfaction of every body but themselves. To such an extent did the virtuous indignation of one of these directors proceed against those third class passengers whom he thought were not in their proper place, that he mooted the proposition of employing sweeps to go in amongst them, and thus effectually drive out every man or woman who should find it in any way disagreeable to come in contact with those gentry; – but, indeed, there has been no occasion to proceed to such extreme measures, the object has been otherwise as effectually obtained. At the general meeting of the Great Western Railway Company last February, a shareholder observed 'That he did not think they were carrying out the intention of the legislature in providing accommodation so scanty for that most numerous class of the community whose previous modes of conveyance railways had superseded; thus the passengers had to leave London either at nine o'clock at night, exposed in an open carriage to all weather, and reaching Bristol at an hour in the morning (20 minutes past 5) when there were few facilities of obtaining shelter and refreshment; or they must be at the station at four o'clock in the morning, and in that case also exposed to the weather during a great part of the night. He felt an improvement in this respect would contribute to the convenience and comfort of a large class of the population'. The worthy proprietor also wished to know the number of passengers who had travelled by the third class trains. The secretary replied, that 'the directors considered that ample accommodation had been provided; he could not consider it as travelling by night, when it was partly travelling by day'. The reason why there were not third class passengers conveyed by other trains was 'that travellers at a speed of 40 miles an hour could not possibly endure the privation and exposure to weather which would have to be encountered by this class'. The excellent secretary, it would seem, would not let those third class passengers make that discovery for themselves, although they would first have to discover how a distance of 118¼ miles, performed by the quickest trains in 4¾ hours, is at the rate of 40 miles per hour; it is but little more than 24, and, exclusive of stoppages, is only 30 miles per hour. According to this gentleman, there does not appear any grievance in a passenger being obliged to get up at three o'clock on a raw winter's morning and finding his way to the railway as he best can, for of course there are no omnibuses at that early hour. It is certainly a kind of 'day travelling' which is rather novel in its way. The journey from London to Taunton by the mail trains is performed in about six hours, by the mixed trains in seven hours, and by the 'waggons' in *sixteen hours and a half!* Is it an exaggeration to say that nothing but the direst necessity will compel any man, however poor he may be, to travel by these legalized nuisances? And that if he have any regard to either health or comfort, he is obliged, however ill he can afford it, to go by a second class open carriage, which is not very comfortable either.

The result of this system is evident; the secretary of this company declined to state the number of third class passengers which had been conveyed; the entire number for the year, of all classes, was 1,606,015, and for the information of the worthy proprietor, who could attain no information from the secretary, I may add that the number of third class passengers did not exceed 100,000.

Another great annoyance to which third class passengers are exposed is occasioned by the want of protection from the sparks and particles of coke which escape from the furnace. Complaints are constantly being made in the public prints of their clothes being burnt, and it is needless to add, that they never receive the slightest indemnification for such loss. To the press in general, and the 'Morning Herald' and 'Times' in particular, the poor of this country are indebted for being able to travel at all on railways. The following extract is from a leading article in the Times: – 'We have received communications from several correspondents imploring us to maintain an advocacy for the poorer class of railway travellers who have to avail themselves of the stinted accommodation afforded by the leading lines, and desire us to urge the necessity of more comfort and facility in their transit than they at present enjoy. It would appear from the facts stated in the several letters received, that little choice exists in one more than another, and that all the great lines are as parsimonious as they possibly can be in providing comfort or convenience for those having the misfortune to travel in the third class conveyances. The manner in which the Great Western Company treat this class of passengers is described as worse than any other pursued, the only trains by which they forward them being those used for the transit of cattle, coals, and merchandize of all descriptions. For instance, it is stated that a third class passenger leaves Paddington in an open carriage, no difference being made to counteract wind or weather, at half-past 4 A. M. When he arrives at Swindon he is detained upwards of an hour, and at last gets to Bristol, if the train keeps its time, in 9½ hours, while the first and second class carriages make the same journey in less than half the time. If a third class traveller wish to go on to Taunton from any place east of Bristol, it is alleged to be still more inconvenient, since he is detained from four to five hours in Bristol, and is kept on the road at a moderate calculation from 14 to 16 hours; whereas, on the other hand, first and second class passengers arrive at the same destination in 6½ hours. These are strong statements, and, unless satisfactorily explained away, must sooner or later bring these undertakings within the managerial scope of the Board of Trade, the authorities of which body would do well to see that fair and adequate provision is made by all the railway companies for the conveyance of the poorer classes, during seasonable hours of the day. Railway directors have at present the exercise of too much irresponsible power, and therefore imagine that they can deal with the public as they choose. They, however, must be mindful not to carry it beyond proper bounds, for though much good may have been achieved by the construction and successful completion of intercourse by means of this system of communication, it remains to be seen what will be the actual results of this description of management should it without some superintending control be left entirely to the judgment of the persons who have the sole exercise of this power. It may possibly prove a useful hint to have said thus much on the subject, without pressing more severely on the attention of the respective railway boards the necessity existing for some amelioration of the plan at present adopted in the conveyance of third class passengers; for, regarding them in the light of national improvements raised on the foundation of the nation's wealth, they must be considered as intended to furnish a comparative convenience to one class of the public as well as to the other. The French, who are now following out the system of railways extensively, are provided against these deficiencies, should they arise, in a much better manner than we are at home, because the Government of that country having identified itself in close alliance with these undertakings by affording assistance in a pecuniary point of view, have the superior right of interfering without encountering the condemnation of that part of the public who may be interested in the maintenance of the supremacy of railway directorates against such supervision. It is a favourite expression among our railway interest, and one that certainly has once or twice occasioned strong opposition against the inspection of the Board of Trade in these matters, viz., that the Government having in the first instance refused all responsibility, and allowed private capitalists to surmount the difficulties which these undertakings presented, ought now not to provoke or desire an immediate connexion with their management. But the great answer to all this is, that where the safety or convenience of the public is concerned, there the Government have the power of inspection, and will exercise it for their benefit'.

But here is the difficulty, – how can the Government compel Railway Companies to adopt any measures that the latter may consider detrimental to their interests, without giving them remuneration? A bargain was made with these great Companies to carry passengers at 3½*d.* per mile; it is only within the last couple of years that, for their *own interest*, they carried third class passengers at 1½*d.* per mile; they might abolish 'waggons' altogether to-morrow if they thought proper. They adopt the system of annoyance to third class passengers merely for the purpose of driving them into better carriages, and that they *do* gain by it there can be no doubt. At the time the Croydon Railway proprietors came to the resolution of giving up their carrying traffic, one of them, in reference to the great inconvenience which the public would suffer, asked the chairman if the Government in such a case would not interfere; the chairman justly replied that Government could not oblige any man to inflict a loss upon himself. The Board of Trade *induced* the Company, by a promise of a 'quid pro quo' in support of another bill, to continue their carrying trade. Such is our system!

The London and Birmingham Company state in their report, that the mileage on their line, for the last half-year, was for the first class 11,043,483, second 12,192,051, and for the third only 2,140,705 miles. Now when we compare this account with other railways, where, from peculiar circumstances, the directors find it necessary to give greater accommodation to the poorer class of travellers, we then find that instead of their not constituting more than a fifth or a tenth of the aggregate number they sometimes amount to two thirds or three fourths. When a company has secured to itself the exclusive conveyance of passengers, it raises its third class fares as well as others to the highest point it can do so with safety, the only check on one side being the fear of driving the public to some irregular or chance mode of conveyance, and on the other their inability to pay the fare. Within the last twelve months, many Railway Companies have raised their fares from 20 to 30 per cent., and should a further advance be found profitable, it will of course be made.

It is unnecessary to go into further detail on this point: the same rule applies to this as to every other act of railway management in this country: 'get as much money as you can from the peasant as from the peer, from the artisan as from the merchant', is the universal principle acted on by all Railway Companies. The fears which the Committee of the House of Commons expressed as to the injurious effect of high charges to the poorer class of passengers, has been amply realized.

Such as I have described are some of the manifold evils inherent in the system of granting to private and irresponsible parties a complete monopoly of the means of transit throughout the kingdom, and of converting what should be the means of a great national good into a private speculation for individual gain.

11

'RAILWAY POLITENESS' AND 'THE THIRD CLASS TRAVELLER'S PETITION'

Punch (1845), p. 101

Railway politeness

The classification adopted in the management of Railways is not confined to the carriages; but the distinctions of first, second, and third class are scrupulously observed in the degree of politeness shown by the servants of the company to the passengers. The old maxim that civility costs nothing, seems to be utterly repudiated by Railway Directors, who calculate no doubt that politeness at all events takes time; and as time is money, the servants of the company are not justified in giving it without an equivalent. Any one who doubts the fact of the distinction to which we have alluded being drawn, has only to present himself at different times as an applicant for information at a Railway Terminus in the different characters of a first, a second, and a third class passenger.

If he is going by the first class he will get speedy attention from the clerks in the office; bows, and even smiles, from the policemen on the platform; and perhaps a touch of the hat from the guard. The second class passenger will get bare civility, but rather more of the bear than the civility, from the officials who stamp and deliver the checks; and who are very fond of trying to cheat themselves into the belief that they are quite on a par with the 'gentlemen in the public offices', whom the railway clerks chiefly resemble in an assumed nonchalance, which, however, the plain-speaking of a passenger who *will* be attended to, and who *may* be a shareholder, is pretty sure to dissipate. A second class passenger will get nothing more than a 'Now, Sir', from the policeman, and a 'Come, jump up!' from the guard; while the third class passenger will experience a poke in the chest from the former with his staff, by way of keeping him back till it is convenient to let him enter the carriage. In fact, there are short answers as well as short trains, and each class has a set of rules of politeness applied to it, which the officers are bound to obey as scrupulously as they do the Railway signals.

DOI: 10.4324/9781315400303-15

The Third Class Traveller's Petition

Pity the sorrows of a third class man,
Whose trembling limbs with snow are whitened o'er,
Who for his fare has paid you all he can:
Cover him in, and let him freeze no more!

This dripping hat my roofless pen bespeaks,
So does the puddle reaching to my knees;
Behold my pinch'd red nose – my shrivell'd cheeks:
You should not have such carriages as these.

In vain I stamp to warm my aching feet,
I only paddle in a pool of slush;
My stiffen'd hands in vain I blow and beat;
Tears from my eyes congealing as they gush.

Keen blows the wind; the sleet comes pelting down,
And here I'm standing in the open air!
Long is my dreary journey up to Town,
That is, alive, if ever I get there.

Oh! from the weather, when it snows and rains,
You might as well, at least, defend the Poor;
It would not cost you much, with all your gains:
Cover us in, and luck attend your store.

12

D. T. TIMINS, 'FROM ROOFLESS PEN TO CORRIDOR COACH: THE EVOLUTION OF THE 3RD CLASS CARRIAGE ON THE SOUTH EASTERN RAILWAY' [EXTRACT]

Railway Magazine, 4 (1899), pp. 496–500

It is the object of the present article to give some account of the 3rd class rolling stock belonging to the 'predominant partner' in the newly-founded South Eastern and Chatham and Dover Railway Company, *i.e.*, the South Eastern. We have decided to devote our attention on the present occasion entirely to the 3rd class vehicles, because they are not only the greatest dividend earners, but also because their luxuriousness, or otherwise, vitally affects the comfort of 90% of the users of the line.

Seldom has a railway excited such blazes of sulphurous wrath by reason of its rolling stock as the South Eastern. Frenetic abuse and unstinted bad language have been hurled at everyone connected with the line on account of the 3rd class carriages; but never has the proverb of 'Give a dog a bad name and hang him' found a better exemplification. For ten years past the rolling stock has been steadily and consistently improved, and yet very few of the habitual travellers by the line will be found willing to admit the fact. That some of it is still not up to the standard of modern requirements the officials themselves are fully aware, and this state of affairs is being remedied as rapidly as it is possible to do. To properly understand the difficult position in which they find themselves it is necessary to examine the past history of the line.

Among the early types of rolling stock may he mentioned the 'North Kent' 1st class saloons with straight sides. These were built by Messrs. Adams and Co. in 1849, 39 of these vehicles being still extant, though they are fast being withdrawn from active service, and will enjoy a hard-earned '*otium cum dignitate*' as tool-sheds, platelayers' dinner rooms, and what not. It will perhaps not be out of place to record the actual dimensions of these now historic carriages –

DOI: 10.4324/9781315400303-16

		Height from centre of buffer		
Length	*Width*	*To underside of side cornice*	*To top of roof in centre*	*Size of doorway in the clear*
ft. in.	*ft. in.*	*ft. in.*	*ft. in.*	*ft. in. ft. in.*
20 0	9 0	6 9	7 3	6 0½ by 1 8
		Seats – No. 26	Wheels 6	

The 3rd class coaches at this period were roofless, but there are no surviving drawings from which their dimensions can be taken. In describing the first and later types of 3rd class vehicle of which a record has been preserved, it must not be forgotten that these South Eastern Railway vehicles were quite as commodious, or possibly more so, as contemporary 3rd coaches on other railways. The first authentic design is an eight-wheeled 'teak' coach with boarded sides and ends. Mr. Mansell, at that time Carriage and Wagon Superintendent of the South Eastern Railway caused all passenger rolling stock to be built of teak, with the result that it was quite impossible for it ever to wear out. This fact no doubt accounted to a certain extent for the antiquated appearance of some of the South Eastern carriages which were running until recently. It is pretty safe to assume that these eight-wheeled 'teak' thirds were originally roofless, but in their altered form as four-wheelers they at least afforded shelter from the elements. They were built by Messrs. Williams in 1851, and in their pristine form were capable of seating 50 passengers each, the space allowed for opposing knees being but 16¾ in.

It is highly satisfactory to know that only a single specimen of this bygone race drags out a dishonoured existence as a lamp carriage. It would be highly interesting to listen to the meditations of the mediæval relic when the American car train or the 'Folkestone Vestibuled Limited' flashes by. It can, however, boast of one co-patriarch with whom we venture to think it is not on speaking terms. In the old days Mr. Mansell designed eighteen 'Teak Composites', and the year of their birth was synchronous with that of the 'teak 3rds'. No doubt the composites held their heads very high and refused to have any dealings with the plebeian '3rds', even when the vicissitudes of railway life coupled them together. But their 'gloria mundi' made a rapid 'transit', and the 'composites' were converted into '2nd class' coaches, and finally – breathe it not at Ashford! – fell to the rank of '3rds'! History recordeth not whether the before-mentioned old 3rd class carriage magnanimously forgave the haughty composites when they descended in the social scale. Probably it never meets the 'last of the converts'. The 'teak composites' were 2½ in. higher than their contemporaries of the lower grade, and could seat 45 people; at the same time allowing them 18 in. of leg space. As we have stated, only one of this particular class also is now in use.

About this time the South Eastern Railway commenced to build some of their own rolling stock, and we find that between the years 1851 and 1858 they turned out 56

3rd class vehicles of what may be regarded as their then standard pattern. Twenty-five similar coaches were also constructed by Messrs. Brown, Marshalls and Co. Of these 81 carriages, not a single one is in existence at the present time. It is interesting to note that as lately as 1853 the Company built 17 open '3rds', and during that and the following year 16 more were built to their order by outside contract.

In 1854 and 1855 the South Eastern built eight brake 3rds of their 'standard' type for use on their Greenwich branch. Oddly enough, these eight coaches have now been transferred to the other incorporated line, *i.e.*, the Canterbury and Whitstable, where they are running at the present time.

The following are the particulars of these 'old standard' vehicles: –

	Length	*Width*	*Height from centre of buffer to top of roof in centre*	*No. of seats*
	ft. in. *ft. in.*	*ft. in.*	*ft. in.* *ft. in.*	
	17 6 to 18 0	7 3	6 7 to 6 7¾	32
'Brake 3rds'	19 0	7 3	6 7 to 6 7¾	34

	Space between seats	No. of wheels
	17½ to 18 in.	4
'Brake 3rds'	17½ to 18 in.	

The years from 1862 to 1865 mark a period of great activity on the part of the South Eastern Company. The demand for 3rd class accommodation was steadily on the increase, in spite of all attempts to keep it down and to drive travellers into the two superior classes. No fewer than 186 4-wheeled 3rd class vehicles were constructed in these three years for the ordinary main-line traffic, 55 of them being turned out of the Ashford shops. Of the remainder, 31 were built, in 1863, by the General Rolling Stock Company, and 100 in 1864 by the Gloucester Wagon Company. They presented no new features, and their dimensions were almost identical with those of the 'old standard' class, save that the new rolling stock was 6 inches longer. The seating capacity was the same, and boarded sides and ends were still universally adopted.

The year 1865, however, saw an entirely new type of train placed upon the 'Greenwich' line. We refer to the 'close-coupled' trains, in the use of which the South Eastern were, if not actually the pioneers, at any rate one of the very first companies. We believe that the North London were their only predecessors. For running in these trains some new 'brake 3rds' were designed, which marked a considerable advance upon anything hitherto constructed. They were 4-wheeled coaches, with panel sides of 3 in. timber, 24 ft. in length, 7 ft. 10 in. in height, and with accommodation for 30 passengers. A space of 20 in. was allowed between the seats, implying an enormous increase in the comfort of the passengers. Eighteen of the 'close-coupled' 3rds possessed a guard's and luggage compartment, which latter have recently been enlarged, for these carriages, in company with most of the 'old standard' vehicles, are still at work. In all, 37 cars were built for the Greenwich line, 17 by the South Eastern Company, in the years 1864, 1869, and 1871 and 20 by the Metropolitan Carriage and Wagon Company, in 1865.

It became necessary to use 'close-coupled' vehicles for suburban traffic by reason of the increasing length of the trains, which often severely taxed the platform accommodation provided for them. Indeed, railway travel was now becoming one of the common incidents of every-day life, and a passenger was no longer regarded with wondering awe as an intrepid explorer.

From 1868 until 1872 no new design of 3rd class coach made its appearance. We will therefore pause awhile in our survey, and make a fictitious rise in the social scale to '2nd class' – fictitious because all the vehicles of which we wish to treat subsequently became 'converted', i.e., degraded to 3rd class rank. No doubt they saw the error of their ways as they grew older, and no longer considered it to be right that they should palm themselves off on the public as 2nd class coaches.

[. . .]

Up to this time all third-class rolling-stock had been exceedingly niggardly as to space. Ten corpulent persons would have split any of the carriages into fragments.

The year 1872 was distinguished by the first real concessions being made to the needs of third-class travellers. An entirely new variety of vehicle was designed, of a size more closely approximating to modern requirements, and giving an amount of light and roominess hitherto undreamt of. One such coach, was built more or less as an experiment at Ashford, and gave results so satisfactory that 30 more were ordered from the Midland Wagon Company in 1873, whilst the South Eastern themselves turned out a further 19 in 1874. The new carriages were 27 ft. in length, 8 ft. 4 in. in width, 7 ft. 10 in. in height from the centre of the buffer to the centre of the top of the roof, and provided seating accommodation for 50 passengers. The single particular in which they showed no improvement worth speaking of was in the matter of space between the seats, a paltry inch representing the sole advance upon former types. As against this must be set off the fact that the side windows were 8 in. higher and 2 in. broader than those of any previous cars. In 1878 six similar carriages, with luggage compartment and guard's observatory, were constructed in the South Eastern shops. Though 30 ft. long the new thirds only seated 40 travellers.

2.2

Metropolitan underground railway

DOI: 10.4324/9781315400303-17

2.2 Metropolitan underground railway

J. Hain Friswell, 'A Journey Underground', *Once a Week* (20 Sept. 1862), pp. 361–363.

Simon Sterne, 'The Greathead Underground Electric Railway' [extract], *Forum*, 11 (1891), pp. 683–687.

Fred T. Jane, 'The Romance of Modern London, III: Round the Underground on an Engine', *English Illustrated Magazine*, 10 (1892/1893), pp. 787–792.

In contrast to the preceding descriptions of early third-class railway travel, James Hain Friswell's 1862 account of taking an inaugural journey on London's Metropolitan Railway praises the fresh air and well-lit stations, predicting a fall in the popularity of the cabs, omnibuses and luggage vans that jam the streets of central London above. The world's first underground passenger railway line, the Metropolitan was undertaken as a new means of connecting London's busy northern and western railway stations to the central City of London. But its management of practical issues such as the venting of smoke and the provision of passenger access to below-ground platforms – as well as its popularity with riders – helped to inspire the creation of further London underground railways by other companies, as well as extensions and the construction of new branch lines on the Metropolitan Railway itself. As the network of underground railway routes grew, it would also help to promote the creation of ever more distant London suburbs along its branches – sometimes even on land controlled by the railways themselves. Along with other rail services, as well as urban omnibuses and tramways, the underground contributed to the rise of one of the mundane experiences of modern life, the daily urban commute.

The Metropolitan used smoky, coal-powered engines and was built largely by means of the cut-and-cover method: digging trenches from the surface, constructing the tunnel, and then topping it to rebuild a new surface. Nearly three decades after the Met's establishment, the engineer James Greathead's City and South London Railway (the 'Greathead Underground Electric Railway') was explicitly devised as an improvement on such older underground lines. It was built by means of deep tube tunneling rather than the disruptive cut-and-cover technique, and it was the world's first major electric railway line. The 'tube' was becoming an ordinary part of London life, but even at the turn of the century, a complete circumnavigation of the District Railway's 'inner circle' (the forerunner of the modern Circle Line on the London Underground) could be the stuff of romance – at least for the sake of an article in a magazine.[1]

Note

1 For accounts of the history of the Victorian underground railways, see Alan A. Jackson, *London's Metropolitan Railway* (Newton Abbot: David and Charles, 1986); Desmond F. Croome and Alan A. Jackson, *Rails Through the Clay: A History of London's Tube Railways*, 2nd ed. (Harrow Weald: Capital Transport, 1993); Christian Volmer, *The*

Subterranean Railway: How the London Underground Was Built and How It Changed the City Forever, revised Ed. (London: Atlantic, 2012). The underground railway could be experienced as part of a new subterranean urban world; see David L. Pike, *Subterranean Cities: The World Beneath Paris and London, 1800–1945* (Ithaca, NY: Cornell University Press, 2005). On the literary history of the London underground, see David Welsh, *Underground Writing: The London Tube from George Gissing to Virginia Woolf* (Liverpool: Liverpool University Press, 2010).

13

J. HAIN FRISWELL, 'A JOURNEY UNDERGROUND'

Once a Week (20 Sept. 1862), pp. 361–363

In the 'Voyages Imaginaires de Milord Céton', written about the year 1780, by the ingenious Marie-Anne de Roumier, we have an account of his lordship's journey to the moon and six other planets. The lunatics, his lordship finds, are given up to many light and frivolous diversions, as would become the people of so changeable a planet. In Mercury we meet with misers, and those given to hiding and hoarding useless heaps of gold. In Mars the people think of nothing but going to war, and snatching by conquest the lands of others. In Venus, on the contrary, we have a Paphian court and inhabitants, who delight in compliments, courtship, and what is termed the 'gentle passion'. In Saturn we find the good old Saturian times restored; times which gentlemen of a certain age longed for in the days of Virgil and Horace. In the Sun we meet with people deeply immersed in the pursuits of science and the cultivation of 'pure reason'. Whilst in Jupiter everybody cultivates his own conceit and pride, each one thinking himself, in the true Jovian method, considerably better off than his neighbour.

This is tolerable fooling, indeed, and might have been written in our own days by the Prophet Zadkiel, or any one who had fancy enough to adapt the old tales of the stars to the assumed characters assigned them by the astrologers. But neither Milord Céton, nor his imaginative authoress, ever dreamt of describing a voyage such as we have realised to-day, under the surface of the earth, beneath the largest city in the world, whilst thousands, nay millions, of its inhabitants were pursuing their avocations over our heads.

Of course everybody will at once see that this talk about Milord Céton and his imaginary voyage, is merely introduced to bring in our description of the first journey on the Metropolitan Railway, commonly called the 'Underground Railway', and they shall not be disappointed.

On Saturday, the 30th of August, 1862, a great number of impatient shareholders and of the equally impatient public (of which latter the writer was one), were invited to take the first trip throughout the entire length of a subterranean and subaqueous undertaking to which the Thames Tunnel is a flea-bite. Had not the shareholders been for two years on the tenterhooks of suspense? Had not the public been turned out of its accustomed route by huge hoardings, immense cuttings, and gigantic pitfalls? Had it not got lost in the purlieus of Clerkenwell, been

DOI: 10.4324/9781315400303-18

upset in the Euston Road, frightened at night by the continued roar and puff of the steam engines? Had not relays of navvies worked noiselessly at the very back of the wine and coal cellars of the public? Had not old landmarks disappeared, and was not the very site of 'King George's statue at King's Cross' tumbled up and down in railway barrows, and all for this gigantic undertaking? Did not Messrs. Croaker and Hare – the one dissatisfied, the other timorous – prophecy [sic] a complete failure and a final crash, like an earthquake, in which the two sides of London streets should first nod to each other, then fall in, and finally topple over each other like a house of cards? We know that all this, and much more, was the case. We also all know that seldom has a great scheme been brought to bear, or a ship sailed, or a plough-coulter cut the sod for the first time, but that some wise-acre shook his head, and with lamenting face prophesied a failure.

But the Underground Railway is now an 'accomplished fact', as our translators say. Already several part journeys have been taken, and the public by its representatives virtually made the trip on the Saturday aforesaid. On the 12th of August, a number of directors, shareholders, and city magnates, had gone through a portion of the works, walking along part of the way, and drawn in trucks over the other. On the 20th of the same month, the grand difficulties of tumbling sides, crumbling foundations, and finally the eruption of the Fleet Ditch, having been overcome, the contractors assembled their workmen and gave them a feast on the occasion. It was a kind of under-ground harvest home, only the crop had been thousands of tons of earth and of London clay instead of corn. After they had dispatched dinner, and done honour to the Queen, they drank the health of the carpenters and bricklayers, and of the navvies too, whereat the latter, at some forty feet below the surface, raised a shout like that which Milton says was given in another place.

All this is now a matter of the past. On the 30th of August, rails had been laid down from one end of the line to within a few feet of the other; the stations had been very nearly finished, and the engines (Fowler's patent improved by Gooch), with smoke-consuming and steam-condensing apparatus, had been brought upon the line with several first and second class carriages and trucks. To these, in the thick darkness which enveloped the commencement of the tunnel, nearly six hundred people clambered up, after walking there from the city terminus in Victoria Street, to which the lines had not yet been joined, and then, doubtless not without some misgivings in the hearts of many, we commenced our journey.

Slowly we went on the first expedition, so that one might inspect the works, and on reaching the first station, that of King's Cross, the train stopped. From this runs a trumpet-shaped tunnel, communicating with the Great Northern Railway, and to join this we believe another branch of the railway will run to a terminus in Finsbury Square. The next stopping-point reached was that of Gower Street, which may as well be described, as a favourable specimen of all the stations. Even upon the earth's surface the only ornamental part of railways really consists of their stations and termini; and underground the same rule seems to be observed. 'Gower Street' is a very pretty station, lighted from the top, from the fore-courts of the gardens and the pavement, whence thick glass panes transmit a soft light to horizontal cuttings lined with white, and from these cuttings oval eyelet holes, lined with Minton's white-glazed tiles, admit both light and air to the station. The reflection of the light from so many surfaces has a very pretty effect; there is no darkness about the matter, but quite as much light as need be, like the soft evening of a June day. Neither is there any smell of damp or confined air; in fact, the air is not confined, and the damp does not exist, and on our hot August trip a dry and pleasant atmosphere was preserved throughout; indeed, the air in the tunnel must always be kept pure by the current passing from terminus to terminus, and from the frequent passage of engines and carriages, which will carry all before them.

Naturally, the pretty station and the agreeable temperature elicited a good deal of cheering and cheerful praise. There was also an evident care in the construction of the work, and the shareholders' money, it was plain to see, had not been carelessly spent. The Portland Road station, which we next reached, is as simple as that at Gower Street, but differs in its mode of lighting, the light being admitted by two glass domes and a flat skylight; at Baker Street we have almost a copy of that of Gower Street, and at all very handsome and wide staircases run on each side up to the surface. The Edgeware Road station, near Praed Street, is not an underground one, and is therefore lighted horizontally; and from thence to the terminus, at the Great Western Railway, the line is single. On reaching the terminus all of us dismounted, and as soon as we had wandered over the works, we remounted our carriages, and proceeded home, my scientific fellow-travellers expressing a firm belief in the success of the undertaking, although nearly 1,500,000*l*. have been spent upon it.

Of the merit and utility of this great triumph of engineering skill there can be no doubt. London is over-crowded with vehicles, and the number seems to increase every day. Cabs, trucks, carts, carriages of all sorts, omnibusses with two or three horses, and gigantic railway-vans driven by furious and reckless Jehus, over-crowd our streets every day, form blocks and stoppages at all our principal thoroughfares, and all but convince the stranger that finally London will find itself tied up in one eternal dead-lock, from which there will be no escape. Time and temper – two very valuable articles – are continually lost in these stoppages, and indeed it is very evident that something must be done to relieve them. Thanks to the security enjoyed by vested interests, it would be an almost hopeless task to widen the main thoroughfares sufficiently. In the widest streets these dead-locks occur; for instance, in Regent Street, in the height of the season. Nay, they would occur in Nevskoï Prospect, or the broadest streets of Paris or Pekin, if those cities had the population, the material wealth, and the eagerness for business, which mark London and the Londoners. Naturally enough, the concourse of vehicles has increased as the railway traffic has increased, and therefore it is but fair that a railway should be applied to abate the nuisance.

A penny-fare from Praed Street to the City will lessen the number of riders in the City omnibusses, and men of business proceeding from the centre of London to any part of England will pack their luggage in the Underground Railway car more safely and expeditiously than in a cab. At the same time, many of our luggage-vans themselves will be superseded, since the goods will be brought right into the midst of the City warehouses from the manufacturing districts, without passing all our public thoroughfares.

That it may interfere with some branches of industry is likely enough; but those branches are capable of being transferred to any other towns, where those who are employed in them will flourish all the more for being taken away from Cobbett's 'Huge Wen'.

14

SIMON STERNE, 'THE GREATHEAD UNDERGROUND ELECTRIC RAILWAY' [EXTRACT]

Forum, 11 (1891), pp. 683–687

On November 4, 1890, there was opened with much ceremony in London a subterranean railway, carrying passengers from the Monument in the city to the Swan in South Lambeth, a distance of about three and a half miles, and at a depth of between 40 and 60 feet below the surface of the streets. This road is called the City and South London Railway. It is composed of two tunnels, which in their course underlie the River Thames, and pass under the mammoth Hibernia Wharf warehouses, the abutments of London Bridge, and the massive viaducts of the Southeastern Railway. The mode of traction is electricity, which at the same time serves to light the carriages and the stations.

When Mr. James H. Greathead, the inventor of the system of tunneling which is known by his name, proposed this line from London Bridge through the densely populated portions of the southern or Surrey side of London, and succeeded in obtaining the indorsement of Sir John Fowler and Sir Benjamin Baker, two of the leading engineers of England, he had, notwithstanding this indorsement, to fight, at the outset, many very serious difficulties in the way of inducing capital to enter into the project and of obtaining the necessary parliamentary concessions for the work of construction in the metropolis of London.

The old underground railway system of London, although carrying an enormous traffic, had not been a financial success. It is also a constant source of complaint to its patrons by reason of the offensive odors which permeate the tunnel, and its dampness and draughtiness. The traction of the old underground railway of London is by steam locomotives; and however successful the smoke-consuming contrivances of the engines, they cannot destroy wholly the emanations of ashes, and sulphurous gases of various kinds, which arise from the decomposition and direct consumption of coal, this being of necessity bituminous, as England has no anthracite coal. The contents of gas pipes, sewer pipes, and water-service pipes, all of which are more or less leaky, saturate and drench the brick arches of the old underground railway system of London with unwholesome moistures and smells, each brick being a lung which takes in and inhales this moisture and these odors

DOI: 10.4324/9781315400303-19

from surrounding material and exudes and exhales them into the tunnel. These were the main reasons that caused Londoners and the English Parliament to be reluctant to extend a system of subways which in one form or another were open to such strong objections.

Mr. Greathead was compelled, therefore, to prove theoretically to both Parliament and the capitalists of England that his system overcame these objections, one and all, before he could obtain either concession or cash. That accomplished, he, for two and a half years, proceeded to build his road; and from the first day of its opening, on November 4, 1890, until the present day, every train has passed through the tunnel successfully, and, with trivial exceptions, on time. The passage of the first train demonstrated the validity of the inventor's claims before Parliament in behalf of this intermural system of rapid transit, and of its superiority over every other system yet devised, as a means of moving daily the population of a great city from one point to another. Every successive train brushed aside objections and objectors until at present there is a consensus of opinion, in England at least, that the solution of the question of rapid transit for cities has been found.

Given a built-up city with its lines of traffic and intercommunication already established, a new system which is to supplement and, in part, replace the existing lines, should meet six serious and important requirements:

> (1) During construction, there must be no opening of streets to interfere with existing traffic; (2) in its operation, it must not impede existing means of traffic, by carriage, omnibus, street cars, and the like; (3) it must do little or no damage to property during its construction and by reason of its operation; (4) it must, when in operation, be a wholesome and pleasant means of transit; (5) it must be rapid; and (6) it must pay its projectors and promoters.

The Greathead system of tunnelling places the tunnel so far below the streets and houses of the city that the land occupied by it is of no value practically, and but of nominal value theoretically. There is no warehouse in any large city the cellars or foundations of which go 60 feet below the surface of the street. The land, therefore, that is occupied is wholly additional space recovered from the domain of no value and made of great value for this special purpose. The very depth at which the work proceeds makes it impracticable, after the sinking of the first shaft, that there should be one continuous open cut from the surface down; the road must be driven through the bowels of the earth. On the surface there is as little indication of its progress as was observable on the fields of the St. Gothard mountain, by the shepherds who fed their flocks thereon, of the advance of the St. Gothard tunnel, thousands of feet below their *sabots*.

The tunnel is circular, is driven through sand, clay, gravel, or rock, by instruments specially devised for such purpose, and is constructed after the opening is made, of sections of rings bolted and riveted together, with tarred rope to fill up the interstices. An inch and a half of grouting surrounds the whole outer surface left vacant by the cutting shield as it advances, making one uniform coating of Roman cement around this iron tube, which, when completed, is thereby forever protected from all gases or water percolating through the earth. Moisture, which heretofore has been an enemy to tunnelling operations, is, by Greathead's system, made a friend, which, at the moment he strikes it, he sets to work as a water shovel by building a diaphragm behind it, and then sucks the gravel, clay, or silt through his pumps and pipes to the surface. The surface openings are made in the interior of dwellings or warehouses which are purchased at different points and which ultimately become the entrances to the stations; therefrom the shafts are sunk and the levels driven after the shafts have reached their proper depth, precisely as in deep mining. The work proceeds without consciousness on the part of the people who use the streets that it has been going on, until the place which before was used for the purpose of removing the waste and of introducing the material necessary for construction, is converted into a beautiful passenger station. Into this station great hydraulic elevators, capable of holding 75 persons each, are introduced, and carry passengers from the street to the depth of 60 feet or more and back again to the thoroughfare. More technically speaking, the manner of construction is about as follows: After a proper depth for the tunnels has been ascertained, a shaft is sunk and solidly bricked around. From this shaft the tunnels are started. The tunnel headings are side by side, or one above the other, as the ground and other circumstances favor, and are continued a sufficient distance to permit of the introduction of the hydraulic shield. (The City and South London tunnels are each a little more than ten feet six inches in diameter.) A dozen or more such tunnel-headings may be working from various sections toward each other to expedite construction. The shield consists of an iron tube of rather more than the full dimensions of the exterior of the tunnel tube, so as to slide over it like the cap of a telescope. In the rear of this shield there are built up two or three rings of the tunnel, formed of segments 20 inches in length, each ring being bolted to the next by a flange three inches in depth, and the outer space between the exterior of the iron tube and the excavation being filled with concrete, blown through small orifices in the tube. The shield carries, in circular arrangement within it, six or eight hydraulic presses, and when the pressure water is pumped into them their rams protrude against the flange of the last ring of the tunnel tube, and the shield is driven forward, its sharp edge cutting away another eighteen inches of the material to be displaced, and permitting the insertion behind it of another tube-ring built up from within. The heading in front of the shield is driven by hand, as in ordinary mining; but where water is encountered, a portion of the tunnel is built off by a diaphragm, with a door in it, in the rear of the shield. Again, in the rear of this a second diaphragm with a door is built. In this way the iron tunnel tube is laid and built in rings in regular consecutive order.

As fast as a segment ring of the tunnel is completed, it is thoroughly and compactly grouted. For this purpose a grouting machine is used. A grouting composition made of Roman cement is mixed in this machine and forced, under an air pressure of 30 pounds, through small holes in the cast-iron segments, into the vacancies left around the tunnel by the shield. Beginning at the bottom, the cement is forced to the outside until it shows at holes in the side. Then the lower holes are permanently plugged and the cement is forced through the side holes until it flows in at the top; and finally it is forced through the top holes until no more can be forced through. By this means a solid casing, impenetrable to water, or even to gas, is secured. It serves more perfectly than a sheathing of solid masonry to protect the tunnel from moisture and to stiffen and sustain it.

The cars are supplied with longitudinal seats, lit by electricity, and luxuriously cushioned, the passengers facing each other. The locomotive is an electric motor, picking up its electricity from a central rail through which the electric current is conducted by a copper wire; and inasmuch as, for each track, there is a separate tunnel only a trifle larger than the train (which fills almost the whole of the annular space, except only at stations) each train acts as a piston, driving out, from station to station, the air through which the preceding train has passed. The stations are connected with the open air and are not more than three-quarters of a mile apart; any foul air which gathers in the tunnel is thus expelled by each passing train. Indeed, the air in the tunnel is of a more equable temperature, and is kept more constantly moved and freshened, than the air on the surface; and frequently on dark and murky days it has been noticed that the air and atmosphere, strange as it may appear, are far more pleasant in the tunnel than on the street surface.

15

FRED T. JANE, 'THE ROMANCE OF MODERN LONDON, III: ROUND THE UNDERGROUND ON AN ENGINE'

English Illustrated Magazine, 10 (1892/1893), pp. 787–792

By the courtesy of Mr. Powell, manager of the District Railway, I was provided with an 'engine-pass' for the 'Inner Circle'; and on a bright June morning I made my way to St. James's Park station. There I met Chief-Inspector Exall, who was detailed to accompany and look after me generally.

The train selected was a District 'down' one. 'Down', by the way, signifies up to the Mansion House; the explanation of this apparent paradox being that the northern part of the 'Circle' was opened first. In those days the line was only some three and a half miles long and yet cost over a million pounds to construct.

In a short time our train rushed into the station, and a moment later we had boarded the engine. I was accommodated with a position near the left-hand tank, whence I could get an uninterrupted view ahead; but it had its drawbacks as the water in that tank was hot.

No time is wasted at stations on the Underground, and a minute later the train was off – off into a black wall ahead with the shrieking of ten thousand demons rising above the thunder of the wheels. The sensation altogether was much like the inhalation of gas preparatory to having a tooth drawn. I would have given a good deal to have waited just a minute or so longer. Visions of accidents, collisions, and crumbling tunnels floated through my mind; a fierce wind took away my breath, and innumerable blacks filled my eyes. I crouched low and held on like grim death to a little rail near me. Driver, stoker, inspector, and engine – all had vanished. Before and behind and on either side was blackness, heavy, dense and impenetrable. Westminster Bridge, Charing Cross, and The Temple were passed before I could do or think of anything beyond holding on to that rolling, rushing engine: then finding that I was still alive and sound, I began to look about me. Inspector Exall put his head to my ear and shouted something at the top of his voice, but I could only catch the word 'Blackfriars'. I looked ahead. Far off in the distance was a small square-shaped hole, seemingly high up in the air, and from it came four silver threads palpitating like gossamers in the morning breeze. Larger and

DOI: 10.4324/9781315400303-20

larger grew the hole, the threads became rails, and the hole a station; Blackfriars, with rays of golden sunlight piercing through the gloom.

Off again, a fierce light now trailing out behind us from the open furnace door, lighting up the fireman as he shovelled more coal on to the furnace, throwing great shadows into the air, and revealing overhead a low creamy roof with black lines upon it that seemed to chase and follow us. Ever and anon the guard's face could be dimly seen at his window, more like a ghost than man; while in the glass of the look-out holes were reflected the forms of the engine-men, like spirits of the tunnel mocking us from the black pit into which we were plunging. Then again we would seem to stop, and to fall down, down, down, with always the wild shrieking surge and ceaseless clatter of the iron wheels.

Soon ahead of us gleamed pillars of crimson stars, the signal lights of the Mansion House. Between this station and Mark Lane there is nothing particularly noticeable, saving the approach to the latter; where ghostly looking figures paced a hidden platform across which fell great golden beams that looked like impassable barriers. Yet, ere one could take a second glance, the beams were riven asunder and a black engine blotted them out with clouds of writhing steam. Next to Mark Lane, and almost close to it, is the old Tower station, now disused. We sped past its deserted platforms and limp signal posts, and a few minutes later steamed into the central station, Aldgate. The firemen at once jumped off the engine and made the necessary arrangements for filling our water tanks. So quickly was this done that probably none of the passengers noticed any difference in the length of the stoppage, and in a very short while we were off again into the tunnels, two minutes sufficing to bring us round a sharp curve into Bishopsgate.

Aldersgate, the next station, was opened in 1865, and for many years was comparatively deserted by passengers. The opening of the markets hard by has altered all this, and it is now one of the principal stations on the line. All about this section we encountered other lines which sometimes dived under us, at other times merely diverged in various directions. Outside Aldersgate the line is ventilated by a series of arches, which give a fine effect of light and shade, making the tunnel look like an old-time dungeon.

From Farringdon Street to King's Cross is the longest stretch without a station, and the driver here gave us an exhibition of full speed, and No. 18 came into King's Cross at the rate of some forty miles an hour. The average speed of trains between one station and another is from twenty to twenty-five miles.

The road now began to be uphill, and at the same time the air grew more foul. From King's Cross to Edgware Road the ventilation is defective, and the atmosphere on a par with the ''tween decks, forrud' of a modern ironclad in bad weather, and that is saying a good deal. By the time we reached Gower Street I was coughing and spluttering like a boy with his first cigar. 'It is a little unpleasant when you ain't used to it', said the driver with the composure born of long usage, 'but you ought to come on a hot summer day to get the real thing!' Fog on the underground appears to cause less inconvenience than do the sultry days of July; then the atmosphere is killing. With the exception of this one section (between

King's Cross and Edgware Road) I found the air far purer than I had expected, and the bad air so much complained of by the 'sewer-rats' – as those who habitually use this circle are called in 'the City' – is due in a great measure to their almost universal habit of keeping all the windows and ventilators closed.

The finest bit of scenery on the underground is the Baker Street Junction, where a second tunnel leading to the St. John's Wood line branches out of the main one. It is no longer used for through trains, however, owing to a fearful accident that occurred here some time ago, and Baker Street is now the terminus of that line. On the left through the main tunnel lies the station, a medley in crimson and gold; on the right the daylight creeps in, and the picture is a harmony in blue and silver. It is a novel and unexpected sight to see the ordinary black coat of respectability look crimson, as it does when seen after the intense blackness of the tunnel. But like all the other scenes, this was brief and momentary; then a dream of the past.

There is a similar and much-used junction before Praed Street, but it is provided with a big signal box where the tunnels meet.

The ventilating holes in the tunnel roof all about this part give a beautiful effect of light striking into darkness; especially one before Edgware Road is reached, where the silver column of light fell on a green signal lamp, set low in the permanent way. Just before Praed Street we got into daylight again – the line passing through a sort of valley formed by high houses on either side.

Hitherto, though we had passed many, I had scarcely noticed the trains that we met; but about here I changed over to the right side of the engine in order to get a better view of a coming train. I had not long to wait. Far away in the distance was an ever-increasing speck of light – the head light of an approaching train. A moment later, it had come and gone – a silent flash of light, so silent that it might have been a phantom; our own engine made too much noise for any other sound to be audible. Curiously enough, an approaching train is totally unlike what one would imagine it ought to look like. A strong light bursts from the furnace if it chances to be open, and illuminates the tunnel overhead, the carriage windows and brass work make lines of light that run off and die in the distance, but the engine itself is lost in the blackness through which it is rushing.

At High Street, Kensington, engines are changed so we jumped off – at least my guide did – my attempt to follow his example being calculated to cause an impression that I had taken the platform to be a seat – but all this is by the way. Engine No. 18 went off into a shed to rest awhile, and No. 7, a precisely similar one, backed on to the train in her place. This resting of engines is rendered a frequent necessity from the strain caused by the numerous stoppages; incessant running in one direction has also been found bad for them as it wears away the wheels on one side sooner than on the other. To remedy this, the engines half their time run 'backwards forwards', as they say in the West of England.

Off again; and this time down-hill. We dashed rapidly through the grass embankments outside Gloucester Road, past some men posting bills on the advertisement hoardings that border the line below South Kensington, now deep in a tunnel, now traversing a cutting open to the sky; until we shot once more into St. James's

Park, seventy minutes after leaving it. We had covered some thirteen miles in our trip round London; seemingly no great distance for the time occupied; till one recollects that it entailed no less than twenty-seven stoppages, with a watering and change of engines into the bargain.

It is these stoppages that make the journey as long as it is; if a train went round at its usual rate it would be back at the starting point in less than forty minutes, while if it went full speed some twenty minutes would suffice.

However, the seventy-minute trip is quite rapid enough for all practical purposes, and is only rendered possible by the excellence of the brake arrangements, and the perfection to which the block-system of signalling has now been brought. The length of the stoppages could not well be reduced, indeed they are already too short if we are to believe the tale now current of a wandering Jew sort of passenger – a lady of advanced years who can only alight from a train backwards. Every time she begins to get out a porter rushes up crying, 'Hurry up, ma'am; train's going!' – and pushes her in again!

'This finishes our journey', said the inspector, as, taught by previous experience, I cautiously crawled off the engine, – 'unless you'd like to go round again'.

I declined.

2.3

Tricycle and bicycle

DOI: 10.4324/9781315400303-21

2.3 Tricycle and bicycle

'Women on Wheels', *Cassell's Family Magazine* (1885), pp. 589–591.
'The Social Effect of Bicycling', *Spectator*, 76 (30 May 1896), pp. 769–770.
E. B. Turner, 'Health on the Bicycle' *Contemporary Review*, 73 (1898), pp. 640–648.
Cesare Lombroso, 'The Bicycle and Crime', *Pall Mall Magazine*, 20 (1900), pp. 310–316.

Since the beginning of the nineteenth century, artisans and hobbyists had experimented with a variety of two-wheeled devices for personal transport. By the 1860s, there were French *velocipedes* with pedals attached to their front wheels, and a decade later, there were tall, penny-farthing bicycles with a tiny rear wheel and a huge front wheel above which a rider would perch precariously. Such vehicles were uncomfortable or dangerous enough to attract few riders except for adventurous young men, although there were also safer penny-farthing-style tricycles to appeal to less reckless cyclists. But in the late 1880s, the development of the 'safety bicycle' – combining features such as pedals that used a chain to drive the rear wheel, air-filled tyres and two wheels of similar sizes – dramatically broadened the appeal of bicycling and helped to turn cycling into an enduring part of modern life.

Although the tricycle and bicycle lacked the bulk, speed and sublime spectacle of the railway, they constituted a transport revolution with far-reaching implications even beyond individual mobility, and writers could present them as epochal developments in their own right. The vision of a 'lady cyclist' might symbolise modernity, freedom and health for women; indeed, the young woman on a bicycle would become an icon of the 'New Woman' in 1890s print culture.[1] But by increasing the locomotive power of the human body, the bicycle might have social effects that included the scattering of communities, a diminution of neighborliness and perhaps even the rise of the sociable lunch and the decline of dinner. Would the bicycle increase bodily health or shatter it? For the physician and criminologist Cesare Lombroso, the bicycle might help conquer working-class alcoholism, but in its convenience and its novelty it would also act as a spur to crime.[2]

Notes

1 See Patricia Marks, *Bicycles, Bangs, and Bloomers: The New Woman in the Popular Press* (Lexington, KY: University Press of Kentucky, 1990).

2 For further reading on the history and design of bicycles, see David V. Herlihy, *Bicycle: The History* (New Haven, CT: Yale University Press, 2004); Tony Hadland and Hans-Erhard Lessing, *Bicycle Design: An Illustrated History* (Cambridge, MA: MIT Press, 2014).

16

'WOMEN ON WHEELS'

Cassell's Family Magazine (1885), pp. 589–591

BY A LADY CYCLIST.

In these days of the higher education of women, people have gradually come to recognise the fact that if a man's field of study is equally open to a woman, a certain amount of exercise and recreation, hitherto regarded as exclusively the heritage of man, must become the right of woman too. This fact is, as I say, pretty well understood and appreciated nowadays, and lawn-tennis, skating, and boating are as important factors in the amusements of a woman's life as the classics, algebra, and Euclid are in her education.

But of all the healthful and enjoyable modes of exercise now thrown open to women, there is none so beneficial to health and spirits, none so conducive to pleasure, interest, and wholesome excitement, as that to be obtained by the use of the tricycle.

Four years ago a woman on wheels was a rare and conspicuous sight; but today there are few parts of England – perhaps I may say of the United Kingdom – where a tricycling maid or matron excites any wonder in the mind of the spectator.

Certainly no more delightful means of locomotion was ever placed within my sex's reach. Women are seldom good walkers; their duties and pursuits confine them far more within-doors than do those of men, and even those who are most ardent over tennis or archery think, as a rule, that they have rather achieved a deed of prowess when they have taken a ten-mile walk. But the tricycle gives them at once a means of wandering far afield; of exploring forest glades and heathery moorlands; of finding close to their own familiar haunts beauties hitherto undreamed of, which, without such aid, they would never have been able to discover. We have slowly grown to realise that, in these days of over-brain-work and over-civilisation, no medicine but fresh air can calm the restless pulses and soothe the fevered mind, and the tricycle offers to women that panacea for over-wrought nerves and tried tempers.

'Why not ride instead?' asks some one. Certainly almost all that can be said in praise of the tricycle applies equally to the horse; but while thousands may enjoy the former, the latter is within the reach of the rich alone. And it is particularly to the women of the middle class that I wish to recommend the use of the tricycle;

DOI: 10.4324/9781315400303-22

that class which suffers most from what we have grown to call the 'little health of women'; the class whose lives are the busiest, and whose minds the most heavily taxed, and who, just in proportion to that taxation and that business, need some relaxation which shall offer them the most complete change and rest from their ordinary occupations.

For it is the very charm of the tricycle that it affords instant change of scene and thought. All worrying cares, all fretting petty details of daily life, seem to fall from one like an ugly shadow when one mounts one's iron steed. Who can keep a wrinkled brow or a heavy heart as one darts swiftly and smoothly through the sweet keen air; or glides down some long descent with an exhilarating rush which is more akin to flying than any known motion? Suppose yourself a dweller in some great dull town, where the air is heavy with the smoke of a hundred thousand chimneys, and your heart is sick with the endless roar of the streets. The country seems a dozen miles away; life seems all grime, and ugliness, and money-getting, with an upper-current of housekeeping cares, or the commonplace round of daily monotonous duties. Your tricycle is at the door; you mount your saddle, and press the pedals with feet which seem as languid and spiritless as the heart within you. A few turns, and the quickened circulation begins to act upon you. Your sad eye brightens; the colour mounts to your pale cheek; you draw a longer breath, and settle down, no longer languidly, to your work. A few minutes, and the dreary town surroundings are left behind. God's own fresh, pure country stretches before you, with smiling meadow and budding hedgerow; there is a burst of heavenly melody from the lark that hangs on quivering wing bathed in the sunlight glory; a rush of perfume in the delicious air that touches with its soft sweet lips your glowing cheeks. You ride and ride, till the calm fair beauty of wood and stream sinks deep into your weary heart, and you feel young and strong, and happy again all on a sudden, and you reach home refreshed and invigorated in body and in mind, feeling as you alight as if you were treading on air, and could scarcely keep from bursting out into singing as blithe as that of the soaring lark you left behind you an hour ago.

That night you sleep the sleep of tired childhood, and you wake to feel the world a very good place. after all, and duties not so irksome by half as you thought them yesterday.

Or if you are fortunate enough to own a lot cast in country places already, your tricycle opens up to you a thousand new joys. What pic-nic parties may be yours in summer! What long rides with a merry party to visit some distant ruin, or quaint cathedral town! What pleasant teas in quiet village inns, or gipsy-meals beneath forest oak, or beside the sounding shore! What nutting parties in the autumn, and what brisk rides to the meet on cold winter mornings, when cowering over the fire doesn't seem to warm one in the least, and only your tricycle-ride sends the quick blood tingling and dancing through every vein! Ah! the woman who has never been on wheels has not tasted half the innocent joys of life!

At first there was some amount of prejudice against tricycling for women. People looked askance, perhaps rather confounding three wheels with two, and fancying that anything of a cycling description must needs be unfeminine. Time has, as usual, proved the best advocate of a good cause, and there are few districts, and still fewer families, where tricycling now suggests anything fast or unwomanly.

That any prejudice against tricycling for women still exists is due, I fear I must own, a good deal to women themselves. Such lamentable spectacles as those afforded to the public from time to time by some riding women go far towards injuring the whole cause of tricycling in the eyes of the world at large; and the unwomanly desire to compete in tricycle races, which lately gave rise to such hot discussions in the cycling press, has done still more. But it is palpably unfair to condemn tricycling for women at large because a few clumsy girls dress unsuitably, ride awkwardly, and attract a good deal of unflattering notice; or because a small minority of silly women pant to win prizes in competition with men in the racing-field.

Of course in tricycling the first consideration must be the tricycle. The question of expense often disposes one to invest in one of those second-hand articles so temptingly advertised on all sides, but as a general rule the few pounds so saved are dearly saved. Never buy a tricycle without a personal examination and as prolonged a trial as possible. Faults, at first unsuspected, often make themselves apparent by use. Avoid rear-steerers – a class of machine which, for some occult reason, were considered, until quite recently, as appropriate for a lady's use. They are less easy, less pleasant, and far more dangerous than the front-steering build.

The tricycle being secured, the next step is to ride it. Very little practice is needed by any woman of average quickness and common-sense, the motion is so easy. The steering is, of course, the difficult part, and a little usage is required before one grows aware how almost unconscious one's touch must be – as light and delicate as that on the tiller-lines of a boat, or the rein of a horse. Of course, as in all else, it is experience that teaches in tricycling. One learns by degrees to save oneself much hard labour by letting the pedals do most of the work for themselves, and by economising all that outlay of strength and breath with which one was at first so over-lavish. One great secret of graceful and easy riding is having the saddle sufficiently high – *i.e.*, just so that the instep rests on the lower pedal as one sits at full height. To sit low is infallibly to ride awkwardly and to exhaust oneself.

Dress is the next important question in the female mind. The great fault of most costumes devised by men is their excessive weight and warmth. Men never seem able to comprehend that a woman cannot carry what would be a light burden to themselves. The Touring Club uniform, otherwise neat and appropriate, suffers from this grave defect; also from being too expensive for many lady riders. The taste and fancy of the wearer can best decide how much and what quality of clothing should be worn, but there are two or three indispensable points to be considered. The gown must not be over two yards in width, or it may catch in the wheels; it must be guiltless of steels, or other dress-improving arrangements; it must be long enough to touch the instep as it reaches the lowest pedal; it must be made plainly and simply, with no floating flounces or frills. A colour calculated to withstand dust and grease is the most sensible wear, and jewellery, coloured ribbons, artificial flowers, &c., are all entirely out of place. Shoes should always be worn, and the head-gear should be chosen with a view to wind, sun, and possible showers.

I have found it a good plan to carry with me a small fur cape – just sufficient to protect my shoulders in a sudden storm, or to prevent a chill when overheated.

Beginners should be careful to avoid long distances at first; it is better never to attempt riding after one is tired, or to ride up ascents if one feels one's breath failing. By degrees the distance can be increased to almost any extent, and at last one grows to feel it far easier to ride up most hills than to push up the machine.

Touring is one of the great pleasures that tricycling brings with it. I should have mentioned, as another proof of the growing popularity of tricycling as an exercise for women, the fact that the club lists of the Cyclists' Touring Club show monthly an ever-increasing number of ladies' names. This Cyclists' Touring Club, which is open to all amateur riders, offers certain very real advantages to its members in the shape of official maps, hand-books, &c., as well as a settled tariff of charges at reduced rates at all inns bearing the club badge, of which there is at least one to be found in almost every town in the kingdom. Besides this, there are consuls appointed for the different divisions of the country, whose duty it is to supply information and assistance to all touring members applying for their aid. The subscription to the club is half-a-crown annually, with an additional shilling as entrance fee. Uniform is worn at option.

The club already numbers over sixteen thousand members, and any lady-tricyclist who contemplates touring should certainly add her name to the sixteen thousand.

And what form of touring can equal the utter enjoyment of the tricycle tour? Far longer distances can be covered with less than half the fatigue of walking, and there is far greater independence than in driving, and even riding does not afford such varied pleasure as the tricycle. To rise betimes on a sweet fresh summer morning, to mount one's steed after an early breakfast, and to whirl away mile after mile through fragrant hedgerows, or amid cool forest shades; to rest at some roadside inn through the burden and heat of the day, only to start once more as the sun is waning in the west, and to ride again under broadening shadows or by rising moon; to sleep in quaint old-fashioned hostelries, where the fare is sweet and hearty and the welcome warm and kind; to gain daily strength and health, and tone of mind and body; to learn that the pure healthful joys of life outweigh all its feverish intoxicating pleasures, as the gold outweighs the thistledown – all that is to have lived, and not to have lived in vain! And that is the happy possibility that every tricycle opens up to its possessor.

17

'THE SOCIAL EFFECT OF BICYCLING'

Spectator, 76 (30 May 1896), pp. 769–770

Bicycling will, we believe, within a few years produce social effects of some importance. The notion that it is a mere fashion or 'craze', like the skating on little wheels which some years ago led to an investment of scores of thousands of pounds in a speculation that proved absolutely futile, is, we are convinced, a pure delusion. The bicycle has greatly added to human powers, and will no more be given up by those who have once learned to use it than horse-riding will be given up or travelling by railway. The number of those who cycle increases day by day, as the objections raised by prejudice or custom disappear, none of those who acquire the art show the slightest disposition to give up the practice, and the probability is that in a very short time it will become far more popular than riding or swimming, or even walking for amusement ever has been. It has been discovered that every one who chooses, and who has any kind of vigour remaining, can learn to ride in about a fortnight, the exercise distinctly improves the health of all who use it in moderation, and as soon as an obstacle or two have been surmounted not to cycle will be nearly as unusual as not to walk. The cost of a wheel is at present considerable, but that is a result only of monopolies, and must sooner or later disappear. There is no reason in the world why a thin wheel of steel, every part of which except the tyre can be made by machinery, should cost from £10 to £30, and, as a matter of fact, people who cannot pay those sums already contrive to possess themselves of very serviceable machines. Poor students, domestic servants, and artisans may be encountered in the evening in scores on every road out of the great cities, and regular systems of selling bicycles at cheaper rates have been invented with an ingenuity most creditable to everything but the dealers' moral sense. You may buy certain machines 'for export' at little more than half the advertised prices, or you may buy 'second-hand' articles, which have perhaps been taken out three times, or you may buy machines 'which have been superseded' by some trivial or, if you are tolerably sharp, some imperceptible improvement. The manufacturers are just now making fortunes, but the moment the demand slackens and the markets are a little glutted, competition will bring prices down with a run until they settle at between five and seven pounds, according to perfection of finish. The remaining difficulty, that of the tyre, will disappear when inventors seriously

DOI: 10.4324/9781315400303-23

set their minds to it. We shall annoy the holders of shares in pneumatic tyre companies by the remark, but we are entirely unable to believe in the permanence of those costly and aggravating 'improvements'. They are much too apt to leave the rider stranded twenty miles away from home, and unless they can be 'improved' again by some lacquer, which we fancy a clever Japanese could invent, and which would be impermeable to a knife or a nail or a flint-stone, they will be superseded by some contrivance for obtaining 'resilience' either from spring coils rising from the spokes under a rim of thin steel, or by pads between the axle and the wheel, or by some new material which will spring and yield, and yet defy any injury short of a total smash. In India, where you have flat roads hundreds of miles long, and where, for climatic and other reasons, indiarubber is out of favour, men glide about all day in the cold weather on wheels of tenacious steel. The moment the cycle costs five pounds as a pivot price, will last ten years, and is independent of repairs, cycles will become for all the healthy the universal means of locomotion, and will be hired out in thousands instead of tens for pennies an hour where shillings are now charged. A register of bicycles will soon be established by law, new rules of the road will be enforced at once by law and by opinion, wilful injury to bicyclists will be declared a separate and a serious offence, and all men and women will find that they have suddenly gained a new power, have become more free, and will henceforward enjoy a much enlarged horizon.

That will be the essence of the social change. At present all but the comparative few who can command carriages at will are limited, especially in the country, in seeking their friends or enjoying scenery, to a radius of about three miles. Many of our readers will exclaim at that, and declare that they are ready to walk three times the distance; but we would ask them, if they are not born Londoners, and therefore accustomed to be on foot all day – Londoners, and Londoners only, really forget distance – to reflect for a moment, and then say truthfully whether they care to walk six miles for a mere visit, and especially whether they even so much as think of paying two such visits in one day. They will acknowledge, we fancy, that they will no more do it frequently or habitually than Americans will, and the American who, in Europe at all events, will voluntarily walk two miles, much less six, has yet to be discovered. The skilled cyclist, however, who has developed the proper muscles, and has got rid of the sense of fatigue which haunts the beginner, just as it haunts, and daunts, the man who is learning to swim, can keep on his bicycle all day, and if his frame is not shaken by a fall, or his temper tried by the pricking of those infernal tyres, he will return in the evening with his nerves in perfect order and his limbs as little tired as if he had been strolling for the same time up and down a terrace or a lawn. This means that he can choose friends or do business within half a county instead of within two villages, and that his powers of locomotion at will are multiplied at least five-fold, or in the case of the really skilled and healthy eight or ten fold. That is a new freedom, a great multiplication of power for men, and especially for women, who, we notice, enjoy it much more than men do, and contrive somehow to avoid the look of care which is the special mark of the bicyclist, and we shall be curious to note, when time has been given for the change to operate fully, what its precise effects are. They will not all be good. They will probably increase the general happiness, for let the cynics say what they like, friendship is a great sweetener of life, and pleasant conversation one of the few really enjoyable occupations, but they will impair neighbourliness, which rests in a degree we none of us like to formulate upon the sense that we must not quarrel with, or avoid, or even sharply criticise, those among whom it is our lot to live. Our neighbour is the man who is nigh us, and in that compulsory association, is a root of kindliness, of forbearance, and of mutual readiness to assist, which life in a great city seriously impairs, and which extreme freedom of locomotion will impair also. That will not benefit the general nature, and we are not sure that it will even benefit the intelligence, though at first sight that should be the result. We all fancy we are the brighter for choosing our own friends at our own discretion, but like tends to seek like, and it may be doubted whether the real intellectual gain of human intercourse is not derived from the unlike. We learn as much from the stupid as the wise. At least, if that as a general axiom is an impossible paradox, we notice that those who live only among the bright are apt to become narrow in a novel way, to misread human nature as it really is, and to fancy that everything is easy, especially in politics, when it is really next to impracticable, or so difficult that to attempt it is waste of energy. Just listen to the advocates of peace, usually able men, talking among themselves, and note the kind of dreams in which they firmly believe. Neighbourliness is a useful virtue as well as a Christian one, and a certain monotony in life which is fostered by a narrow radius of locomotion tends, as we have always maintained, to deeper thought and reflection. The constant habit of the bicycle dissipates the mind just as a constant immersion in society does, and for the same reason, – it renders reflection less frequent and less enjoyable. Why think when you can reach a pleasant circle five miles off in half an hour, and with no perceptible fatigue? Let those who doubt that this effect will be produced in the country note the curious increase the cycle is causing in the habit of meeting at lunch, and indeed in the substitution of lunch for dinner. You cannot bicycle back on a dark night with your wife or sister in full dress, but you can lunch at 2 o'clock and cycle back in the cool of the evening with great enjoyment and no danger. Cycling, in fact, will increase the scattering and moveability of country society, to the increase of its pleasures and the loss of much of its steadfastness and quiet. The ancient 'rootedness' of the country sides will be greatly diminished, and we are old-fashioned enough to believe that in that quality was much not only of charm but of utility. It is a horrid thing to say nowadays, and one which excites a ridicule not untinged with dislike, but we confess to a sympathy with that old world which read into the epithet 'gadabout' such a richness of contempt. All life, they say, is change, but the most mutable thing in the world is a candle, which perishes unrenewed. The cycle will stay, and its influence, though enfranchising – which is one reason that women take to it more eagerly than men – will, socially, always be centrifugal.

18

E. B. TURNER, 'HEALTH ON THE BICYCLE'

Contemporary Review, 73 (1898), pp. 640–648

There can be no doubt but that the health of the people of this country must be influenced one way or the other, for good or for bad, by the almost universal craze for bicycling which during the last few years has become the fashion. The cult of the bicycle is by no means new – it has had its votaries for now about thirty years; but while the high, difficult, yet withal graceful 'Ordinary' machine held sway, both sport and pastime were practically confined to practised athletes, and the question of health or fitness for the exercise in their case was never raised. But the invention in the first place of the tricycle and of the low, equal-wheeled 'Safety', and in the second of the pneumatic tyre, changed all this, and has brought an exercise both fascinating and exhilarating within the reach of all, old and young, man, woman, and child. Of course, a great number of men who have recently commenced to ride are either those who in their younger days were given to some form or other of athletic exercise, or else are now at school or university engaged in running, rowing, cricket, football, or other competitive sports, and so do not suddenly, and in an untrained state, commence to throw an unaccustomed strain on their muscular and circulatory systems. But these experts are not the only recruits to the new army of cyclists. Men who have passed the greater part of their lives in sedentary occupations, women whose only exercise has been 'carriage', young children, and old people, have with one accord fallen victims to the fascinations of this alluring form of locomotion. It stands to reason, therefore, that among those in this second category there must be many on whom a sudden increase of bodily exertion must produce a great effect, and it is the object of this paper to lay down such rules and indicate such precautions as may be necessary to insure that the change in their habits may be productive of good, and not the means of laying the foundations of disease and injury.

There are few exercises or sports more healthful to the ordinary individual than bicycling in a moderate and discreet fashion, and experience has shown that in many cases of functional ailments, and even in some of organic delicacy, its regulated use has materially aided the physician in his efforts to restore health. The reason for this is not far to seek. A person riding a bicycle has not to carry his own weight. He is rolled on wheels, and only has to propel himself; the machine carries him. A simple

DOI: 10.4324/9781315400303-24

experiment will prove the truth of this. Let any one carry a man of twelve stone weight on his back for, say, one hundred yards, and afterwards seat him on a tricycle and push him over the same course, and compare the amount of force needed to accomplish the distance. He will find that a finger-touch is sufficient to propel both man and machine, while very considerable fatigue results from carrying him. A bicycle ride, therefore, combines the maximum of fresh air and change of scene with the minimum of injurious effort, and to the delicate will afford exercise without exhaustion, and to the strong will open up the country and give access to places which otherwise would be unattainable to those not blessed with riding horses.

Granting, then, that cycling properly regulated is in itself a good and healthful recreation, it is well to examine the question, and endeavour to point out the pitfalls which, in its pursuit, should be avoided, and give any hints which may conduce to its becoming a healthful as well as a pleasurable amusement.

First of all, to take the case of persons who are sound and well. At what age may a child commence to ride? At what age should a man decide that the time is past for him to learn? As a general rule, it may be stated that seven years is quite the earliest age at which a boy or girl should be allowed to mount a cycle, and even then great care is necessary to see that the machine is in every way fitted to the child. The reach must be carefully adjusted according to the length of leg; the saddle must be accurately adapted to the rider; the crank should not be too long, four to five inches is quite sufficient for a child of such an age; and the gear should not exceed fifty-two inches. Young growing tissues are easily distorted, and therefore it is most important to see that the handle-bar is raised to such a height that the rider can easily sit quite upright. If it were too low and the handles set too far forward, the child would adopt the ungainly 'scorcher' attitude, and a permanently humped spine would be the result. Then when he is properly mounted and the machine rightly adjusted he must not be allowed to do too much. Excessive distance is bad, excessive speed is worse, and excessive hill-riding is worst. It is impossible to lay down in miles and furlongs how far each particular boy or girl may ride. The capacity of each for active exercise differs, and each by practice will become capable of doing more. If after any ride the child is found to refuse his food, and to be feverish, restless, and sleepless at night and thirsty the next day, it is a sure and certain sign that he has done too much, and such over-exertion persisted in must lead to disaster. If, on the contrary, on returning home the young cyclist eats well, sleeps well, and is bright and lively the next day, then the ride has not been pushed too far, and has done him good and not harm.

It is difficult to say when a man is too old to commence to ride. Some men of advanced years have all their life long been used to regular athletic exercise, and in consequence come to any new form of bodily exertion with heart and muscles well prepared, and long experience teaches them how much or how little they can do without injury. Of such was the late Major Knox Holmes, who, an athlete from his youth upwards, at the age of about seventy-four years exchanged his arm-chair and chronic rheumatism for a tricycle, and died of influenza at the age of eighty-five, having the year before his death ridden over one hundred miles in the day on the great North Road.

There are several other instances of men who, having passed the allotted span of threescore years and ten, have learned to cycle, and are still living instances of the benefits to be obtained therefrom. But old arteries are inelastic, old muscles are brittle, and any veteran who has passed a sedentary existence should count well the cost before he risks the chances of over-strain which might easily ensue on his attempting a new and unaccustomed pastime for the first time in his old age.

This warning applies with double force to women – as those who have at the present time attained a mature age, passed their youth in the days when the only exercise considered 'ladylike' was dancing or a mild walk, and who consequently are quite unprepared to suddenly change their habits. No old man or elderly woman should, under any circumstances, commence to cycle unless passed sound, and even then the greatest care must be taken never to venture beyond the bounds of extreme moderation. Those, however, who are already expert cyclists may look forward with confidence to being able to continue their riding through a green old age, and to reap health and length of days from their habits of regular exercise.

One of the most frequent questions asked is whether persons who are physically unsound may cycle; and if they may, how much should they be allowed to do? It is quite impossible to discuss this thoroughly, except in the pages of a purely medical work; but a broad rule may be laid down that no one who is unsound or delicate should commence to cycle, except under the advice of a competent physician. There are some ailments in which cycling, properly regulated, acts like a charm in restoring health; there are others in which to mount a bicycle would be simple suicide. It does most good in functional diseases, and in such as arise from insufficient exercise. It prevents and assists in the cure of such ailments as gout and rheumatism, and few regular cyclists are troubled with indigestion. In the bloodlessness of young girls it sometimes does more good than pints of iron drops, though in such cases moderation is most essential until the heart is well drilled in its new work, and very few instances of pure 'nervousness' survive a regular course of bicycle rides. Its use is not so apparent when there is organic mischief and change of structure in any organ, though sometimes it is used as a palliative, and enables the sufferer to take that exercise which is good for his general health, and which he could not manage on his feet. No person, however, with any organic disease, especially if the heart be affected, should attempt to cycle, except under the direct orders of his physician.

When it is decided that it is right and wise for a person to commence riding, a most important question is the distance he should cover and the pace at which he should cover it. From what has been written above, it will be seen that the answer to this depends entirely on the physique and condition of the rider. Because Cordang, an exceptional athlete, trained to the hour and perfectly paced, can compass over 600 miles in twenty-four hours on a cement track, it does not follow that a delicate girl or weak man can ride fifty miles in the same time on a country road.

In all probability, were they to attempt it, they would be more harmed by their exertions and more exhausted at the finish than the experienced professional was after racing over twelve times the distance. Each novice, commencing to ride, must feel his or her way gingerly; condition will come with practice, and in a few weeks it will be possible to accomplish a distance at a speed which seemed quite impossible when viewed through the glasses of inexperience and unfitness. But, even when in condition, to the ordinary rider moderation, both in pace and mileage, should be the watchword. It is extremely easy to 'over-do' it cycling. The exercise is so easy and the exertion seems so slight that much mischief has been done to many, especially women, who, tempted by a leading wind and favourable gradients, have exceeded their usual distance riding away from home, and, on returning, have found that the adverse conditions of wind and hill entail a struggle which, if persisted in, may leave its mark on their constitutions for years. The old hand, especially when not quite fit, carefully arranges his ride so that he has the difficulties to contend with when fresh, and takes the help of the breeze and formation of the country to bring him home without undue exertion.

It is very easy to know if any ride has overtaxed the strength and caused over-fatigue. Under such circumstances the rider will be unable to eat, he will be thirsty, hot, restless, and feverish at night, and quite unable to sleep, and the next day will suffer from lassitude and a distinct disinclination for any form of exertion. If a rest be taken, these symptoms of 'fatigue fever' will rapidly subside; but if they be disregarded, and the offence repeated, nature will step in to exact the penalty due to her outraged laws.

For the great majority of cyclists there is no doubt but that the bicycle is a better machine than the tricycle. It has the advantage in weight and ease of propulsion, and can be used more easily when the road is bad, because it is a 'one-track' machine, and can pick its way along any smooth portion of the highway; whereas the tricycle requires three tracks, one for each of its wheels. In case of accident also the bicycle is the safer, as it is possible to jump clear when it is impossible to avoid the danger; while the tricycle rider, especially if of the female sex, is wedged in between the seat-pillar behind and the handle-bar in front, and has to sink or swim with the machine. The disadvantages of the bicycle are the tendency to 'side-slip' in greasy mud, the difficulty in mounting and dismounting, which require a certain amount of agility in the rider, and the fact that it requires a trick-rider to remain seated when not in motion. For ladies with a tendency to *embonpoint* a well-built tricycle is decidedly the more graceful steed.

With regard to the saddle, each person must suit himself. There are dozens of good patterns on the market, but, as it has been well said, 'one man's saddle is another man's blisters'. It is most necessary to be careful about the adjustment and position of the saddle; if too high or too low it cannot be comfortable, even if the pressure in the wrong places is not injurious. It should be placed just so high that when the rider is sitting at ease and upright he can touch the pedal with his heel when it is at its lowest point. This will give him perfect command over the machine, and allow him to use his ankles in pedalling to the best advantage.

Riders, especially ladies, are inclined to transgress this rule for two reasons. The first is, that it is much easier to mount the cycle if the saddle be placed too low; the second is, that persons of short stature look more elegant and graceful if their seat is raised to such a height that they can only just touch the pedal with the ball of the foot when extended. Either error is injurious. If the saddle be too low, it is impossible to use the full power of the muscles of the leg, as the knee must always be kept bent, and so they have to act at a great disadvantage, because the force has to be applied by a pull rather than by a push; sitting in such a cramped and doubled-up position, it is extremely difficult to make any use of the weight of the body as an agent of propulsion, and so the rider has to depend entirely on his muscular efforts to drive the machine, and they, handicapped by his incorrect position, are frequently at fault, especially when climbing a hill. It is much better to have a machine built with a low frame, or to carefully cultivate the art of mounting, than to struggle on with the saddle some inches too low.

When, on the other hand, the reach is set too long, it is positively injurious to the rider. He (or it is generally a 'she') is at the mercy of every stone or rough place in the road, and is quite unable to humour the bicycle over ruts or bumps by distributing the weight between handles, pedals, and saddle, and is consequently tossed about as if riding on a rail, while the position is unsteady and a great deal of injurious pressure is exercised where it will do most harm. At the same time, the danger of side-slip and of losing control of the bicycle in an emergency is doubled, as the guiding power of the feet on the pedals is lost for about half the stroke and the ankle-action is much impaired. If any cycling beyond mere park-riding be contemplated, it is better by far to sacrifice a little appearance to safety and comfort, and shorten the reach according to the rule given above. Each different person, according to his length of limb, will probably require the peak of the saddle to be in a different position with regard to the crank-axle. Experience will alone determine this, but for the majority it will be found that if a plumb-line be dropped from the peak and fall about four or five inches behind the crank axle, the most suitable place will have been discovered. Some are able to do better with a more forward, some with a more backward position, but in either case extremes should be avoided.

With regard to the actual shape of the saddle, it should be sufficiently broad at the back to allow of the rider sitting fairly and squarely upon it, and using for that purpose his ischial tuberosities, the bones intended by nature to support the weight of the sitting body. Most persons prefer some sort of a peak, as it gives a sense of security in descending hills, and also assists them in guiding the cycle. The saddle should be most carefully adjusted, so that this peak shall cause no undue pressure anywhere, and when the right angle is found, the nuts should be firmly fixed, and never moved. There are numerous patented arrangements, all intended to produce the great cycling desideratum – a perfect saddle; each rider must discover that which is perfect for himself. But it is essential, whatever be the shape of the saddle, that the springs be adapted to the weight of him who sits thereon. Springs for a fourteen-stone man are absurd for a nine-stone girl. For a novice, rubber or felt pedals are best; for an expert, rat-trap. For these last a special pair of shoes should be kept, and if vibration, causing numbness of the feet, be complained of, it is well to have the soles made of a sheet of rubber fixed between two layers of leather. To both sexes, when cycling, certain rules as to dress are common. All underclothing should be of wool, with a thickness regulated according to the temperature; shoes always; boots never should be worn; and no garment should be at all tight. For men little more need be said. Golfing or shooting costume, with rather thinner stockings, suits every cycling requirement, it being understood that knickerbockers are far preferable to trousers. For women the skirt should be well cut and not too large round the hem; three yards will be found sufficient, and it should clear the ground by about four inches when the wearer is not on her machine. Knickerbockers should take the place of the petticoat, and thin woollen stockings should be worn by those who mean to ride more than a mile or two. Some women are disposed to discard the skirt when cycling, on the ground that 'rational dress' is both more convenient and safer, as well as allowing a diamond-framed machine to be used instead of the more cumbrous drop-framed ladies' bicycle. In these contentions they are undoubtedly right, but, beyond the proto-martyrs and pioneers of the movement, it does not seem likely that many women, in this country at least, will adopt the new fashion, as, with two or three exceptions necessary to prove the rule, the all-powerful looking-glass forbids. It is as well for ladies riding in the early spring and winter, or who are likely to return against a wind or after dark, to carry an extra wrap. It may save many a chill. Very little beyond common sense is necessary to point out a proper diet for cycling. Whatever the rider may have been accustomed to, and has found to suit him, is best. It is not necessary to be a vegetarian, a teetotaler, an excessive meat-eater, or large consumer of alcohol, to excel on the cycle. Nature and experience point out that a simple mixed diet is best for man, and simple regular meals are best for the man who cycles. It is unwise for any one to start riding directly after food, and stimulants between meals, even in case of fatigue, must be bad. Their effect soon passes off, and the reaction leaves the rider worse than he was before.

So long as human nature remains what it is, it may be taken as absolutely certain that racing and speed competitions will find favour among the young, and that not only the young, but those even of more mature years, will be tempted to descend into the arena and test their speed and stamina against their fellows. For years it has been a matter of controversy whether racing, either on foot, in boats, or on cycles, is dangerous to health, or whether it may be indulged in with impunity, and be expected to improve rather than damage the physical condition of its votaries. The last five-and-thirty years have witnessed a great athletic revival, which has spread downwards to all ranks of the community, and in the present day the number of young men engaged in all sorts of occupations and avocations, who take part in hard competitive exercises such as football, rowing, cross-country running, short and long distance walking, running, and cycle racing, is simply legion; and, if the after-effects of all this athletic strain be as bad as some pessimists delight to paint them, it stands to reason that the general health of the community must show a marked and increasing deterioration as a result. Studying this question from an active experience of over thirty years, it appears that, if no harm is to be done to the individual, and through him to the community, by indulging in the practice of this athleticism, the love of which is inherent in the human race, two stringent rules should be laid down: the one, that no person should take part in any competition unless he be properly trained and fit; the other, that no person organically unsound should, under any circumstances, be allowed to commence training. It is impossible that an untrained man can pass through the ordeal of a fast and keenly contested race without throwing such a stress upon his heart, lungs, and muscular system that some mischief must be done, and some organ, weaker perhaps than its fellows, receive a strain which, though perhaps not appreciated at the time, is painfully apparent later on, and may wreck a whole lifetime with the curse of chronic ill-health. This danger is more real to the old hand, who may be tempted to compete when out of condition, than to the novice who has no experience of the race-path. The one knows exactly how to make the most of himself, and his nervous system, stamped with the mark of many previous contests, enables him to overtax his strength, and goads him on to the extreme limits of exhaustion. The other is unskilled; his nervous energy is misapplied, and, though his pluck may equal that of the more skilled performer, nature steps in before he can do himself much real injury and compels him to cease from his ill-advised efforts. That any one whose organs are unsound should not be encouraged to subject them to the trials and labours of that sort of preparation which is necessary in the present day before it is possible to excel on the race-track must be clear to every one who takes the trouble to consider the matter. No young man whose heart, lungs, or joints are in any way diseased can hope to do more than jog on through life. Cracked plates are not used to build a war-ship, and guns with flaws are condemned. Such persons can be very useful members of society, but they are not fitted for the fierce joy of contest. The weak spot must under such circumstances be found out, and the greater their pluck and determination the worse will be their ultimate fate. It must not be concluded from the above that all men organically unsound are to be prohibited from every form of bodily exercise. Moderate and proper use of their limbs will be beneficial, and many a wise physician will order them exercise, and so direct it that it will lighten their burden and sweeten their days. But there is a great difference between a quiet potter on a bicycle and a well-fought-out race. A bruised reed may accomplish the one unharmed, but break on attempting the other.

When it is decided that a young man is fit to go into training, it is necessary that he should train with care. The object of proper training is to bring the body to the highest perfection in health and efficiency, and this process must be accomplished gradually; and pains must be taken not to overdo the work, but by degrees fit and accustom each organ to the extra strain which will be laid upon it, and build up the whole system to withstand such strain without sustaining injury. It is impossible to lay down in a short paper any more than the most general rules which should be observed to attain this end. Each man trains differently, and must be humoured accordingly. Common-sense and moderation are the best trainers, and regularity in sleep, food and exercise is the best regimen. It is wonderful what feats can be accomplished by a sound athlete, when properly fit, without any apparent harm. The competitors in many twenty-four hours' races and record feats have been thoroughly examined by competent observers and found perfectly healthy and but little exhausted by their arduous labours. The time has not yet arrived to say with certainty how these long-distance races will affect the future health of those who have participated in them; suffice it to state that at present they show no signs of unsoundness. It is hardly necessary to mention races of a duration of six days, such as have recently been held in America, except unhesitatingly to condemn them. Let it be hoped that the National Cyclists Union will never permit any such exhibition to take place in England under its rules. For the sound, moderate racing, after proper training, is good, and many a man owes to his athletic career improved health and physique, as well as habits of temperance and self-denial, which, necessary for success on the path, have influenced the whole of his subsequent life. For the unsound, racing is a snare and a delusion, and many a useful career has been cut short in the pitfall of athletic ambition.

Cyclists should take heart; their pastime is healthful and pleasing, and, though it is possible for any one to do himself harm by over-riding, it is not the only sport which has this failing; men, and women too, have over-walked, over-run, over-climbed, and over-rowed, and but little notice has been taken of it. Cycling, for the many, is a new sport, and we live in the days of evening papers, and at present every accident and every injury which in any way can be attributed to it is commented and enlarged upon more than its merits deserve. The bicycle-face, the bicycle-hand, the bicycle-foot are myths, and even 'kyphosis bicyclistarum' need but provoke a smile, provided only that the reader observe the good old cycling rule: 'Sit easily upright, and keep your eyes well in front of you'.

19

CESARE LOMBROSO, 'THE BICYCLE AND CRIME'

Pall Mall Magazine, 20 (1900), pp. 310–316

Every new mechanism adopted in our daily life multiplies the causes and the number of crimes. Electricity and magnetism in the hands of delirious degenerates have lent themselves to murder; and as they enter into new instruments they develop fresh forms of crime – as, for instance, the use in highway robbery of the *assommoir électrique*, which knocks down a passenger with a single blow, the employment of chloroform to deprive the thief's victim of consciousness or of dynamite to force the strong-room. No sooner were railways laid than up sprang a whole crop of railway offences, not the least of which was the de-railing of trains. The increasing growth of insurance companies, and of journalism, has evolved offences as modern as they are wide-spread, offences appalling in the difficulty of their discovery, such as bribery of the press, or poisoning for the sake of insurance money. And now the phonograph is pressed into the service of calumny and crime.

But no modern mechanism has assumed the extraordinary importance of the bicycle, either as a cause or as an instrument of crime. So marked is this that, whereas it used to be the somewhat intemperate fashion to seek in woman the mainspring of every masculine offence, – *cherchez la femme*, – we might now say with perhaps less exaggeration *cherchez la bicyclette* in the majority of offences committed by young men, and, in Italy at all events, by young men of good social standing. This may be explained in many ways. First there is the enormously popular use of the bicycle, not only as a vehicle of conveyance and pleasure, but as a means of gain both by 'record' riding and by sale. Then there is the increased intercourse among men, which, as I have pointed out in my *Delinquent Man*, always augments vice; the more so when, as in this case, such intercourse arises about the very age (from fifteen to twenty-five years) when the tendency towards vice is most marked, and amongst men of leisure, and men of extraordinary agility, who, as I have also long ago observed, have a strong propensity to crime. The very general use of a fairly valuable machine encourages swindling, just as bills of exchange and postal and telegraphic orders, which facilitate the circulation of money, encourage it in a form which had no existence before their invention.

 DOI: 10.4324/9781315400303-25

The bicycle a cause of crime

It is certain that many muscular young men, consumed with vanity, desire to make their way in the world rapidly. The longing to surpass others without possessing any special mental qualification for so doing is one of the strongest tendencies of our times; and it is most marked amongst youths who, not being rich enough to buy a costly bicycle which shall enable them to 'break the record', are moved to commit theft, perhaps even highway robbery involving homicide, to gain their end. We must remember that the born criminal, who is most addicted to such crimes, unlike the average person, is a *neophile* – a lover of the new, an anti-conservative. He has therefore a predilection for this new machine, and knows better than others how to derive advantage from it. For him it has special sources of pride; for, being by nature an idler, an enemy to labour, he is free from the class-scruples of clergymen, magistrates or doctors, for whom the bicycle is a source of possible public contempt and professional damage. He is free, too, from the shrinking of the average man or woman from an instrument but recently adopted (in Italy at any rate) into social habits.

Two very young brothers came under my notice in Turin. They were of good family, but addicted to bad company, precocious in passion and the use of wine; and whilst still mere lads they were led to become thieves on account of the bicycle. The elder brother of a fine but somewhat effeminate countenance, hoping to become a great cyclist (he was already a great gymnast), at the age of eighteen incited two friends to join him in breaking into a cycle shop. They were caught red-handed, and he then obstinately feigned dumbness, refused food and tore his clothing, so that he eventually succeeded in getting himself pardoned.

His brother aged sixteen, of fair complexion, with abnormal cranial and facial peculiarities – note the projecting lower jaw – was consumed with the desire of possessing a bicycle. He was a mechanic in a small cycle factory; so he waited until several bicycles came into the shop, and handed one over to the custody of a friend, intending to use it for a time and then restore it. But ere the day of restitution came he was caught. In prison he, like his brother, had fits of mania, in one of which he threw himself from a height and broke his arm. When after a few months of confinement he was set at liberty, he sickened and died of consumption.

I recall another case of a lad of sixteen. He was a gymnastic student, and came of a wealthy family. His countenance was sympathetic, but childish; he too had a projecting jaw, and was of precocious physical development; he had, besides, an extraordinary passion for gambling and sport. He hired a bicycle for an hour, intending, he said, to take it back in a day or two. In the meantime, however he deposited it for the night in the porter's lodge of a friend's house far distant from his own home. The next day he rode out of the town to enjoy his machine in greater security, but was presently arrested. In prison he showed no shame; he only complained that his cell was small, his bed hard, and his soup unsavoury: he was obviously devoid of all moral sense. His sentence was a few months' imprisonment, but no sooner was he free than he stole some graphophone tubes.

[Another young man] has all the characteristics of the born delinquent: cranium hydrocephalic, vision oblique, passions precocious; probably epileptic too, having had a blow on the head in infancy. By the time he was twenty-two he had been a waiter, a custodian, a typographer, a soldier. Having obtained a post as office messenger, he considered it necessary to have a bicycle; 'so of course', said he, 'I had to take it'. And take it he did, and kept it for seven months.

Sometimes the offence is much slighter. The desire for a bicycle being appeased, the offender (fundamentally honest, or, at worst, having but a slight criminal tendency) feels the first sting of remorse, and restores the stolen object. Occasionally, with peculiar prudence, he returns it, with a note of apology, through a third person.

Not seldom, however, the bicycle craze leads to bloodshed. On July 15th, 1895, a youth of nineteen entered a neighbour's house by night to steal a bicycle. The neighbour being awakened, the intruder killed him with such violence that he also wounded himself. He returned to his own house, washed, changed his clothes, and joined the neighbours and the police, who, attracted by the cries of the victim, had come to the rescue. He even expressed pity for the dead man, 'lying there', he said, 'with his throat cut like a calf'. But his own blood-tracks between the two houses promptly betrayed him. When arrested he confessed that the murder was premeditated. He had sharpened the knife two days before, and had dexterously procured the key of his victim's house. Shortly afterwards he feigned madness, dressed up like Hamlet, spouted verses and refused food. I unmasked him, however.

He was a fine young fellow – although his expression was sinister – with a massive skull; his sensibility to touch and pain was obtuse; the visual field was restricted, and he had some epileptic symptoms. But the most noteworthy point about him was his double personality. The son of a butcher, and himself a butcher, it nevertheless pained him to kill a chicken or a wasp. Amongst his friends he was the general peacemaker; he appeared so benevolent that the mere reading of the plague episode in the *Promessi Sposi* caused him to weep and remain silent for hours. And yet he felt no remorse for the murder, because, as he said, it was justified by the great object of becoming the best bicyclist in the world. With a bicycle he could have escaped from his father's house, which he hated, and have become rich and famous. What was the life of a man compared with that? It must, however, be noted that his mother was hysterical – a mere cipher morally; that an epileptic uncle on the father's side had committed suicide, and that he had an epileptic cousin on his mother's side. As a child he had himself suffered from hysteria and epilepsy – a fact which throws light on his double personality, of excessive benevolence on the one hand and excessive egoism on the other, a balance of characteristics which his morbid vanity, whetted by the cycling craze, weighed down on the side of crime.

The bicycle an instrument of crime

The spread of the bicycle, and its comparatively high price, make it not only an object but a means of thieving and swindling even amongst fairly well-to-do people. Take the example of a rich banker's son, aged twenty-two, a student at the Military Academy. From the time he was fifteen he was addicted to more display than his means warranted, and it was said that he used to feed his large St. Bernard dog on sweet cakes. He used to hire bicycles under false names, and then, wearing a military uniform to which he had no longer any right, he would sell them at very low prices.

Then of course there is the regular professional thief. Bicycle thieves frequently club together in gangs, from three up to fifteen or so, with branches in the country or in neighbouring towns. They begin by stealing wayside bicycles left by the unwary; then, waxing bolder and more expert, they steal them from dealers' doorways, and take them to other towns, where they promptly make them unrecognisable by altering the most conspicuous parts. The chief of one gang which came under my observation had almost unwittingly stolen a bicycle whilst he was in a state of intoxication. Another gang started with a young man of nineteen as captain; he was of the criminal type, by trade a saddler. At the age of sixteen, being too poor to gratify his passion for cycling, he appropriated an unguarded bicycle, which after a few days' use he sold. Some months later, no longer out of enthusiasm for cycling, but from sheer vice, he contrived to steal no fewer than six. His companion, a metal founder, stole, altered, and sold ten more. These two joined two others, and formed a gang who stole altogether about seventy or eighty bicycles.

Very often swindling is added to theft. A travelling vendor of jewellery, who had been convicted of forgery, hired a furnished room and searched the newspapers for advertisements of bicycles for sale. As a result of his quest he went to a lady's house, struck a bargain for a bicycle and arranged that it should be delivered at his new residence. When it arrived he mounted in the courtyard under pretext of trying it, and rode off without paying to a distance of fifty kilometres. The next day, however, he returned to the town, nay, to the very same street, and was promptly arrested. This was his third offence of the kind.

The next portrait is that of an ex-officer who married a music-hall singer, and who, in order to cut a great figure, purchased with promissory notes, three bicycles, which he immediately sold again, omitting to redeem the notes. This trick he repeated to procure fifteen bicycles and a carriage; and, to crown his dishonesty, he managed to lay the blame on others – protesting that, rich, married, an officer and a gentleman, he was incapable of such actions. To shop-keepers he always presented himself in full uniform. Now and then he would borrow large sums from wealthy persons and give them a bicycle on account of the payment, which he never concluded. This man also, for the better accomplishment of his schemes, joined three others who completed the *mise-en-scène* of his greatness. I should add that these bicycle swindles were supplemented by others for obtaining a pianoforte, horses and carriages. He was not even above robbing the till; for now and then he would steal bank notes from the cash desks of bicycle dealers, who of course could entertain no suspicion of such a great personage, such a noble warrior.

The bicycle as a means of highway robbery

The bicycle is so mobile that it falls an easy prey to the thief. This same mobility, however, makes it a most serviceable instrument for the accomplishment of other crimes; for what so well facilitates flight and *alibi* as the bicycle – swifter than the horse, safer than the railway with its blabbing telegraph? Thus a rich lady in broad daylight was ascending the doorsteps of a large house in the Boulevard S. Germain, when a bicyclist who had jumped off his machine at the foot of the steps followed and passed her, pushed her down, robbed her, and, before she could cry out or rise, remounted his cycle and got clear away.

Then there is the wealthy young cyclist, who, with his brother, started on a tour round the world, according to a fashion lately revived and much in vogue with budding criminals. At an hotel in Savoy they met a lady, with whom they opened a grand flirtation, and, having ascertained where she kept her jewels and money, they helped themselves and rode away to a discreet distance, where the sole slender chance of their discovery lay in the possible recognition of some of the stolen jewels. (As it turned out, however, this really happened a few months later.)

A ferocious highway robber, who was an expert cyclist, found one day by the roadside an idiot who had been robbed, and advised the poor creature to recoup himself by robbing the next person he met. The two of them then joining forces, brutally maltreated an unfortunate bicyclist who chanced to be the next passenger on the highroad. They stripped him of his money and rode off with his cycle to a place sixty kilomètres away. For the most part these highwaymen are very young, very alert, enthusiastic cyclists, and of good social standing; they are frequently military or ex-military men, or students.

Minor or pseudo crimes

In addition to serious cycle crimes culminating in the delinquency of associates or in highway robbery, we have minor cycle crimes, such as those practised by boys who scatter nails on the ground or puncture tyres with pins, or who run under bicycles on purpose to upset them, and to get knocked down so that they may claim damages. Then again, in districts where the bicycle makes its appearance for the first time, we have the offences of brutal persons who deliberately drive their horses into the new machine and injure the rider out of sheer hatred of anything new. On the other hand, we have the careless cyclist who, through inattention or awkwardness, runs over the pedestrian. In tax-laden Italy it was inevitable that this machine should be burdened with taxes, sufficiently vexatious in themselves but particularly so in the methods of their payment. No cycle is permitted to circulate unless it bears a special stamp, which is impressed upon it when the tax is assessed. The unwary foreigner, coming into our country from happier lands where cycle taxation is unknown, is as promptly fined as any heedless Italian who may have neglected to register his machine. The stamp in its turn gives rise to a new variety of offence. It not seldom happens that on railways and tramways ill-disposed persons remove the stamp from one bicycle to transfer it to some unstamped machine. Innocent persons are frequently fined for this offence. I once heard a worthy father and five sons, each the possessor of a bicycle, seriously accused of fraud because one of their cycle stamps had been accidentally injured.

But for the most part these cases and the graver ones in which persons are run over are accidental, rather than deliberate offences; and at any rate they would never have been committed save, on the one hand, for the existence of the cycle, and, on the other, for the police regulations controlling its use.

Advantages of the bicycle, hygienic and social

It must, however, be admitted that if the bicycle has augmented the causes and means of crime, it has increased the well-being and civilising tendencies of life; lessening the isolation of the small centres and bringing the country within a few minutes' distance of the large centres. In the elections it was a powerful ally of those political parties which were most advanced and best able to avail themselves of modern means of contest.

Again, if the bicycle gives rise to fresh forms of crime, it offers new and merciful means for the suppression of crime. Here is an illustration of the tandem cycle used in the State of Ohio for the conveyance of criminals. The seat at each end is occupied by a policeman, whilst the prisoner sits in the middle with hands and feet secured to prevent his moving or escaping. Truly we have travelled a long way from the famous *Boite à Salade* of old France and Italy! Not only so, but the bicycle promises substantial improvement to our race; and that in most important ways. In an age in which excess of mental work is making neurasthenia endemic, the bicycle presents itself as a vehicle which stimulates locomotion without the exhaustion produced by excessive climbing or boxing. The healthier men are, the better they are; and in so far as the bicycle makes for health it indirectly diminishes the causes of crime. A remedy is everywhere being vainly sought for alcoholism, a disease which is based on an ever-increasing craving for cerebral excitement. Now, it seems to me that a passion for cycling, which is incompatible with the degrading use of alcohol so common amongst the lower classes, offers the finest of all remedies for this terrible evil. In our rides along the country roads most frequented by cyclists, my son and I have observed that the public-houses have quite changed their character, and now sell all sorts of mineral waters, syrups, and coffee. As a mental specialist I have seen the gravest forms of neurasthenia and melancholia yield before this marvellous machine, and I am sure that your great English specialists will bear me out. A satirical forecast describes the *cyclo-anthropos* of the twentieth century as a doubled-up hunchback with atrophic arms. For my part, I venture to predict that the real *cyclo-anthropos* of the twentieth century will suffer less from his nerves and will be more muscular than the man of the nineteenth century. And certainly, for one evil which the bicycle now provokes, it will yield us a hundred benefits in time to come.

2.4

Horseless carriage

DOI: 10.4324/9781315400303-26

2.4 Horseless carriage

J. Munro, 'Carriages Without Horses', *Cassell's Family Magazine* (1896), pp. 529–532.
[H. Cunningham], 'Horseless Carriages' [extract], *Edinburgh Review*, 183 (1896), pp. 408–420.

Many nineteenth-century inventors designed prototypes of passenger vehicles that would operate without tracks, under the power of their own steam or internal combustion engines or electric motors. By the turn of the century, various versions of the horseless carriage or automobile were beginning to seem viable as technologies. Yet any widespread use of them would require extensive infrastructure that was not yet in place. The cultural position of the late-Victorian automobile – the status of an incipient technology that remained on the verge of further development and popular adoption – could make it an object of scepticism, exaggeration and misinformation. This state of potentiality or incipience, of being a future technology that remained just over the horizon, would become a familiar one for any number of technologies during the following decades and the next century.[1]

Note

1 The most detailed account of the early history of the automobile in Great Britain is provided in T. R. Nicholson's three-volume *The Birth of the British Motor Car, 1769–1897* (London: Macmillan, 1982). For engaging accounts that take the story of the automobile from the late nineteenth century to the end of the twentieth, see L. J. K. Setright, *Drive On!: A Social History of the Motor Car* (London: Granta, 2003); Rudi Volti, *Cars and Culture: The Life Story of a Technology* (Westport, CT: Greenwood, 2004).

20

J. MUNRO, 'CARRIAGES WITHOUT HORSES'

Cassell's Family Magazine (1896), pp. 529–532

'Carriages without horses!'

The phrase occurs in a popular rhyme, which is held to be a prophecy of Mother Shipton, the wise woman of Yorkshire, but is really of doubtful and perhaps recent origin. In any case, the advent of horseless carriages was predicted by Friar Bacon six hundred years ago, that is to say, two centuries before Mother Shipton was born. 'We will be able to construct machines', he wrote, 'which will propel large ships with greater speed than a whole garrison of rowers, and which will need only one pilot to direct them; we will be able to propel carriages with incredible speed without the assistance of any animal; and we will be able to make machines which, by means of wings, will enable us to fly in the air like birds'.

The idea of mechanical carriages was itself 'in the air' during succeeding centuries, and the great Sir Isaac Newton designed a steam coach of a very simple order in the year 1680.

But it was not until 1763 that Nicholas Cugnot, a French inventor, actually made one which carried four passengers along the streets of Paris at a speed of two and a quarter miles an hour, to the amazement of the multitude. In turning the corner of a street near what is now the Madeleine, however, the plucky little engine fell over on its side with a loud crash, and was promptly 'run in' by the bold *gens d'armes*. The experiments were stopped and the machine finally relegated to the museum of the Conservatoire des Arts et Métiers, where it can still be seen. Cugnot himself, like many another pioneer of science, was imprisoned, and afterwards endured miserable privations, until he was relieved by Napoleon I.

This fascinating problem then occupied the minds of Benjamin Franklin, James Watt, Dr. Erasmus Darwin, William Murdoch, inventor of gas lighting, and many others. Murdoch built a working model, which was tried at Redruth, Cornwall, in 1784; and the famous Richard Trevithick, his assistant, made a carriage which ran in London at a speed of ten miles an hour.

Among later inventors, James Nasmyth in 1827 ran a steam coach on the Queensferry Road at Edinburgh; and, above all, Hancock, of London, constructed many coaches and brakes, which plied for months between London, Romford, and other towns, carrying thousands of passengers sixty years ago.

DOI: 10.4324/9781315400303-27

These and other brave attempts aroused the opposition of horse and land owners, and in 1862 an Act was passed prohibiting sham engines from travelling at a greater speed than four miles an hour on public highways. This measure has seriously checked the development of horseless carriages in the United Kingdom, but it did not prevent Mr. R. W. Thompson, of Edinburgh, from introducing the slow steam traction engine, or road locomotive, and the indiarubber tyre.

But how were they 'managing in France'? Here the self-moving carriage has been brought into practical use within recent years. In 1888 Serpollet and others devised steam carriages so convenient and safe that they were permitted to travel through the streets of Paris at a speed of ten miles an hour. In England electricity was applied to the propulsion of dog-carts and bath-chairs by Mr. Magnus Volk, of Brighton, but only on a small scale.

Within the last few years, however, a great impetus has been given to the subject by the invention of the Daimler motor, a kind of gas engine in which the piston is driven up and down in the cylinder, not by the admission of steam under pressure, but by small explosions of the vapour of rectified petroleum, such as gasoline or benzine. A supply of the petroleum to last out the journey is carried in a reservoir and fed to the motor engine, in which it is exploded under the piston by means of a flame or the electric spark from a small induction coil excited by a voltaic battery, and the motion of the piston is communicated to the wheels of the carriage by suitable gearing.

The long-distance race of these 'automobile' carriages from Paris to Bordeaux and back has proved the superiority of the petroleum over the steam carriage, which may now be regarded as out-of-date. The 'struggle for existence', terminating in the 'survival of the fittest', will henceforth lie between the electric and the petroleum carriage.

For the benefit of those who may be thinking of investing in an 'auto-car', it will be useful to consider these two kinds in relation to each other and to the ordinary horse-carriage.

The horse, as a beautiful and intelligent creature, and often an affectionate friend, is, of course, more interesting than a lifeless mechanism, and it is not to be supposed that he will be entirely driven from the field; but, on the other hand, the horse is often ill-treated and over-wrought, his life is made a burden to him by cruel or thoughtless masters, and no one can deny that where mechanical power can do the work of *suffering* flesh and blood it should be allowed to do it.

Moreover, the horse is subject to illness, and is frequently dangerous through fright; but there is no fear of an auto-car 'shieing' on the road, and although the motor might break down or the petroleum reservoir explode, these contingencies are somewhat remote.

In case the injury to the motor is such that an ordinary blacksmith or working engineer could not repair it, the motor could easily be made detachable and sent to the manufacturer for amendment.

It is probable, however, that makers will provide against such a mishap by supplying spare parts with which an intelligent smith can replace the broken ones in a very short time. Even now the danger of explosion is reduced to something very small, by removing the reservoir as far as possible from the igniting apparatus, and still further improvements will doubtless be made in this respect.

The electric car is, of course, quite free from any such danger, since the motive mechanism consists of an electric motor, fed by the current of an accumulator or a primary battery stowed in the car, under the box-seat, or elsewhere. Should the apparatus break down, the services of a practical electrician would have to be called in or the apparatus disconnected and sent to the makers.

This question of breakdown is, however, a secondary one, and will not deter people in general from getting an auto-car if the ordinary working advantages justify them.

Electric carriages are even now almost entirely free from vibration, and they will be made still freer in future. The great advantage of the petroleum car over the electric one is that sufficient fuel or rectified petroleum for a long journey can be carried in smaller bulk and weight than a supply of electricity. Moreover, it is much easier to procure a fresh supply of petroleum than electricity. The petroleum car is therefore better adapted for general and country use than the electric car, which, however, is convenient enough in large towns, or in plying between fixed stations, where the batteries can be replenished without much trouble.

Coming now to the important matter of cost and maintenance, the auto-cars are much more expensive to buy than horse carriages, owing to the motor and gearing; but they are easier to maintain. The price of an auto-car ranges from £150 to £300, according to its size and beauty; but the cost of a mile of travel varies from a halfpenny to a penny. A ten-mile drive can be enjoyed for sixpence or a shilling, and it must be borne in mind that neither coachman nor groom is required for the auto-car, which can be managed by an intelligent gardener. The proprietor himself can drive the machine, for it requires no particular skill to work the handles which start and stop the engine or control the brakes.

The difference in price between the auto-car and the carriage and horses will therefore soon be made up by the saving in maintenance. To those who only require a carriage during a portion of the year, the advantages of the auto-car are obvious. At the same time, we would counsel all who are not in a hurry to wait a little before investing in an auto-car. There is no doubt whatever that in the course of the next year or two the improvements made in them will much increase their efficiency and convenience, as well as reduce their price.

21

[H. CUNNINGHAM], 'HORSELESS CARRIAGES' [EXTRACT]

Edinburgh Review, 183 (1896), pp. 408–420

It is a melancholy reflection that most of the great improvements which have been introduced into the world, whether in religion, science, or art, have at first been received with incredulity and derision. Even those mechanical discoveries which have proved most valuable have not escaped, and almost down to our own days the verdict of the public upon a new invention has been – first, that it will not work, next, that it is too dangerous, and finally, that every one knew it before. The developement [sic] of mechanical road carriages has offered no exception to these general principles. They were invented towards the close of the last century; they were made completely successful about the year 1857. As soon as there was no doubt that they would work well, they were prohibited as dangerous by an Act passed in 1861. This law, however, permitted them to run at about two-thirds of the speed of a stage coach, and as they still continued to progress towards perfection, a further Act was passed in 1865 which had the effect of rendering their use impossible. For thirty years they were lost sight of; but in 1893 they were again revived by the French and Germans, and having been proved to be neither dangerous nor impossible, they are now recognised as matters of common knowledge, possessing in principle but few features of novelty.

No useful purpose would be served by tracing in detail the series of steps which led from the first crude ideas of early inventors to the more perfect machines of later days. Cugnot in France and Murdoch in England were among the pioneers of the movement. Murdoch, who was at that time one of the foremen in Boulton & Watt's engineering works, was severely blamed by Watt for wasting his employers' time in useless experiments. In France society seems, in the case of Cugnot, to have been irresolute whether to treat him as a malefactor or as a genius. So both plans were adopted. In 1770, after an accident which occurred to a machine which he was driving in Paris, he was sent to the Bastille, from which, however, he was soon afterwards liberated with a pension.

It may seem strange to us now to reflect that one of the great difficulties which in early days beset the inventors of locomotives, whether for use on road or rail, was to believe it possible to drive a carriage effectively without either pushing or dragging it along. To propel it by placing a machine inside it arranged so as to twist the wheels round appeared altogether an error. This prejudice was no

 DOI: 10.4324/9781315400303-28

doubt increased by the ill success of the early attempts at velocipedes, and in consequence many primitive machines were provided not only with wheels, but with iron legs and feet, which were designed to push them forward with an action resembling a walking man. By the year 1820 it became recognised that carriages could be propelled by causing the pistons of steam engines to work cranks affixed to their wheels, and in the period between 1820 and 1830 the rail locomotive was perfected.

No idea at first seems to have been entertained of the speeds which would soon be reached. On the hearing of the case for the first railway Bill by a parliamentary committee in 1822, 4½ miles an hour was urged as the utmost that could be expected, and a leading periodical which reflected public opinion very accurately, published the following passage in 1825: –

> 'As to the persons who speculate in making railways general throughout the kingdom, and superseding all the canals, all the wagons, mail and stage coaches, post-chaises, and, in short, every other mode of conveyance by land and by water, we deem them and their visionary schemes unworthy of notice. . . . It is certainly some consolation to those who are to be whirled at the rate of eighteen or twenty miles an hour by means of a high-pressure engine to be told that they are in no danger of being sea-sick when on shore; . . . but with all these assurances, we should as soon expect the people of Woolwich to suffer themselves to be fired off upon one of Congreve's ricochet rockets as trust themselves to the mercy of such a machine going at such a rate. . . . We trust that Parliament will, in all the railways which it may sanction, limit the speed to eight or nine miles an hour, which is as great as can be ventured upon with safety.'

The speed fixed by the early railway Bills as a maximum was twelve miles an hour.

The contest between road and rail locomotives which occupied the first thirty years of this century was ultimately terminated by the complete victory of the railways, but road locomotives were pronounced perfectly practicable by a parliamentary committee which sat in 1832. In the year 1834 a road car made by Messrs. Summers & Ogle attained a speed of thirty-two miles an hour, and ran long distances at an average speed of twenty-four miles an hour. In the same year also, Hancock organised a regular steam-coach service at from twelve to fifteen miles an hour. But these performances were altogether eclipsed on rails. For in 1834 Hackworth, the foreman of George Stephenson's works, whose name will be for ever connected with railways, ran a locomotive on the Stockton and Darlington Railway at fifty miles an hour. It is true that four years afterwards the boiler of this engine burst; but about the same time a road locomotive designed by Scott Russell, who afterwards became celebrated as the designer of the 'Great Eastern' steamship, was overturned, and the boiler burst, and killed five people. This circumstance demonstrates, what without demonstration is sufficiently obvious, that boilers at high pressure and containing large volumes of water may prove very dangerous if they are suddenly subjected to the strain caused by an overthrow.

The complete and decisive superiority of railway lomocotives not only in speed, but also in the weights which they could draw and the far smaller consumption of fuel which they required, led after the year 1840 to a temporary cessation of the manufacture of road cars. It is difficult to see how it could have been otherwise, when it is remembered that to drag a weight upon wheels along an ordinary road requires the expenditure of about seven times the energy necessary for an equal load upon rails. But in 1857 fresh interest was aroused in road engines. There were many routes too unimportant to warrant the construction of a railway, and yet sufficiently frequented to require regular coach service. Accordingly, Rickett and others constructed some excellent carriages designed to run at a speed of from twelve to fifteen miles an hour. At this date it may be said that the problem of road-engine locomotion had been solved. Much remained to be done in points of detail, but a possible speed of over thirty miles an hour had been reached, and regular coach services had been run. It is difficult to single out as deserving of special recognition any one name from among the multitude of engineers whose efforts led to the above results. What had been attained had been due rather to a great number of small improvements than to any radical change introduced by a master-mind. But if it be thought necessary to associate any one man with the success of road cars, Hancock will probably be considered to have done more than any other individual. Even at this day his coach would serve as an excellent point of departure for modern improvements.

No sooner had the possibility of road-engine locomotion been demonstrated, than all the opposition which had been fruitlessly exerted to prevent the developement [sic] of railway engines became concentrated upon their unfortunate rivals. They were hooted at; they were refused admission into inns; stones were placed to impede their progress, and holes dug in the roads over which they were to pass. Even the local authorities joined in the attack. Such methods, of course, were insufficient of themselves. The engines were, according to the law as it then stood, perfectly legal, provided they were so run as not to constitute a nuisance. They had been proved to be safe and cheap. It was necessary, therefore, to devise some more effective measures to suppress them. At last it was discovered that they were not subject to the Turnpike Acts, which only related to vehicles drawn by horses. This gave the supporters of horse traffic their opportunity. Although it could not be shown that the coaches were dangerous to life, they were represented as causing the most extraordinary wear upon roads and destruction to bridges; and in 1859 a Bill was introduced imposing heavy tolls upon them. The Bill was in due course referred to a committee, which only examined three witnesses, among whom was the celebrated Mr. Macadam. Mere tolls alone, it was felt, would be easily borne by coaches which could run at half the cost of horse-hire. The report of the committee was somewhat hesitating. There occurred, therefore, a brief period before the first epoch of persecution; but in 1861 the blow fell, and the first Act for regulating the use of locomotives upon common roads was passed. It placed the making of regulations for these vehicles in the hands of a Secretary of State, but provided, in addition, that the tires of the wheels were to be three inches wide, that the engines were to consume their own smoke, that they were to have at least two drivers, and were not to exceed ten miles an hour in the country and five miles an hour in towns. The Act concluded that no locomotive might be used so as to be a nuisance.

This law seemed sufficiently severe. Under it, however, further progress was made, and Fisher and Rickett continued to construct successful coaches. But in 1865 it seems to have been determined to destroy all prospect of ever driving coaches or carriages by steam. The power of a Secretary of State to make rules was abolished; three persons were required to conduct each locomotive, one of whom was to precede it on foot with a red flag; no whistles were to be sounded, no steam to be blown off. Any person in a carriage drawn by horses had, by merely putting up his hand, a right to require the locomotive to stop. Four miles an hour in the country and two in towns was specified as the maximum speed. Added to this, the name and residence of the owner were to be painted upon it in a conspicuous manner, and the hours during which it might be used in any borough or town were to be subject to the control of the local authority.

The work of legislation was virtually completed in 1878 by additional restrictions upon points of detail. The Act passed in that year enabled local authorities in counties to make bye-laws, as well as those in boroughs, and also conferred upon them the power, which they have liberally exercised, of charging a fee not exceeding 10*l*. for a license to use a locomotive in their counties, to be applied as part of the county rate. By this time the progress of invention had rendered it possible that steam engines would not be the only means of propelling locomotives. Gas engines had been invented, and petroleum engines proposed. Even the prospect of electric traction had dawned. In order, therefore, to prevent the possibility of any of these new powers being tried in road carriages, it was thought expedient to widen the application of the Acts which hitherto had only applied to steam engines. Therefore, in the Act of 1878, a locomotive was defined as 'a locomotive propelled by steam or by other than animal power'. Thus armed, the county authorities (which then were the justices of the peace) proceeded vigorously to work. They did not, apparently, consider it necessary to consult any experts, or even to take counsel with one another with a view to common action. The only point upon which they seemed all agreed was to levy in each county the very highest licensing fee which the law would allow.

It is difficult to divine the reasons which, in the present depressed condition of agriculture, induce the local authorities still to maintain these fees. One would have thought their desire would be in every way to encourage the new locomotives. In France, so far from taxing the use of agricultural engines, they are bought at the county expense and loaned out to small farmers. Besides, when carts and carriages paid turnpike tolls, it might have seemed fair to place a tax upon road locomotives; but now that roads are toll free, it seems hard that agricultural engines should be exceptionally treated.

The views of the local authorities as to the proper hours during which locomotives ought to be permitted to travel varied very considerably. In Gloucestershire traffic was only allowed at night, the roads being open from 8 in the evening till 4 in the morning. But in the adjoining county of Monmouth it was determined that the only traffic allowed should be by day, the roads being closed from 12 noon till 8 the next morning. This rendered it necessary for a car coming from Gloucestershire to Monmouth to start so as to arrive at the boundary by 4 in the morning, then wait four hours, and then stop again at noon. The car would have to pay a total license of 16*l.* for the two counties, Monmouthshire only requiring a fee of 6*l.* But such moderation was rare. In twenty-six of the counties of England the full license fee of 10*l.* was, and is still, demanded. In only six counties is the fee as low as 5*l.* So that practically, as the law now stands, a person with an autocar who desires to go from London to Newcastle must take out nine separate licenses at a cost of 85*l.* He must take a week at least over the journey. He must procure nine sets of conflicting bye-laws, which he must be careful to obey, and his groom must walk in front of him the whole way with a red flag.

Thus perished the nascent industry. From 1865 invention was entirely confined to the manufacture of heavy locomotives, and the promotion of light locomotive carts and carriages practically ceased. It is true that a few spasmodic attempts were made. In 1868 Mr. Knight, an engineer now living, the inventor of the 'Trusty' petroleum engine, made a small carriage, but it was hardly used. In 1881 Sir Thomas Parkyn (who died last year) employed Mr. Bateman (a manufacturer of emery wheels, now living) to construct a steam tricycle. Sir Thomas Parkyn was at once prosecuted; although his machine emitted no steam and made so little noise that the policeman who gave evidence respecting it was doubtful how it was driven, the magistrate had no option but to enforce the law, and the sentence was ratified by the High Court of Justice. Since the revival last year of road cars, some five or six persons have been punished for using them in different parts of the kingdom. Rarely have the combined efforts of Parliament, the local authority, the magistrates' courts, and the police been exerted with such signal success.

The revival of public interest in autocars commenced in France and Germany. It is very characteristic of the French genius that it has originated a number of adaptations of scientific ideas to practical life which have been completed by other nations. Gramme, a Parisian, developed the dynamo out of Paccinotti's machine while the Germans were encamped around Paris. Faure first showed the practicability of accumulators; and to French ingenuity we owe the bicycle. The machines used in France in 1893 were, as a rule, German petroleum engines fixed into French carriages. About the same time several of them were tried in Berlin. But the first great impetus to the movement was given by the race in the summer of 1894, from Paris to Rouen, organised by the proprietors of 'Le Petit Journal'. After several days wisely spent in preliminary trials, to accustom the drivers of the vehicles to the rules of the competition, the race came off on Sunday, July 22. Amid a large concourse of spectators, on a bright summer morning, the line of carriages placed themselves in order, five yards one behind the other, at the

Porte Maillot. By eight o'clock nineteen competitors had arrived and were in line, and were started with a break containing the jury, and enveloped by a crowd of cyclists and persons on foot. Most of the cars were driven by petroleum engines, but there were several steam carriages. The day was exceedingly hot, and the road covered with the thick white dust which travellers in France know so well. It was observed that only one of the horses encountered on the route appeared frightened by the procession of cars, which must have afforded a scene truly characteristic of that light-hearted nation which can make a festival out of a trial of engineering. The mayors of the villages through which they passed fired off cannon, and the houses were adorned with flags. Proprietors of fruit gardens appeared with baskets of apricots to refresh the engine drivers. Seventeen of the carriages arrived at Rouen, a distance of seventy-nine miles, in times varying from eight to thirteen and a half hours. The first to arrive was driven by steam, but the first prize was divided between two carriages driven by the Daimler petroleum motor. The greatest speed attained by any carriage was about eighteen miles an hour. Seven dogs were run over on the route, one lady cyclist injured, and one of the boilers burst.

In the next year (1895) it was determined by 'Le Petit Journal' to organise another race on a larger scale. This time the course arranged was from Paris to Bordeaux and back, a distance of 744 miles. Sixteen petroleum carriages, seven steam vehicles, two electric carriages, and two petroleum bicycles started. The first four carriages that came in were driven by petroleum motors; the shortest time taken was 48 hours 47 minutes, not counting stoppages, being an average of almost fifteen miles an hour. This was a great improvement in speed on the race of the previous year. Last autumn a race took place upon a 100-mile course near Chicago. A number of carriages entered, but not many came up to the post. The winning one was a French petroleum carriage.

It is to be regretted that the American press tolerates at present in its columns an exaggeration of which the best Americans are ashamed. The most absurd accounts have reached this country of machines which would go over sixty miles an hour on roads, of carriages driven by compressed springs wound up at starting, of absurdly light accumulators which never are produced, and of marvellous gas engines which automatically cool themselves. No one can doubt that in the future the nation which produces the best and most ingenious steel tools in the world will play a worthy part in the developement [sic] of any mechanical invention, however difficult; meanwhile America is too great a nation in mechanics to have need of all this silly bombast, which only obscures, not enhances, her great reputation for engineering skill.

Another competition has been arranged for this year in France, organised by the members of the Automobile Club. The editors of an English mechanical journal, 'Engineering', are also to award prizes amounting to 1,000*l.* for the best carriages. They have already issued notice of the conditions of the competition. It is to be regretted that they have totally forbidden the use of light petroleum spirit, restricting petroleum engines to those which use heavy oil. There can be no doubt, as will presently be shown, that heavy oil carriages are preferable on the score of safety to those propelled by spirit, but it is perhaps a pity that some one of the prizes was not left open to light petroleum motors. By this action all chance of comparing the two is destroyed. A somewhat capricious rule has also been made, that speed over ten miles an hour is not to count at all. So that there can be no true race in any sense of the term, for it may be safely predicted that every carriage that enters for the race at all will go at a greater pace. Although, as will presently be shown, there is no such thing yet in existence as a really perfect carriage, the problem has been solved, and it may with certainty be predicted that ere long these cars will be common in our streets.

It is now time to give some description of the different genera into which motor cars may be divided. Those which have hitherto been the most successful are driven by small engines fixed either under the seat or in front. They all have either three or four wheels. The apparatus consists of one or more cylinders, the pistons of which are driven, not by steam, but by the explosion of a small quantity of the vapour of petroleum. It is, of course, well known that all carbonaceous inflammable gases become explosive when mixed with air, and therefore at each alternate stroke a small quantity of air and carbon vapour is introduced into the cylinder and exploded at the right instant. This seems at first sight likely to be a very dangerous proceeding; but in practice there is no danger attendant on it, and the force of the explosion being all converted into work, there is no energy left to be expended in making a noise. The explosions, therefore, are quite silent. The cylinders by virtue of these explosions become heated, and require jackets of water to cool them. This is a great disadvantage, because a heavy tank of water, containing about ten gallons, must be carried in the carriage, and must be replenished with cold water from time to time upon the road. The fuel used is either what is known as petroleum spirit – that is to say, light petroleum, or 'benzoline', or else the heavy oil which is burnt in ordinary paraffin lamps, called petroleum oil. The advantage of the former is that it is clean, it does not clog the engine with soot, it contains great working power in a small bulk, and, being volatile, the smell of it soon passes off. Any one who has used a carriage or launch driven by petroleum spirit, and also one driven by heavy oil, will easily recognise these advantages.

But all petroleum motors have grave inconveniences. In practice, the proper operation of these engines, and the due ignition of the mixture of vapour and air above mentioned, depend upon the uniformity and regularity of the speed at which they are driven. They do not admit of great changes of velocity. Hence, therefore, in order to adapt them to carriages it is necessary to have some means of varying the speed of the carriage, while that of the engine remains constant. This, as is well known, is very difficult to accomplish for machinery doing work at high speeds. Cogwheels are apt to clank and jar when thrown in and out of gear, bands upon cones slip and break; so that it is not very easy rapidly to alter the speed of the vehicle.

Again, the high speed of the motors, say from 200 to 400 revolutions per minute, causes great vibration, and in all the carriages of this type hitherto made the whole frame trembles, and when they are standing still, the wheels being disengaged from the engines, the vibration is most unpleasant. To get rid of vibration when in motion it is expedient that the engines should be what is termed 'well balanced' – that is to say, arranged so that each rapid movement of any part is exactly counterpoised by an equal movement of an equally heavy part in the opposite direction. It is also desirable that the vibration should be horizontal, because when it is vertical it jumps directly upon the springs of the carriage, which are much more sensitive to vertical than to horizontal shocks.

There is also a further disadvantage in that petroleum engines will not start themselves. In order to start them it is necessary, just as in the case of gas engines, to get down and turn a handle rapidly round for a few times; so that if it be desired to stop the carriage without descending, this can only be done by disconnecting the wheels from the engine by a lever, and letting the engines run, doing as little work as possible, but what they do being turned into heat, or noise and vibration. Thus, when a short stoppage is made, and it is not worth while to stop the engine, it is left running, but disconnected from the wheels. All its work is therefore turned into shaking the carriage. To prevent this the best method is to give it some work to do, such as rubbing against a break. But this disadvantage will be surmounted. Several admirable inventions have been made for starting gas engines, and before long there is no doubt that they will be applied to autocars.

In those which employ petroleum spirit there is a further disadvantage, which amounts to a positive danger. Not only does benzine take fire when a match is put to it, but even when a light is brought near its vapour. So that any spilling of the liquid on the floor renders the whole building in which it is liable to be set on fire. Indeed, the vapour of petroleum spirit has been known to roll along the floor, and form a train of vapour, by which the spirit is ignited by a light a considerable distance away; and when it burns the violence of its combustion is excessive. It has been found by experiment that one volume of petroleum spirit will evaporate into 141 volumes of vapour, which are capable of rendering 5,000 volumes of air strongly explosive, and more than three times that quantity inflammable. So dangerous is this spirit that its use is regulated by two Acts of Parliament, by which no petroleum spirit can be kept without a license, unless it is under three gallons in quantity, and kept in separate stoppered vessels containing each not more than one pint. Of course these regulations, unless they are repealed, would entirely prevent the use for autocars of engines in which petroleum spirit is employed. On the other hand, petroleum oil is not under any statutory restrictions.

When steam is talked of for driving road cars, there naturally rises to the mind an idea of a boiler with more or fewer tubes in it, filled with water, the vapour of which, when it has done its work in a small pair of cylinders, would be allowed to escape into the air. But such a contrivance would be altogether out of place in a carriage. The only boilers permissible there would be of an entirely different type. Instead of a receptacle for water, we must conceive of a network of small tubes with no water space at all. When the engine is required to start, these tubes are heated almost to a low red heat, no water being in them. If a drop of water is now introduced into the hot coils, it will at once be converted into highly heated steam, and the engines will make a few rotations. If no more water were added they would stop, but by the carefully regulated introduction of drop after drop into the boiler just so much steam is produced as is needful. The pace may be made slow or quick, and if the engines are compound there will be no snorting noise from the exhaust and but little vibration. The fire can be a furnace burning gas produced from the vapour of petroleum. This sounds a tempting solution of the difficulty. No water is required to cool the cylinders, and there is no likelihood of the engine stopping. But there are other drawbacks. If the steam were allowed to escape into the air, not only would dense clouds of white vapour be produced, but the water-supply would soon be exhausted. This can be prevented by arranging apparatus for condensing the steam into water again, and putting it back into the boiler. Unfortunately it is not easy to design a condensing apparatus of a sufficiently small size to be carried in a road car. A large quantity of water and a large extent of cooling surface are required. The invention of a good condenser of small size and of little weight is wanted before steam autocars can be made completely successful. In order to reduce the size of the condenser, and at the same time to cause less loss of heat, petroleum spirit has been successfully employed in the boilers, so that the vapour of benzine replaces steam. The furnace may be fed with petroleum oil, and thus be less dangerous. It has been also proposed to drive carriages with a carbonic acid gas engine, in which carbonic acid is used instead of steam.

This whole subject is full of interest. Mr. Maxim, in his extraordinary flying machine, has shown that a steamengine, boiler and all, can be made which will give one-horse power for every eleven pounds of weight. This engine is far lighter than would be needed for an autocar; but of course the rapid rush through the air would cool his condenser in a way that would be hopeless in a road carriage, and hence, if his engine were applied to road traction, far larger condensers would have to be added, which would considerably increase the weight. The difficulty of obtaining a metal which will bear heating to the temperature sufficient to work the boilers above described has not yet been entirely surmounted. Upon the whole it may be safely pronounced that we have not heard the last of steam for motor carriages, and that the problem of adapting them to this use presents no features of very exceptional difficulty.

We must next turn to electricity. Energy can, of course, not be originated: it can only be transformed. The energy of all electrical engines is obtained from coal, and thus indirectly from the rays of the sun in prehistoric times. As, however, it would be impossible, or hardly practicable, to carry with the carriages the engines necessary to convert the heat into electricity, some means must be found of storing or bottling up the electricity. This is done by causing it to flow into large plates of lead immersed in dilute sulphuric acid. These are called 'accumulators', or 'storage batteries'. Each pound of the lead is capable of absorbing the energy that one horse can put out in about twenty seconds, and therefore, if we wish to store up a horse-power to last, say, for eight hours, we must have about 1,440 lb. of lead. Whence, then, in practice a four-wheeled carriage ought not to have less than about a ton of accumulators in addition to the dynamo. This is a considerable weight; and if 600 lb. is put down for the carriage, 600 lb. for the dynamo, and 800 lb. for four passengers and their luggage, we should obtain a vehicle just weighing two tons, and capable of exerting practically about two-horse power for six or seven hours. It is calculated that for ordinary carriages about half a ton is the maximum weight that should be put upon each of the ordinary wheels with 2½-inch tires; but two-horse power would be fully required to drag a two-ton carriage at any reasonable speed over a fairly rough road. Hence, then, it is clear that the weight of accumulators is a great obstacle to their use. When, however, this has been overcome the advantage of electrical carriages will be very great. They will be quite free from vibration, from smell, and from danger. They will want no attention; they can be stopped and started at pleasure. It will require some new arrangements to enable their speed to be varied, but there seems no reasonable doubt that a dynamo can be contrived which, by suitable arrangements of switches, can be made to vary its speed at pleasure.

Here, then, we have the interesting spectacle of three forms of engine, moved by petroleum, steam, and electricity, about to compete in the solution of the problem of driving a carriage which shall be manageable, safe, economical, and comfortable. By none of them has the feat been yet accomplished; but each of these three competitors seems to have about an equal chance of success.

Up to the present time the engines which have succeeded the best are the Daimler and Benz petroleum engines; but they leave much to be desired, and will in time, no doubt, be superseded by far better ones. So far as a forecast can be made, it seems probable that some form of petroleum engine will eventually be the most successful.

PART 3

Illumination

3.1

Gas light and electric light

DOI: 10.4324/9781315400303-30

3.1 Gas light and electric light

'Electric Lighting', *Cornhill Magazine*, 39 (1879), pp. 157–172.
J. Munro, 'From Candles to Gas', *Cassell's Family Magazine* (1880), pp. 225–228.
J. Munro, 'From Gas to Electricity', *Cassell's Family Magazine* (1880), pp. 282–284.
Charles W. Vincent, 'The Dangers of Electric Lighting', *Nineteenth Century*, 27 (January 1890), pp. 145–149.

Long before an incandescent electric light bulb became a cartoon image for a sudden idea, metaphors of light and enlightenment were already being used to stand for reason, knowledge or understanding, as with the use of the words *bright* and *brilliant* to denote intelligence. But the nineteenth century brought important advances in illumination, from Sir Humphry Davy's safety lamp for miners to gas lighting and multiple types of electric lights. Like many of the era's great projects in transport, communication and sanitation, new light sources such as gas and electricity also required new types of infrastructure that further interwove new technologies into the daily lives of many Victorians.

The texts included here illuminate the history and state of artificial lighting in the nineteenth century. First used on the streets of early nineteenth-century London, gas lighting lit up many towns as well as some public buildings and houses by mid-century. But the light produced by gas remained rather sickly and faint, at least by modern standards. The work of Thomas Edison in the United States and Joseph Swan in England, both of whom received important and profitable patents on incandescent light bulbs in 1879, provides the immediate context for the first three pieces. Edison and Swan were hardly the first to produce or even to commercialise electric lighting; by the late 1870s, bright electric arc lights (originally based on another of Sir Humphry Davy's inventions) had recently been installed in the Thames Embankment and elsewhere in London. But the incandescent bulbs of Swan and Edison represented not only technical advances but the integration of electric lighting into emerging systems for the generation and use of electricity.[1]

In the staid and solidly upper-middlebrow *Cornhill Magazine*, a timely interest in the state and prospects of electrical illumination – the 'glowing reports' on Edison's recent work – now prompts and frames a look at the modern understanding of electricity, as well as at various kinds of lighting. The airier, more modern *Cassell's Family Magazine* looks back on the history of illumination that has culminated in the recent ascent of electricity (although, as the articles make clear, electric lighting remains an emerging technology, not yet a dominant one). A decade later, more alarmingly, the *Nineteenth Century* spotlights the dangers of electricity as the world becomes electrified, although – notwithstanding the article's title – there is little here that actually deals with the hazards of electric lighting in itself. Rather, the piece argues that the contemporary scramble for electric light has sidelined the issue of electrical safety; with the admonitory phrase 'in

America', the essay looks across the ocean to a country that has perhaps embraced electrical modernity too quickly and with too few restraints or regulations.[2]

Notes

1 Thomas P. Hughes argues that a view of technologies as whole 'systems' was the key to American invention and industry in the nineteenth and twentieth centuries. In Hughes' account, Swan 'erred in trying to integrate his electric lamp into a system with a generator designed by others for other purposes', whereas Edison developed and promoted his light bulb as part of 'a coherent system' developed by his company [*American Genesis: A Century of Invention and Technological Enthusiasm, 1870–1970* (New York: Viking, 1989), p. 55]. In Britain, Swan and Edison merged their interests to establish a joint electric light company in the early 1880s.

2 For a lucid overview of the history of artificial lighting, especially in the nineteenth and twentieth centuries, see Brian Bowers, *Lengthening the Day: A History of Lighting Technology* (Oxford and New York: Oxford University Press, 1998); a popular, essayistic account of this history is provided by Jane Brox, *Brilliant: The Evolution of Artificial Light* (Boston: Houghton Mifflin Harcourt, 2010). Developments in lighting over the course of the nineteenth century intersected with larger changes in cities, government and vision; see Chris Otter, *The Victorian Eye: A Political History of Light and Vision in Britain, 1800–1910* (Chicago: University of Chicago Press, 2008).

22

'ELECTRIC LIGHTING'

Cornhill Magazine, 39 (1879), pp. 157–172

Although we certainly have no reason to complain of the infrequency of attempts in newspapers, &c., as well as in scientific journals, to explain the principles on which electric lighting depends, it does not seem that very clear ideas are entertained on this subject by unscientific persons. Nor is this, perhaps, to be wondered at, when we observe that in nearly all the explanations which have appeared, technical expressions are quite freely used, while those matters about which the general reader especially desires information are passed over as points with which every one is familiar. Now without going quite so far as to say that there is no exaggeration in the picture presented some time back in *Punch*, of one who asked whether the electric fluid was 'anything like beer, for instance', we may confidently assert that the very vaguest notions are entertained by nine-tenths of those who hear about the electric light, respecting the nature of electricity. Of course, we are not here referring to the doubts and difficulties of electricians on this subject. It is well known that Faraday, after a life of research into electrical phenomena, said that when he had studied electricity for a few years he thought he understood much, but when he had nearly finished his observational work he found he knew nothing. In the sense in which Faraday spoke the most advanced students of science must admit that they know nothing about electricity. But the greater number of those who read about the electric light are not familiar even with electrical phenomena, as distinguished from the interpretation of such phenomena. We are satisfied that there is no exaggeration in a passage which appeared recently in the 'Table Talk' of the *Gentleman's Magazine*, describing an account of the electric light as obtained from some new kind of gas, carried in pipes from central reservoirs, and chiefly differing from common gas in this, that the heat resulting from its consumption melted ordinary burners, so that only burners of carbon or platinum could be safely employed.

We do not propose here to discuss, or even to describe (in the proper sense of the word) the various methods of electric lighting which have been either used or suggested. What we wish to do is to give a simple explanation of the general principles on which illumination by electricity depends, and to consider the advantages which this method of illumination appears to promise or possess.

DOI: 10.4324/9781315400303-31

Novel as the idea of using electricity for illuminating large spaces may appear to many, we have all of us been long familiar with the fact that electricity is capable of replacing the darkness of night by the light of broad day over areas far larger than those which our electricians hope to illuminate. The lightning flash makes in an instant every object visible on the darkest night, not only in the open air, but in the interior of carefully darkened rooms. Nay, even if the shutters of a room are carefully closed and the room strongly illuminated, the lightning flash can yet be clearly recognised. And it must be remembered that though the suddenness of the flash makes us the more readily perceive it (under such circumstances, for instance), yet its short duration diminishes its apparent intensity. This may appear a contradiction in terms, but is not so in reality. The perception that there has been a sudden lighting up of the sky or of a room, is distinct from the recognition of the actual intensity of the illumination thus momentarily produced. Now it is quite certain that the eye cannot assign less than a twenty-fifth of a second or so to the duration of the lightning flash, for, as Newton long since showed, the retina retains the sensation of light for at least this interval after the light has disappeared. It is equally certain, from Wheatstone's experiments, that the lightning flash does not actually endure for the 100,000th part of a second. Adopting this last number, though it falls far short of the truth – the actual duration being probably less than 1,000,000th of a second – we see that so far as the eye is concerned, an amount of light which was really emitted during the 100,000th part of a second, is by the eye judged to have been emitted during an interval 4,000 times as long. It is certain, then, that the eye's estimate of the intensity of the illumination resulting from a lightning flash is far short of the truth. This is equally true even in those cases where lightning is said to be for awhile continuous. If the flashes for a time succeed each other at less intervals than a twenty-fifth of a second, the illumination will appear continuous. But it is not really so. To be so the flashes should succeed each other at the rate of at least 100,000, and probably of more than 1,000,000 per second.

While the lightning flash shows the brilliancy which the electric illumination can attain, it shows also the intense heat resulting from the electric discharge. This might, indeed, be inferred simply from the brilliancy of the light, since we know that this brilliancy can only be due to the intense heat to which the particles along the track of the electric flash have been raised. But it is shown in a more convincing manner to ordinary apprehension by the effects which the lightning flash produces where – in the common way of speaking – it strikes. The least fusible substances are melted. Effects are produced also which, though at first not seemingly attributable to intense heat, yet in reality can be no otherwise explained. Thus, when the trunk of a tree is torn into fragments by the lightning stroke, though the tree is scorched and blackened, a small amount of heat would account for that particular effect, while the destruction of the tree seems attributable to mechanical causes. It is, indeed, from effects such as these that the idea of the fall of thunderbolts has doubtless had its origin, the notion being that some material substance has struck the body thus shattered or destroyed. In reality, however, such destructive effects are due entirely to the intense heat excited during the passage of the electricity. Thus in the case of a tree destroyed by lightning, the shattering of boughs and trunk results from the sudden conversion of the moisture of the tree (that is, the moisture present in the substance of the tree) into steam, a change accompanied of course by great and sudden expansion. The tree is as certainly destroyed by the effects of heat as is a boiler which has burst, though in each case the expansive power of steam directly works the mischief.

It is the more useful for our present purpose thus to note at the outset both the illuminating and the heating power of the lightning flash (or rather of the electric discharge), because, as will presently be seen, the electric light, while in all cases depending on intensity of heat, may either be obtained in the form of a series of flashes succeeding each other so quickly as to be to all intents and purposes continuous, or from the incandescence of some suitable substance in the path of the electric current.

Let us now consider briefly the general nature of electrical phenomena, or at least of those electrical phenomena which are related to our present subject.

Formerly, when light was supposed to be a material emanation, and heat was regarded as an actual fluid, electricity was in like manner regarded as some subtle fluid which could be generated or dispersed in various ways. At present, it is safer to speak of electricity as a state or condition of matter. If it were not that some very eminent electricians (and one especially whose eminence as a practical electrician is indisputable) are said to believe still that there is such a thing as an electric fluid, we should have simply asserted that in the present position of scientific research, with the known velocity at which the so-called electric current flows, and the known relations between electricity, heat, and light, the theory of an electric fluid is altogether untenable. It will suffice, under the actual circumstances, to speak simply of electrical properties, without expressing any definite opinion respecting their interpretation.

A certain property, called electricity, is excited in any substance by any cause affecting the condition of the substance, whether that cause be mechanical, chemical, thermal, or otherwise. No change can take place in the physical condition of any body without the generation of a greater or less amount of electricity, although in far the greater number of cases there may be no obvious evidence of the fact, while in many cases no evidence may be obtainable even by the use of the most delicate scientific tests.

We have spoken here of the generation of a greater or less amount of electricity, but in reality it would be more correct to speak simply of a change in the electrical condition of the substance. Electricians speak of positive and negative electricity as though there actually were two distinct forms of this peculiar property of matter. But it may be questioned whether it would not be more correct to speak of electricity as we do of heat. We might speak of cold as negative heat precisely as electricians give the name of negative electricity to a relative deficiency of what they call positive electricity; but in the case of heat and cold it is found more convenient, and is more correct, to speak of different degrees of one and the same quality. The difficulty in the case of electricity is that at present science has no means of deciding whether positive or negative electricity has in reality the better claim to be regarded as absolute electricity. Making comparison between electrical and thermal relations, the process which we call the generation of positive electricity may in reality involve the dispersion of absolute electricity, and so correspond to cooling, not to heating. In this case the generation of what we call negative electricity would in reality be the positive process. However, it is not necessary to discuss this point, nor can any error arise from the use of the ordinary method of expression, so long as we carefully hold in remembrance that it is only employed for convenience, and must not be regarded as scientifically precise.

Electricity may be excited, as we have said, in many ways. With the ordinary electrical machine it is excited by the friction of a glass disc or cylinder against suitable rubbers of leather and silk. The galvanic battery develops electricity by the chemical action of acid solutions on metal plates. We may speak of the electricity generated by a machine as frictional electricity, and of that generated by a galvanic battery as voltaic electricity; but in reality these are not different kinds of electricity, but one and the same property developed in different ways. So also of what is sometimes called magnetic electricity, of which we shall presently have much to say. It is electricity produced by means of magnets, but is in no respect different from frictional or voltaic electricity. Of course, however, it will be understood that for special purposes one method of producing electricity may be more advantageously used than another. Just as heat produced by burning coal is more convenient for a number of purposes than heat produced by burning wood, though there is no scientific distinction between coal-produced heat and wood-produced heat, so for some purposes voltaic electricity is more convenient than frictional electricity, though there is no real distinction between them.

Every one knows that when by means of an ordinary electrical machine electricity has been generated in sufficient quantity and under suitable conditions to prevent its dispersion, a spark of intense brilliancy and greater or less length, according to the amount of electricity thus collected can be obtained when some body, not similarly electrified, is brought near to what is called the conductor of the machine. The old-fashioned explanation, still repeated in many of our books, ran somewhat as follows: – 'The positive electricity of the conductor decomposes the neutral or mixed fluid of the body, attracting the negative fluid and repelling the positive. When the tension of the opposite electricities is great enough to overcome the resistance of the air, they re-combine, the spark resulting from the heat generated in the process of their combination.' This explanation is all very well; but it assumes much that is in reality by no means certain or even likely. All we *know* is that whereas before the spark is seen the electrical conditions of the conductor and the object presented to it were different, they are no longer different after the flashing forth of the spark. It is as though a certain line (straight, crooked, or branched) in the air had formed a channel of communication by which electricity had passed, either from the conductor to the object or from the object to the conductor, – or *possibly* in both directions, two different kinds of electricity existing (before the flash) in the conductor and the object, as the old-fashioned explanation assumes. Again, we know that the passage of electricity along the air-track, supposing there really is such a passage, but in any case the observed change in the relative electrical conditions of the conductor and the object, is accompanied by the generation of an intense heat along the aërial track where the spark is seen.

In the case of electricity generated by means of a galvanic battery, we do not note the same phenomena unless the battery is a strong one. We have in such a battery a steady source of electricity, but unless the battery is powerful, the electricity is of low intensity, and not competent to produce the most striking phenomena of frictional electricity. For instance, voltaic electricity, as used in telegraphic communication, is far weaker than that obtained from even a small electrical machine. What is called the positive extremity of the battery neither gives a spark, nor attracts light bodies. The same is true of the other, or negative extremity. The difference of the condition of these extremities can only be ascertained by delicate tests – the deflections of the needle, in fact, by which telegraphic communications are made, may in reality be regarded as the indications of a very delicate electroscope.

But when the strength of a galvanic battery is sufficiently great, or, in other words, when the total amount of chemical action brought into play to generate electricity is sufficient, we obtain voltaic electricity not only surpassing in intensity what can be obtained from electrical machines, but capable of producing spark after spark in a succession so rapid (so infinitely rapid one may almost say) that the light is to all intents and purposes continuous.

Without considering the details of the construction of a galvanic battery, which would occupy more space than can here be spared, and even with fullest explanation would scarcely be intelligible (except to those already familiar with the subject), unless illustrations unsuited to these pages were employed, let us consider what we have in the case of every powerful galvanic battery, on whatever system arranged. We have a series of simple batteries, each consisting of two plates of different metal placed in dilute acid. Whereas, in the case of a simple battery, however, the two different metals are connected together by wires to let the electric current pass (the current ceasing to pass when the wires are disconnected), in a compound battery, in which (let us say) the metals are zinc and copper, the zinc of one battery is connected with the copper of the next, the zinc of this with the copper of another, and so on, the wire *to* the copper of the first battery and the wire *from* the zinc of the last battery being free, and forming what are called the poles of the compound battery – the former the positive pole, the latter the negative pole. When these free wires are connected, the current of electricity passes, when they are disconnected the current ceases to pass, unless the break between them is such only that the electricity can, as it were, force its way across the gap. When the wires are connected, so that the current flows, it is as though there were a channel for some fluid which flowed readily and easily along the channel. When the circuit is absolutely broken, it is as though such a channel were dammed completely across. If, however, while the poles are not connected by copper wires or by other freely conducting substances, yet the gap is such as the electricity can pass over, the case may be compared to the partial interruption of a channel at some spot where, though the fluid which passes freely along the channel is not able to move so freely, it can yet force its way along, with much disturbance and resistance. Just as at such a part of the course of a liquid stream – say a river – we find, instead of the quiet flow observed elsewhere, a great noise and tumult, so where the current of electricity is not able to pass readily we perceive evidence of resistance in the generation of much heat and light (if the resistance is great enough).

It will be observed that we have spoken in the preceding paragraph of the passage of a current along the wire connecting the two poles of a powerful electric battery, or along any substance connecting those poles which possesses the property of being what is called a good conductor of electricity. But the reader is not to assume that there is such a current, or that it is known to flow either from the positive to the negative pole, or from negative to positive pole; or, again, that, as some have suggested, there are two currents which flow simultaneously in opposite directions. We speak conventionally of the current, and for convenience we speak as though some fluid really made its way (when the circuit is complete) from the positive to the negative pole of the compound battery. But the existence of such a current, or of any current at all, is purely hypothetical. We should be disposed, for our part, to believe that the motion is of the nature of wave-motion, with no actual transference of matter, at least when the circuit is complete. According to this view, where resistance takes place we might conceive that the waves are converted into rollers or breakers, according to the nature of the resistance – actual transference of matter taking place through the action of these changed waves, just as waves which have traversed the free surface of ocean without carrying onward whatever matter may be floating on the surface, cast such matter ashore when, by the resistance of the shoaling bottom or of rocks, they become converted either into rollers or into breakers.

We may also notice, with regard to good conductors and bad conductors of electricity, that they may be compared to substances respectively transparent and opaque for light-waves, or again to substances which allow heat to pass freely or the reverse. Just as light-waves fail to illuminate a transparent body, and as heat-waves fail to warm a body which allows them free passage, so electricity-waves (if electricity really is undulatory, as we imagine) fail to affect any substance along which they travel freely. But as light-waves illuminate an opaque substance, and heat-waves raise the temperature of a substance which impedes their progress, so waves of electricity, when their course is impeded, produce effects which are indicated to us by the resulting heat and light.

A powerful galvanic battery is capable of producing light of intense brilliancy. For this purpose, instead of taking sparks between the two metallic poles, each of these is connected with a piece of carbon (which is nearly as good a conductor as the metal), and the sparks are taken between these two pieces of carbon, usually set so that the one connected with the negative pole is virtually above the one connected with the positive pole, and at a distance of a tenth of an inch from each other or more, according to the strength of the battery. Across this gap between the carbons an arc of light is seen, which in reality results from a series of electric sparks following each other in rapid succession. This arc, called the voltaic arc, is brilliant, but it is not from this arc that the chief part of the light comes. The ends of the carbon become intensely bright, being raised to a white heat. Both the positive and negative carbons are fiercely heated, but the positive is heated most. As (ordinarily) both carbons are thus heated in the open air, combustion necessarily takes place, though it is to be noticed that the lustre of the carbons is not due to combustion, and would remain undiminished if combustion were prevented. The carbons are thus gradually consumed, the positive nearly twice as fast as the negative. If they are left untouched, this process of combustion soon increases the distance between them beyond that which the electricity can pass over. Then the light disappears, the current ceasing to flow. But by bringing the carbon points near to each other (they must, indeed, be made to touch for an instant), the current is made to flow again, and the light is restored.

The following remarks by M. H. Fontaine (translated by Dr. Higgs) may help to explain the nature of the voltaic arc: – 'In truth the voltaic arc is a portion of the electric circuit possessing the properties of all other parts of the same circuit. The molecules swept away from point to point' (that is, from one carbon end to the other) 'constitute between these points a mobile chain, more or less conductive, and more or less heated, according to the intensity of the current and the nature and separation of the electrodes' (that is, the quality and distance apart of the carbon or other substances between which the arc is formed). 'These things happen exactly as if the electrodes were united by a metallic wire or carbon rod of small section' (so as to make the resistance to the current great), 'which is but saying that the light produced by the voltaic arc and that obtained by incandescence arise from the same cause – that is, the heating of a resisting substance interposed in the circuit'.

The intensity of the light from the voltaic arc and the carbon points varies with circumstances, but depends chiefly on the amount of electricity generated by the battery. A fair idea of its brilliancy, as compared with all other lights, will be gained from the following statements: – If we represent the brightness of the sun at noon on a clear day as 1,000, the brightness of lime glowing under the intense heat of the oxyhydrogen flame is about 7; that of the electric light obtained with a battery of 46 elements (Bunsen's) 235. With a battery of 80 elements the brightness is only 238. (These results were obtained in experiments by Fizeau and Foucault). The intensity does not therefore increase much with the number of the component elements after a certain number is passed. But it increases greatly with the surface, for the experimentors found that with a battery of 46 elements, each composed of 3, with their zinc and copper respectively united to form one element of triple surface, the brightness became 385, or more than one-third of the midday brightness of the sun (that is, the apparent intrinsic lustre of his disc's surface), and 55 times the brightness of the oxyhydrogen lime-light.

Another way of obtaining an intense heat and light from the electric current generated by a strong battery is to introduce into the electric circuit a substance of small conducting power, and capable of sustaining an intense heat without disintegration, combustion, or melting. Platinum has been used for this purpose. If the conductive power of copper be represented by 100, that of platinum will be represented by 18 only. Thus the resistance experienced by a current in passing through platinum is relatively so great that if the current is strong the platinum becomes intensely heated, and shines with a brilliant light. A difficulty arises in using this light practically, from the circumstance that when the strength of the current reaches a certain point, the platinum melts, and, the circuit being thus broken, the light immediately goes out.

The use of galvanic batteries to generate an electric current strong enough for the production of a brilliant light, is open to several objections, especially on the score of expense. It may, indeed, be safely said that if no other way of obtaining currents of sufficient intensity had ever been devised, the electric light would scarcely have been thought of for purposes of general illumination, however useful in special cases. (In the electric lighting of the New Opera House at Paris batteries are used.) The discovery by Oersted that an electric current can make iron magnetic, and the series of discoveries by Faraday, in which the relation between magnetism and electricity was explained, made electric lighting practically possible. One of these shows that if a properly insulated wire coil is rapidly rotated in front of a fixed permanent magnet (or of a set of such magnets), currents will be induced in the coil, which may be made to produce either alternating currents or currents in one direction only, in wire conductors. An instrument for generating electric currents in this way, by rapidly rotating a coil in front of a series of powerful permanent magnets fixed symmetrically around it, is called a magneto-electric machine. Another method, now generally preferred, depends on the rotation of a coil in front of an electro-magnet; that is, of a bar of soft iron (bent in horseshoe form), which can be rendered magnetic by the passage of an electric current through a coil surrounding it. The rapid rotation of the coil in front of the soft iron generates a weak current, because iron always has some traces of magnetism in it, especially if it has once been magnetised. This weak current being caused to traverse the coil surrounding the soft iron increases its magnetism, so that somewhat stronger currents are produced in the revolving coil. These carried round the soft iron still further increase its magnetism, and so still further strengthen the current. In this way coil and magnet act and react on each other, until from the small effects due to the initial slight magnetism of the iron, both coil and the magnet become, so to speak, saturated. Machines constructed on this principle are called dynamo-electric machines, because the generation of electricity depends on the dynamical force employed in rapidly rotating the coils.

We need not consider here the various forms which magneto-electric and dynamo-electric machines have received. It is sufficient that the reader should recognise how we obtain electric currents of great intensity in one case from mechanical action and permanent magnetism, and in the other from mechanical action and the mere residue of magnetism always present in iron.

In the cases here considered it is in reality the sudden presentation of the coil (twice at each rotation) before the positive and negative poles of the magnet, which induces a momentary but intense current of electricity. The rotation being exceedingly rapid, these currents succeed each other with sufficient rapidity to be appreciably continuous. A similar principle is involved in the use of what is called the inductive coil, except that in this case the sudden beginning and ceasing of a current in one coil (and not magnetic action) induces a momentary but strong current: matters are so arranged that the current induced by the starting of the inducing current, immediately causes this to cease; while the current induced by the cessation of the inducing current immediately causes this current to begin again: so that by a self-acting process we have a constant series of intense induced currents, succeeding each other with great rapidity, so as to be practically continuous, as with those produced by magneto-electric and dynamo-electric machines.

All that we have said about the voltaic arc, the incandescence resulting from resistance to the current's flow, and so forth, in relation to electricity generated by galvanic batteries, applies to electricity generated by induction coils, or by magneto-electric and by dynamo-electric machines. Only it is to be noticed that in some of these machines the currents alternate in direction with each revolution of the swiftly turning coil, in others the currents are always in the same direction, and in yet others the currents may be made to alternate or not, as may be most convenient.

We have now to consider how light suitable for purposes of illumination may be obtained from the electric current. Hitherto we have considered only light such as might be used for special purposes, where a bright and very intense light was required, where, perhaps, expense and complexity of construction might not be open to special objections, and where in general the absolute steadiness of the light was not an essential point. But those who have seen the electric light used even by the most experienced manipulators for the illustration of lectures, will know that the light as so obtained, though of intense brilliancy, is altogether unsuited for purposes of ordinary illumination.

If we consider a few of the methods which have been devised for overcoming the difficulties inherent in the problem of electric lighting, the reader will recognise at once the nature of these difficulties, and the probability of their being effectually overcome in the future, for though much has been done, much yet remains to be done in mastering them.

Let us consider first the Jablochkoff candle, the invention of which brought about, in July 1877, the first great fall in the value of gas property.

The Jablochkoff candle consists of two carbons placed side by side (instead of one above the other in a vertical line). Thus placed, with a slight interval between them, the carbon rods would allow the passage of the electric current at the place of nearest approach, and therefore of least resistance to its passage. A variable and imperfect illumination would result. M. Jablochkoff, however, interposes between the separate carbon rods a strip of plaster of Paris, which is a non-conducting material. The upper points of the carbon rods are thus the only parts at which the current can cross. They are connected by a little bridge of carbon, which is necessary for the starting of the light – just as in the case of the ordinary electric light, the two carbons must, in order to start the light, be brought into contact. When the current flows, the small bridge of carbon connecting the two points is presently consumed, but the arc between the points is still maintained: for the plaster becomes vitrified by the intense heat of the two carbon points on each side, and melts down as the carbons are consumed. If the light is in any way put out, however, a small piece of carbon must be set again, to form a bridge between the carbon points. Throughout the burning of the Jablochkoff candle the fused portion of the insulating layer forms a conducting bridge between the carbon points; and hence there is a considerable loss of electric force (probably about thirty per cent), which in the ordinary arrangement would increase the intensity of the light. The great advantage of the candle consists in the circumstance that throughout its consumption the carbon ends are at a constant distance from each other without any mechanical or other arrangement being necessary to maintain them in due position.

One point should be noticed here. In the ordinary arrangement of carbon points, the positive carbon, as we have already said, is much more intensely heated, and consumes twice as fast as the negative carbon. Now if one carbon of the Jablochkoff candle were connected with the positive, and the other with the negative pole of the battery or of a machine, the former side would consume twice as fast as the latter, and the two points would no longer remain at the same horizontal level, which is essential to the proper burning of the Jablochkoff candle. By using a machine which produces alternating currents, M. Jablochkoff obviates this difficulty, the carbons being alternately positive and negative (in extremely rapid succession), and therefore consuming at the same rate.

The Jablochkoff candle lasts only about an hour and a half. But four, six, or more candles may be used in the same globe or lantern, and automatic arrangements adopted to cause a fresh candle to be ignited at the moment when its predecessor is burnt out.

In Paris and elsewhere (as in Holborn for instance), each Jablochkoff lamp is enclosed in an opal glass globe. Mr. Hepworth remarks on this, that in his opinion the use of the opal globe is a mistake, as it shuts off quite 50 per cent of the light without any corresponding advantage, except the correction of the glare. 'This wasteful disadvantage will no doubt be remedied in the future', he says, by the use of some less dense medium. 'Mr. Shoolbred states that from a series of careful photometric experiments carried out by the municipal authorities with the Jablochkoff lights, each naked light is found to possess a maximum intensity of 300 candles. With the opal globe this was reduced to 180 candles, showing a loss of 40 per cent, while during the darker periods through which the light passed the light was as low as 90 candles'. It may be mentioned here that Mr.

Van der Weyde, who has long used the electric light for photographic purposes, has given much attention to the important problem of rendering the electric light available as an illuminator without wasting it, and yet without throwing the rays directly upon the object to be illuminated. The rays are intercepted by an opal disc about four inches in diameter, and the whole body of the rays is gathered up by a concave reflector (lined with a white material), and thrown out in a flood of pure white light, in which the most delicate shades of tint are discernible. He can use any form of electric candle in this way. Only it should be noticed, before the employment of his method is advocated for street illumination, that there is a difference between the problems which the photographer and the street-lighter have to solve. The Jablochkoff candle, for instance, must be screened on all sides, and even above, when used to illuminate the streets. If its direct light is allowed to escape in any direction, there will be a mischievous and unsightly beam, and from every point along the path of the beam, the intensely bright light of the candle will be directly visible. Again it is essential that whatever substance is used to screen the light should be dense enough to cause the whole globe to seem uniformly bright or nearly so. The only modification which seems available (when these essential points have been secured) is that the tint of the globe should be such as to correct any colour which the light may be found to have in injurious excess. We may, however, remark that the objection which has been often raised against the colour of the electric light can hardly be just – the injury to the eyes in certain cases arising probably from the strong contrast between the light and the background on which it is projected. For, as to colour, the electric light derived either from the glowing carbon or from incandescent metal is appreciably the same as sunlight.

The Rapieff burner, employed in the *Times* Office, consists of four carbon pencils, arranged thus $\substack{\vee \\ \wedge}$ (except that the two v's are not in the same plane, but in planes at right angles to each other). The spark crosses the space between the points of the v's, and arrangements are made for keeping the two points at the right distance from each other, and also for keeping the ends of the two pencils which form each point in their proper position. If the current is from any cause interrupted, an automatic arrangement is adopted to allow the current to pass to the other lamps in the same circuit. There are six lamps in circuit at the *Times* Office; and M. Rapieff has exhibited as many as ten. The advantages claimed for this light are the following: – 'First, its production by any description of dynamo-electric machine with either alternating or continuous currents; secondly, great divisibility and complete independence of the several lights, and long duration without change of carbons; and lastly, the extreme facility with which any ordinary workman or servant can renew the carbons when necessary, without extinguishing the lights'. The last-named advantage results, it need hardly perhaps be said, from the use of two carbons to form each point. One can be removed, the other remaining to keep the voltaic arc intact until a new carbon has been substituted for its fellow; then it in turn can be replaced by a new carbon, the new carbon already inserted keeping the voltaic arc intact.

The six lamps at the *Times* Office thoroughly illuminate the room, and give light for working the eight Walter presses used in printing the paper. The light has been thus used since the middle of last October, and it is said that other rooms in the building are shortly to be illuminated in the same manner. 'Each lamp is enclosed in an opal globe of about four inches in diameter, and so little heat is given off, that the hand can be placed on the globe without inconvenience, even after the light has been burning for some time'.

In the Wallace lamp, there are two horizontal plates of carbon, about nine inches in diameter, instead of mere carbon points. When the current is passing, these carbon plates are separated by a suitable small distance which remains unchanged. The electric arc, being started at the point along the edge of the carbons where there is least resistance to the passage of the current, gradually passes along the edge of the carbons as combustion goes on, changing the position of the place of nearest approach and consequently of least resistance. The light will thus burn for many hours (even for a hundred with large carbon plates), and any number of lights up to ten can be worked from the machine. The objection to the Wallace lamp is, that the light does not remain at one point, but travels along the whole extent of the carbons. It will not be easy to design a glass shade which will be suitable for a light thus changing in position.

The Werdermann regulator is on an entirely new plan; but it has not yet been submitted to the test of practical working outside the laboratory. The positive carbon, which is lowest, ends in a sharp point, which strangely enough retains its figure, while the carbon burns away at the rate of about two inches per hour. The negative carbon is a block having its under side, against which the positive carbon presses, slightly convex. The positive carbon is pressed steadily against the negative, by the action of a weight. The increased resistance to the passage of the current, at the sharp point of the positive carbon, generates sufficient heat to produce a powerful light. The light resembles a steadily radiant star, but 'with all its softness and purity of tint, it is so intense, that adjacent gas-flames are thrown on the wall as transparent shadows'. The light will last for fifteen hours without attention, the positive carbon rod being used in lengths of three feet. The carbon block hardly undergoes any change. When the lamp has been burning a long time, a slight depression can be seen at the place where the positive carbon touches it, but by shifting the carbon in its holder this is easily remedied'. Mr. Werdermann lately exhibited a row of ten small lamps burning side by side at the same time. 'The two wires from the machine', says Mr. Hepworth, 'were carried one on either side of this row of lamps, branch wires being led from them for the service of each lamp. Mr. Werdermann says that his perfected lamps will be furnished with keys, by which the current can be turned on or off, as in the case of gas. We may say in fact, that in the nature of its connections and various arrangements, it ("the Werdermann lamp") most nearly comes up in convenience to the use of gas'.

We do not yet know certainly what arrangement Mr. Edison employs to obtain the light of which so much has been heard. It is asserted that his light is obtained from the incandescence of an alloy of iridium and platinum, which will bear without fusion a heat of 5,000 degrees Fahrenheit. It would be unsafe, however, to assume that this account is trustworthy, or to infer (as we might in the case of almost any other inventor), that such being the nature of his plan, it could lead to no result of practical value. As has been well remarked by a contemporary writer, whatever Edison's invention may be, 'it is certain to be something to command respect, even if it does not quite come up to the glowing accounts which have reached us in advance'.

The following passage from one of these accounts, which appeared in the *New York Herald*, will be read with interest, and may be accepted as trustworthy so far as it goes. 'The writer last night saw the invention in operation in Mr. Edison's laboratory. The inventor was deep in experimental researches. What he called the apparatus consisted of a small metal stand placed on the table. Surrounding the light was a small glass globe. Near by was a gas jet burning low. The Professor looked up from his work, to greet the reporter, and in reply to a request to view the invention, waved his hand towards the light, with the exclamation, "There she is!" The illumination was such as would come from a brilliant gas jet surrounded with ground glass, only that the light was clearer and more brilliant. "Now I extinguish it and light the gas, and you can see the difference," said Mr. Edison, and he touched the spring. Instantly all was darkness. Then he turned on the gas. The difference was quite perceptible. The light from the gas appeared in comparison tinted with yellow. In a moment, however, the eye had become accustomed to it, and the yellowish tint disappeared. Then the Professor turned on the electric light, giving the writer the opportunity of seeing both side by side. The electric light seemed much softer; a continuous view of it for three minutes did not pain the eye; whereas looking at the gas for the same length of time, caused some little pain and confusion of sight. One of the noticeable features of the light, when fully turned on, was that all the colours could be distinguished as readily as by sunlight. "When do you expect to have the invention completed, Mr. Edison," asked the reporter. "The substance of it is all right now," he answered, putting the apparatus away and turning on the gas. "But there are the usual little details that must be attended to before it goes to the people. For instance, we have got to devise some arrangement for registering, a sort of meter, and again, there are several different forms that we are experimenting on now, in order to select the best." "Are the lights to be all of the same degree of brilliancy?" asked the reporter. "All the same!" "Have you come across any serious difficulties in it as yet?" "Well no," replied the inventor, "and that's what worries me, for in the telephone I found about a thousand; and so in the quadruplex. I worked on both over two years before I overcame them"'.

Other methods, as the Sawyer-Man system, and the Brush system, need not at present detain us, as little is certainly known respecting them. In the former it is said that the light is obtained from an incandescent carbon pencil, within a space containing nitrogen and no oxygen, so that there is no combustion. In the latter the carbon points are placed as in the ordinary electric lamp, but are so suspended in the clasp of a regulator, that they burn 14 inches of carbon without adjustment, the carbons lasting eight hours, and producing a flood of intense white light, estimated as equivalent to 3,000 candles.

We have no space to consider the cost of electric lighting, even if the question were one which could be suitably dealt with in these pages. Opinions are very much divided as to the relative cost of lighting by gas and by electricity; but the balance of opinion seems to be in favour of the belief that in America and France certainly, and probably in this country, where gas is cheap, electric lighting will on the whole be as cheap as lighting by gas. It should be noticed, in making a comparison between this country and others in which coal is dearer, that the cheapness of coal here, though favourable in the main to gas illumination, is also favourable, though in less degree (relatively) to electric lighting. Machines for generating electricity can be worked more cheaply here than in America. Nay, it has even been found advantageous in some cases to use a gas engine to generate electricity. Thus Mr. Van der Weyde used an Otto gas engine driven at the cost of 6*d*. an hour for gas, to produce the light which he exhibited publicly on the night of November 9. So that the cheapness of gas may make the electric light cheaper. Then it is to be remembered that important though the question of cost is, it is far from being all-important. The advantages of electric lighting for many purposes, as in public libraries, in cases where many persons work together, under conditions rendering the vitiation of the air by gas lighting exceedingly mischievous, and in cases where the recognition of delicate differences of tint or texture is essential, must far more than compensate for some slight difference in cost. The possibility (shown by actual experience to be a real possibility) of employing natural sources of power to drive machines for generating electricity, is another interesting element of the subject, but could not be properly dealt with save in greater space than is here and now available.

23

J. MUNRO, 'FROM CANDLES TO GAS'

Cassell's Family Magazine (1880), pp. 225–228

To satisfy his wants, man takes at first the means which lie nearest to his hand; but as these become spent, or as his art increases, he brings into requisition deeper stores of material and more occult sources of energy. Thus it is that to supply himself with artificial light he has successively advanced from the torch and rush-light of early times to the modern candle and oil-lamp, and from these again to the gas-jet and electric light. For public illumination, oil-lamps have in turn superseded torches, gas has superseded oil-lamps, and the time may possibly come when electricity will take the place of gas.

Before considering these different sources of light, let us first see what is the nature of a flame. Flame is a stream of gaseous matter in a state of ignition, or at a very high temperature. Where the flame is produced by burning, or combustion, as with candles, oil, and gas, the high temperature is created by chemical combination of hydrogen and carbon in the fuel with the oxygen of the surrounding air to form water on the one hand, and carbonic acid gas on the other. In the case of oils and candles, the hydrogen and carbon are liberated by the destructive distillation under heat of the fats which they contain. The flame of a candle, which is a type of other flames, consists of three parts, one within the other: an interior cell or reservoir of unignited gases surrounding the wick, a middle zone of bright white flame, and an outer shell of dimmer flame. The middle zone is the principal source of light, and owes its brilliance to the fact that the combustion is incomplete there, and particles of solid carbon are heated to whiteness; while the outer shell or fringe, where the ignited gas meets the air and the carbon is completely burned, gives off little or no light. Of the products of combustion, water is, of course, harmless; but the carbonic acid poisons the air, and if it be in excess will in time impair vitality, as well as the strength of the flame, by stinting both of their proper meed of oxygen. It is the same gas which is given off by a person in breathing, and it has been estimated that two burning candles give off as much of it as a living adult. Smoke, or unconsumed particles of carbon, are also shed by an oil or candle flame, but only when it is getting an insufficient supply of oxygen. This supply of oxygen is maintained by the indraught of cold air from below to fill the place of the uprising heated air over the flame. The fuel, or liquid fat, to be distilled into its constituent gases is fed to the flame through the *wick* by capillary suction.

DOI: 10.4324/9781315400303-32

In the ancient torch, which was usually made by steeping a strand of tow in melted resin or pitch, the tow was the wick, and the pitch the fuel; and in the Anglo-Saxon rush-light grease was consumed by means of a wick of rush-pith. Both of these illuminators in time gave place to the modern candles, which were formerly made of tallow and wax alone, but since Chevreul's discovery, in 1825, that all fats are composed of certain fatty acids and a comparatively uninflammable substance termed glycerine, a variety of materials, such as stearine, paraffin, spermaceti, ozokerit, or mineral wax, palm oil, and cocoa-nut oil, have been used for candles.

These inflammable acids are separated from the glycerine by stirring the melted fat with lime and water, whereat the lime combines with the acids to form a soap and leaves the glycerine free. The soap is then decomposed under heat by adding sulphuric acid to unite with the lime, and the oleic acid after being purified is ready to be moulded into stearine candles.

Candle-wicking is usually a loose spiral of cotton yarn, but plaited wicks to obviate snuffing, and wicks of spun glass, and felting, have also been introduced. In stearine candles the combustion is sometimes aided by impregnating the wick with boracic acid.

Candles are made by either dipping the wicks again and again into the melted fat, by means of a simple rotating frame, or moulded by immersing sets of polished pewter moulds, each charged with its wick, in the vat of melted fat. Wax candles, being liable to crack, are made by ladling the fluid wax on the wick. Presses have been invented for making a continuous candle, which was then cut into lengths, but they are not in general use. Wax tapers, however, are made in this way, and shaped by drawing them through draw-holes, like metal wires. Paraffin, which is obtained from petroleum, or by distillation of peat, lignite, and ozokerit, is made into candles by mixing it with stearine and moulding it hot, then cooling in cold water to preserve the transparency. Spermaceti, a solid substance filtered from the oil of the sperm whale, is mixed with wax or paraffin before being moulded, and the result is a costly but very fine candle. Composite candles are a mixture of the acid from palm-oil and the stearine from cocoa-nut oil. Belmont sperm candles are made of palm-acid hot-pressed into shape; and the well-known *night-lights* are short, thick cylinders of wax shod with tin, and provided with a cotton wick forced up a hole in their centres.

We have seen that the candle is a means for burning those fats which are solid at ordinary temperatures; the lamp, on the other hand, is a contrivance for burning those fats, or oils, which are fluid at ordinary temperatures. The kind of oil burned varies very much with the sources of supply; for example, in England whale oil was for a long time used, until the introduction of coal-gas and the later mineral oils. In Paris oil from rape and poppy seeds is still employed; in Italy they make use of oil from the grape-pip; in Piedmont, oil from the walnut; in China, oil from the sesamum seed; and in tropical countries, oil from the cocoa-nut; while, as is well known, the Eskimo of the Arctic regions burn seal oil.

Naphtha, the most liquid of all the oils, was once distilled from coal and burned in the London street lamps. Alcohol is chiefly used as a source of heat in spirit lamps on account of its sootless flame.

The antique lamp was a flat cruse or dish, beautifully shaped and having an unspun wick rising through a hole in the beak; but it gave a very poor smoky flame. The requirements of a good lamp are that there shall be as complete combustion of the hydrogen and carbon of the oil as possible, that the wick shall be fed with a constant and regular supply of oil, and that the form shall be such as to throw as little shadow as possible. All the earlier lamps were more or less imperfect, especially as regards the first of these conditions; and it was not until the year 1789, when Ami Argand invented what is now known as the Argand burner, that a really brilliant lamp was known. Argand's discovery created such a revolution in this mode of lighting that he was publicly persecuted by the tinners, locksmiths, and ironmongers of his time, who disputed his right to infringe the charter of their vocation by any improvements soever. This invention simply consisted in forming the burner of two concentric cylinders, the intermediate space being filled by the wick, which was of a hollow cylindrical form, and the oil to be consumed. The interior cylinder was left open at top and bottom, so that a current of air could enter at the bottom and supply a constant stream of oxygen to the *centre* of the flame. In ordinary lamps the middle part of the flame is taken up with unconsumed gases, which pass away in smoke, but Argand directed a current of oxygen through these so as to effect their combustion. The difference between the common lamp and the candle flame has, indeed, been aptly compared to the difference between a fire made in the open air without any forced method of supplying it with oxygen, and a fire made in a furnace to which a rapid supply of oxygen is furnished by means of the central tube and the draught of the chimney which encloses the whole. Argand's burner has become so general over the world, not only for oil lamps, but for gas lamps, and for heating in chemical analysis, that it is entitled to be reckoned a first-rate invention.

Lamps are so various in their forms and qualities, that we can only briefly describe a few of the better-known modern kinds. In order to get rid of shadows the Fountain Reservoir lamp was early introduced, and still exists in the Student's Reading-lamp, in which the oil-vessel is removed to one side of the burner, so that its shadow may fall to that side of the room where the light is least wanted. In this lamp the Argand burner is adopted.

To abolish the shadow entirely, however, the reservoir is now generally placed below the flame, and in order to supply more oil to the latter than can rise by capillarity, different processes have been applied. For instance, in the Carcel lamp the oil is pumped up from the bottom of the lamp by clockwork, in such a quantity as to exceed that consumed during the whole period of burning, and the unconsumed portion flows back to the reservoir over the outside of the burner. This lamp gives an excellent light, but is somewhat expensive. In the Moderator lamp, the oil is forced up the wick by means of a spiral spring, pressing on a disc immersed in the oil. The spring of this lamp, like the clock-work of the Carcel, requires to be periodically wound up. The flow of the oil to the wick is *moderated* by means of a tapering rod of iron wire which is placed in the ascending tube, and as the pressure of the oil increases it is forced more into the tube, thereby checking the ascent of the oil.

Owing to the extreme fluidity of the mineral oils, such as naphtha, camphine, petroleum, and paraffin, the capillarity of the wick is sufficient of itself to raise enough oil to the flame. Naphtha is sometimes burned in lamps without a wick, such as the Steam and Vapour lamp, in which a current of air traverses the naphtha and becomes saturated with it; or the lamp, so common on our hucksters' stalls, where the flame proceeds from a knob perforated with a circle of holes. Camphine, or turpentine deprived of its water and smell, is a powerful illuminant if well supplied with air, but very obnoxious owing to the disagreeable fumes and soot which it gives off if stinted of oxygen.

Among the most serviceable lamps now in use are the Silber lamp, the Indicator, the Paragon, the Duplex, and the Triplex. The Silber is a Moderator lamp, made to burn petroleum and colza. It has an Argand burner, and a large cylindrical split wick with a metal cone over it, to converge the outer draught on the flame, and various minor improvements. It yields a light at full power equal to twenty-four candles, and will burn for seven hours or more without replenishing with oil. The Indicator, also a form of Moderator, has an adjustable funnel for regulating the combustion. It burns colza oil, and yields a smaller light than the Silber. The Paragon, a petroleum lamp very common in the colonies and America, has a single flat wick made very wide, so as to give a large flame, and a cone over it. It gives a light of twenty-three candles, and burns for seven hours. The Duplex lamp, as its name implies, has two flat wicks, side by side, both movable by one thumbscrew, and a cone over them. It burns crystal oil, or purified petroleum, and yields a full light of twenty-five candles. Opinion is divided as to the relative merits of the Silber, the Paragon, and the Duplex lamps, but we may mention that a recent writer on the subject gives the palm to the improved Silber, and deems the Paragon somewhat more economical than the Duplex in point of oil, though it is more difficult to manage, and its chimneys are apt to break; on the other hand, we have seen the Duplex preferred to the other two. All three are good lamps, and the Duplex and Silber are the best known in this country. The Triplex lamp has three wicks arranged so as to give a Δ section. Like the Cylindrical and Duplex wicks, it is not so economical as a single flat-wicked lamp – that is, it does not give so much light for the same quantity of oil – but it yields a very large flame, and is suitable for dining and billiard-rooms, where expense is not so much the object as a good light. And here, before leaving the subject, let us recommend consumers of paraffin and petroleum to buy it from a respectable firm.

We have seen that the flame of a candle or an oil lamp is fed by inflammable gases yielded by the destructive distillation of the wax, tallow, or oil. In the manufacture of coal-gas those hydro-carbon gases are produced on a large scale by the destructive distillation of coal; and they are consumed in the flame of a lighted gas-burner just as they are consumed in the flame of a candle or a lamp. In fact, the only essential difference between oil or candle-lights and gas-jets is that in the case of the former the destructive distillation is immediate, and takes place at the light itself, whereas in the case of the latter it is a general process apart, the gases being generated and stored at a distance from the points where they are consumed.

Inflammable gas occurs in nature in great quantities among certain carbonaceous deposits in America, the Caspian Sea, and elsewhere, as well as among beds of rock-salt in China and Hungary. The merit of discovering and utilising artificial gas belongs among the nations to our own country, and the chief credit, as is well known, is due to a Scotchman, Robert Murdoch. Before Murdoch's time there had been many attempts to use coal-gas for lighting purposes, but none of these trials led to any marked success. In 1792, however, Murdoch, who was then residing at Redruth in Cornwall, began to study the subject, and five years later lighted up the workshop of Messrs. Boulton and Watt in Birmingham with coal-gas manufactured on the premises. From that time the introduction of gas proceeded apace in private establishments, but it was not until 1810 that the first public company, the Gaslight and Coke Company, was formed by Act of Parliament for the manufacture and supply of gas for streets and homes. In 1813 Westminster Bridge was first lighted with gas; and three years later gas was common in London.

24

J. MUNRO, 'FROM GAS TO ELECTRICITY'

Cassell's Family Magazine (1880), pp. 282–284

Aritificial gas is now distilled from a great variety of substances, among which are coal, shale, lignite, petroleum, turf, wood, resins, oil, fats, and vegetable refuse. The best of these processes for general purposes is the ordinary coal distillation now so common. The best kind of coal for gas-making is bituminous coal of the pitch and cannel sorts. As a rule, the coals which yield the highest percentage of gas furnish also that of highest illuminating power. The cannel or 'gas-coals' of Scotland and Lancashire are the richest in gas, and hence it is that gas-lighting is so prevalent in Scotland, where, in the towns at least, every bedroom and passage has its jet.

The following simple experiment illustrates very well the distillation of coal-gas. 'When', says a recent writer, 'the bowl of an ordinary clay pipe is filled with small fragments of bituminous coal, covered over with clay, and placed in a bright fire, immediately smoke is seen to issue from the stalk which projects beyond the fire. The smoke soon ceases, and if a light is then applied to the orifice of the stalk, the issuing gas burns with a bright steady flame, while a proportion of a black, thin, tarry liquid oozes out from the stalk. After the combustion ceases, there is left in the bowl of the pipe a quantity of char or coke'. As practised on a large scale, retorts of iron, clay, or brick take the place of the pipe. These are heated to a bright red in retort furnaces having fires of coke and coal, and charged or cleared by manual labour as the distillation proceeds. From the retorts within the furnace the crude gas passes by vertical 'ascension' pipes to a long chamber containing water, termed the 'hydraulic main', where tar is condensed out of it, and flows by a pipe to the tar-well. From the hydraulic main the gas, which is still of a high temperature, is next passed through a series of long pipes termed the 'condenser', to cool it, and thereby free it from the heavier hydro-carbons which adulterate it. These pipes open at one end into a series of troughs filled with water, and the tar and ammoniacal liquor collect in these, the tar sinking to the bottom while the liquor floats on the top. The gas has yet to pass through the purifiers, and to help it on its way, and prevent a too great back pressure in the retorts, it is subjected to exhaustion by means of various contrivances termed 'exhausters', which have in general a fan-like action. After this process the gas is relieved of ammonia,

 DOI: 10.4324/9781315400303-33

sulphuretted hydrogen, carbonic acid, and other impurities. The ammonia is separated by passing the gas through the 'scrubber', which is usually a hollow tower divided vertically into two compartments, which are filled with coke and water. The gas flows up one side and down the other; the ammonia unites with the water, and the ammoniacal liquor is discharged at the top. The sulphuretted hydrogen and carbonic acid are both freed from the gas by the 'lime purifier', which, consists of a chamber stored with tiers of trays containing slaked lime. The gas is allowed to diffuse itself over the surface of the lime, and thereby delivers up its impurities. Instead of slaked lime, quicklime and hydrated oxide of iron are also employed to separate the carbonic acid and sulphuretted hydrogen from the gas, the latter uniting with the oxide to form a sulphide of iron, while the quicklime absorbs the carbonic acid.

The gas is now ready for use, and after traversing the station meter it is stored in the gas-holders, from which it is distributed by main and service pipes to the consumers' homes, where a meter is placed to register the amount consumed.

Meters are of two kinds, wet and dry. In the wet meter the gas drives round a kind of drum partially immersed in water, and the drum actuates the hands on the indicating dial. In the dry meter the gas enters a kind of double bellows, which it causes, by means of valves, to expand and contract in such a way as to communicate motion to the hands of the indicator through the medium of a train of mechanism.

In order to make gas burn with perfect steadiness, the pressure at the burner itself should be quite uniform; but this is not so unless a special 'consumer's governor' be employed. The principle of this device is the same as that which regulates the larger governor at the gas-works, namely, causing the pressure of the gas to regulate mechanically the size of the orifice through which the gas escapes to the flame. Among the best of these governors are those now so extensively applied to street lamps. In one kind the gas flows into an expansible chamber, or holder, the expansion of which under the pressure of the gas regulates the size of the outlet by means of a half-ball valve; while in the latter the same object is effected by causing the gas to press upon a thin diaphragm.

The gas-burners in common use are of a very inferior sort, and it is estimated that they only give about one-half of the light which the amount of gas consumed is capable of giving. This is chiefly due to the fact that it is against the interests of the gas companies to improve private burners; but when the enormous waste of gas and the vitiated air, as well as the trying light, which result from bad combustion, are considered, the great importance of securing good burners comes home to all. As rich cannel (or 30-candle) gas requires to be burnt in a thinner stream than poor coal (or 14-candle) gas, the slits in burners for the former require to be much thinner than for the latter. There are two kinds of burners in use – the Argand and the flat-flame. The Argand, which only burns poor gas, consists of an annular tube with a circle of small holes pierced in the end of the ring, and it consequently gives a tubular flame. It is principally used in offices, and is protected by a cylindrical glass chimney. That known as Sugg's No. 1 is the best, and has been adopted by Act of Parliament as the standard burner for the United Kingdom. Last winter, in order to compete with the electric light, Mr. Sugg devised a compound Argand consisting of several concentric simple burners, and these lights may now be seen illuminating several of the wider London streets – the four-ring pattern yielding a light of 200 candles. Flat-flame burners are of two kinds, the 'fish-tail' and the 'bat-wing'. The former has two holes drilled at an angle, so that the two jets of gas impinge on one another in issuing, and the velocity of the particles being thereby impeded, a more complete combustion is the result. The light of a fish-tail is sensibly increased by inserting a 'Scholl's platinum perfecter', which is simply a tiny slip or thin partition of platinum between the two jets. The bat-wing burner has a narrow slit cut across the point, and from this the gas issues. In all the best burners now used the tops are made of steatite or of 'adamas' pottery. In the 'Christiania' burner, the slit is circular, and the light issues in two thin sheets which blend in their upper parts, and produce a great increase of light over the ordinary burner. As the common metal and steatite burners allow the gas to rush from their orifices without any attempt at regulation, various devices have been patented for retarding the escaping current. The simplest and best of these is Brönner's burner, which has the opening in its lower part smaller than the upper orifice; and the width of either opening can be readily varied at will so as to suit different qualities and pressures of gas. Of all burners the ordinary fish-tails in general use give the poorest light. From experiments made by Mr. Pattison, with the usual 14-candle gas, it appears that the illuminating powers of different burners, each consuming five cubic feet of gas per hour, were represented by the following numbers: – Fish-tail, No. 3, steatite top, 3.75; do., do., metal top, 5.85; do., No. 4, steatite top, 5.31; do., No. 5, steatite top, 7.80; Bat-wing, metal top, 9.26; Fish-tail, Bray's No. 4, 6.28; do., Bray's No. 8, 11.80 and 10.15; Bat-wing, Brönner's No. 4, 12.62 and 11.60; Bat-wing, Sugg's No. 4, 10.50 and 10.90. From these figures it is evident that there are burners in use which for the same amount of gas consumed give three times the amount of light obtained from others, and if the best Argand burner be taken into account the range is actually from one to five times.

The latest competitor for public favour as an illuminant is the electric light, and though it has been in existence under some form or other for the last seventy years, it has only now established a sure footing in practice, a footing which has but to be advanced by a train of improvements in order to render it the chief light of the future.

Every solid body, whatever its nature, becomes luminous when raised to a temperature of 1,000° of Fahrenheit's thermometer, and emits a dull red light. As this temperature is increased the light comes brighter, in a proportion exceeding the corresponding rise of temperature. Thus at 1,300° the body emits orange rays, at 1,500° blue rays, at 2,000° violet rays, so that a body heated to a temperature of over 2,000° will yield all the rays of the sun. With candles, lamps, and gas, the heat necessary to produce these high temperatures of luminosity is generated, as we have seen, by chemical combination, but in the electric light is generated by a current of electricity. There are two modes of applying the current so as to transform it into heat and light: one is to make it jump through the air across a gap in the conducting circuit between two pieces of carbon or other refractory conductor; and the other is simply to make it flow through a narrow pencil of carbon, or a fine metal wire. In the first of these cases the current encounters great resistance in bridging the non-conducting air-space, and spends its energy in overcoming it, while at the same time it tears away the atoms of one of the carbon 'poles' and, raising them to a dazzling white heat, produces the brilliant stream of light known as the 'voltaic arc'. In the second case the current, meeting with great resistance in the narrow channel of carbon or wire provided for it, raises the latter to a high temperature and a state of glow.

A good electric light should be brilliant, steady, and lasting; but while the first of these qualities is easily obtained with electricity, the other two are very difficult to achieve. Those lamps which depend on the 'voltaic arc' are especially subject to variableness in the light, owing to the irregular wasting of one of the carbons; and the duration of the light is, because of this wasting, confined to the time which the carbon requires to be entirely consumed. Those lamps, on the other hand, which depend on the incandescence of a solid conductor are, if not the most brilliant, at least the steadiest and most durable; for in them, since there is no break in the circuit, it is only necessary to keep the current flowing and prevent the fusing of the wire or the oxidation of the carbon through which it flows, to secure a perfectly steady light, and hence Mr. Edison was on the right track when he adopted the incandescent mode. The 'arc' is, however, by far the most economical source of the two, it being found that the same current will yield two and a half times the light by means of the arc that it will by the incandescence of a wire; and Mr. Edison, when he startled the world a year ago, overlooked this fact. The light obtained from platinum or iridium wire, heated by electricity, is all that the most exacting could require, but it is too costly as yet. The important fact that the amount of light emitted by a heated body increases in a greater ratio than the temperature, affords good hope for the success of incandescent lights. For instance, platinum at 2,600° emits forty times more light than at 1,900°, therefore if a substance could be found which would bear a prodigious temperature without melting it might be possible to make incandescent lighting cheap; and it is with this aim that Mr. Edison has tried to render the highly infusible metals, platinum and iridium, more infusible still by tempering them *in vacuo*, and more recently has abandoned metals in favour of a thin arch or slip of charred drawing-paper, through which the current is passed.

There are various electric lamps of both kinds, but the best of these are – for the arc, the Serrin, which is very brilliant; the Rapieff, which is both brilliant and steady; the new Siemens, which is so perhaps in a lesser degree; and the Jablochkoff, which has for some time past been illuminating the Thames Embankment; while for incandescence may be cited the carbon lamps of Berderman and Reynier, and the platinum-iridium and carbon-flake lights of Edison.

The relative intensities of artificial lights are measured by instruments termed photometers, which all depend upon the estimate of the eye as regards brightness, and therefore are more or less inaccurate. In some the eye judges by the intensities of the shadows thrown by the two lights compared, in others by the intensities of the direct reflections. In order to compare lights properly, a fixed criterion of illumination is required. In England, this is the standard candle made of pure spermaceti, weighing a sixth of a pound, and burning 130 grains of spermaceti in an hour; in France it is the Carcel jet, consuming 42 grammes of pure colza oil an hour, and yielding about ten times more light than the standard candle. In Rumford's photometer the two lights to be compared are made simultaneously to project two shadows of an upright rod upon a screen behind, and the stronger light is shifted back until the eye judges the two shadows equally dark, when the intensities of the lights are respectively proportional to the *squares* of their distances from the shadows. For example, if one light be *twice* as far from the screen as the other when the shadows on the latter are equally dark, its intensity is *four* (2×2) times greater than the intensity of the other light; if *three* times as far, its intensity is *nine* (3×3) times that of the other, and so on. Bunsen's photometer, again, consists of a paper screen having a grease spot made with spermaceti dissolved in naphtha on it. One light is placed in front of the screen so as to cause the spot to appear dark, the other is then placed behind the screen, and since it tends to make the grease-spot appear bright it is shifted back until the spot is neither dark nor bright, but resembles the rest of the paper. The relative intensities of the two lights are then proportional to the squares of their distances from the screen. There are several other photometers, but those of Rumford and Bunsen are perhaps the best known.

According to trustworthy measurements by the photometer, the intensity of sunlight is equal to the light from 5,500 wax candles at the distance of a foot. The electric light produced by the current from a voltaic battery of fifty Bunsen cells is equal to about one-fourth of sunlight, or 1,400 candles; but some of the great electric lamps now employed in our lighthouses instead of oil lamps, with several concentric wicks, and fed by the current from a Siemens dynamo-electric machine, out-rival the sun himself in generating a light equivalent to 20,000 candles. The Drummond oxy-hydrogen or *lime-light* is almost as intense as the electric light. It is formed by a jet of oxygen gas and a jet of hydrogen impinging and mingling together on a small cylinder of lime, which is heated to whiteness by the heat from the combining gases. The lime-light, the 'bude' light, produced by forcing an oil-flame with a current of oxygen, and gas, have all been tried for lighthouse purposes, but they are defective in practice. The ordinary gas-flame is equivalent to from 11 to 16 standard candles. According to Dr. Letheby, 754 ozokerit candles are equivalent to 891 paraffin ones, and 1,150 wax ones; and as regards economy, an estimate given by Dr. Ure represents the relative costs of different kinds of candles by the following scale: – For tallow candles, 6 to the pound, 9.8; for ditto, 8 to the pound, 12; for pressed tallow candles, 5 to the pound, 23.7; for wax, 5 to the pound, 48.6; for spermaceti, 5 to the pound 47.8; and for stearine, 5 to the pound, 37.1. Wax candles are therefore the dearest of all, and spermaceti candles come next.

From a recent comparison of oil lamps with gas, made by a chemist to a petroleum association, we gather that the cost of a light of one-candle for 1,000 hours is, for petroleum oil at 1s. per gallon, 9¾d.; and for colza oil, at 3s. 6d. per gallon, 8d.; while for gas, at 3s. 6d. per 1,000 cubic feet, the cost for the same amount of light is only about 4½d., taking the ordinary light of a gas-jet as equivalent to twelve candles.

The cost of electric lighting is not yet well determined, but we may safely assume that for streets it will ultimately be as cheap as gas, while for large buildings and factories it is considerably cheaper.

25

CHARLES W. VINCENT, 'THE DANGERS OF ELECTRIC LIGHTING'

Nineteenth Century, 27 (January 1890), pp. 145–149

Dread of lightning is of all ages; it is not much lessened by knowledge of its nature, even though that knowledge enables neutralisation of its most violent effects. Indeed, the awe may well be increased when we learn that the lightning flash, splitting the steeple from pinnacle to base, rending the oak, scattering herds in lifeless heaps, may be rivalled by the electricity obtained by separating the gaseous constituents of a single drop of water.

Happily deaths from artificially produced electricity have in this country been rare. In America, where the protean force is in every-day use for lighting streets and houses, and driving machinery, accidents have been numerous, and are increasing in frequency. Upwards of 100 lives have been lost in New York alone during the past twelve months. Day by day we read that men are killed by the very force which flashes the news of their death across the world. One is at work on a telegraph cable: he touches a lightning wire; instantly he hangs lifeless and burning above the head of a horror-stricken, shrieking crowd. (It is said that a woman died of the sight.) A few days later a shopman moving a metal show-case was done to death; in his shoe a projecting nail pierced the stocking, and thus helped on his fate. Quite recently a workman died on the roof of a building alone, unseen, and for some hours unsought for: the wire he was at work upon, by some mismanagement, carried a greater current than it was intended to do. In consequence of these accidents some 80,000 miles of overhead electric wires in New York are ordered to be taken down.

The electric conductors laid in subways are at times sources of danger. A succession of tremendous lightning flashes from the sky would be required to equal the effect of an accidental concentration of electricity in one of these conductors which Mr. Edison thus describes: –

> Near the corner of William and Wall Streets, New York, the underground conductors of the Edison Illuminating Company became crossed, and the current, which was passing through them at a pressure of only 110 volts, melted not only the wires, but several feet of iron tubing in which

DOI: 10.4324/9781315400303-34

they were encased, and reduced the paving stones within a radius of three or four feet to a molten mass.

According to Mr. Westinghouse, the Edison underground lines leak in a short time after they have been laid, and it is possible to draw off a sufficient quantity of electricity to light a number of lamps when connection is made between a water pipe and one of the mains.

The American municipalities have some ground for their contention that the enormous expansion of the new industry has created a somewhat contemptuous familiarity with its dangers in place of the wholesome dread which sought for every possible safeguard.

Our own experience is yet to come. Already are overhead wires and underground conductors being laid in every direction to supply electricity in quantity and of intensity hitherto unknown in England.

The public have the right to insist that the users of force dangerous to life and property shall have ascertained and secured the conditions necessary for their own safety, and, above all, that they shall not in any way interfere with the physical or mental comfort of those who do not use it.

Even in the interest of the electric lighting and power companies it is imperative that the public shall be assured that telegraph and telephone wires, gas and water pipes, railings, and gratings of houses, posts and pavements will always be as absolutely free to their use as now.

Sufficiently stringent regulations will no doubt be made at some future time. Would it not be better that they should be made before accidents happen rather than after?

Electricity is dangerous in three ways. When in great quantity but of small intensity, it destroys by fusion conductors of insufficient capacity and semi-conductors. When of high intensity it destroys insufficient or semi-conductors by disruption or heating or both, and has the tendency to leave the road laid down for it and cut out a new path for itself. Thirdly, whenever electricity enters or leaves an electric conductor, it, by its mere presence in one, evokes a momentary current of electricity in neighbouring conductors: this is termed induction.

Voltaic electricity, the current produced between a zinc and a copper plate sunk in an oxidising liquid, is electricity of low tension; if the plates are large and the liquid active, the quantity will be great. Two plates coiled in a tank as big round as the dome of St. Paul's would produce electricity sufficient in quantity to light a great part of the City, to melt a bar of iron like a tallow candle; its current turned into a system of conductors of insufficient size would carry fire and destruction wherever it went. Nevertheless, the intensity would be scarcely more than that of a cell made up of a brass thimble and a bit of zinc, viz., about one 'volt', and would be unfelt by the human body. The equivalent of one hundred such cells, in dynamo-electric machines, is proposed for a London district. When voltaic cells are connected in sequence, *i.e.* so that the current passes through all in succession, the intensity is multiplied, the quantity remaining constant. The late Dr. De la Rue, with a battery of 11,000 cells, obtained electricity of sufficient intensity at the terminals to leap across a space in the air of nearly three-quarters of an inch. The shock from this battery would have caused instant death, and extraordinary precautions were taken to avoid chance contact with any part of it or its connections. Dynamo machines of nearly equal potency are being constructed.

The apparatus so often seen in the streets, whereby a moderate amount of electric tetanus can be experienced for a penny, is an example of electric induction. The current of a few cells is made to circulate round a bobbin or reel of insulated wires, on its way back having to pass through a little magnetic arrangement which makes and breaks the circuit many times in a second. Outside this primary coil of wires, but not in contact with it, is wound a large coil of much finer wire, the two extremities of which are connected to brass handles to be grasped by the experimenter. There is no connection between the first and the second coil. Every time the low-tension current enters or leaves the primary or inner coil a current of higher 'potential' passes through the secondary or outer coil; thus a 'potential' of two or three volts is made to *induce* a potential (ten or fifteen volts in the case quoted) dependent on the relative length and fineness of the two separate coils. Induction coils have been made of great capacity. Dr. Spottiswoode constructed one which when worked with a few cells producing an imperceptible shock induced in the secondary coil electricity of tension sufficient to flash across four or five feet of air, and pierce glass a quarter of an inch thick.

In electric lighting induction coils of converse construction are employed, the primary coil being of fine wire, and the secondary or induction coil of the thicker wire. These coils convert high-tension into low-tension electricity, and under the name of 'converters' are already in use in several electric lighting systems.

Electricity for lighting and other purposes is now universally produced by means of dynamo machines founded on Faraday's discovery of magneto-electricity. Momentary currents in alternate directions are induced in coils of wire passing the poles of powerful magnets, by rotating these coils between the poles. In some machines these induced currents are immediately carried off to do the required work; these are termed alternating-current machines. They are commonly worked at an electric tension of 1,000 volts, enabling a large number of arc or other lamps to be worked in series – or the current passes into a 'converter' as above described, and is thus reduced to a tension of 100 volts.

Generally, however, the alternating current is by an ingenious arrangement twisted round upon itself in the machine, so that when the separate impulses leave it they are all in the same direction. These machines are termed continuous current machines. They, like the alternating-current machines, can be made of any desired 'potential' or electric pressure.

The physiological effects of alternating currents of electricity are very different from those of continuous currents. In the former case 10 to 15 volts are as much as can be borne for any length of time, whereas in the latter as much as 100 volts can be endured, though even here much depends on the quantity. Westinghouse says, 'With even less than 100 volts it is painful beyond endurance to grasp firmly with the hands the brushes or any bright brass work of a large dynamo or to grasp any metal connected with the wires.'

A 220 volt continuous current will burn the human body if the flesh is in contact with the conductors, that is if the skin is broken. A current of 90 volts will burn meat, boil water, melt cast iron. In Mr. Edison's experiments a continuous current of 400 volts killed a dog in 40 seconds; 304 volts did not kill in 30 seconds. A current of 1,000 volts killed a large strong dog instantly. The alternating current he found to be much more hurtful; 120 volts killed, and 100 volts may cause death; 200 certainly will. The hands are unable to relinquish the grasp of a conductor carrying an alternating current of more than about 20 volts; this adds materially to the danger of this system.

Death by electricity is not always instantaneous. A person fixed to the conductors by an alternating current might live some time before death released him from his sufferings; and it is to be feared that this sometimes happens.

In America the alternating currents pass through the streets at a pressure of 1,000 volts. Arriving at the place to be lit, the wires pass into a converter as described above, and the lights are worked at a pressure of 100 volts. There is always some danger of the 'converter' being pierced, in which case the house wires would be fused if nothing worse happened, and the house would almost certainly be set on fire. This is no imaginary danger. Mr. Edison, corroborating the experience of many other workers, points out that the insulating material, under the continued stress of millions of strong currents in opposite directions, undergoes molecular change, and ultimately becomes so disintegrated that piercing and disruption follows. It is common experience that such is the end of an induction coil.

The conditions of absolute safety, as we know them at present, are, conducting wires of large size and great capacity and conductivity, perfect insulation, currents of low tension, and installations for limited areas.

It is commonly said that, to save cost of conductors, a higher potential than any known in New York will be carried through the streets of London, and the appalling intensity of 10,000 to 15,000 volts is talked of! Apparently the following regulation of the Board of Trade contemplates such action: – 'Every high-pressure aërial conductor must be insulated with a durable and efficient material, to be approved by the Board of Trade, to a thickness of not less than one-tenth of an inch, and in cases where the extreme potential in the circuit exceeds 2,000 volts, the thickness of insulation must not be less in inches or parts of an inch than the number obtained by dividing the number expressing the volts by 20,000.'

Thus it appears that the existing regulations permit any pressure the electric companies may desire to use.

Sir William Thomson holds that 'nothing beyond 200 volts, on any account, should be admitted into a house or ship'. It may be asked – Why, then, into the streets? 8,000 volts' pressure was surely safer in Dr. De la Rue's house than in the highways and byways of London, where the insulation is liable to be disturbed every time a gas- or water-pipe is hunted for or the road opened for drainage purposes.

Beyond this there is a further and perhaps still greater because unrecognised danger. Currents of 10,000 to 20,000 volts have power of inducing currents in surrounding conductors at a very considerable distance. At the Royal Institution recently a rapid succession of discharges of a Leyden jar, through a wire running round the front of the gallery, caused by induction at a distance of 8 or 10 feet the points and interstices of the gold leaves ornamenting the wall of the theatre and the metal gratings of the ventilators to scintillate with bright sparks: given an escape of gas, and the theatre might have been fired.

In the neighbourhood of a wire carrying an alternating current of 20,000 volts, wires carrying harmless currents become dangerous, for in addition to the risk of contamination by leakage, they are liable to carry induced currents.

Large installations of electricity introduce fresh risks. There is danger to property if quantity is very great, even though potential be low. There is danger to life if potential be high.

Fortunately it is ordered 'that the Board of Trade may from time to time make such regulations as they may think expedient for securing the safety of the public from personal injury or from fire or otherwise'.

Many people think that the time for such regulations is *now*!

3.2

Lucifer match

DOI: 10.4324/9781315400303-35

3.2 Lucifer match

Charles Knight, 'Illustrations of Cheapness: The Lucifer Match', *Household Words*, 1 (13 April 1850), pp. 54–57.

[Henry Morley], 'Letter from a Highly Respectable Old Lady', *Household Words*, 1 (18 May 1850), pp. 186–187.

T. E. Thorpe, T. Oliver, and G. Cunningham, *Report on the Use of Phosphorus in Manufacture of Lucifer Matches* [extract] (HMSO: London, 1899), pp. 11–12, 17–18.

The price of modern convenience and productivity could be steep, even when an invention did not involve elaborate infrastructure and high technology. The first friction matches were invented in the 1820s, and the popular phosphorus match (which was easier to strike) dates from the next decade. Matches might seem a small thing, but they brought easy, reliable access to fire within the reach of even many of the poorest Victorians. Charles Knight was the great editor behind projects in education and mass publishing such as the *Penny Magazine* and the Society for the Diffusion of Useful Knowledge. Writing in Dickens' brand-new journal *Household Words* in the early 1850s, Knight hails the science and manufacture of the Lucifer match (which used so-called 'white' or 'yellow' phosphorous) as a 'fire revolution' that combined advances in the science of chemistry with the efficiencies of the factory system – the revolutionary modern method of manufacturing based on the division of labour.

But this triumph of cheapness did not look so successful from all points of view. Indeed, the cheapness of matches reflected the cruel conditions under which they were produced. Adopting the persona of an old lady sceptical about modern ways, the health reformer and man of letters Henry Morley replies to Knight in *Household Words* by pointing out that the workers who make the matches are often afflicted by the phosphorous-induced necrosis of the teeth and jawbones that was becoming notorious as 'phossy jaw'. It is not merely that human labour transforms raw materials; labouring with those materials can also alter human bodies. The danger remained through the end of the century, as a late-Victorian government report confirms. The adoption of the newer red phosphorous match would have eliminated phossy jaw among workers, but the 'safety match' was more expensive to produce as well as less convenient for its users, because it could only be ignited by being struck on its box. The 1888 Match Girls' Strike over low wages, punitive fines from supervisors and poor working conditions at the Bryant and May match factory in East London became one of the most famous instances of successful industrial action by Victorian women. Still, it would be years until Parliament completely banned the manufacture of dangerous white phosphorous matches.[1]

Note

1 The great, definitive work on the humble match – a ubiquitous, inexpensive technology that placed the power to create fire in any pocket or bag – perhaps has yet to be written.

But for insight into the history of the match in Victorian Britain, see Asa Briggs, *Victorian Things* (London: Penguin, 1990), pp. 187–205. On the stories of phosphorous and of the strikers at Bryant and May, see, respectively, John Emsley, *The Shocking History of Phosphorus: A Biography of the Devil's Element* (London: Macmillan, 2000), and Louise Raw, *Striking a Light: The Bryant and May Matchwomen and Their Place in History* (London: Continuum, 2009).

26

CHARLES KNIGHT, 'ILLUSTRATIONS OF CHEAPNESS: THE LUCIFER MATCH'

Household Words, 1 (13 April 1850), pp. 54–57

Some twenty years ago the process of obtaining fire, in every house in England, with few exceptions, was as rude, as laborious, and as uncertain, as the effort of the Indian to produce a flame by the friction of two dry sticks.

The nightlamp and the rushlight were for the comparatively luxurious. In the bedrooms of the cottager, the artisan, and the small tradesman, the infant at its mother's side too often awoke, like Milton's nightingale, 'darkling', – but that 'nocturnal note' was something different from 'harmonious numbers'. The mother was soon on her feet; the friendly tinder-box was duly sought. Click, click, click; not a spark tells upon the sullen blackness. More rapidly does the flint ply the sympathetic steel. The room is bright with the radiant shower. But the child, familiar enough with the operation, is impatient at its tediousness, and shouts till the mother is frantic. At length one lucky spark does its office – the tinder is alight.

Now for the match. It will not burn. A gentle breath is wafted into the murky box; the face that leans over the tinder is in a glow. Another match, and another, and another. They are all damp. The toil-worn father 'swears a prayer or two'; the baby is inexorable; and the misery is only ended when the goodman has gone to the street door, and after long shivering has obtained a light from the watchman.

In this, the beginning of our series of Illustrations of Cheapness, let us trace this antique machinery through the various stages of its production.

The tinder-box and the steel had nothing peculiar. The tinman made the one as he made the saucepan, with hammer and shears; the other was forged at the great metal factories of Sheffield and Birmingham; and happy was it for the purchaser if it were something better than a rude piece of iron, very uncomfortable to grasp. The nearest chalk quarry supplied the flint. The domestic manufacture of the tinder was a serious affair. At due seasons, and very often if the premises were damp, a stifling smell rose from the kitchen, which, to those who were not intimate with the process, suggested doubts whether the house were not on fire. The best linen rag was periodically burnt, and its ashes deposited in the tinman's box, pressed down with a close fitting lid upon which the flint and steel reposed. The match was chiefly an article of itinerant traffic. The chandler's shop was

DOI: 10.4324/9781315400303-36

almost ashamed of it. The mendicant was the universal match-seller. The girl who led the blind beggar had invariably a basket of matches. In the day they were vendors of matches – in the evening manufacturers. On the floor of the hovel sit two or three squalid children, splitting deal with a common knife. The matron is watching a pipkin upon a slow fire. The fumes which it gives forth are blinding as the brimstone is liquifying. Little bundles of split deal are ready to be dipped, three or four at a time. When the pennyworth of brimstone is used up, when the capital is exhausted, the night's labour is over. In the summer, the manufacture is suspended, or conducted upon fraudulent principles. Fire is then needless; so delusive matches must be produced – wet splints dipped in powdered sulphur. They will never burn, but they will do to sell to the unwary maid-of-all-work.

About twenty years ago Chemistry discovered that the tinder-box might be abolished. But Chemistry set about its function with especial reference to the wants and the means of the rich few. In the same way the first printed books were designed to have a great resemblance to manuscripts, and those of the wealthy class were alone looked to as the purchasers of the skilful imitations. The first chemical light-producer was a complex and ornamental casket, sold at a guinea. In a year or so, there were pretty portable cases of a phial and matches, which enthusiastic young housekeepers regarded as the cheapest of all treasures at five shillings. By and bye the light-box was sold as low as a shilling. The fire revolution was slowly approaching. The old dynasty of the tinder-box maintained its predominance for a short while in kitchen and garret, in farmhouse and cottage. At length some bold adventurer saw that the new chemical discovery might be employed for the production of a large article of trade – that matches, in themselves the vehicles of fire without aid of spark and tinder, might be manufactured upon the factory system – that the humblest in the land might have a new and indispensable comfort at the very lowest rate of cheapness. When Chemistry saw that phosphorus, having an affinity for oxygen at the lowest temperature, would ignite upon slight friction, – and so ignited would ignite sulphur, which required a much higher temperature to become inflammable, thus making the phosphorus do the work of the old tinder with far greater certainty; or when Chemistry found that chlorate of potash by slight friction might be exploded so as to produce combustion, and might be safely used in the same combination – a blessing was bestowed upon society that can scarcely be measured by those who have had no former knowledge of the miseries and privations of the tinder-box. The Penny Box of Lucifers, or Congreves, or by whatever name called, is a real triumph of Science, and an advance in Civilisation.

Let us now look somewhat closely and practically into the manufacture of a Lucifer-match.

The combustible materials used in the manufacture render the process an unsafe one. It cannot be carried on in the heart of towns without being regarded as a common nuisance. We must therefore go somewhere in the suburbs of London to find such a trade. In the neighbourhood of Bethnal Green there is a large open space called Wisker's Gardens. This is not a place of courts and alleys, but a

considerable area, literally divided into small gardens, where just now the crocus and the snowdrop are telling hopefully of the spring-time. Each garden has the smallest of cottages – for the most part wooden – which have been converted from summer-houses into dwellings. The whole place reminds one of numberless passages in the old dramatists, in which the citizens' wives are described in their garden-houses of Finsbury, or Hogsden, sipping syllabub and talking fine on summer holidays. In one of these garden-houses, not far from the public road, is the little factory of 'Henry Lester, Patentee of the Domestic Safety Match-box', as his label proclaims. He is very ready to show his processes, which in many respects are curious and interesting.

Adam Smith has instructed us that the business of making a pin is divided into about eighteen distinct operations; and further, that ten persons could make upwards of forty-eight thousand pins a day with the division of labour; while if they had all wrought independently and separately, and without any of them having been educated to this peculiar business, they certainly could not each of them have made twenty. The Lucifer Match is a similar example of division of labour, and the skill of long practice. At a separate factory, where there is a steam-engine, not the refuse of the carpenter's shop, but the best Norway deals are cut into splints by machinery, and are supplied to the match-maker. These little pieces, beautifully accurate in their minute squareness, and in their precise length of five inches, are made up into bundles, each of which contains eighteen hundred. They are daily brought on a truck to the dipping-house, as it is called – the average number of matches finished off daily requiring two hundred of these bundles. Up to this point we have had several hands employed in the preparation of the match, in connection with the machinery that cuts the wood. Let us follow one of these bundles through the subsequent processes. Without being separated, each end of the bundle is first dipped into sulphur. When dry, the splints, adhering to each other by means of the sulphur, must be parted by what is called dusting. A boy sitting on the floor, with a bundle before him, strikes the matches with a sort of a mallet on the dipped ends till they become thoroughly loosened. In the best matches the process of sulphur-dipping and dusting is repeated. They have now to be plunged into a preparation of phosphorus or chlorate of potash, according to the quality of the match. The phosphorus produces the pale, noiseless fire; the chlorate of potash the sharp cracking illumination. After this application of the more inflammable substance, the matches are separated, and dried in racks. Thoroughly dried, they are gathered up again into bundles of the same quantity; and are taken to the boys who cut them; for the reader will have observed that the bundles have been dipped at each end. There are few things more remarkable in manufactures than the extraordinary rapidity of this cutting process, and that which is connected with it. The boy stands before a bench, the bundle on his right hand, a pile of half opened empty boxes on his left, which have been manufactured at another division of this establishment. These boxes are formed of scale-board, that is, thin slices of wood, planed or scaled off a plank. The box itself is a marvel of neatness and cheapness. It consists of an inner box, without a top, in which the matches are placed, and of an outer case, open at each end, into which the first box slides. The matches, then, are to be cut, and the empty boxes filled, by one boy. A bundle is opened; he seizes a portion, knowing by long habit the required number with sufficient exactness; puts them rapidly into a sort of frame, knocks the ends evenly together, confines them with a strap which he tightens with his foot, and cuts them in two parts with a knife on a hinge, which he brings down with a strong leverage: the halves lie projecting over each end of the frame; he grasps the left portion and thrusts it into a half open box, which he instantly closes, and repeats the process with the matches on his right hand. This series of movements is performed with a rapidity almost unexampled; for in this way, two hundred thousand matches are cut, and two thousand boxes filled in a day, by one boy, at the wages of three halfpence per gross of boxes. Each dozen boxes is then papered up, and they are ready for the retailer. The number of boxes daily filled at this factory is from fifty to sixty gross.

The *wholesale* price per dozen boxes of the best matches, is FOURPENCE, of the second quality, THREEPENCE.

There are about ten Lucifer Match manufactories in London. There are others in large provincial towns. The wholesale business is chiefly confined to the supply of the metropolis and immediate neighbourhood by the London makers; for the railroad carriers refuse to receive the article, which is considered dangerous in transit. But we must not therefore assume that the metropolitan population consume the metropolitan matches. Taking the population at upwards of two millions, and the inhabited houses at about three hundred thousand, let us endeavour to estimate the distribution of these little articles of domestic comfort.

At the manufactory at Wisker's Gardens there are fifty gross, or seven thousand two hundred boxes, turned out daily, made from two hundred bundles, which will produce seven hundred and twenty thousand matches. Taking three hundred working days in the year, this will give for one factory, two hundred and sixteen millions of matches annually, or two millions one hundred and sixty thousand boxes, being a box of one hundred matches for every individual of the London population. But there are ten other Lucifer manufactories, which are estimated to produce about four or five times as many more. London certainly cannot absorb ten millions of Lucifer boxes annually, which would be at the rate of thirty three boxes to each inhabited house. London, perhaps, demands a third of the supply for its own consumption; and at this rate the annual retail cost for each house is eightpence, averaging those boxes sold at a half-penny, and those at a penny. The manufacturer sells this article, produced with such care as we have described, at one farthing and a fraction per box.

And thus, for the retail expenditure of three farthings per month, every house in London, from the highest to the lowest, may secure the inestimable blessing of constant fire at all seasons, and at all hours. London buys this for ten thousand pounds annually.

The excessive cheapness is produced by the extension of the demand, enforcing the factory division of labour, and the most exact saving of material. The scientific discovery was the foundation of the cheapness. But connected with this general principle of cheapness, there are one or two remarkable points, which deserve attention.

It is a law of this manufacture that the demand is greater in the summer than in the winter. The old match maker, as we have mentioned, was idle in the summer – without fire for heating the brimstone – or engaged in more profitable field-work. A worthy woman who once kept a chandler's shop in a village, informs us, that in summer she could buy no matches for retail, but was obliged to make them for her customers. The increased summer demand for the Lucifer Matches shows that the great consumption is amongst the masses – the labouring population – those who make up the vast majority of the contributors to duties of customs and excise. In the houses of the wealthy there is always fire; in the houses of the poor, fire in summer is a needless hourly expense. Then comes the Lucifer Match to supply the want; to light the candle to look in the dark cupboard – to light the afternoon fire to boil the kettle. It is now unnecessary to run to the neighbour for a light, or, as a desperate resource, to work at the tinder-box. The Lucifer Matches sometimes fail, but they cost little, and so they are freely used, even by the poorest.

And this involves another great principle. The demand for the Lucifer Match is always continuous, for it is a perishable article. The demand never ceases. Every match burnt demands a new match to supply its place. This continuity of demand renders the supply always equal to the demand. The peculiar nature of the commodity prevents any accumulation of stock; its combustible character – requiring the simple agency of friction to ignite it – renders it dangerous for large quantities of the article to be kept in one place. Therefore no one makes for store, but all for immediate sale. The average price, therefore, must always yield a profit, or the production would altogether cease. But these essential qualities limit the profit. The manufacturers cannot be rich without secret processes or monopoly. The contest is to obtain the largest profit by economical management. The amount of skill required in the labourers, and the facility of habit, which makes fingers act with the precision of machines, limit the number of labourers, and prevent their impoverishment. Every condition of this cheapness is a natural and beneficial result of the laws that govern production.

27

[HENRY MORLEY], 'LETTER FROM A HIGHLY RESPECTABLE OLD LADY'

Household Words, 1 (18 May 1850), pp. 186–187

Some one of you gentlemen has been a writing about Lucifer-matches. Lucifers, indeed! Is that your improvement of the people? Yah! If folks were wise they would send Lucifer his matches back, and not be indebted to him any longer for them. None of us ever lost our jawbones over a tinder-box in my young days. But you must have improvements. Don't you know that you pay for civilisation with health. Look at me. I am eighty-two; but we used flint and steel when I was young. Turn to the British and Foreign Medical Review of a few years ago, there you will see what I mean. There's an account in it, of the new disease begotten by lucifer-matches; by the phosphorus. It's this: a worker in the manufactory has a hollow tooth, it generally begins there, resembles tooth-ache; then there is inflammation about it; the periosteum of the lower jaw becomes inflamed; the bone dies: a man is recorded to have picked his lower jawbone out of his chin as we pulled winkles out of their shells, when winkles were eaten, in the good old times. It's true that forewarned is forearmed. Great care is taken in lucifer factories on a large scale; those who work over the phosphorus have their mouths shielded, I believe, and so on: but then, what a thing it is! Here's your march of improvement! A new luxury, a new disease.

 DOI: 10.4324/9781315400303-37

28

T. E. THORPE, T. OLIVER, AND G. CUNNINGHAM, *REPORT ON THE USE OF PHOSPHORUS IN MANUFACTURE OF LUCIFER MATCHES* [EXTRACT]

(HMSO: London, 1899), pp. 11–12, 17–18

It may be desirable to describe briefly the mode of manufacture of lucifer matches in this country. The splints are about 4½ inches long, and about one-ninth of an inch thick. These, at the larger works, are received in large cases and are transferred in batches of 20,000 or so on to trays, technically known as 'monkeys'. They are next filled into 'frames' or 'clamps', and are so placed that each splint is separated from its neighbour by a space sufficiently large to prevent the tipping composition from cementing the whole together at the ends. The mode of filling the 'frames' varies slightly in the different works. In one of the commonest of these a rectangular box at the top of the filling machine is charged with splints lying parallel to each other and at right angles to the face of the machine. The box or 'hopper' has given to it a jogging motion by means of machinery, usually worked by steam power, whereby a row of splints is dropped from the box, and by pulling a lever these are pushed over by wires into notches cut in a thin lath placed in the frame; a second lath, the bottom of which is coated with a strip of felt or woollen list, is placed over the row of splints, and another row of splints is immediately brought into the notches by the action of the lever; the operation being repeated until the 'clamp' or 'frame' has received its complement of 4,000 splints, destined to make twice that number of matches. A skilful hand will deliver to the 'dipper' as many as 100 frames a day, that is, 400,000 splints, to be coated at each end with the igniting composition.

Occasionally the splints are slightly charred at the end by being pressed upon a heated iron plate. They are next dipped into a thin layer of melted paraffin wax or crude paraffin scales, or in a mixture of paraffin and stearin, or Japan wax, substances first introduced into the match industry by Letchford in 1861. The paraffin is necessary to insure the ignition of the wood, as probably not 1 match in 50 would take fire without its intervention. Formerly sulphur was exclusively employed for this purpose. Brimstone matches are, however, now rarely seen, although, if procurable, they are preferred by sailors, lamplighters, and cabmen,

DOI: 10.4324/9781315400303-38

as, from the low igniting point of sulphur, they are not so readily extinguished by the wind as the ordinary lucifer.

The composition is made by first 'melting' the glue in the requisite quantity of water heated by steam, and adding to it, little by little, the phosphorus, weighed out either in the form of sticks, or in segments of the cheese-shaped masses in which it is supplied to the manufacturers. As the phosphorus melts, it is thoroughly incorporated with the glue, with which it forms a thick white emulsion, giving off more or less 'fume', mainly of oxides of phosphorus. The colouring matter is then added, and afterwards the mixture of chlorate of potash, whiting, powdered glass, &c., previously intimately mixed in a mill with sufficient water to make the whole thoroughly wet. The entire paste is then once more thoroughly mixed so as to render it of uniform composition.

The pasty mass, which always evolves more or less 'fume', is poured, a ladleful or so at a time, on to a horizontal slab, usually of iron, kept at a regulated temperature by means of steam or a water jacket, and is spread out to a layer of uniform depth by means of a gauge or 'doctor'. The dipper then immerses the ends of the splints on one side of the 'frame' or 'clamp' into the viscid mass when it is immediately removed to the drying room by an assistant or 'carrier-away', who places it with the dipped ends downwards so that the composition gradually sets, forming a well-rounded head. A second 'frame' is meanwhile handed to the dipper, and one end of the splints is in like manner dipped into the pasty composition, and is afterwards transferred to the drying room by the 'carrier-away'. The dipper proceeds in this way until the whole batch of framed splints is dipped at one end only. By the time he has finished, the heads first dipped are usually hard enough to allow of the clamp being reversed and the other ends dipped; each splint, it being remembered, forming two matches. The dipped 'clamps' are allowed to remain in the drying chamber for some hours, the time varying with the humidity and temperature of the air, until the heads are sufficiently set to allow of the splints being cut and the matches filled into the boxes. A clever dipper can dip 1,400 frames in a day of 10 hours, that is, in round numbers, some 11 million matches.

The air of the drying room is always impregnated with more or less of the fumes from the phosphorus and a thin white smoke is usually observed playing about the dipped ends of the matches. The drying rooms, as a rule, are provided with large fans so as to effect a rapid interchange of the air and thus expedite the drying and incidentally to remove the fumes. If all parts of a match factory were as well ventilated as the drying chambers, phosphorus necrosis would happen less frequently.

The next operation consists in dividing the splints and boxing the matches. The dipped and dry splints are removed from the 'clamps', or, as it is technically called, are 'racked-off' or 'laid-out' and taken to benches at which stand a number of girls or women, each provided with a hinged lever-knife and a supply of empty boxes. The boxer throws back the knife, seizes a number of the splints lying beside her – her sense of touch tells her to a match or two whether she has the required number – places them on the wooden support carrying the knife, slings a weighted cord across them to keep them in position, and with a downward stroke of the knife cuts through the 70, 80, or 100 splints. As she again throws back the knife, she takes up one of the half-open boxes before her and drives into it, with a single stroke of the hand, its complement of matches. A very considerable number of matches are necessarily lost in this operation, if they are at all 'quick' or tender'. The operation of 'racking-off' or the friction of the heads against each other in the cutting and boxing not infrequently causes the ignition of the whole batch. Occasionally it happens that the whole of a half day's make will ignite in the drying chamber; a plentiful supply of sawdust in which to bury the inflamed splints will promptly stop the spread of the burning.

[. . .]

As the result of my inquiries and observation I conclude –

1 That no satisfactory substitute for phosphorus in either the one form or the other in the manufacture of matches has yet been found.
2 That inasmuch as phosphorus must continue to be employed, the only modification of it which confers complete immunity from phosphorus necrosis is the red or so-called amorphous variety.
3 That, as yet, no method of using this substance in a 'strike-anywhere' match is commercially practicable. The risk in the manufacture of a paste in which red phosphorus and chlorate of potash are commingled, and the dangers attending the packing and transport of matches tipped with such a compound would enormously outweigh the evil caused by phosphorus necrosis. The only practicable method of applying red phosphorus at present known is that of Böttger, as worked out by Fürth and Lundström, in the match in which the red phosphorus is placed upon the rubbing surface, that is, the so-called 'safety' match.
4 The total prohibition of the use of ordinary phosphorus is probably impossible without international co-operation. 'Strike-anywhere' matches are apparently demanded, and will therefore continue to be supplied. Whether, however, all the arguments which are employed in favour of their continued adoption, other than that of price, are valid is open to question. There is no doubt, as regards many of the larger manufacturers abroad, that any general legislative action which compels the use of red phosphorus would be welcomed. It is significant that every Ministerial declaration in Belgium which accompanies any promulgation of the law relating to the conditions under which matches are made in that country, makes reference to a time when red phosphorus will alone be employed.

It is, nevertheless, certain, judging from the experience of other countries in which the special rules have been made sufficiently stringent, and where they are effectively complied with, that the evils attending the use of ordinary phosphorus can be greatly minimised. The remedial measures are comparatively simple. They are: –

1 Proper medical supervision and inspection of the operatives.
2 Periodical inspection of the teeth of all those who in any way come in contact with the fumes of phosphorus.
3 Efficient ventilation of all workshops in which processes involving the use of ordinary phosphorus are carried on.
4 Proper lavatory appliances and vestiary accommodation under efficient control.

As regards medical inspection the special rules of most continental countries require that this shall be at least quarterly. In the case of Holland, it is two-monthly, whilst, as will be seen from the Report, certain manufacturers require the medical man to attend once a month. The Act of 1895 enjoins that the occurrence of phosphorus necrosis shall be at once notified. Even cases in which the premonitory symptoms are consistent with the existence of but slight necrosis should be brought to the knowledge of the medical department of the Home Office. It will be observed that in the Dutch special rules power is given to the factory inspectors to invoke the assistance, through the central authority, of a medical man paid by the State in all cases in which he has reason to suspect that any collusion exists between the employer and the visiting medical man.

It is clearly established that carious teeth constitute the main channel by means of which the phosphorus fumes are enabled to attack the maxillary bones. This, indeed, seems to be everywhere recognised, and a dental examination is placed among the chief remedial measures which are adopted abroad. Many of the larger firms in this country have now voluntarily adopted this examination, and the dental arrangements at Bryant and May's, and of the Diamond Match Company are excellent.

PART 4

Communication

4.1

Postage stamp and letter

DOI: 10.4324/9781315400303-40

4.1 Postage stamp and letter

Rowland Hill, *Postal Reform: Its Importance and Practicability* [extract] (London: Knight, 1837), pp. 27–30.
Charles Dickens and W. H. Wills, 'Valentine's Day at the Post Office' [extract], *Household Words*, 1 (30 March 1850), pp. 7–8.

The Victorians produced an extraordinary array of new forms of media and communication, many of them based on epochal advances in electricity or chemistry. But one of their most significant revolutions in communication required a breakthrough in thought and organisation rather than in science or manufacture. At the beginning of the Victorian era, every letter was assessed an individual charge on the basis of factors such as the distance it travelled and the number of sheets of paper enclosed – with these fees paid by the letter's recipient upon its delivery. Many large cities had separate local postal services with their own sorters, letter carriers and schedules of charges. The expense and complication of exchanging letters also encouraged various frauds and workarounds, which were further impediments to the efficiency and the finances of the postal system.

The great postal reformer Rowland Hill's critical insight was to realise that the actual cost of transporting and delivering a letter was vanishingly low, even though the complications of calculating and collecting its postage were often high. Rather than carefully assessing the composition and destination of every letter and collecting fees on delivery, he concluded, the post office should charge the sender a uniform, low rate of postage to put a letter into the system, whether its destination lay across town or across the country. Furthermore, Hill argued that under such a simplified system, the more letters were posted, the lower the cost per letter would become. After substantial debate, Parliament adopted Hill's plan, creating a uniform rate of just a penny to send a regular letter. As Hill had predicted, the change dramatically increased not only public use of the post office but also its revenues and profitability.

Hill imagined that most people would pay for postage by purchasing special prepaid 'covers' (envelopes), but as an afterthought to this proposal, he describes the postage stamp as another option. For the inaugural issue of his new journal *Household Words*, Dickens and his subeditor W. H. Wills surveyed the reformed postal system by tracking pre-stamped, cash-paid and unpaid letters through the main London post office at St. Martins-le-Grand. Always fascinated by systems and industrial processes, Dickens had visited Rowland Hill at home to discuss postal matters with him before writing the piece, which would become the prototype for what Dickens called his journal's 'process' articles, essays that approach an everyday industrial or institutional process with a sense of romance and wonder.[1]

Note

1 On Dickens' 'process' articles, see Harry Stone, 'Introduction', *The Uncollected Writings of Charles Dickens, Household Words, 1850–59*, by Charles Dickens, ed. Harry Stone, 2 vols. (Bloomington, IN: Indiana University Press, 1968; London: Allen Lane/Penguin, 1969), Vol. 1, p. 53.

For insight into Victorian postal reform, see Gavin Fryer and Clive Akerman (eds.), *The Reform of the Post Office in the Victorian Era and Its Impact on Social and Economic Activity*, 2 vols. (London: Royal Philatelic Society); Douglas N. Muir, *Postal Reform and the Penny Black: A New Appreciation* (London: National Postal Museum, 1990). The most comprehensive and readable accounts of Victorian postal history remain Howard Robinson, *The British Post Office: A History* (Princeton, NJ: Princeton University Press, 1948), and Charles R. Perry, *The Victorian Post Office: The Growth of a Bureaucracy* (Woodbridge: Royal Historical Society Office, 1992).

By inventing the postage stamp, the Victorians also inaugurated philately (the study and collection of stamps and other postal products), which had its own extensive specialised literature even before the end of the nineteenth century. Two useful resources are Robson Lowe, *The British Postage Stamps of the Nineteenth Century*, 2nd ed. (London: National Postal Museum, 1979), and James Mackay, *British Stamps* (London: Longman, 1985).

29

ROWLAND HILL, *POSTAL REFORM: ITS IMPORTANCE AND PRACTICABILITY* [EXTRACT]

(London: Knight, 1837), pp. 27–30

Having shown the practicability and even fairness of a uniform and low rate of postage, (the primary conditions of the simplicity of arrangements, and of the extension in the number of letters which we have contemplated,) our next step is to show the means by which such postage might be conveniently collected in advance.

In former editions two modes of collection were submitted for consideration; but the public having evinced a decided preference for one, the other is here, for the sake of brevity, omitted.

The following is a sketch of the mode of collection which I propose. It is drawn out with reference to the metropolis, but a few very slight and obvious modifications would adapt it to any other town.

A few years ago, when the expediency of entirely abolishing the newspaper stamp, and allowing newspapers to pass through the Post Office for one penny each, was under consideration, it was suggested by Mr. Charles Knight, that the postage on newspapers might be collected by selling stamped wrappers at one penny each. Availing myself of this excellent suggestion, I propose the following arrangement:

Let stamped covers and sheets of paper be supplied to the public from the Stamp Office or Post Office, or both, as may be most convenient, and sold at such a price as to include the postage. Letters so stamped would be treated in all respects as franks.

Covers at various prices would be required for packets of various weights; and each should have the weight it is entitled to carry legibly printed with the stamp. The Keeper of the Receiving-house should take the packets from time to time from the box, examine them to see that the allowance of weight was not exceeded, and assort them as hereafter described. If any packet exceeded the proper weight, it should be sent to the dead-letter office, opened, and returned to the writer: the delay thus occasioned, and the loss of the frank-stamp, being the penalty for carelessness. As a check on the Receiver, a few packets taken at random should be examined at the Central Office, and a fine levied for negligence.

DOI: 10.4324/9781315400303-41

Economy and the public convenience would require that sheets of letter paper of every description should be stamped in the part used for the address; that wrappers, such as are used for newspapers, as well as covers made of cheap paper, should also be stamped; and that every Deputy Postmaster and Letter Receiver, all over the kingdom, should be required to keep them on sale; a discount, such as is now given on stamps, would render it their interest to do so. Stationers also would be induced to keep them.

The stamp of the receiving-house should be struck upon the frank-stamp, to prevent the latter being used a second time.

For the forgery of these stamps their low price would leave but little temptation; and the account of their issue, compared with the account of the number of letters passed through the Post Office, (kept as hereafter described,) would lead to the detection of any extensive fraud.

Should experience warrant the Government in making the use of stamped covers universal, most important advantages would be secured; advantages, indeed, of such magnitude, that before any exception whatever is admitted, the policy of such exception should be very fully considered.

1 The Post Office would be relieved altogether from the collection of the Revenue, and from all accounts relating to that collection. Distribution would be its only function.
2 The receipt of letters would be much more simple than it now is; as the present trouble of receiving money for the post-paid letters would be avoided.
3 Any necessary exception to the uniform rate of postage (1*d.* per half-ounce) would, under this arrangement, be productive of comparatively little inconvenience. For instance, the greater weights proposed to be allowed in the local posts would be readily managed. Penny covers, and sheets for local posts, might be marked thus, when stamped,

 'For Local Distribution. – The weight allowed is two ounces.'

Or all penny covers and sheets might be marked thus:

> 'For General Distribution. – The weight allowed is half an ounce.'
> 'For Local Distribution. – The weight allowed is two ounces.'

It may, perhaps, be said that this plan only transfers the receipt of postage from the Post Office to the Stamp Office; but it will be recollected that at the latter the postage would be collected in large sums, the number of payments being reduced, probably, in the ratio of at least a thousand to one.

The cost of stamping such an enormous number of papers may appear to be a formidable objection to this arrangement. With the aid of machinery, however, this cost may be reduced to a mere trifle.

The only objection which occurs to me to the universal adoption of this plan is the following: Persons unaccustomed to write letters, would, perhaps, be at a loss how to proceed. They might send or take their letters to the Post Office without having had recourse to the stamp. It is true that on presentation of the letter, the Receiver, instead of accepting the money as postage, might take it as the price of a cover, or band, in which the bringer might immediately inclose the letter, and then re-direct it. But the bringer would sometimes be unable to write. Perhaps this difficulty might be obviated by using a bit of paper just large enough to bear the stamp, and covered at the back with a glutinous wash, which the bringer might, by applying a little moisture, attach to the back of the letter, so as to avoid the necessity for re-directing it. If the bringer should put the letter into the letter-box, there would be no resource but to send it to the dead letter office; but, if proper pains were taken to inform the public, and legibly to mark the letter-box, 'For Stamped Letters, Franks, and Newspapers only', such cases could seldom occur.

I am aware that many consider the required payment in advance objectionable.

30

CHARLES DICKENS AND W. H. WILLS, 'VALENTINE'S DAY AT THE POST OFFICE' [EXTRACT]

Household Words, 1 (30 March 1850), pp. 7–8

Having been led through a maze of offices and passages more or less dark, they found themselves – like knights-errant in a fairy tale – 'in an enormous hall, illumined by myriads of lights'. Without being exactly transformed into statues, or stricken fast asleep, the occupants of this hall (whose name was Legion) appeared to be in an enchanted state of idleness. Among a wilderness of long tables, and of desks not unlike those on which butter-men perform their active parts of legerdemain in making 'pats' – only these desks were covered with black cloth – they were reading books, talking together, wandering about, lying down, or drinking coffee – apparently quite unused to doing any work, and not at all expectant of ever having anything to do, but die.

In a few minutes, and without any preparation, a great stir began at one end of this hall, and an immense train of private performers, in the highest state of excitement, poured in, getting up, on an immense scale, the first scene in the 'Miller and his Men'. Each had a sack on his back; each bent under its weight; and the bare sight of these sacks, as if by magic, changed all the readers, all the talkers, all the wanderers, all the liers-down, all the coffee-drinkers, into a colony of human ants!

For the sacks were great sheepskin bags of letters tumbling in from the receiving-houses. Anon they looked like whole flocks suddenly struck all of a heap, ready for slaughter; for a ruthless individual stood at a table, with sleeves tucked up and knife in hand, who rapidly cut their throats, dived into their insides, abstracted their contents, and finally skinned them. 'For every letter we leave behind', said the bag-opener, in answer to an inquiry, 'we are fined half-a-crown. That's why we turn them inside out'.

The mysterious visitors closely scrutinised the letters that were disgorged. These were *from* all parts of London *to* all parts of London and to the provinces and to the far-off quarters of the globe. An acute postman might guess the broad tenour of their contents by their covers: – business letters are in big envelopes, official letters in long ones, and lawyers' letters in none at all; the tinted and lace-bordered mean Valentines, the black-bordered tell of grief, and the radiant with white enamel announce marriage. When the Fleet Street dispatch appeared, the

 DOI: 10.4324/9781315400303-42

visitors tracked it, and the operations of the clerk who separated the three bundles of which it consisted were closely followed. With the prying curiosity which now only began to show itself, one of the intruders actually took a copy of the bill which accompanied the letters. It set forth in three lines that there were so many 'Stamped', so many 'Prepaid', and so many 'Unpaid'.

The clerk counted the stamped letters like lightning, and a flash of red gleaming past showed the inquirers that one of their epistles was safe. Suddenly the motion was stopped; the official had instinctively detected that one letter was insufficiently adorned with the Queen's profile, and he weighed and taxed it double in a twinkling. Having proved the number of stamped letters to be exactly as per account rendered, he went on checking off the prepaid, turning up the sender's green missive in the process. He then dealt with the unpaid, amongst which the lookers-on perceived their yellow one. The cash column was computed and cast in a single thought, and a short-hand mark, signifying 'quite correct', dismissed the Fleet Street bill upon a file, for the leisurely scrutiny of the Receiver-General's office. All the other letters, and all the other bills of all the other receiving-houses, were going through the same routine at all the other tables; and these performances are repeated ten times in every day, all the year round, Sundays excepted!

'You perceived', said one of the two friends, 'that in the rapid process of counting, our stamped letter gleamed past like a meteor, whilst our money-paid and unpaid epistles remained long enough under observation for a careful reading of the superscriptions'.

'That delay', said an intelligent official, 'is occasioned because the latter are unstamped. Such letters cause a great complication of trouble, wholly avoided by the use of Queen's heads. Every officer through whose hands they pass – from the receiving-house-keeper to the carriers who deliver them at their destinations – has to give and take a cash account of each. If the public would put stamps on *all* letters, it would save us, and therefore *itself*, some thousands a-year.

'What are the proportions of the stamped to the prepaid and unpaid letters which pass through all the post-offices during the year?'

'We can tell within a very near approximation to correctness: – 337,500,000 passed through the post-offices of the United Kingdom during last year, and to every 100 of them about fifty had stamps; 46 were prepaid with pennies; and only 4 were committed to the box unpaid.'

While one of the visitors was receiving this information, the other had followed his variegated letters to the next process; which was that of stamping on the sealed face, in red ink, the date and hour of despatch. The letters are ranged in a long row, like a pack of cards thrown across a table, and so fast does the stamper's hand move, that he can mark 3000 in an hour. While defacing the Queen's heads on the other side, he counts as he thumps, till he enumerates fifty, when he dodges his stamp on one side to put his black mark on a piece of plain paper. All these memoranda are afterwards collected by the president, who, reckoning fifty letters to every black mark, gets a near approximation to the number that have passed through the office.

It was by this means that our friends obtained the following account of the number of district letters that passed through this office on St. Valentine's Day: –

Feb. 14th, 1850.	*Paid.*	*Unpaid.*		*Stamped.*	*Total.*
	1d.	*1d.*	*2d.*		
Collections.					
8 o'clock.	6,872	52	1,216	20,082	28,222
10 "	6,212	19	607	13,629	20,467
12 "	7,069	36	612	15,240	22,957
1 "	2,989	17	277	6,395	9,678
2 "	6,520	39	535	13,696	20,790
3 "	2,456	36	328	6,909	9,729
4 "	4,873	36	375	13,478	13,478
5 "	3,340	28	317	8,207	11,892
6 "	9,300	129	958	27,950	38,337
8 "	3,903	32	812	6,650	11,487
	53,624	424	6,037	126,952	187,037

To this total are to be added 6,000 'bye' letters – or those which passed from village to village within the suburban limits of the district post without reaching the chief office – and 100,000 destined for the provinces and places beyond sea, which were transferred to the Inland Department. The grand total for the day, therefore, rose to nearly 300,000. Thus the sacrifices to the fane of St. Valentine – consisting of hearts, darts, Cupid peeping out of paper-roses, Hymen embowered in hot-pressed embossing, swains in very blue coats and nymphs in very opaque muslin, coarse caricatures and tender verses – caused an augmentation to the revenue on this anniversary equal to about 70,000 missives; 123,000 being the usual daily average for district and 'byes' during the month of February. This increase, being peculiar to cross and district posts, does not so much affect the Inland Office, for lovers and sweethearts are generally neighbours. The entire correspondence of the three kingdoms is augmented on each St. Valentine's day to the extent of about 400,000 letters.

'Is it possible?' exclaimed one of the visitors, regarding the piles of epistles on the numerous tables, 'that this mass of letters can be arranged and sent away to their respective addresses in time to receive the next collection, which will arrive in less than an hour?'

'Quite', replied an obliging informant, 'I'll tell you how we do it. We have divided London into seventeen sections. There they are, you perceive.' He then pointed to the tables with pigeon-holes numbered from one to seventeen; one marked 'blind', with a nineteenth labelled 'general'. It was explained that the proper arrangement of the letters in these compartments constitutes the first sorting. They are then sorted into sub-divisions; then into districts, and finally handed over to the letter-carriers, who, in another room, arrange them for their own convenience into 'walks'. As the visitors looked round they perceived their coloured envelopes – which were all addressed to Scotland – suddenly emerge from a chaotic heap, and lodge in the division marked 'general', as magically as a conjurer causes any card you may choose to fly out of the whole pack. 'These letters', remarked the expositor, 'being for the country will be presently passed into the Inland Office through a tunnel under the hall. The 'blind' letters have superscriptions which the sorters cannot decypher, and are sent to the 'blind' table where a gentleman presides, to whom, from the extreme sharpness of his vision, we give the *lucus à non lucendo* name of the "blind clerk." You will have a specimen of his powers presently.'

While this dialogue was going on there was a general abatement of the noise of stamping, and shuffling letters, and when the visitors looked round, the place had relapsed into its former tranquillity. It was scarcely credible that from 30,000 to 40,000 letters had been received, stamped, counted, sorted, and sent away in so short a time. 'A judicious division of labour', remarked one of our friends, 'must work these miracles.'

'Yes, sir', was the reply of an official, 'and there are from 1200 to 1700 of us to do the work of the district post alone. When it was removed from Gerard Street to this building there was not a quarter of that number. For instance – then, three carriers sufficed for the Paddington district; but, by the dispatch you have just seen completed, we have sent off 2000 letters to that single locality by the hands of twenty-five carriers.'

'The increase is attributable to the penny system?' interrogated one of our inquiring friends.

'Entirely.'

The questioner then referred to a Parliamentary paper of which he had obtained possession. It showed him the history of general postal increase since the era of dear distance rates. In 1839 – under the old system – the number of letters which passed through the post was 76,000,000. In 1840 came the uniform penny, and for that year the number was 162,000,000, or an increase of 93,000,000, equal to 123 per cent. That was the grand start; afterwards the rate of increase subsided from 36 per cent. in 1841, to 16 per cent. in 1842 and 1843. In 1845, and the three following years, the increase was respectively, 39, 37, and 30 per cent. Then succeeded a sudden drop; perhaps the culminating point had been attained. The Post-Office is, however, a thermometer of commerce: during the depressing year 1848, the number of letters increased no more than 9 per cent. But last year 37,500,000 epistles passed through the office, being an augmentation of 8,500,000 upon the preceding year, or 11 per cent. of progressive increase. Another Parliamentary document shows, that, although the business is now exactly four-and-a-half times more than it was in 1839, the expense of doing it has only doubled. In the former year the cost of the establishment was not quite 690,000*l*.; in 1849 it was about 1,400,000*l*.

4.2

Electric telegraph

DOI: 10.4324/9781315400303-43

4.2 Electric telegraph

'A Few Weeks from Home: The Electric Telegraph', *Chambers's Edinburgh Journal*, 9 (25 July 1840), pp. 209–210.

George Wilson, 'The Electric Telegraph' [extract], *Edinburgh Review*, 90 (1849), pp. 459–463.

Andrew Wynter, 'The Electric Telegraph' [extract], *Quarterly Review*, 95 (June 1854), pp. 131–139.

Anthony Trollope, 'The Young Women at the Telegraph Office' [extract], *Good Words* (1877), pp. 377–381.

The Victorian era did not merely witness or inspire new forms of communication; it invented the modern sense of communication itself, superseding the idea of communication as proximity (as when we speak of adjacent rooms as 'communicating') and decisively freeing long-distance transmission from the constraints of physical transport. Even more than Hill's call for a uniform rate of postage for all domestic letters, the electric telegraph promised to help liberate communication from the tyranny of distance and geography.

The roots of the electric telegraph extend back to experiments that began at the turn of the nineteenth century. But the forms of the device that actually left the laboratory and changed the world were invented more or less simultaneously in 1837 by Samuel F. B. Morse in the United States and by the team of William Fothergill Cooke and Charles Wheatstone in the United Kingdom. The early account of electric telegraphy in *Chambers's Edinburgh Journal* regards it with appropriate wonder, but what may be more striking is the attempt here to find a way to describe just what it transmits, to capture the new sense of communication: the telegraphed sequence of letters seems to appear instantly on the receiving apparatus, notes the author, but the 'idea' of the word has actually travelled miles across the wire. In this passage, the meaning of communication – its potential to include transmission not only by means of speech or a physical text but via an intangible set of patterns – seems to be changing before our eyes.

Once telegraphy has been adopted, partly as an adjunct to the railway in mid-Victorian Britain, the technology professor George Wilson and the journalist Andrew Wynter provide descriptions of its apparatus, pre-eminently at first the needle telegraph invented by Cooke and Wheatstone as opposed to the clicking telegraph associated with Morse, which is probably more familiar today. Yet the implementation of a technological system involves not only the specific arrangements of particular objects or devices but also issues of ownership, access and labour. Anthony Trollope combined the profession of postal bureaucrat and novelist for years, but after his retirement from the post office, he returned to consider its newest branch, the telegraph department, created by the nationalisation of domestic telegraphy in 1870. This political development presaged the British state's future involvement in electronic communication, including the establishment of the British Broadcasting Corporation in the next century. For his part, however, Trollope was more interested in the post office's training and hiring of young women as telegraph clerks, perhaps the earliest systematic movement of women into such information work. By the turn of the century, women would gain wide employment not only as telegraphists but also as secretaries, stenographers, typists, office clerks and switchboard operators.[1]

Note

1 For further reading on the history of the electric telegraph, see Jeffrey L. Kieve, *The Electric Telegraph: A Social and Economic History* (Newton Abbot: David and Charles, 1973); Geoffrey Hubbard, *Cooke and Wheatstone and the Invention of the Electric Telegraph* (London: Routledge, 1965); Ken Beauchamp, *History of Telegraphy: Its Technology and Application* (London: Institution of Electrical Engineers, 2001); Roland Wenzlhuemer, *Connecting the Nineteenth-Century World: The Telegraph and Globalization* (Cambridge: Cambridge University Press, 2015). Useful accounts of the nationalisation of the domestic telegraph lines appear in Kieve, *The Electric Telegraph*; Robinson, *The British Post Office*; and Perry, *The Victorian Post Office*.

Important discussions of the rise of women's information work in the late nineteenth century include Meta Zimmeck, 'Jobs for the Girls: The Expansion of Clerical Work for Women, 1850–1914', in *Unequal Opportunities: Women's Employment in England, 1800–1918*, ed. Angela V. John (London: Blackwell, 1986), pp. 153–177; Jane E. Lewis, 'Women Clerical Workers in the Late Nineteenth and Early Twentieth Centuries', in *The White-Blouse Revolution: Female Office Workers since 1870*, ed. Gregory Anderson (Manchester: Manchester University Press, 1988), pp. 27–47; and Thomas C. Jepsen, *My Sisters Telegraphic: Women in the Telegraph Office, 1846–1950* (Athens, OH: Ohio University Press, 2000). On the connections between the feminisation of information work and that of spirit mediumship in the nineteenth century, see Jill Galvan, *The Sympathetic Medium: Feminine Channeling, the Occult, and Communication Technologies, 1859–1919* (Ithaca, NY: Cornell University Press, 2010).

31

'A FEW WEEKS FROM HOME: THE ELECTRIC TELEGRAPH'

Chambers's Edinburgh Journal, 9 (25 July 1840), pp. 209–210

June, in London, is the most fashionably busy season of the year. Every body is in town. The Houses are sitting. All the places of public amusement are open. Epsom races – that admirable national engine for improving the breed of horses and deteriorating the race of men – come on in all their glory. And now generally occur those meetings of an important nature which attract strangers from all quarters of the united kingdom. This, then, is one of the most agreeable months in the year for visiting the metropolis, and it was on one of its finest evenings that, having arrived from the north at the railway station in Euston Square, we were whirled in a cab through the dusty streets to the domicile hospitably opened for our reception.

The following sketches of what fell under my observation during a short stay in town, may perhaps serve to amuse a leisure hour of that class of readers who, by circumstances, are shut out from personally visiting the scenes of my inquiry.

One evening, shortly after my arrival in London, I had the pleasure of meeting Professor Wheatstone at the house of a mutual friend, along with fifteen or twenty other gentlemen, all in some manner distinguished by their scientific or literary abilities. I cannot say that I remember having ever spent a few hours more agreeably. The company, besides being eminent in their respective lines of pursuit, were all, less or more, the friends of an advancing intelligence, or at least did not belong to the formidable order of retarders. I was particularly delighted with the opportunity of knowing Professor Wheatstone personally, and of conversing with him on a subject of experimental philosophy in which he is known to be engaged, and which, indeed, he may be said to have already made his own; I allude to that very surprising result of human ingenuity operating on a mysterious principle in nature – the *electric telegraph*. With much kindness, the professor invited me to attend a private exhibition of the apparatus and its operations on the ensuing Saturday, at King's College. As may be supposed, I readily accepted the offer; and if the reader pleases, he shall accompany me along the Strand to the lecture-room on the day in question.

The professor was present, with an assistant, while the apparatus required in the experiments lay before and around him on tables, or hung on the wall at his side.

DOI: 10.4324/9781315400303-44

The electric telegraph, it is essential to explain, is a means of transmitting any piece of intelligence, through the medium of wires, to any assignable distance, by night or by day, and in a moment of time. The wires do not move, or are in any way drawn, neither do they emit any sound. They lie perfectly still and quiescent, and the transmission is effected simply by electric or galvanic influence, passing along invisibly from one extremity to the other. The transmission of an electric shock through a wire, or any other metallic body, is well understood, and there must be few who are not acquainted with the instantaneous manner in which it acts; the only thing peculiar, therefore, in the present matter, is causing the shock to affect a moveable object at the extremity of the wire, and so produce a certain telegraphic sign. The production of signs by galvanic shocks, may on this account be defined as the principle on which this new species of communication is made to act.

The discovery of this kind of telegraphic action is by no means new. From a passage in Arthur Young's Travels in France, published in 1787, it appears to have been at that period known, and to some extent practised by a M. Lomond. But like many other remarkably ingenious devices – gas-lighting and steam-boating, for example – it was long in being heard of popularly after science had established its capabilities. Even now, it is one of those practical improvements which, to a certain extent, remain under public suspicion. Twelve years ago, Dr Ritchie made some attempts to complete the plan of an electric telegraph; Sir Humphry Davy and others also engaged in a similar undertaking. In 1837, the model of an apparatus for communicating by galvanic action, was exhibited by Mr Alexander before the Society of Arts in Edinburgh; and this, as far as I know, was the first time the thing was brought in a tangible form before the public. Mr Alexander's telegraph was in the form of a chest, containing thirty copper wires, answering to the twenty-six letters of the alphabet, three points, and an asterisk to denote the termination of a word. At one end, in connexion with the wires, were keys like those of a piano-forte, and underneath these were a pair of plates, zinc and copper, forming a galvanic trough: at the other extremity of the wires were thirty steel magnets, and, any one of these being affected by the electric agency produced by touching the key, it was turned to the right or left, and unveiled a particular letter. On removing the finger from the key, the magnet sprung back, and the letter was screened from observation. Thus any letter could be instantaneously exposed, or words spelled letter by letter, according to the will of the operator. As galvanism requires a complete circuit for its operation – that is, a wire must not only go from but return to the trough where it receives its influence – it might be supposed that a duplication of the thirty wires would have been necessary, but by a happy arrangement of Mr Alexander, with one return wire to serve for all, this encumbering of the apparatus was avoided.

Since this time, considerable improvements have been effected on the mechanism of electric telegraphs, chiefly by Professor Wheatstone, one material object having been the reduction of the number of wires, which has been effected with a surprising degree of skill. The professor has spent several laborious years, and, as is understood, some thousands of pounds, in perfecting the apparatus. In the early stage of the discovery, he effected a patent for a particular mode of operating, but that, though possessing very remarkable powers, he has some time ago superseded by one much more simple, and which I can see no reason for not immediately coming into general use.

On the occasion of my visit, to which I must now return, the professor showed two varieties of the apparatus, one being the latest invention, and the most deeply interesting from its simplicity. It may be briefly described as consisting of two small galvanic troughs or batteries; four lengths of copper wire; an object resembling a brass clock, with a small opening or dial on the surface sufficient to show a single letter at a time; close by this case of mechanism stood an upright pivot of brass about three inches high, having a circular top inscribed with the letters of the alphabet all round, and from each letter a spike pointing outwards like the spokes from a capstan. The whole stood on a table, except the wires, which, being four miles in length, and warped in numerous convolutions through the vaults of the college, were observable only at their extremities in connexion with the apparatus.

I need not confuse the reader by attempting an explanation of the principle of the process, which has been already adverted to; it will suffice to state, that the electricity or galvanic property generated in the batteries, was made to proceed along the wires, and in its passage to affect the mechanism in the case. In the construction of this mechanism, the great merit of the invention consists. It is a beautiful combination of brass wheels, and other details, the object of which is to produce a desired letter or figure at the exterior opening or dial. To bring any particular letter into view, the capstan is turned by the finger till the metal point projecting from a similar letter upon it, is made to touch a corresponding point near the side of the case. Thus, there is a sympathy, as I may call it, between the letters in the case and the letters on the capstan. A touch of the point opposite L, will bring L into view on the dial, and so on with any other letter. Nothing can be more perfect, or apparently simple. To appearance, the letters can be exposed at the rate of two in every moment of time. A lady, turning the capstan with her finger, brought into view the word L o n d o n, in the time it could be uttered letter by letter, although the idea had to travel through four miles of wire.

In the transmission of the electric influence through the wires of this or any other apparatus, distance is of no consequence as respects time, for electricity is supposed, with some degree of probability, to travel with the velocity of light, or 192,000 miles in the space of a second. In point of fact, therefore, no longer time would be occupied in transmitting intelligence to the uttermost ends of the earth, than would be required for sending it across a room or a table. Distance is a matter for consideration only as regards expenditure of galvanic force. The electric agency has a tendency to weaken in its progress, according to circumstances, and this must necessarily be provided for by increasing the number of batteries to the desired amount and power. It has been supposed that the difficulty of perfectly isolating and preserving the wires from injury in their course, would be an insuperable bar to their establishment on an effective footing; but fears need be no longer entertained on this score. Each of the four wires in Professor Wheatstone's apparatus is wrapped round with a well-rosined thread, and the whole are then tied together with a cord possessing a similar coating, so as to present the appearance of a tightly-bound rope. This it is proposed to place in a small iron tube like that used for bringing gas into houses, and the tubes, united to any length, are laid below the ground, or in a wooden case on the surface, to preserve them from injury. Yet another difficulty here presents itself. What if the rope, or any particular wire, should be fractured somewhere in its course? How would the precise point of injury be discoverable? This the professor has likewise provided for, as far as it possibly can be. He proposes that there shall be a signal-case at an interval of every few miles along the whole line, and therefore should any injury be sustained by the wires, it will be speedily discovered in what portion it has taken place, and a new and complete section of rope inserted in connexion with the other pieces. To avoid a very remote chance of delay in the transmission of intelligence from this cause, it would be easy to lay two sets of wires, one of which could be employed while the other was in course of being repaired.

It was impossible to observe the beautifully rapid and exact process of communication effected by the apparatus before me, without entertaining the conviction that I saw the rudimentary working of an engine, which ere long must force itself on the attention of the world, and come into universal use. Whether in the form to which it has been brought by Mr Wheatstone, or in some other modification of the principle, it is indisputable that it possesses the power of an effectual, and at all times ready, messenger of intelligence. Its capabilities have indeed been fully tested in a practical manner on the line of the Great Western Railway, to a distance, I believe, of fifteen miles; the apparatus employed being somewhat different from that which I have already described. Last September, when the wires of this electric telegraph were carried as far as West Drayton, the following account was given of it in one of the London papers: –

> 'The space occupied by the case containing the machinery (which simply stands upon a table, and can be removed at pleasure to any part of the room) is little more than that required for a gentleman's hatbox. The telegraph is worked by merely pressing small brass keys (similar to those of a keyed bugle), which, acting by means of galvanic power upon various hands placed upon a dial-plate at the other end of the telegraphic line, as far as now opened, point not only to each letter of the alphabet (as each key may be struck or pressed), but the numerals are indicated by the same means, as well as the various points, from a comma to a colon, with notes of admiration and interjection. There is likewise a cross (+) upon the dial, which indicates that where this key is struck, a mistake has been committed in some part of the sentence telegraphed, and that an erasure is intended. To a question – such, for instance, as the following: "How many passengers started from Drayton by the ten o'clock

> train?" – the answer could be transmitted from the terminus to Drayton and back in less than two minutes. This was proved on Saturday. This mode of communication is only completed as far as West Drayton station, which is about 13½ miles from Paddington. There are wires (as may be imagined) communicating with each end, thus far completed, passing through a hollow iron tube, not more than an inch and a half in diameter, which is fixed about six inches above the ground parallel with the railway, and about two or three feet distant from it. It is the intention of the Great Western Railway Company to carry the tube along the line as fast as the completion of the rails takes place, and ultimately throughout the whole distance to Bristol. The machinery, and the mode of working it, are so exceedingly simple, that a child who could read would, after an hour or two's instruction, be enabled efficiently to transmit and receive information'.

It being thus ascertained, by practical working, that the electric telegraph can perform all that its designers have proposed, it only remains that it should be spread in different directions over the country, or at the least laid in communication from London along the great lines of thoroughfare. The railways already formed and in course of construction, offer peculiarly eligible channels for the lines of wires. It is not to be expected, however, that any telegraph of this description is to be constructed at the public expense. It will require to be the private undertaking of a joint-stock company, and its services given at a price which would more than repay the outlay. The expense of tube, wires, and apparatus for a distance of four hundred miles, as from London to Edinburgh – provided a railway line were employed – would probably amount to L.25,000; and, once put in operation, the outlay is at an end, for the fresh supply of material for the batteries is almost too inconsiderable to be worthy of notice.

The method of working the apparatus will be readily understood. At each extremity of the line of rope – for it would work both ways – there would be an office for receiving and communicating intelligence, at a price conformable to the extent of the message. Being dispatched from one end, the communication would be instantaneously received at the other by an officiating clerk, and forthwith made known by a note to the party concerned. Thus, intelligence of the rise and fall of stocks, foreign news, orders for goods, or any other species of communication of an urgent nature, might, with the utmost facility, and at a trifling cost, be transmitted to any imaginable distance. To all merchants, capitalists, and, in particular, newspaper publishers, such a means of procuring intelligence would prove invaluable, and of course the benefit would be reflected on the public at large. The principle being placed beyond the reach of cavil, any attempt to put it in practice would depend exclusively on the question of expense and the necessity for its services. If it be reckoned of importance to possess speedy and correct intelligence on any given subject, here is the engine by which it can be attained. Do the people of Manchester, Liverpool, and other great seats of manufacture and commerce in the west and north of England, wish to possess the news of London as speedily as the people of London themselves, here is a means of indulging their wish ready to their hands. They have only to organise a very small establishment of officials, and expend a few thousands of pounds, and the matter is effectually accomplished.

Here I leave this extraordinary invention to the speculations of the reader. What may be its influence in aiding the progress of social improvement, uniting different nations in one common brotherhood, and extending the boundaries of knowledge, involves an inquiry too vast and intricate for solution in these pages.

32

GEORGE WILSON, 'THE ELECTRIC TELEGRAPH' [EXTRACT]

Edinburgh Review, 90 (1849), pp. 459–463

[. . .]The ultimate and only important *fact* in reference to the telegraph is, that by the marvellously simple device of dissolving a few pieces of metal connected with a long wire, we can develope [sic] instantaneously, a thousand miles off, a force which will speak for us, write for us, print for us, and so far as the conveyance of our thoughts is concerned, annihilate space and time. This annihilation is not of course complete, but in reference to practice it may be called so. Shakspeare's [sic] Juliet refers to 'the lightning which doth cease to be, ere one can say it lightens'. The exact velocity of electricity along a copper wire is 288,000 miles in a second. It is calculated, accordingly, that we could telegraph to our antipodes in rather less than the five hundredth part of one second of time!

The most impatient of correspondents may be satisfied with this velocity; and we may now inquire in what way electricity is made to produce signals. In discussing this we shall recur to the provisional theory adopted at the outset, that electricity flows in currents; and in conformity with the universal practice of expositors of these phenomena, write as if there were but a single current of positive electricity flowing at once along a telegraph wire. The other and opposite negative current may conveniently be disregarded, just as in navigation a compass-needle is referred to as if it had but one pole, pointing to the north.

Having secured the means of transmitting at will a current of electricity with great velocity, it remains to determine what phenomenon we shall cause it to produce at the distant station.

The phenomena most easily produced by electricity are *magnetic* ones; and these, accordingly, are now preferred as the sources of signals. The electric telegraph, indeed, remained an unrealised idea in the minds of ingenious men, till the famous Danish philosopher Oersted discovered, that a current of electricity, even though of very small intensity, if passing near a compass-needle poised on a pivot, will cause the needle to change its position, and point in a new direction. Let the telegraph-wire for example, whilst connected with a battery, be placed so that the needle of a mariner's compass shall be directly below or above and parallel to the wire, and the needle, no longer 'true to the pole', will whirl

DOI: 10.4324/9781315400303-45

round and stand east and west, instead of as before north and south. It depends upon the direction in which the current of electricity is sent, which pole of the compass-needle points east or west. Let the telegraph-wire stretching from London to Edinburgh and back again, be considered as consisting of an upper and a lower wire. If the London end of the upper wire be connected with the copper extremity of the battery, whilst the termination of the lower wire is connected with the zinc, the current of positive electricity (the only one of which we now take cognisance) will flow along the upper wire to Edinburgh, and return by the lower one to London. If the upper wire be now attached to the zinc, and the lower to the copper, the current will travel north by the lower wire, and come south by the upper. Now, without entering into details for which we have not room, and which are not essential to the comprehension of the telegraph, it may suffice to say, that the pole of the compass-needle, which points east if the electrical current passing near it be sent in one direction, points west if it be sent in the opposite one: while, if the passage of electricity be discontinued, the needle resumes its original position. We have it thus in our power to cause a compass-needle to move to either side at will; and we can bring it in a moment to rest. All those effects are produced still more strikingly if the wire, instead of being stretched above or below the compass-needle, be coiled many times round the compass-box, or case containing the magnetic needle. The wire, in that case, is covered with thread; which allows its coils to be put close together, without risk of the electricity passing *across* from coil to coil where they touch, as it would do, if the thread, which is a non-conductor, did not insulate the electricity. It is more convenient that the magnetic needle should originally stand vertically, so as to move from right to left, or *vice versâ* – like the index of a wheel barometer, than that it should revolve in a horizontal plane like the mariner's compass. It is also much more easily moved, if the effect of the earth's magnetism on it be neutralised. This is done by placing *two* magnetic needles on the same axis, with their poles reversed, so that the north pole of the one is opposite the south pole of the other. Such an arrangement, if the needles are of equal power, has no tendency towards one point of the compass more than another; and by making what are to be the lower ends of the needles somewhat heavier than the opposite extremities, the needles, when not under the influence of electric currents, will at once resume their vertical position.

Now, the one needle which is to act as the visible index, appears in front of a dial plate; the other surrounded by the coil of covered wire, which is continuous with one of the telegraph-wires, is placed behind the dial. An arrangement of this kind is provided at Edinburgh, the upper telegraph-wire being drawn out there into a long loop, which consists of soft copper wire covered with thread. This is wound round the concealed magnetic needle, so that a current of electricity moving along the upper wire follows the coiled loop, moves the needles in passing, and returns to London. At London, for a reason to be mentioned immediately, there is a similar loop or coil of covered copper wire surrounding a double magnetic needle, and then rejoining the upper main wire from which it proceeded. From the copper end of the battery, a wire is conducted to one of the strands of this coil, and soldered to it. From the zinc end a wire also is conducted, which is soldered to the lower telegraph-wire. The current setting off from the one end of the London battery, deflects the needles at London and at Edinburgh before it returns to the former. That the needles may be deflected to either side at will, a contrivance is supplied for cutting off and letting on, as well as for reversing the electric current from the battery. It is a little difficult, without a diagram, to explain distinctly this important portion of the telegraph. The following description, however, will perhaps make it sufficiently clear. Let the upper end of the double telegraph wire at London be marked A, and the lower end B. If A be connected to the copper of the battery, and B to its zinc, the current of electricity setting off from A, and returning to B, moves the index-needle to one side, for example to the left. If the arrangement be now reversed, so that A is connected to the zinc, and B to the copper, the current flows from B to A, and moves the needle to the right.

In actual practice, however, the wires are not shifted from the zinc to the copper, but are *cut across* between the battery on the one hand, and the telegraph-wires and coil round the magnetic needles on the other. The gap thus made is left vacant when no message is to be sent. When a signal is to be transmitted, a metallic cylinder is moved by a handle so as *to fill up the gap*, and establish continuity between the wires and the copper and zinc respectively, of the battery. This bridge, however, is so contrived, that when the handle which controls it is moved to the left, it stretches in such a manner as to connect the end A of the telegraph-wire with the copper, and the end B with the zinc, and the needle moves to the left. When the handle is moved to the right, it shifts the cylinder or bridge so as to establish a communication between A and the zinc, and between B and the copper; and the needle moves to the right. When the handle is placed vertically the current is cut off from both wires.

It only remains that an arrangement be made between the parties in Edinburgh and London, as to *the signification* of these deflections of the needle. This having been settled, the message-sender in the Metropolis, seated before his dial, moves the handle which determines the transmission and direction of the electricity along the wires. Every motion of the handle to the right or to the left, causes the index-needles at London and Edinburgh to move simultaneously to the same sides. We may suppose for example, that an answer in the negative is to be telegraphed from London to an interrogation from Edinburgh. It has been pre-arranged that one movement of the needle to the left shall signify N, and one to the right O. The respondent accordingly moves his handle to the left; thereby transmits the current of electricity in such a direction as to move the index-needle at Edinburgh to the left also; and so represents N. He then places the handle vertically so as to cut off the current, and permit the needle to resume its vertical position; and, after a brief pause, carries his handle to the right, which moves the Edinburgh needle also to the right, – which indicates O, and thus completes the answer.

The signal-dial at London is not essential, if London is not to receive messages; but as it must be provided with a view to their reception, it is so arranged that the electricity moves its index-needle before it passes on to Edinburgh. The party transmitting a message, has thus figured before him deflections of the index-needles, identical with those which his correspondent is watching and deciphering, at the same moment hundreds of miles away.

33

ANDREW WYNTER, 'THE ELECTRIC TELEGRAPH' [EXTRACT]

Quarterly Review, 95 (June 1854), pp. 131–139

At the same time that the first working telegraph was being simplified and improved, the system was gradually spreading, and, by the end of the year 1845, lines exceeding 500 miles in extent were in operation in England, working Messrs. Wheatstone and Cooke's patents. In the following year, capital, as represented by the powerful Electric Telegraph Company, commenced its operations, and an immediate and rapid development of the new method of carrying intelligence was the result.

'A period of eight years has elapsed', as they say in a certain class of drama, and let us now look upon the condition of electro-telegraphy in England. We left it exerting its influence in a disjointed manner over a few railways, and striking out its wires here and there at random, without governing head or organization; and how do we find it?

Jammed in between lofty houses at the bottom of a narrow court in Lothbury, we see before us a stuccoed wall, ornamented with an electric illuminated clock. Who would think that behind this narrow forehead lay the great brain – if we may so term it – of the nervous system of Britain, or that beneath the narrow pavement of the alley lies its spinal chord, composed of 224 fibres, which transmit intelligence as unperceived as does the medulla oblongata beneath the skin? Emerging from this narrow channel, the 'efferent' wires branch off beneath the different footways, ramify in certain plexuses within the great centre of intelligence itself, and then shoot out along the different lines of railway until the shores of the island would seem to interpose a limit to their further progress. Not so, however: beneath the seas, under the heaving waves covered with stately navies, they take their darksome way, until, with the burthen of their moving fire, they emerge once more upon the foreign strand, and commence afresh their career over the wide expanse of the Continent.

And now, like a curious physiologist, let us examine the various parts of this ingeniously constructed sensorium, and endeavour to show our readers how in this high chamber, fashioned by human hands, thoughts circulate, and ideas come and go. The door of the 'Central Telegraph Station' leads immediately into the Central Hall, an oblong space, open quite up to the roof, which presents an appearance something like the Coal Exchange or the Geological Museum, two

DOI: 10.4324/9781315400303-46

tiers of galleries being suspended from the bare walls, and affording communication to the different parts of the building. If we ascend the first gallery and lean over the balustrade, we shall get a very clear bird's eye view of the method in which messages are received and transmitted. Here, man, like the watchful spider, sits centered within his radiating web, and 'lives along the line'. Beneath us runs a sweep of counter forming three sides of a quadrangle, divided into compartments of about a square yard, by green curtains. A desk and printed forms, to be filled up, are placed in each of these isolated cells, towards which we see individuals immediately make, and then bury themselves, being for the time profoundly intent upon the printed form.

We all know the jocose excuse of the correspondent for having written a long letter – that he had not time to make it shorter. And truly it requires some art to be laconic enough to satisfy the pocket in this establishment. Let us watch for instance yonder youth: he seems to have filled his sheet very close – now he gives it in to the receiving clerk, and something evidently is wrong, for he looks perplexed – it is some hitch about the charge, for his attention is directed to the scale of prices printed at the head of the paper.

> 'Messages (not exceeding 20 words) can be sent between all the principal towns in Great Britain at a charge of 1*s*. within a circuit of 50 miles, of 2*s*. 6*d.* within a circuit of 100 miles (geographical distance), and of 5*s*. beyond a circuit of 100 miles, with an additional sum of 6*d.* porterage within half a mile of the station.'

'Economy', says a French writer, M. de Courcy, 'teaches conciseness. The telegraphic style banishes all the forms of politeness. "May I ask you to do me the favour" is 6*d.* for a distance of 50 miles.' How many of those fond adjectives therefore must our poor fellow relentlessly strike out to bring his billet down to a reasonable charge! What food for speculation each person affords, as he writes his hurried epistle, dictated either by fear, or greed, or more powerful love! – for we have not yet got into the habit of employing the telegraph like the Americans, on the mere everyday business of life. Every message – and of these there are 350,000 transmitted by this Company yearly for the public, and upwards of 3,500,000 for the Railways – is faithfully copied, and put by in fire-proof safes – those sent by the Recording Telegraph being wound in tape-like lengths upon a roller, and appearing exactly like discs of sarcenet ribbon. Fancy some future Macaulay rummaging among such a store, and painting therefrom the salient features of the social and commercial life of England in the nineteenth century. If from the Household-book of the Duke of Northumberland, or still later, from the Paston Letters, we can catch such glimpses of the manners of an early age, what might not be gathered some day in the twenty-first century from a record of the correspondence of an entire people?

'Softly, softly', interposes the Secretary of the Company, 'we have no such intention of gratifying posterity, for after a certain brief period all copies of communications are destroyed. No person unconnected with the office is under any consideration allowed to have access to them, and the servants of the Company are under a bond not to divulge "the secrets of the prison house".' Very good as far as the present generation is concerned, nevertheless it is devoutly to be wished that an odd box or two of these sarcenet ribbons, with their linear language, may escape for future Rawlinsons to puzzle over and decipher for the instruction of mankind.

Whilst we have been thus speculating, however, a dozen messages for all parts of the kingdom have successively ascended through the long lift before us, to the instrument rooms, of which there are two, situated in the attics of the establishment, on either side of the top gallery of the central hall: – these, to carry out our anatomical simile, might be called the two hemispheres of the establishment's cerebrum. The instruments of one of these rooms are worked by youths, while those of the other are manipulated by young ladies; and it seems to us as though the directors were pitting them against each other – establishing a kind of industrial tournament – to see which description of labourer is worthiest. As yet little or no difference can be detected: this however is in itself a triumph for the fair sex, as it proves their capacity for a species of employment well calculated for their habits and physical powers, and opens another door for that superabundance of female labour of a superior kind which has hitherto sought employment in vain.

Click, click, go the needles on every hand as we enter. Here we see the iron tongues of the telegraph wagging, and talking as fast as a tea-table full of old maids. London is holding communication with Manchester. Plymouth is listening attentively to a long story, and every now and then intimates by a slight movement that he perfectly comprehends. But there is one speaker whose nimble tongue seems to be saying important things by the stir around him – that is *the Hague* whispering underneath the North Sea the news he has heard an hour or so ago from Vienna of a great victory just gained by the Turks. We are witness to a series of conversations carried on with all corners of the island, and between the metropolis of the world and every capital of northern and central Europe, as intimately as though the speakers were bending their heads over the dinner table and talking confidentially to the host. And by what agency is this extraordinary conversation carried on? All that the visitor sees is a number of little mahogany cases, very similar to those of American clocks, each having a dial with two lozenge-shaped needles working by pivots, which hang, when at rest, perpendicularly upon it. Two dependent handles, situated at the base of this instrument, which the operator grasps and moves from side to side at his will, suffice to make and break the currents or reverse them, and consequently to deflect the needles either to the right or left. Two little stops of ivory are placed about half an inch apart, on either side of the needle, to prevent its deflecting too much, and to check all vibration. It is the sound of the iron tongue striking against these stops that makes the clicking, and to which the telegraphists are sensitively alive. In the early days of telegraphy the operator's attention, at all the stations, was drawn to the instrument, by the sudden ringing of an alarum, which was effected by the agency of an electro magnet; but the horrid din it occasioned became insupportable to persons in constant attendance, and this part of the instrument was speedily given up, the clicking of the needle being found quite sufficient to draw his attention to the arrival or passing of a message. We say *or passing* of a message, because when a communication is made, as for instance, between London and Edinburgh, the needles of all the telegraph stations on the line are simultaneously deflected, but the attendant has only to take notice of what is going on when a special signal is made to his particular locality, informing him that *he* is spoken with. A story is told of a certain somnolent station clerk, who, in order to enjoy his nap, trained his terrier to scratch and awaken him at the first sound of the clicking needles.

There are but two kinds of telegraph used by the Company, the Needle Telegraph and a few of the Chemical Recording Telegraph of Bain. The latter instrument strikes the spectator more perhaps than the nimble working needle apparatus, but its action is equally simple. Slits of variable length representing letters, according to the alphabet in the note,[1] are punched out from a long strip of paper called the message-strip, which is placed between a revolving cylinder and a toothed spring. The battery is connected with the cylinder; the wire, which goes from station to station, is joined to the spring. As dry paper is a non-conductor, no electricity passes while the unpierced portion of the message-slip interposes between the cylinder and the tooth; but when the tooth drops into a space and comes in contact with the cylinder the current flows. If we now transfer our attention to the station at which the message is received we find a similar cylinder revolving at a regular rate, and a metal pin, depending from the end of the telegraph-wire, pressing upon it; but in this case the paper between the cylinder and the pin has been washed with a solution of prussiate of potash, which electricity has the effect of changing to Prussian blue at the point where the pin touches it. Therefore, as the chemically-prepared paper moves under the pin, a blue line is formed of the same length as the slits at the other end, which regulate the duration of the electric current; and thus every letter punched upon the message-strip is faithfully transferred to its distant fellow. Such is the celerity with which the notation is transmitted by this method, that 'in an experiment performed by M. Le Verrier and Dr. Lardner before Committees of the Institute and the Legislative Assembly at Paris, dispatches were sent 1000 miles at the rate of nearly 20,000 words an hour.' In ordinary practice, however, the speed is limited to the rate at which an expert clerk can punch out the holes, which is not much above a hundred per minute. Where the object was to forward long documents, such as a speech, a number of persons could be employed simultaneously in punching out different portions of the message, and the message-strips would then be supplied as fast as the machine could work.

This system is used on 1199 miles in America. A weaker current of electricity than what is required for deflecting needles or magnetising iron, suffices to effect the requisite chemical decomposition. The conducting power of vapour or rain carries much of the electricity from the wires in certain states of the atmosphere, 'and in such cases, where both Morse's and Bain's telegraphs are used by an amalgamated company in the same office, it is found convenient to remove the wires from Morse's instruments and connect them with Bain's, on which it is practicable to operate when communication by Morse's system is interrupted.'

This Chemical Telegraph has also the advantage, in common with all recording instruments, that it leaves an indelible record of every message transmitted, and therefore is very useful when the mistake of a single figure or letter might be of consequence, which we will illustrate by a case which happened very lately. A stockbroker in the City received, during a very agitated state of the funds, an order to buy for a client in a distant part of the country, by a certain time of the day, 80,000*l.* of Consols. This order being unusually large for the individual, the broker doubted its accuracy, and immediately made inquiries at the office. The message had luckily been sent by the recording instrument, and upon looking at the record it was immediately seen that the order was for 8,000*l.* – the transcriber having put in an 0 too much, for which, according to the rules of the Company, he was incontinently fined. Now here the error was immediately traced to the person who made it, and there was no need of telegraphing back to inquire if all were right, two matters of vital importance in such a transaction as this, involving so much personal responsibility, for if the purchase had been made and turned out unfortunate, the loss would indubitably have fallen upon the unhappy sharebroker.

In all ordinary transactions, however, the needle instrument is preferable, because it transmits its messages much more quickly. The speed with which the attendants upon these instruments read off the signals made by the needles is really marvellous: they do not in some cases even wait to spell the words letter by letter, but jump at the sentence before it is concluded, and they have learned by practice, as Sir Francis Head says in 'Stokers and Pokers', to recognise immediately who is telegraphing to them, say at York, by the peculiar *expression of the needles* – the long drawn wires thus forming a kind of human antennæ by which individual peculiarities of touch are projected to an infinite distance. To catalogue the kind of messages which pass through the room, either on their way from London or in course of distribution to it, would be to give a history of human affairs. Here, from the shores of this tight island, comes the morning news gathered by watchers, telescopes in hand, on remote headlands, of what ships have just hove in sight, or what craft have foundered or come ashore – to this room, swifter beyond comparison than the carrier-dove of old, the wire speeds the name of the winner of the Derby or the Oaks. How the four winds are blowing throughout the island; how Stocks rise or fall every hour of the day in all the great towns and in the continental capitals; what corn is at Mark Lane, and what farmer Giles got a quarter of an hour since in a country town in Yorkshire, are equally known in the telegraph room. Intermixed with quotations of tallow and the price of Wall's End coals, now and then comes a love-billet, which excites no more sympathy in the clerk than in the iron that conveys it; or a notice that the sudden dart of death has struck some distant friend is transmitted and received as unconcernedly as an account of the fall in Russian Stock. When business is slack the telegraphists sometimes amuse themselves by an interchange of badinage with their distant friends. Sir

Francis Head informs us that an absolute quarrel once took place by telegraph, and the two irritated manipulators were obliged to be separated in consequence.

In addition to this Private Message department there is, below stairs, an Intelligence Office, in which news published in the London morning papers is condensed and forwarded to the Exchanges of Liverpool, Bristol, Manchester, Glasgow, &c. A few years since the Company opened subscription rooms in all the large towns of the North, in which intelligence of every kind was posted immediately after its arrival in London; but the craving for early intelligence was not sufficient to induce the people to incur the expense, and, with the exception of the room at Hull, the establishments have all been shut up.

On Friday evening especially this department is very busy condensing for the country papers the news which appears in that exciting column headed By Electric Telegraph, London, 2 A.M. Thus the telegraph rides express through the night for the broad sheets of the entire kingdom, and even steps across from Portpatrick to Donaghadee into the sister country, with its budget of latest intelligence, by which means the extremities of the two islands are kept as well *up* in the progress of important events as London itself. Upwards of 120 provincial papers each receive in this manner their column of parliamentary news of the night, and the Daily Mail published in Glasgow gets sometimes as much as three columns of the Debates forwarded whilst the House is sitting. A superintendent and four clerks are expressly employed in this department; and early in the day towards the end of the week the office presents all the appearance of an Editor's room. At seven in the morning the clerks are to be seen deep in the Times and other Daily papers, just hot from the press, making extracts, and condensing into short paragraphs all the most important events, which are immediately sent off to the country papers to form 'Second Editions'. Neither does the work cease here, for no sooner is a second edition published in town, than its news, if of more than ordinary interest, is transmitted to the provinces. For instance, whilst we were in the Company's telegraph room a short time since, the following intelligence was being served out to Liverpool, York, Manchester, Leeds, Bristol, Birmingham, and Hull: –

> 'EASTERN WAR – BATTLE ON THE DANUBE – FROM EVENING EDITION OF THE MORNING CHRONICLE.
>
> '*Vienna, Saturday, April 8th.*
>
> 'The journal Fremden Blatt announces, under date of Bucharest, 4th April, that a great battle was being fought at Rassova, about midway between Hirsova and Silistria, in the Dobrudscha. The result was not known. Mustapha Pasha is at the head of 50,000 men.'

Arrived at the above-mentioned places, swifter than a rocket could fly the distance, like a rocket it bursts and is again carried by the diverging wires into a dozen neighbouring towns. The announcement we have quoted comes opportunely to remind us that intelligence, thus hastily gathered and transmitted, has also its drawbacks, and is not so trustworthy as the news which starts later and travels slower. The 'great battle of Rassova' has not yet been fought, and the general action announced through the telegraph was only a sanguinary skirmish.

The telegraphic organization of London, meagre as it is at present, would form alone a curious paper: 'a province covered with houses', it demands a special arrangement, and accordingly we see day by day new branches opened within its precincts, by which means every part of the metropolis is being put in communication with the country and Europe.

Note

1

a -	*f* — —	*k* - — — -	*q* — - — -	*x* — - - —
b - — -	*g* - — - -	*l* - —	*r* —	*y* — - —
c — - -	*h* — — —	*m* - — - —	*s* — -	*z* — - - -
d - - —	*i* – - - -	*n* - — —	*t* – —	
e – –	*j* - - — - -	*o* - - - -	*u* - - - - -	
		p - - — -	*v* — — -	
			w — — - -	

34

ANTHONY TROLLOPE, 'THE YOUNG WOMEN AT THE TELEGRAPH OFFICE' [EXTRACT]

Good Words (1877), pp. 377–381

Eight hundred young women at work, all in one room, all looking comfortable, most of them looking pretty, earning fair wages at easy work, – work fit for women to do, work at which they can sit and rest and not be weary, with a kitchen at hand and a hot dinner in the middle of the day, with leave of absence without stoppage of pay every year, with a doctor for sickness, and a pension for old age and incompetence, – for the young women as years roll on will become old, – with only eight hours of work, never before eight in the morning and never after eight at night, with female superintendents, and the chance of rising to be a superintendent open to each girl! Is not that the kind of institution that philanthropic friends of the weaker sex have been looking for and desiring for years? What would Hood have thought of such an institution when he sang his 'Song of the Shirt', – what those beneficent friends of distressed incompetent governesses who are using all their efforts so nobly to provide bread for poor females in distant lands? And all this in a government office, under government surveillance, which, in this country, is of all surveillance the most tender, – though there be and ever will be grumblers. That such surveillance is tender will, I think, be admitted when I have described the position of these eight hundred females. And all this has sprung into existence during the last eight years! By those who have watched the efforts made for female employment in other branches of business, at printing, for instance, and watchmaking, sometimes with but moderate effects, sometimes with heartrending failure, will not this be welcomed as a great success?

The Civil Service of the country has been a rock of safety to very many men, a haven of refuge when no other haven could be reached. And it is so still, in spite of that great barrier at the mouth of the harbour which we call competitive examination. There is a security in it, an absence of cruelty, a justice, a clemency leaning a little too much, perhaps, to the side of faulty servants, a philanthropy and consideration forced upon it, both by its magnitude and its publicity, which no other employment can enjoy to the same extent. If we put aside the question of direct remuneration – the amount of salary paid – and look to the other circumstances of

DOI: 10.4324/9781315400303-47

a clerk's position, we shall find that the man employed by the Crown has shorter hours of labour and longer hours of absence than he who is in private service, that he has an infinitely stronger right to his position, that he is less likely to be dismissed from personal dislike, less liable to arbitrary punishment, more gently considered in illness, and very much more generously treated in regard to pension. Eight years ago all these good things were enjoyed only by the stronger sex. Luckily the stronger sex is prone to take a wife to itself in prosperous circumstances, and in this way the benefits became common to men and women. But the stronger sex does not always take a wife – does not do so quite so often as it ought – sometimes cannot afford to do so till middle life. And therefore women have not had quite their share of government nourishment. But when we see eight hundred women at work in one room – eight hundred female government clerks – we feel that something has been done for them.

Everybody knows the General Post-Office in St. Martin's-le-Grand, near St. Paul's. Everybody knows that there are now two great post-offices at the same place, facing each other, the elder one having been found altogether insufficient for the purposes required, though when it was first opened, about forty-five years years ago, it was supposed to be absurdly too large for any possible requirements which the country could have for such a building. Those who pass from Cheapside into Newgate Street after the lamps have been lighted may observe, on looking up, that the whole top floor of this new building is illuminated. It is here that the eight hundred young women are at work, and their business consists in the receipt and dispatch of telegraph messages.

The work on which they are all engaged is performed in one large room, – a room that appears to be low because of its great size but which is in truth of considerable altitude, and is lighted by roof-windows. I wish I could say that it is well ventilated; – but that difficulty of giving a sufficiency of fresh air without too much of it to a large body of men or women working together has not as yet been solved at the Telegraph Office. Open the windows, is the easy solution to which the unpractised ventilating theorist would come; yes, or take off the roof, and you certainly would get plenty of fresh air. But these eight hundred human beings – here there are many more than eight hundred – are tender subjects, who, as to their own immediate perceptions, are much more affected by cold than by unwholesome air. The difficulty in ventilation consists very much in this, – that the person to be ventilated does not know that he wants ventilation. You shall find five travellers in a railway carriage – you, joining them suddenly as an unhappy sixth – who do not know that they are being smothered. Tell them so, and they will bitterly resent your interference. Remain with them for an hour, and you shall not know that you are being smothered yourself. These eight hundred lady friends of mine require some process of ventilation of which they themselves shall be kept in ignorance. It is to be hoped that some such process may soon be found.

This great room is divided, something like a church, into transepts and naves; such, at least, is the first idea, though the form of it when studied does, in fact, assume the shape of a great letter **H**. It contains an area of very nearly two thousand feet, and those who are curious in statistics may be glad to know that the length of the instrument desks amounts to two thousand four hundred feet. Though it is all one room, it has its well-marked divisions, its east end and its west end; and thus the Indian telegrams and the foreign telegrams are no more mixed up with the Liverpool and Glasgow business, or those with the internal metropolitan telegrams, than is Grosvenor Square with the Victoria Docks, or Regent's Park with Kennington Oval. It is a 'mighty maze', and certainly appears so to the stranger when he first finds himself among all these young women, but he soon finds that it is 'not without a plan'.

The stranger, if he be at all such a stranger as I was, will think a great deal more about the young women than the telegraphy. To those who are the masters in the place, who have used their skill and science in concentrating so much that is useful in one place, and who are thoroughly aware of the importance of the interests which are confided to their charge, the security and expedition and cheapness of the messages are, of course, the points of attraction. To me it was the condition of the girls – their appearance, their welfare, their respectability, their immediate comfort, their future prospects, their coming husbands, their capabilities, their utility, and their appropriateness in that place – or inappropriateness. The reader may, therefore, know at once that he will learn nothing from me about telegraphy; whether he will learn anything about the telegraph girls I will not say, but it is my ambition to tell him something. Even those prolonged iron spouts down which came and up which went the metropolitan messages, which are not communicated by wires but which are dispatched bodily by atmospheric pressure within two miles of the building at the rate of about thirty miles per hour, did not interest me much, because they are waited upon by boys and not by young women.

My first point of interest in the matter was to know how the girls got there. Though there be at present eight hundred of them – the actual total in the principal office is eight hundred and forty-three – even though there were eight thousand there would certainly be great competition for the service. And then of those who would want to be employed so many would be unfit! And then again, that question of character – what we may call respectability – is one much more difficult among women than men, but one which so imperatively demands to be asked and answered. A young man of bad character will do harm to his associates – very great harm; but he will not be held to be so fatally noxious as a young woman of bad character among those who are pure. Mothers and fathers, if they will think of their own children, will feel that it is so. They are anxious no doubt to keep their sons from evil contact; but for their girls – ! I felt at once that it was a very delicate matter – this of selecting these young women for the public service.

And then what did the girls do when they were there? Of course they would send messages and receive them – more or less expeditiously, according to the adroitness of their fingers, eyes, ears, and intellects. But it is not only the work which is done by any great mass of persons working together which is interesting, but all that which must necessarily be done beyond the work. For mere production, a well-arranged machine is more interesting perhaps than a human being.

They who look only to what labourers can be made to produce are too apt to regard these living souls as though they were wound up by some key or windlass, or set in motion by the power of heat, and that they would so do a certain fixed task, and that then there would be an end of them. To me, when I have seen a half-naked, brawny puddler turning the iron, or a miner digging out the gold-containing rock, or the ploughman in his tucked-up frock striving to drive his furrows straight and deep, I have felt more interest in the man's willingness to serve, or in his mutiny, in his conversation, if I could hear what he was talking, or even in his silence, in the expenditure of his wages, in his bread-and-cheese and beer, in his hilarity or sadness as he sits during his allotted minutes of idleness with his pipe in his mouth, than I have in the profit or loss accruing from his work. And so with these girls. There were the messages to send and receive – of course. But what else was there done in that large room? Did they talk? Oh! – if I could only know what those two pretty girls in the distance were talking about! – not from curiosity, but that I might judge somewhat of their inward natures, – whether they were good or bad, happy or unhappy, pure or impure. They looked to be good, and happy, and pure; and I thought to myself that I should like to take them to the Zoological Gardens, and to make them feed the bears and ride upon the elephant, and then to hear what they would have to say about Madame Tussaud's horrors, and after that to give them their dinners and send them home happy. As I was thinking of all this, the newest system of telegraphy by sound was being clearly and skilfully explained to me; – but I did not pay by any means as much attention as I ought to have done to the new system, so much was my attention taken up with those two pretty girls – and with others.

And what was their conduct generally? I found it difficult to frame my questions so as not to betray any improper curiosity. But I was very anxious to know whether they – flirted, for there are young men in the same room. I thought that had I been a young man there I might have been tempted. As far as I could judge by looking round, there did not seem to be anything of the kind. And then, in other respects, how did they behave themselves? Were they punctual, attentive, and obedient? Was it often necessary to punish them, and, if so, in what manner? Were there frequent dismissals?

And then what did they get – what in immediate money, what in prospects, what in comforts, what in privileges, what in respectability? They were all then, of course, congregated in that one room, and busy in accommodating the instant haste of a hurrying world, only for the sake of what they could get. Was it enough to make them happy and comfortable; enough to give them plenty to eat, and decent rooms to live in? I could see that they were all nicely dressed; but when a large number of girls have come together, each girl will spend her last sixpence in dress rather than be less well accoutred than her neighbours.

And how did they live at home? As to that I knew that I could learn very little. With their parents, generally, I hoped. But there must have been many there whose parents were at a distance – many orphans – many so far alone in the world as to have to look out for their own lives as most young men are called upon to do.

These would come and go to and from their offices independently, as do the clerks in the Treasury or War Office. What sort of life do they make of it?

As I had imagined, I found the competition for the situation to be very great. Who does not know how many girls there are, somewhat above the rank of domestic service, who have been taught their three Rs with more or less success, and to whom there comes early in life the necessity of either earning their bread or else of eating very little bread? Indeed, for what service, especially for what government service, is there not competition? Great efforts have been made to do away with the horrors of competitive patronage, that is with the giving away of situations by favouritism. These horrors need to be the more horrid because the favouritism displayed was not generally that of open friendship but of political adherence. Active manipulators of votes in small boroughs, or even in large cities, would think themselves entitled to a proportion of these favours, and the distributors of patronage would find themselves unable to resist the claims made upon them. This was bad on all sides, but to none was it so bad as to those who were obliged to distribute the prizes. Had they nothing to give, they would be asked for nothing. But while the bestowal of these gifts was a necessity to them, there was no resisting the political cormorants who had supported them, or who would hereafter support them in their political combats. It was this feeling, I think, even more than the desire for increased educational excellence, which prompted our official chieftains to open the public service generally to competitive examination, so that they might rid themselves of the incubus of patronage. For almost any clerkship in the Civil Service almost any aspirant may now compete.

But in regard to these young women, a nomination is still made by some officer high in the department. I will not name Lord A. or Sir C. B., lest the unfortunate official pundit should be at once overwhelmed with applications by young ladies who read GOOD WORDS. As vacancies occur from six to a dozen are nominated together, and the fortunate ones – not as yet quite fortunate – have to submit themselves on a fixed day to the tender mercies of Sir George Dasent and the other official examiners at Westminster. They are examined in reading, writing, and arithmetic, and if they come up to a given standard then they are appointed on probation. But in addition to this there must have been medical approval, and for this and other purposes the telegraph department keeps a doctor of its own. And references are made as to character to three householders. In regard to these references we cannot but feel how hard it would be – how almost impossible – for any tender-hearted householder not to say a kind word.

But after the terrors of the examination there are the subsequent terrors of the telegraph school. It is to be understood that no girl is allowed to enter after eighteen, and that they may become candidates at fourteen, so that the schooling is for the most part undergone at an age appropriate for tuition. The school is in Telegraph Street, near Moorgate Street, and here telegraphy is inculcated for a period of two or three months. If a poor girl cannot learn the art, there is an end of the matter. If by that time she has gone so far as to show that she probably will learn it, she is sent to the big room at the top of the building in St. Martin's-le-Grand.

Here she begins to receive wages. During these school days she receives nothing, nor does she perform any service, but she receives her tuition gratis.

On her first entrance into the great world of the telegraph office – that which is to be her world till she becomes a married woman, or during her life of celibacy – she is put in possession of 8*s*. a week. But at this period she is hardly of much use as a telegraphist. During half her day she still undergoes instruction, performing light services about the office for the other half. Then, when she is declared to be competent, she is seated proudly at her table, becomes a full-fledged government clerk, and is made the mistress of a weekly stipend of 12*s*.

From this time her duty consists in sending and receiving telegrams, or rather in passing on the telegrams which other public servants have received in other parts of the world. A telegram, for instance, from New Zealand to the Brazils would pass through this room – or from Hammersmith to Poplar, or from San Francisco to Sydney, or from Liverpool to Southampton. But no one desiring to send a message goes here, nor are the messenger boys dispatched by these young women. They live secluded and apart, in a world of their own, harassed by no interruptions from without, and might, for aught that they feel in the matter, be accelerating communications from one star to another. As I have said before, it is not my purpose here to explain the various systems of telegraphy used, but there are two distinct modes – very distinct as far as the aptitudes and capabilities of the young women are concerned: that, namely, by eye, and that by ear. The former may be learned almost by any one who can learn to read – though, as some pupils can read well and rapidly, while others hardly get beyond an elementary use of their letters, so, of course, it will be with those who learn the alphabet of the wires. The second system, that by ear, can only be acquired by those whose organs of hearing are subtle and appreciative. And as there is a preference at present for those tinkling sounds by which words can be noted coming from a distance of as many thousand miles as the world is round – as there is less labour and cost in this method, the clerk receiving the sounds without any interposition of marked paper – they who are so gifted are held to be the most useful. No difference in pay is made, nor has it been acknowledged to me that the ear-gifted girl is better off than she who is less fortunate; but I cannot but think that higher capability will in the long run lead to higher rewards in the Telegraph Office, as in all other positions.

After three years of service the wages average 16*s*. a week, and then it is supposed that the girl is fully able to support herself, that is, she can then pay, not only for her clothes and her food, but an adequate proportion of the other expenses of the home she may occupy. Of the total number employed I found that the average wages were at the period of my inquiry 18*s*. a week, and that the maximum wages of those working at the desks were 30*s*. The wages are paid once a fortnight, on every alternate Friday. The average will of course become higher than it is at present, as the whole thing is new, having been commenced in the service of the Crown within the last eight years. The greater number of the girls live with their families, and not unfrequently two or three sisters are employed together. I was assured that in many cases these girls had thus become the support of their parents. There are thirty female superintendents at higher salaries, and to these offices the clerks are of course eligible; and there is one matron over them all, to whom I presume is confided those delicate questions as to propriety and discipline at which I have hinted.

4.3

Telephone

DOI: 10.4324/9781315400303-48

4.3 Telephone

'The Telephone' [extract], *Westminster Review*, 53 (1878), pp. 208–211.
'The Telephone: A Domestic Tragedy', *Temple Bar*, 107 (1896), pp. 106–110.
Arthur Mee, 'The Pleasure Telephone', *Strand Magazine* (1898), pp. 208–214.

As the earliest of a series of new, nineteenth-century communication technologies to appear and become established, the electric telegraph shaped the discussion of technologies to follow. Writing soon after the invention of the telephone, the *Westminster Review* introduces this new form of communication by comparing it to the telegraph, assuming that its readers will be long familiar with that device. The author of this piece anticipates readers' questions: are the electric signals discontinuous, like the pulse of a telegraph message? Do you have to be an expert or learn a special code in order to use a telephone?

Despite the Victorians' interest in telephony, late-Victorian Britain adopted the telephone more slowly than did many countries in Europe and North America. Perhaps the most significant factor behind the lag was the recent nationalisation of the domestic telegraph system. In contrast to the profitable Penny Post, the new postal telegraph system was losing money because the charges for sending telegrams had been set artificially low. This meant that customers had access to cheap, rapid communication via telegram, while the post office had little appetite – and few financial resources – for constructing or acquiring another electric communication network. Instead, an assortment of private telephone companies with disparate equipment and charges arose to cover different localities. Even once these companies consolidated, the status of the telephone in Britain did not greatly improve until after 1912, when the post office effectively nationalised telephony.

Although it was not yet a popular technology, the telephone did begin to appear in late-Victorian offices, in public places and – as its comic possibilities began to emerge – in light literature. Two decades after its first appearance, the domestic telephone became the cause of semi-farcical tragedy in a short story from the periodical *Temple Bar* – an example of what might be the first depiction of someone distracted by constantly checking her phone. The fact that the telephone was well-known but not yet widely adopted probably also helped to inspire excited reflections about its potential future. The journalist and editor Arthur Mee looked forward to the use of the telephone as a democratic medium that would transmit news and entertainment into every household. Despite efforts in Hungary and in London to create such a role for telephony, it was really in a later medium that this model of audio broadcast as a mass medium would be realised: radio.[1]

Note

1 A useful starting point for reading about the telephone and other 'new' electric communication technologies in their nineteenth-century contexts remains Carolyn Marvin, *When Old Technologies Were New: Thinking about Electric Communication in the Late Nineteenth Century* (Oxford: Oxford University Press, 1988). On the telephone in Britain before the post office largely took over the industry, see Charles R. Perry, 'The British Experience 1876–1912: The Impact of the Telephone During the Years of Delay', in *The Social Impact of the Telephone*, ed. Ithiel de Sola Pool (Cambridge, MA: MIT Press, 1977), pp. 69–96. For more on early telephone 'broadcasts', see Asa Briggs, 'The Pleasure Telephone: A Chapter in the Prehistory of Media', in *The Social Impact of the Telephone*, ed. I. Pool, pp. 40–65.

35

'THE TELEPHONE' [EXTRACT]

Westminster Review, 53 (1878), pp. 208–211

Of all modern inventions connected with the transmission of telegraphic signals, the telephone, devised by Mr. Alexander Graham Bell, has excited the most widespread interest and wonder. Wherever Mr. Bell has appeared before the public to give an account of his invention and the researches which have led up to it, crowds have assembled to hear him. Nor is this astonishing; for the telephone professes not only to convey intelligible signals to great distances without the use of a battery, but to transmit in facsimile the tones of the human voice, so that a voice shall be as certainly recognised when heard over a distance of a few hundreds of miles as if its owner were speaking in the room by our side. And the telephone does not fall short of its profession. Scientific men have had their wonder and curiosity aroused even more than the unscientific public, since a scientific man appreciates the enormous difficulties to be overcome before such an instrument can be realised. Had any hardy speculator a few years ago proposed a telephone which should act on the principle, and be constructed in the form, of Mr. Bell's instrument, he would probably have been considered a lunatic. The effects are so marvellous; the exciting causes at first sight so entirely inadequate to produce them. For a telephonic message differs as widely from an ordinary telegraphic message as a highly finished oil-painting differs from a page of print. In the one you have only white and black, black symbols on a white ground, the symbols being limited in number, and recurring again and again with mere differences of order. The painting, on the other hand, discloses every variety of colour and arrangement. No sharp lines of discontinuity offend the eye; on the contrary, the tints shade off gradually and softly into each other, presenting tone and depth in endless variety. The page of print is unintelligible without the aid of a key; the painting tells its story plainly enough to any one who has eyes to see.

Let us inquire for a moment what is the nature of the apparatus which we have been using for the last thirty or forty years for the transmission of telegraphic signals. The instruments chiefly employed have been the single-needle telegraph and the Morse instrument. In the former a coil of wire surrounds a magnetised needle, which is suspended in a vertical position. When an electrical current passes through the coil, the needle is deflected, to right or left, according to the direction of the current. The sender by means of a handle can pass either positive

DOI: 10.4324/9781315400303-49

or negative currents into the circuit. The right and left deflections of the needle are combined in various ways to form the letters of the alphabet, and the letters form words. Thus at the sending station a message is broken up into little bits, each bit or part of a bit transmitted separately, and the process of building these up again performed at the receiving station. Some of the letters of the alphabet are indicated by a single movement of the needle, that is, by a single current; for others, as many as four are required.

In the Morse instrument only one current is utilised, which may be either positive or negative, and the requisite variety is obtained by allowing the current to pass through the circuit for a longer or shorter interval. The essential part of the instrument consists of an electro-magnet with an iron armature attached to one end of a lever. At the other end of the lever is a pointer or pencil, and a paper ribbon moves at a constant rate in front of the end of the pointer. When the coils of the electro-magnet are traversed by a current, the iron armature is attracted, and the pointer comes in contact with the paper ribbon, on which it makes a mark, long or short, according to the duration of the current. Thus are produced the dots and dashes. These are combined in a similar way to the right and left movements of the needle in the needle instrument. In some of the more refined instruments letters are indicated and even printed directly at the receiving station. This is of course a great simplification; but with such arrangements we cannot have more than this. The page of print represents the limit of what such instruments and methods can do for us. It is true that a skilled operator with the Morse instrument can interpret the signals as they arrive without looking at the marks on the paper, simply by using his ears. Every time the circuit is made or broken a click is heard, and long practice has taught him to rely on the evidence of his ears with as much confidence as one less accustomed to the work would trust his eyes. Nevertheless he hears only a succession of clicks, which must be interpreted before they become intelligible to any one but himself.

In these forms of apparatus, it will be observed, the currents are intermittent; each current, circulating through the coil, is followed by an interval of rest. They begin and end abruptly, and all perform the same kind of work; that is, they deflect a needle, or produce marks on a piece of paper. Telephonic currents, on the other hand, rise and fall, ebb and flow, change in intensity within comparatively wide limits, but preserve their continuity so long as continuous sounds are being uttered in the neighbourhood of the telephone. They are called undulatory currents, to distinguish them from the intermittent currents of the ordinary telegraphic apparatus; and their peculiar character is an essential feature of the telephone.

No skill or training is required for the effective use of the telephone. The operator has merely to press the instrument to his ear to hear distinctly every sound transmitted from the distant end. For this, it is true, an effort of attention is required, and some persons use the instrument at the first trial with more success than others. Individuals differ in the facility with which they are able to concentrate their attention on one ear, so as to be practically insensible to what goes on around them. But this habit of attention is readily acquired, and when it is once acquired, the telephone may be used by any one who has ears to hear and a tongue to speak. In sending a message, the instrument is held about an inch in front of the mouth, and the sender merely talks into the mouth-piece in his ordinary natural manner. The words are repeated by the instrument at the other end of the circuit with the same pitch, the same cadences, and the same relative loudness. But what strikes one the most is that the *character* of the speaker's voice is faithfully preserved and reproduced. Thus one voice is readily distinguished from another. No peculiarity of inflection is lost. Nor is this result effected over short distances only. No doubt a sentence will be heard with diminishing distinctness as it comes over an increasing distance. In this country experiments have not yet been made, so far as we know, over very long distances; but Mr. Bell states that he carried on a conversation without any difficulty between Boston and New York, 258 miles apart, through an ordinary telegraph wire. A man's breathing was distinctly heard 149 miles away. At the Newport torpedo station, in Rhode Island, speaking was carried on through a line, including five miles of submerged cable and an equal length of land wire. Resistance coils were added, 2000 ohms at a time, until 12,000 ohms were introduced into the circuit, without interfering with the transmission of speech. The importance of this test will be understood when it is remembered that the resistance of the Atlantic cable is equal to 7000 ohms only. The experiments at Newport were continued by the addition of a total resistance of 30,000 ohms, but beyond 12,000 ohms the sound was found to diminish in intensity. Mr. Bell states that the *maximum* amount of resistance through which the undulating current will pass, and yet retain sufficient force to produce an audible sound at the distant end, has yet to be determined. In the laboratory he has conversed through a resistance of 60,000 ohms. There is a practical difficulty in transmitting telephonic signals through a telegraph wire running parallel to a number of other wires which are being used for ordinary telegraphic purposes. Induction currents are produced in the telephone wire, which greatly interfere with the distinctness of the sounds. This difficulty is said to be overcome by having an extra return wire, instead of utilising the earth for a part of the circuit, as is ordinarily done. The two wires are put side by side in close proximity, and the detrimental effect of the inductive currents is thus partially or entirely disposed of.

36

'THE TELEPHONE: A DOMESTIC TRAGEDY'

Temple Bar, 107 (1896), pp. 106–110

Persons represented,
MISS HYPHEN-SMITH, 33.
MR. PAGET, 55.

Scene: A drawing-room in Miss Smith's house near Richmond. In the centre of the room, on a table, is a telephone.

MISS S. (*putting down her book and glancing at clock*). Nearly three, and he said that at three o'clock he would telephone to me from Bristol. What *can* he want to say to me? I – I think – I am nearly sure it must be a proposal. He has been *so* attentive of late. I am sure no one can be less vain than I am, but there has been a look in his eye, a tone in his voice, that is quite unmistakable. (*Looks fondly at telephone.*) What a comfort it is to have a telephone in one's drawing-room! I really don't know how I ever existed without it. If a visitor drops in unexpectedly to dinner and I want a nice little dish of cutlets, I ring up the butcher. If I feel a little low and only a fried sole can tempt my failing appetite, I ring up the fishmonger. The grocer, the butcher, the wine merchant, the livery stables – they are all on the telephone. (*Clock strikes.*) Ah, there's the bell! (*Rushes to telephone and speaks.*) 'Yes; are you there? Is that you, Captain Vavasour? Yes; are you there?' There's no one there, and yet I hear some one speaking in the distance, a faint buzzing like a bee in a bottle. (*Rings off and glances at clock.*) Just three. It was the clock striking, and I thought it was the telephone bell. (*Sits – ring at the bell – she jumps up.*) There it is again! Oh no, it's the door-bell this time (*goes to window*), and there's Mr. Paget coming in – provoking! I should have said, 'Not at home'; too late now, and he *must* come in here; I can't leave the telephone! Not that I don't like Mr. Paget; I like him very much. I might have preferred him to Captain Vavasour, but I have never seen any tendency in *him* to propose to me. Dear me, it's very awkward to have a visitor in the room when I'm expecting a telephonic proposal, and mean to accept it, at the top of my voice! (*Enter Mr. Paget.*)

 DOI: 10.4324/9781315400303-50

MR. P. (*he is very nervous and flurried*). How do you do, Miss Smith? – beg your pardon, Hyphen-Smith. Er – er – lovely day, isn't it?

MISS S. (*shaking hands with effusion*). So *glad* to see you; here is your favourite chair. Let me put your hat down in its accustomed corner.

MR. P. (*aside*). She is really a most charming woman. I wonder if she'll be surprised when I ask her to marry me. It's a little difficult to lead up to, but I like to get these awkward things over quickly. (*Aloud, nervous.*) Ahem – my dear Miss Smith – Hyphen-Smith – I – (*telephone bell rings; she rushes to it*). Confound it, what's that? what's she doing?

MISS S. (*at telephone*). Yes; are you there? What? Is that Captain – Mr. *who?* I can't hear; speak louder. What? what? Six gross of screws? don't keep screws. Who do you want? No, I'm forty-six.

MR. P. Impossible!

MISS S. What? *what?* Well, another time when you want sixty-four don't ring up forty-six! (*Rings off in disgust and sits down.*)

MR. P. My dear Miss Smith, may I ask what that instrument of torture is, and why you are shouting at it?

MISS S. Why, have you never seen a telephone?

MR. P. I suppose I've seen them in offices, but I've never met a – a domesticated telephone – (*aside*) hope I never shall again. (*Aloud.*) I don't care for these new-fangled things; I'm an old-fashioned fellow. Don't you find it a confounded nuisance?

MISS S. No, *indeed!* It's the greatest comfort I possess. (*Clock strikes; she jumps up, then sits.*)

MR. P. Don't you find it a little jumpy? bad for the nerves, eh?

MISS S. Not in the least; most soothing.

MR. P. (*nervous*). My dear Miss Smith – Hyphen-Smith – you – you will be surprised to hear what brought me here to-day.

MISS S. (*absently, looking at telephone*). Cab, I suppose.

MR. P. You will be surprised to hear –

MISS S. (*absent*). Oh, not at all.

MR. P. Eh? I had no idea you had guessed my secret.

MISS S. Secret? what secret? Oh, I beg your pardon, I didn't quite catch what you were saying. I – I was listening for the telephone.

MR. P. (*aside*). Confound the telephone!

MISS S. (*aside, glancing anxiously at clock*). He said about three, and now it's nearly twenty minutes past; surely he must ring me up soon.

MR. P. Well, as I was going to say when the telephone interrupted me, you will hardly have guessed why I came here to-day.

MISS S. (*archly*). Wasn't it to see me?

MR. P. It was, my dear Miss Smith, and –

MISS S. (*laughing*). And to hear the telephone.

MR. P. Apparently. But as I was going to say, it was to tell you – to – to – (*telephone bell rings. Miss S. rushes to it*). Curse the bell!

Miss S. (*at telephone*). Yes; are you there? What? is that you? Captain Vavasour? What? Fish? what fish? I said salmon. *What?* Yes, salmon cutlets. What? No, I didn't! I never said sausages! sausages in July! What? I can't hear. *Salmon cutlets* – S-a-l-m-o-n. Do you hear? Next time you take my orders, please send some one who isn't deaf! (*Rings off and sits down, fuming.*)

Mr. P. (*dryly*). You must find that telephone a great comfort, I am sure. No drawing-room should be without it.

Miss S. It doesn't always go on like this.

Mr. P. I hope not, for the sake of your nerves and your – visitors.

Miss S. Oh, I *am* so sorry; of course it must be very provoking for you, but it isn't my fault, is it? Now sit down and begin again; you were going to tell me something very interesting, I am sure.

Mr. P. (*aside*). I'll make one more attempt, but if I can't get my proposal out before that confounded telephone goes off again I'll give it up, once and for all. (*Aloud.*) My dear Miss Smith – Hyphen-Smith, I am a man of few words.

Miss S. Indeed? (*She listens with perfunctory attention and every sign of impatience, her eyes on the telephone, half starting from her chair at every sound that can suggest a bell.*)

Mr. P. I don't wear my heart upon my sleeve, I keep it in its right place, (*aside*) though it's in my mouth at this moment! (*Aloud.*) I am, as I said before, a man of few words – reticent, taciturn.

Miss S. Yes?

Mr. P. Feeling a great deal, but never saying so – modest, retiring – perhaps you may think me too retiring?

Miss S. Oh no! not at all!

Mr. P. But a man cannot change his nature.

Miss S. Of course not!

Mr. P. I am sure I have kept my secret, that I have never given you reason to think – to imagine – that – in a word, that I – I – do I make myself clear?

Miss S. Oh, perfectly! (*Aside.*) What *is* he talking about? why doesn't he go?

Mr. P. I will be even more explicit. (*Telephone bell rings faintly, she starts up.*) Don't go – it was the clock. In one word, Miss Smith, the feeling I have for you is not friendship.

Miss S. (*her eyes on the telephone*). Oh dear, I am sorry to hear that! why –?

Mr. P. It is more! I ask you to be my (*bell rings loudly, she rushes to telephone*). Damn the bell! *That's* all over!

Miss S. (*at telephone*). Yes? are you there? Are you Captain – what? Speak up, I can't hear! Four-wheeler? no – a Victoria. What? got a fit? the horse? What? not fit? Then why do you keep a Victoria that's not fit to use! (*rings off violently and sits down.*)

Mr. P. This is too bad, Miss Smith – let me tell you this is too much of a good joke! (*Bell rings again, she rushes to telephone*).

Miss S. (*at telephone*). Yes? what? still on? ring off? why did you ever ring on! (*she rings off viciously.*) Ah! (*she falls into a chair and fans herself.*)

MR. P. (*furiously*). Where's my hat? I'm going!

MISS S. Going? why?

MR. P. Because I can't stand it any longer!

MISS S. I'm sure *I've* done all the standing!

MR. P. Don't joke! it's beyond a joke. Do you know what I was going to say to you?

MISS S. The telephone didn't give me a chance.

MR. P. (*with venom*). No, it's lost you a chance! I was going to ask you to marry me – to marry *me*, do you hear?

MISS S. (*starting up with outstretched hands*). To marry me! Oh, Mr. Paget!

MR. P. No, it's too late. I haven't asked, you and I never will now! (*Her hands fall limply to her sides – she listens in crushed silence.*) Never will I ask a woman to marry me who is fool enough to domesticate a tame telephone in her drawing-room! Good-bye – I shall *not* call again. (*He takes up his hat and departs, smiling sardonically.*)

MISS S. (*sinking into chair*). Oh dear, oh dear, I've lost him! Why didn't I guess what he wanted to say, but I couldn't think of anything with that dreadful bell always going. Oh, my head! I feel quite dazed! I begin to think a telephone is a qualified blessing. (*Telephone bell rings.*) Ah! this time it *must* be he! (*She rushes to the telephone.*) Yes? are you there? Is that Captain Vavasour? Yes – yes. You are very unpunctual. What? can't hear – what? *she* was very unpunctual? I don't understand. I can't speak any louder, I'm *shouting*. Yes – yes – oh yes! what? yes, oh *yes!* I have always felt a deep interest in your happiness. (*Aside.*) Now it's coming.

What? what? I can't hear you. What do you say? oh yes, now I do! What? who? Miss who did you say? (*her face falls.*) No, I never met her. Does she live at Bristol? what? (*she becomes vaguely alarmed.*) What? Very what? oh! I'm not a judge of pretty girls. (*Disgusted, and more and more alarmed.*) What? what say? Ah! glad you are in such good spirits. Yes? yes? something to tell me? (*her face brightens.*) Oh, yes! do! Yes? yes? oh yes! What? what? accepted you? what do you mean? What? *what?* did you say marry her? Ah! (*she shrieks and drops receiver*).

I have lost both! both! Oh, why did I ever have that abominable telephone? (*She drops, weeping stormily, into chair. Curtain descends upon her sobs.*)

37

ARTHUR MEE, 'THE PLEASURE TELEPHONE'

Strand Magazine (1898), pp. 208–214

Dreams are fulfilled very rapidly in these days, but even Mr. Bellamy himself would doubtless have been amazed to know that one of his most daring predictions is on the eve of realization. Mr. Bellamy, in that remarkably prophetic book, 'Looking Backward', wrote, ten years ago, of a young man who was amazed by hearing charming music in a room in which there was neither musician nor instrument, and who was still further surprised to be told that the music was supplied 'on the cooperative principle'.

The reply of his hostess is so absolutely prophetic that it is worth quoting here: –

> '"Wait a moment, please," said Edith; "I want to have you listen to this waltz before you ask any questions. I think it is perfectly charming," and as she spoke the sound of violins filled the room with witchery of summer night. When this had also ceased, she said: "There is nothing in the least mysterious about the music, as you seem to imagine. We have simply carried the idea of labour-saving by co-operation into our musical service as into everything else. There are a number of music-rooms in the city, perfectly adapted acoustically to the different sorts of music. These halls are connected by telephone with all the houses of the city whose people care to pay the small fee, and there are none, you may be sure, who do not. The corps of musicians attached to each hall is so large that, although no individual performer, or group of performers, has more than a brief part, each day's programme lasts through the twenty-four hours. There are on that card for to-day, as you will see if you observe closely, distinct programmes of four of these concerts, each of a different order of music from the others, being now simultaneously performed, and any one of the four pieces now going on that you prefer you can hear by merely pressing the button which will connect your house wire with the hall where it is being rendered. The programmes are so co-ordinated that the pieces at any one time simultaneously proceeding in the different halls usually offer a choice, not only between instrumental and vocal, and between different sorts of instruments, but also between different motives, from grave to gay, so that all tastes and moods can be suited."'

 DOI: 10.4324/9781315400303-51

It is probable that before the dawn of the twentieth century this prophetic picture will have been surpassed in actual fact, and the telephone will be a quite indispensable element in English social life. But it will be a much more comprehensive and effective instrument than the telephone as we know it at present, and the likelihood is that it will be fitted in our houses just as gas or electricity is now. It will be so cheap that not to have it would be absurd, and it will be so entertaining and useful that it will make life happier all round, and bring the pleasures of society to the doors of the artisan's cottage.

That, indeed, will be the unique feature of the Pleasure Telephone. It will make millions merry who have never been merry before, and will democratize, if we may so write, many of the social luxuries of the rich. Those who object to the environment of the stage will be able to enjoy the theatre at home, and the fashionable concert will be looked forward to as eagerly by the poor as by their wealthy neighbours. The humblest cottage will be in immediate contact with the city, and the 'private wire' will make all classes kin.

The honour of pioneering this revolution does not belong to England or America. The inventor of the Pleasure Telephone is a native of Hungary, where, for two years, he has been demonstrating the soundness of his invention with great success. The capital of the Hungarian Empire is the only place in the world where the Pleasure Telephone has been in operation, and the restrictions placed on the enterprise by the authorities of Buda-Pesth have not tended to popularize the instrument, or develop it fairly. But the experiment has been sufficiently successful to justify an effort on a wider scale and in a wider field. The new telephone is to be brought to London, and at the present moment arrangements are being made for its installation in the Metropolis.

Though the telephone is likely to effect immense changes, and will no doubt create something like a sensation when introduced into this country, its installation is really a very simple thing. Indeed, the whole ramifications of the Pleasure Telephone – carrying business and pleasure into the homes of thousands, and making next-door neighbours, as it were, of strangers who have never met – will be conducted in one single room by one single man. The power of resistance of the telephone is said to be enormous, and the inventor has declared that it would be possible with its aid for one man's voice to be heard simultaneously by the whole six million inhabitants of London. All that is necessary is a central office, from which the whole of London – if not the whole of England – might be supplied with a constant flow of news and pleasure all day long.

It is proposed that the present telephone machinery shall be largely used in connection with the Pleasure Telephone, the only addition necessary being a new main wire, with which each subscriber will be connected. The wire now in use in Buda-Pesth is 168 miles long, and carries sound as distinctly at the extreme end as an ordinary private wire in this country. There are 6,000 persons dependent on the wire, but, unlike our own telephone, a stoppage at one station – 'station' signifying a subscriber's house – does not affect the main wire, and the rest of the subscribers are not interfered with.

Each subscriber has a time-table of the various items which will be telephoned during the day. Beginning as early as half-past eight in the morning, every hour is amply provided for as long as there is anything going on in the city. At half-past eight the subscriber is given the substance of the principal telegrams received throughout the night, which are condensed so as to be delivered in a quarter of an hour. Only the main facts are given, such as generally satisfy the average man thus early in the day, but in case any of the news is sensational the fresh telegrams are transmitted as they arrive later on. After this foreign matter comes the news of the capital, with a programme of the day's events, and at nine o'clock news of an official nature is given. A little later – after a pause for breakfast – follows a concise review of the principal papers, with the substance of the leading articles. This lasts half an hour, and is followed by reports on the opening of the stock and corn exchanges.

The subscriber who is not interested in these matters has only to put down his receivers and wait a few minutes for the local news, the theatrical, art, or science notices, or the ecclesiastical intelligence. Next come the latest foreign, provincial, and sporting information, and all kinds of society and political matter.

The morning having been devoted to an exhaustive study of all the papers, the afternoon is spent mainly in keeping subscribers up to date concerning current events, which are frequently dispatched within a few minutes of the actual occurrence. Parliamentary reports are given at brief intervals, and the speech of a Minister is often transmitted throughout the capital while the Minister is still speaking. In London, for instance, under this system, the substance of the Budget speech would be known in thousands of houses before the Chancellor of the Exchequer had sat down, and it would be quite possible to acquaint every subscriber with the result of an important division five minutes after the figures were announced in the House. The same with the result of an exciting election. And this news not only comes with extraordinary promptness, but it is brought to one's own fireside, without the trouble of running into the street for the paper.

But the name of the telephone – its full description is the 'News and Entertainment Telephone' – implies that the instrument is not monopolized by news. Perhaps the most popular feature of it is its connection with the theatres, concert halls, and the hundred and one other places of amusement in the city. It is not necessary that sound should be conveyed directly into the telephone. The transmitter has only to be within sound of the singer to carry the song along the scores of miles of wire. By special arrangement, the great concerts in the Hungarian capital are sometimes listened to throughout the whole of the empire, or even beyond its borders. A song sung in Buda-Pesth has been heard with remarkable distinctness in Berlin and other great cities, and there seems to be no limit to possibility in this direction. At night the subscriber is taken round the theatres, each being visited in turn, and weary folk may allow themselves to be lulled to sleep by the strains of some pretty melody sung a hundred miles away.

So popular has the Pleasure Telephone become in Buda-Pesth that it has found its way into every public place of importance. There is not a public building in the capital where it is not in operation, and even the churches have not objected to it, as our illustrations show. The preacher of Buda-Pesth no longer reckons his hearers by the state of the pews, but by the number of telephone subscribers. It may be objected, perhaps, that religious worship by telephone is not calculated to inspire reverence or inculcate virtue; but, at any rate, the system is an inestimable boon to the aged and infirm, the patients in hospitals, and the women who are unable to leave their houses. A single hospital in Buda-Pesth has over thirty installations, which carry brightness and cheer into the lives of the lonely sick.

No hotel in the capital can afford to be without the instrument, which has become, in fact, practically indispensable, and is found not only in private houses and hospitals, but in doctors' waiting-rooms, barbers' shops, coffee-houses, clubs, and business offices of all kinds. Waiting is never tedious in Buda-Pesth: there is always something to interest the waiter. Half the trifling irritations of life disappear under the soothing influence of this universal distributer of pleasure.

It may be urged against the Pleasure Telephone that the subscriber has either to keep the receiver at his ears all day long, or miss half the news, but that objection is answered by the existence of the programme. Everything is transmitted in strict accordance with the programme, so that each subscriber knows exactly when his interesting items are coming. But lest important items of news should be missed, a summary of all the news is given at noon and again in the evening. There is also an ingenious emergency signal, by which all subscribers are 'rung up' on the receipt of any special news.

Though the communication between the central office and the subscribers is really very simple, it necessitates an enormous amount of preparatory labour. In many ways, the routine of the office resembles that of a newspaper, there being a staff of law, police, parliamentary, and news reporters, all of whom hand in their 'copy' to the editor. The whole of the matter to be sent through is approved by the editor before it can be handed over to the 'speaker', who speaks it into the instrument. The 'speaker' must, of course, possess a strong, clear voice, and in order that the message may be perfectly distinct, no single speaker is on duty more than two hours at a time.

The most wonderful feature of the Pleasure Telephone is its cheapness. So trivial is the outlay connected with it that the charge to subscribers is only a penny a day, or 30s. a year – ridiculously cheap when compared with the cost of the ordinary telephone. There are two receivers for each subscriber, to render the message more distinctly, each receiver being about the size of a watch. They are attached to long cords, so that they may be moved to any part of the room. So anxious are the telephonists for the comfort of the subscribers, that the two receivers can be attached to a light spring arrangement which holds them firmly over the ears, thus relieving the hands, and making it possible to walk about or lie down while listening to what is going on in the city. It is perhaps unnecessary to mention that subscribers can only hear through the telephone and not speak back in return. The telephone is, of course, non-political, all controversial news being imparted with strict impartiality. Original articles of general interest are sometimes read, with occasional short stories.

There are, of course, unlimited possibilities in the new telephone. It is quite possible that concert managers and theatrical proprietors will object to the instrument. But the probability is much the other way. The newspapers of Buda-Pesth persistently boycotted the invention on its introduction, but they recognise now that, instead of being taken as a substitute for the newspaper, its effect is to whet the appetite of the public for details of events announced briefly through the telephone. The theatres, too, realize that to give the public a snatch or two from a favourite opera gratis has not, in the long run, an adverse effect on the receipts, and they invariably support the instrument. Should the worst come to the worst, however, it is always possible to organize concerts and entertainments in the editorial office; and for an insignificant outlay on the part of each subscriber, it would not be by any means an impossible or unprofitable thing for the proprietors of the telephone to organize a concert, at which the cream of British vocalists should sing. Mr. Bellamy's prediction of a central hall of music with a twenty-four hours' programme is by no means impossible of realization. Patti and Paderewski may yet entertain us in our own drawing-rooms, and the luxuries of princes may be at the command of us all.

Who knows but that in time we may sit in our arm-chairs listening to the speeches of Her Majesty's Ministers, or allow ourselves to be soothed into blissful unconsciousness by a Parliamentary debate on bimetallism? There would be, at any rate, one blessing in this – the problem of the Ladies' Grille would be solved for ever. Then in the cricket season we shall follow our favourite wielders of the willow without risking cold or sunstroke, and all the unpleasantness of winter travelling will be avoided in the football season by the fixing of a telephone on the football field, which will keep us acquainted minute by minute with the whereabouts of the ball and the prospects of the teams. There is, indeed, no element in our social life which will be unprovided for, and if, as it is said to be not unlikely in the near future – the principle of sight is applied to the telephone as well as that of sound, earth will be in truth a paradise, and distance will lose its enchantment by being abolished altogether.

Where finality is to be reached in this matter is not known. Nothing that has been tried yet has failed, and it is confidently stated that a single wire would carry the same sound over the whole United Kingdom, if not beyond the seas. Whether this claim is exaggerated or not, time alone will prove; but at any rate the Pleasure Telephone opens out a vista of infinite charm which few prophets of to-day have dreamed of, and who dare to say that in twenty years the electric miracle will not bring all the corners of the earth to our own fireside?

4.4

Typewriter

DOI: 10.4324/9781315400303-52

4.4 Typewriter

Ardern Holt, 'The Art of Type-Writing', *Cassell's Family Magazine* (1888), pp. 659–660.
Edward Abbott Parry, 'Mr. Twistleton's Type-Writer', *Cornhill Magazine*, 8 (1889), pp. 62–71.

The first commercially successful typewriters appeared in the 1870s, the culmination of decades of attempts to create a tabletop machine with which an operator could rapidly produce texts whose appearance recalled print rather than laboriously having to write everything by hand. Like many other popular late-nineteenth-century consumer devices such as the sewing machine and the bicycle, the typewriter represented not simply the culmination of years of widespread tinkering but also the emerging technical possibilities of manufacturing complex mechanisms with interchangeable metal parts.[1] Efficient production techniques lowered costs and helped to make these Victorian high-tech products affordable to more and more buyers.

Through most of the nineteenth century, the office had remained largely a male preserve, from the junior copying clerks to the directors in charge, and many of the typewriter's early users were men. But by the early 1880s, more and more women were learning to type and obtaining jobs as typists and other kinds of office workers, part of the late-Victorian rise of women's information work. The lady typist might seem to defy nineteenth-century middle-class norms that tied women and their work to domesticity or children – norms that might also cast a mixed-gender office into suspicion. Yet, women's success at the typewriter keyboard could also reinforce other aspects of everyday sexism; it might be attributed to childhood piano lessons or dismissed as a feminised, craftlike skill in making copies or transcribing documents written by men. (Even Mina Harker, who emerges as the quick-witted typist-heroine in Bram Stoker's 1897 novel *Dracula*, seems to treat her typewriter as a tool for transcription and copying rather than for original composition.)

For the society columnist Ardern Holt, women's ability to become rapid and accurate typists confirmed their potential to outpace men at particular workplace tasks. But the typewriter also epitomised the stresses and struggles of modern life, with its encouragement of competition, standardisation and speed. 'Mr. Twistleton's Typewriter', a short story by the author and judge Edward Abbott Parry, might seem to confirm the typewriter's affiliations with competitiveness, neurosis and male failure.[2]

Notes

1 Simon Winchester, *Exactly: How Precision Engineering Created the Modern World* (London: William Collins, 2018), p. 161n.

2 In addition to the previously recommended sources on women's information work in the nineteenth century, see Christopher Keep, 'The Cultural Work of the Typewriter-Girl', *Victorian Studies*, 40 (1997), pp. 401–426. On the history of the typewriter, see Michael H. Adler, *The Writing Machine: A History of the Typewriter* (London: George Allen and Unwin, 1973); Darren S. Wershler-Henry, *The Iron Whim: A Fragmented History of Typewriting* (Ithaca, NY: Cornell University Press, 2007).

38

ARDERN HOLT, 'THE ART OF TYPE-WRITING'

Cassell's Family Magazine (1888), pp. 659–660

There are very few things that a woman can do better than a man, but there is one, and that is type-writing; her touch is lighter and truer, and up to the present time she has been able to attain a greater speed.

This is an important matter, seeing that the female labour market is over-crowded; and that one of the most difficult social problems of the day is, how educated women, unprovided by fate with incomes, are to earn a living. Up to the present time the supply of proficient typewriters is not equal to the demand.

In America, type-writing clerks are almost universally employed in business houses, and the majority are women. Many of them attend for a stated time daily, take down in shorthand verbatim replies to the contents of the post-bag, type these necessary letters, and pass on elsewhere to repeat the process; thus accomplishing what would otherwise be a morning's work in an hour or so.

Up to the present time type-writing with us has been but little adopted, but the field is widening, and the more efficient workers there are to be had, the more their value will be appreciated.

Education is a necessary adjunct; besides being neat and quick, a good type-writer must be highly educated, a thorough linguist, well versed in literature, and, most essential of all, a shorthand writer. All kinds of work are brought to a type-writing office: many plays and novels, books of all classes in MS., and some with numerous quotations in all tongues. The medical profession has hitherto patronised type-writing a great deal, and the terms and phrases incidental to that profession are not learnt in a day.

Authors are proverbial for illegible writing; and patience, common sense, knowledge, and quickness are all essential in deciphering their manuscripts.

Curiously enough, the first type-writing machine was made by an Englishman, Henry Mill, as far back as 1714 – a clumsy, useless instrument; but it started an idea, and the honour of ultimately attaining a practical result is due to America.

So much depends on the machine that it is impossible to discuss type-writing without making reference to the several kinds of type-writers. For hard business wear the No. 2 Remington is acknowledged to be the best. It costs a little over £20, gets out of order with great difficulty, is simple, though cumbersome. The

DOI: 10.4324/9781315400303-53

Caligraph, which is much after the same order, but with different keys for capitals and small letters, and the No. 1 Remington, which has only capitals, are the next best; then comes the Hammond, which is built on a different model, and is a wheel machine, the type being arranged round the segments of an oscillating wheel. Whatever letter is struck, the whole wheel rotates, causing much more friction, so that it cannot of necessity last so long with hard wear and tear, although for ordinary use it has many merits. There are smaller machines, such as the Hall and the Columbia, which would do very good amateur work, and have the great merit of being portable; but they attain no great speed, which is one of the chief virtues of type-writing. The most ordinary type-writer ought to be able to type twice as fast as writing; forty to sixty words a minute is the lowest computation. An adept can accomplish seventy-five, and the most proficient a hundred words and over.

But all this speed depends on the proper manipulation of the machine. At first sight this seems so easy. The type-writer, with its key-board of four rows of letters and figures, &c., which only have to be pressed, when a word is very easily printed, is in truth a snare and a delusion. The letters are not placed in their natural sequence, and the new operator realises that he or she must master that difficulty; but not one in a dozen understands the amount of slow and patient practice which is required to use the thumb on the narrow wooden bar in front, which divides the words; and the three fingers of each hand on the key-board itself. It is far easier to use four fingers instead of six, and dispense with the thumb; but no speed and no accurate work can be thus accomplished. It is most difficult to avoid employing the wrong letters sometimes, and you never are a good writer until you are so completely master of the machine that you understand all its mechanism, and could do your work blind-fold. Then, and then only, can you achieve the requisite speed and accuracy.

Festina lente – 'Hasten slowly' – should be written up well in sight of all type-writing pupils; slow and sure wins the day, and the more haste in learning the less speed in writing.

Type-writing would have made its way much faster in England had the manipulators been more adept – bad work has acted as a deterrent, but that is being got over now.

Admirable lessons and training can be obtained; but with patience, and the directions for using the type-writer given with the machine, and Mr. Edward F. Underhill's hand-book of instructions, it is quite possible to acquire the art untaught. To do this, however, the inductive exercises should be faithfully carried out. They teach fingering, and a perfect knowledge of the key-board. They are tedious, and most wearisome, but they are worth all the trouble.

Improvements are continually being introduced; indelible ink that will, it is said, last for centuries is now to be had, and in America, where the State archives are mostly typed, this is of great value. Type-written minutes take up much less space than written ones. A new machine has been patented, too, for binding and perforating. This inserts an eyelet-hole into as many pages as are required to be put together, and runs a tape through several inch packets, thus effectually binding them together. A very good testimony to the durability of the ink used in the type-writer is that a document which went down in the *Oregon*, and remained two or three months under water, was quite legible when recovered after its immersion.

Those who have to write much, and continuously, will recognise one or two great merits in this mode of reproducing their thoughts. In the first place, it spares the over-strained muscles of the hand, which have a habit of aching just when a pressure of work must be done; and then during type-writing an upright position may be maintained. No stooping is required, and thus much more continuous work can be carried on.

Printers and editors appreciate its legibility, and authors save much expense in correcting proofs by availing themselves of it. Indeed, in many firms across the Atlantic manuscripts that are likely to be published are typed before they are submitted to the reader. The introduction of type-writing will certainly not take employment from one class to give it to another. On the contrary, it has created a need which women of education are peculiarly well able to supply.

Many type-writing offices now exist in London, where there are only female clerks, and pupils from thence have opened other offices in Scotland, Oxford, Liverpool, and Cambridge. As civilisation grows, the value of the refinement and higher education of gentlewomen becomes more recognised, though the struggles of life grow harder. There is no doubt that a wide and acceptable field is being opened to them through type-writing.

In the United States type-writing has been adopted as part of the curriculum in many schools.

Many perfect copies can be obtained at the same time by placing carbon paper between each sheet, and copies can also be made in the usual way in the copying press. If a specially prepared ink is employed, the writing can be transferred direct to the lithographic stone.

We live at railroad speed in this nineteenth century, and all aids which enable us to do the work of life well and quickly should be recognised and adopted when feasible, or we are apt to be laggards in the race for existence, which perchance may prove too much for us.

39

EDWARD ABBOTT PARRY, 'MR. TWISTLETON'S TYPE-WRITER'

Cornhill Magazine, 8 (1889), pp. 62–71

Several strange things have happened to me in my life that my friends could never account for. They could never understand how I got an introduction to Twistleton, Q.C., nor why that learned gentleman, after allowing me to devil his work for him for ten years without putting anything in my way, suddenly used every effort and influence he was capable of to put an important and valuable junior practice in my hands.

Twistleton, Q.C., was a hard, selfish man. In person he was like a badly dried moth, whose long, old-fashioned whiskers resembled the remains of wings. It was of him that it was originally said that he was the living representative of a tenant in tail after possibility of issue extinct; and there was consequently great surprise when Twistleton married Lucy Travers, who, as you will remember, was the belle of her season. But the Travers were not so well off as they pretended to be, and Twistleton, as we all know, made his fifteen thousand a year, and had, if anything, an ever-increasing practice in the Chancery Division.

Twistleton was undoubtedly a great lawyer, and a man of strong common sense, but he had two fads. He was a believer in ghosts, and he wrote everything in his chambers upon a Remington type-writer.

Twistleton and his wife were staying one June in Norfolk, at Lady Barndore's. Twistleton was due in town to argue the great patent case concerning sewing machines, of Buncombe and Another *v.* Badger, in the Court of Appeal, on Wednesday morning. I expected him back in chambers on the Monday evening, understanding that he intended rejoining his wife at the end of the week; for this case would last at least three days, and Twistleton was in several other cases on the list.

About eight o'clock on Monday evening, I had dined early at my club, and was engaged noting up Twistleton's papers, when he came in, with his Gladstone bag and rug, looking, as I thought, tired and out of spirits. When Twistleton was in town by himself he always slept at his own chambers, as in the old days before he was married; and his breakfast (a chop and two eggs) was sent in from the 'Cock'.

Twistleton, having heard what Foss, his clerk, had to say on the subject of retainers, dismissed him. Then he slammed down the windows, which I had

 DOI: 10.4324/9781315400303-54

opened to let in what fresh air there was in Old Square, carefully closed the door, let himself into the hard chair in front of his writing-table, and idly leaned over the papers which were before him. At length the outer door was heard to close; Foss had departed, and Twistleton broke silence.

'Penrose, my dear fellow, I'm uncomfortable.'

Twistleton, I may here remark, was always on the best of terms with me, and treated me as a friend, for I believe I was useful to him. I had made great way in his affections by solemnly advising him to marry Miss Travers when I saw he was bent on doing so; but, since his marriage, I am not sure that this course of conduct of mine had been altogether to my advantage. I looked to him for a further explanation, which I saw was coming.

'Penrose, my dear fellow, who do you think is at Lady Barndore's?'

I shook my head, being entirely in ignorance.

'Charley Colston,' replied Twistleton, trying to carve his whiskers with the paper-knife. 'Charley Colston.'

Poor Charley Colston! It was well known that he had paid his addresses to pretty Mrs. Twistleton in former days, and report said she had encouraged them. No wonder Twistleton was excited. I knew him to be of an extremely jealous nature.

'Now mark me, Penrose,' said Twistleton, shaking his forefinger at me as he would at Lord Usher in the Appeal Court – 'what took place yesterday when I was playing tennis? The whole time, sir, he and she were talking and chatting together, and laughing – yes, laughing! Perhaps at my play, for I played abominably; I know it. I could not bear to see them.'

Twistleton's tennis was never first rate. He had begun to play too late in life. He was an annoying partner, as he always insisted on leading, taking all the difficult strokes, and failing at them. He was a still more objectionable opponent, as he was always taking technical objections on points of practice. Still, however badly one plays, it is not pleasant to be laughed at, even by one's wife. I tried to soothe Twistleton, but he interrupted me.

'Now, there is another point I desire to urge.' Twistleton always spoke as though he was addressing the Court of Appeal. 'When I asked my wife to come back today, she point blank refused. What do you think of that?'

'Nothing whatever,' I answered. 'She had arranged to stay, and you are going down on Saturday again. I think you are making mountains out of molehills.'

I hope I am, Penrose, I hope I am,' replied Twistleton mournfully; 'but you didn't see them – I did;' and Twistleton sighed deeply.

Then the subject dropped, and we got to work on a small case. Soon, Twistleton, with a self-complacent smile on his countenance, was playing an opinion on his type-writer. It was to him, I believe, as though each note he struck produced a deep mellow tone, and not a capital or small Roman. I can remember when Twistleton first had his type-writer. In those days he used to sit at it for hours, practising; hitting first one note and then the other, at intervals varying between ten seconds and two or three minutes, every now and then using the most horrible language, as he put a capital for a small Roman or missed a space. Then his efforts looked as though they were the productions of six drunken printers who had each taken an absent comrade's work for the day; and they were always copied before they went to clients. Now the machine went click, click, click, evenly and merrily. Twistleton was a perfect master of it. I had seen him write it with his eyes shut. I have no doubt that if he could have stood on his head, and if it had been consonant with the dignity of a Queen's Counsel to do so, he could have played his instrument in that posture.

The opinion finished, Twistleton, who was a very methodical man, put a fresh sheet of paper in readiness to commence again, folded and signed what he had written, and bade me good-night. His last words to me were –

'I hope you are right about Charley Colston.'

'I am sure of it,' I said.

'I wish I were.'

To-morrow we were to have a long day at Buncombe *v*. Badger. When I arrived in the morning, Twistleton was at breakfast. I no sooner entered than he set down his egg-spoon, and, rushing at me with a piece of paper, thrust it into my hands.

'Read that,' he cried excitedly – 'read that.'

I noticed that Twistleton seemed unwell. There was a wild look in his eyes. His chop was untouched – a reversal of Twistleton's procedure at breakfast, which was more extraordinary to me than his strange appearance. The egg he was eating was, to any one with a sense of smell, manifestly a bad one; a most portentous fact to me, who remember hearing Twistleton – who never knew any criminal law – seriously tell the boy from the 'Cock' that he believed a bill of attainder would lie against him for bringing him a bad egg. What did it all mean? I looked at the paper in my hand: on it were two words, neatly printed – 'Charley Colston.'

I stared blankly at Twistleton. What did it mean? Twistleton was shaking visibly.

'Do you believe in ghosts?' he asked anxiously.

'Certainly not,' I replied.

'Ah!' sighed Twistleton; and added sententiously, 'There are more things in heaven and earth than are dreamt of in your philosophy'. This was the only quotation I ever heard him utter that did not come from the Law Reports. I believe he fancied it was a phrase he had invented in his early youth when he first began to believe in ghosts.

'If you don't believe in ghosts, who wrote that message on my type-writer?'

Twistleton's manner was very impressive. I felt like a witness committing perjury.

'I tell you, I found it this morning when I went to write a letter just before breakfast. Who wrote it?' he shouted. 'Who wrote it? I will know.'

'Perhaps Foss,' I suggested.

'He has not been here, and can't use the type-writer.'

I had heard him say so, but did not believe it. Foss was afraid of overworking himself, and so did not choose to learn it, but any fool could use it if he liked to learn. My opinion was that Foss could use it. He was like the monkeys, who, as the negro said, 'could talk if they would, but knew if they did they would be made to work.'

'How about the laundress?' I suggested.

'Ah! the laundress,' repeated Twistleton, thoughtfully; 'the laundress.'

So Mrs. Buttick, the laundress, was sent for when Foss came in; but she denied all knowledge of the type-writer or the writing, making a new suggestion, which did not, to our thinking, much advance the solution of the mystery, and that was that the culprit was the cat.

'It is a message,' said Twistleton mysteriously; 'a message!'

'Nonsense!' I said. 'Some fellow has strolled in, and written the name for fun.'

'Fun!' cried Twistleton indignantly. 'Fun!' And then more quietly: 'No, I am sure of it; it is a message.'

Very little of Buncombe *v.* Badger could I get into Twistleton's head that day. Plans and specifications he seemed not to understand; the seductive literary style of the affidavit had no charm for him. He could only gaze at the paper in his hand, and murmur ever and anon, 'A message!'

I saw it was best to humour him, and at my suggestion the type-writer was locked up that night, and he took the key with him into his bedroom. We had had a rattling good dinner together, and when I left Twistleton he was in much better spirits.

'If the ghost comes to-night, he won't be able to get at the type-writer, anyhow,' I said, laughing.

'Hush! I don't know,' replied Twistleton solemnly. 'It is no jesting subject.'

I went my way, wondering how a man with Twistleton's practice could believe in ghosts, and who the deuce had written Charley Colston's name on the type-writer.

The next morning I walked down to Twistleton's directly after breakfast. I found him in the wildest imaginable condition. He had taken every precaution, locking up the type-writer, placing the key under his pillow; and yet, here was the message, as he called it, printed in clear, faultless style: 'Charley Colston. He is with your wife. Charley Colston.'

'I must go. I must go. Oh! Penrose, what shall I do?' he cried in agony, as I entered the room.

'Go?' I said; 'and who is to lead in Buncombe *v.* Badger?'

He was silent, and buried all of his face, except his whiskers, in his hands. Even his hands, large and uncouth as they were, could not contain his whiskers.'

'Think of Writson and Clame. What will they say?' I urged, seeing the effect that my words had on him. 'They rely on you in this case.'

The name of this eminent firm seemed to calm Twistleton to some extent.

'My dear Penrose,' he said in a trembling voice, 'this is a message; I am sure of it. But I will do my duty; I will stay by my clients.'

'Twistleton, you speak like a Queen's Counsel and a man of honour,' I said, seizing him by the hand, proud to shake it. 'If it is a message,' I added to humour him, 'it will come again to-night. I will tell you what we will do. We will watch the type-writer all night.'

Twistleton wrung my hand with gratitude at this suggestion of mine, and calmed himself. I made him eat some of his cold chop, and sent for some brandy and water for him, instead of the tea, which had already stood in the teapot for more than an hour. Then I endeavoured to coach him in Buncombe *v.* Badger, but with small success. Then we went over to the Appeal Court, in which I took my seat; for though I was not briefed in the case, I had nothing else to do, and was interested in seeing how Twistleton got on with it. He was very able at picking up a case as he went along, and the Court of Appeal stood greatly in awe of him. I had never seen him as nervous as he was to-day – not even on his wedding-day – and I was quite frightened for him.

Lord Usher, M.R., supported by Smugg, L.J., and Summerbosh, L.J., formed the Court. Twistleton came in late; he had been at a consultation. As he entered I heard two solicitors' clerks say to each other –

'Who is that with the whiskers?'

'Twistleton, Q.C.: he has the biggest practice at the bar.'

'He looks like a boiled owl,' suggested his companion.

'Drinks, I believe,' was the reply.

This was horrible, for Twistleton was a follower of Prebendary Falutin, the great teetotaller.

But certainly Twistleton had a dissipated look this morning. His eyes were red, and the lines under his eyes were very dark and hollow; his cheeks were pale and yellow. Something of this kind, I fancy, the Master of the Rolls remarked to Lord Justice Smugg, who nodded assent.

Twistleton rose to open the case, which was a very intricate one, and Lord Usher, according to his constant practice, interrupted him with the regularity of a piece of clockwork every two and a half minutes, and then wondered why he did not understand the case and shook himself impatiently. Much to Lord Usher's astonishment, Twistleton did not deliver any of those stinging retorts by which he was wont to keep the Court of Appeal in order, and frighten their Lordships into deciding in his favour. On noticing this, Lord Usher began to chaff and rally Twistleton in a manner that was the admiration of the junior bar, the two Lords Justices, and, not least of all, of the Master of the Rolls himself. At length Twistleton, in expatiating on the merits of Buncombe's sewing machine, alluded to it as a type-writer. Whereupon Lord Usher said, with a humorous leer, that if it had been a question of type-writers, no doubt Mr. Twistleton would have been called as a specialist to give evidence and would not have been arguing the case before them. At which those in the court who knew of Twistleton's fad tittered; and his Lordship's namesakes who stand about the Court put their hands before their faces and shook visibly for a moment or two, and then called out 'Hush!' and looked angry. But Twistleton lost his temper over this, and asked his Lordship if his Lordship meant to hint that the Court did not want to hear him; and intimated his intention, if such was the case, of sitting down. And then the whole Court was really quite silent for a minute or two, in anticipation of a row; and every one ceased to fidget, and paid close attention to Lord Usher; to hear him, with his blandest and most urbane of smiles, explaining how it was the great privilege of that Court to listen to Mr. Twistleton, and what a high value they set upon that privilege, and how it was quite inconceivable to him (Lord Usher) that he (Mr. Twistleton) could imagine for a moment that this Court or any other Court should wish him to sit down. Whereupon Twistleton murmured that his Lordship was very good, meaning thereby that he should like to be with his Lordship in a small room where he could give him a bit of his mind. Then the case proceeded quite regularly, until Twistleton handed Lord Usher a lot of papers to explain his case; and Lord Usher coming to one, said, with a knowing side-glance at Smugg, L.J., that, from the handwriting, it must be a note of Mr. Twistleton's in another case; as he did not know that any one of the name of Charles Colston was a party to this case. And what would have happened then I don't know; only the Court rose for lunch.

I heard two or three people say that day that 'Twistleton, poor fellow, was doing more work than he ought to;' that 'Twistleton was a clever fellow, but he could not afford to burn the candle at both ends.' Indeed, Twistleton's strange conduct in Buncombe *v.* Badger was the general topic of conversation in the robing-room.

When Twistleton came out of court, I had the greatest difficulty to prevent him rushing down to Norfolk by the night train. He was sure it was true; he believed in the message. I calmed him down, and we had dinner together at my club. He had to continue his speech in the morning. I tried to coach him in Buncombe *v.* Badger, but it was of no avail. I do not think he even knew for which side he was appearing.

We agreed that we would sit up in watches and so keep our eye on the type-writer all night. There was a sofa in the recess of the window, and Twistleton sent me to bed and placed himself on this. I bade him good-night, and took his bed for the first half of the night. About two o'clock in the morning I awoke and went to Twistleton. He was wide awake, reading some papers, on the sofa.

'Have you seen anything?' I asked.

'Nothing whatever,' he replied.

'Nor heard anything?'

'Not a sound.'

We took the lamp to the type-writer and opened it. There was the sheet of paper as he always left it, untouched. Twistleton locked it up again and took the key.

'Put it under your pillow.'

'I will,' he replied; 'it's very good of you to sit up like this.'

'It's nothing at all, I assure you,' I answered.

'Keep strict watch, won't you?'

'I promise you,' I said.

Twistleton shook me by the hand, with emotion, and went out; he looked very ill and wretched, I thought, and was sorry for him. Was it a ghost's message or what, that was making his life a burden to him? Should I solve the mystery to-night?

I waited about an hour and a half. The dawn came peeping through the painted shutters and made the lamp look dim. I was almost dozing – in fact, I had shut my eyes, and lost consciousness for perhaps a minute, perhaps more. A sharp clicking sound awoke me. It was the type-writer. There, seated on a chair in front of it, playing nimbly on the queer instrument, was a white, misty figure. It had finished. It closed the cover down and turned the key. It wheeled round to the door, and I saw the face and whiskers I knew so well; it was Twistleton himself.

My first impulse was to wake him, but I had heard that it was dangerous to wake persons walking in their sleep. He wanted all the sleep he could get, so I decided to let him alone, to walk down to my own chambers and get some more rest myself. When I got out into Old Square I could not help roaring with laughter. It was too funny. The idea of old Twistleton writing messages to himself on the type-writer, and being frightened out of his wits by them. What a story to tell against him! No one would believe it, it was too good to be true.

I awoke a little late the next morning, but went straight down to Old Square before breakfast. Alas! I was too late. There was Foss in misery over a hasty scrawl of Twistleton's. He had gone to Barndore by the early train; Foss was to make any excuse he thought fit to Writson and Clame. There was the type-writer shattered into a thousand pieces, its intricate machinery a shapeless chaos. I shuddered to think what would happen if there was anything between Charley Colston and Mrs. Twistleton.

In town every one was asking what had become of Twistleton. The rumour went round the law courts that he was insane. I maintained a discreet silence. Mr. Clame was almost crying, as Slokoach, murmuring something about 'bad news, and his learned leader,' rose to continue Twistleton's opening. Lord Usher, unrestrained by the presence of Twistleton, made the Court of Appeal a place of fiery torment to that eminent elderly junior, Mr. Slokoach. Bustle, Q.C., for Badger, was not even called upon to reply; Buncombe and Another were dismissed, with costs.

The early train stopped, as I knew, at every station, forty in number. I could imagine poor Twistleton's state of mind as he pottered along in a slow train to Barndore. He arrived at the house about breakfast time – I have the story from Grimbleton, who was there – he came into the breakfast-room, and his appearance elicited a shout of surprise.

'What has become of Buncombe *v.* Badger?' cried Lord Barndore. 'Settled, eh?'

'Not that I know of,' muttered Twistleton, sulkily; and then, looking round fiercely, asked, 'Where's my wife?

'Not down yet,' replied Lord Barndore.

Twistleton looked hastily round, as though in search of some one else, and then tore upstairs to his wife's room. The whole company looked at each other in silence.

There was some explanation about 'bad news,' but the Twistletons never went into mourning; and Mrs. Twistleton seemed very merry all that day. It is true Twistleton was moody and shut himself up a good deal. Grimbleton told me that he never understood the whole business in the least; in fact, in Twistleton's circle it was a nine days' wonder. By-the-by, I almost forgot to mention that Charley

Colston left Barndore to be married in Scotland the day after Twistleton came to town.

When Twistleton returned to Old Square he was a sadder and a wiser man. He gave up believing in ghosts, and did not buy another type-writer. I told Twistleton that I would not let the matter go any further, and I mentioned at the time that he might get me the junior brief in Buncombe *v.* Badger, which went to the House of Lords, where, through Twistleton's clear arguments, Lord Usher and Lords Justices Smugg and Summerbosh were overruled.

That year, mostly through Twistleton's influence, my fee book credited me with 2,000*l*.

I have kept my secret well, but since Twistleton succeeded Lord Usher as Master of the Rolls Lady Twistleton has not called on Mrs. Penrose, and, although my wife assures me that she is rather glad of it, she is always telling me now that she does not think so good a story should be lost to the world as that of 'Twistleton's Type-writer'.

4.5

Linotype

DOI: 10.4324/9781315400303-55

4.5 Linotype

'A Shareholder', *The Linotype Composing Machine: A Retrospect and a Prospect* [extract] (London: Witherby, 1889), pp. 28–31, 47–49.

The typewriter was a writing machine that would let a skilled operator speedily produce readable texts that resembled print. So perhaps it was only natural that its success would help galvanise the effort to invent a more efficient way to set type into place for a printing press. Although the steam-powered rotary presses of the late nineteenth century could print thousands of pages an hour, the work of setting type for them proceeded in much the fashion it had since the days of Johannes Gutenberg and Peter Schöffer. The typesetter would select letters and other characters from cases of movable lead type, compose them into lines, and then transfer those lines into place, assembling all the elements of the page. After the printing was finished, the lines would be broken down again and the individual pieces of type laboriously returned to the cases to be reused.

The inventor Ottmar Mergenthaler's Linotype did away with the traditional compositing process. Instead of hand-assembling bits of type from cases, an operator typed on the Linotype keyboard and the machine assembled molds for the characters into a temporary configuration called a matrix. Once a line was complete, the Linotype poured molten lead into it to create a complete line of type that was ready to be used. After printing, the lines were simply melted down to provide the materials for new lines of type.

Although its output lacked the finesse of traditional typesetting, the fast and efficient Linotype was soon adopted by most publishers of newspapers in the 1890s. Following the success of the typewriter, the promoters of the new Linotype advertised their compositing machine not simply as a tool for streamlining the newsroom and providing inexpensive periodicals to consumers but as a future personal printing press for authors, offices and households – a vision of late-Victorian desktop publishing that would far exceed reality.[1]

Note

1 On the history of the Linotype and mechanical compositing, see Frank Romano, *History of the Linotype Company* (Rochester, NY: RIT Press, 2014); Basil Kahan, *Ottmar Mergenthaler: The Man and His Machine* (New Castle, DE: Oak Knoll Press, 2000); John S. Thompson *The History of Compositing Machines* (Chicago: Inland Printer, 1904; rpt. New York: Garland, 1980). A fascinating view of the Linotype's long heyday and rapid replacement by digital technologies in the 1970s and 1980s is offered by *Linotype: The Film*, dir. by Douglas Wilson (OnPaperWings Productions, 2012).

40

'A SHAREHOLDER,' *THE LINOTYPE COMPOSING MACHINE: A RETROSPECT AND A PROSPECT* [EXTRACT]

(London: Witherby, 1889), pp. 28–31, 47–49

If the profits from the Machines ordered by newspapers are likely to be sufficient, according to the estimates (attenuated in every possible way) in the preceding chapters, to make us seem 'rich beyond the dreams of avarice', what must the result be when the revenue is swelled by the orders of the great mass of general printing houses, book publishers, miscellaneous and job printers, &c., &c., who constitute considerably more than one-half – possibly, nearer three-fourths – of the entire printing industry of the country?

Unfortunately, the statistics of the population, and the proportions of the classes employed in the different branches of the industry, do not enable us accurately to gauge the fulness and extent of the inroad which the Linotype can make into these branches.

But in book printing it must effect possibly a greater '*revolution*' than in newspapers.

The shilling and sixpenny novels, for example, as sold on the bookstalls by hundreds of thousands must come under its sway. It is stated that in America a book – of the class sometimes irreverently called a 'shilling shocker' – can be set up, printed, folded, cut, and covered (with paper), for *one cent*, or *one halfpenny* per copy! This price is for a 320-paged book, ordered in quantities of twenty-five thousand copies – a usual order in America for one edition. It does not, of course, include the material – *i.e.*, the cost of the paper itself – only the labour and printing. The operation is first and mainly effected with the aid of Linotype bars, and copies struck off, thirty-two pages at a time, by the Fowler-Henkle Press, a rotary Machine, with eight flat surfaces, doing over four thousand copies per hour.

It is claimed that novelists and authors by the score will certainly, when they know it, hold up both hands for the Invention. Many a hundred authors, like many a peripatetic newspaper owner, has been crushed outright, or very nearly ruined, by the first cost of production in printing, viz., *composition*, with which the Linotype alone deals.

DOI: 10.4324/9781315400303-56

In every other branch of printing and paper-making we have achieved vast economies and increase of speed; but the first step in printing, the doorway, in fact, to everything, the *cost of composition*, practically remains, in point of methods, the same to-day as in Caxton's and Guthenberg's days. In fact, as compared with twenty years ago, the cost of composition is even *dearer*.

Can there be any doubt that in any department wherein the public, as in book-printing, can in the distribution of patronage, influence or control the price of work, and demand through the means of competition cheaper terms, they will adopt it?

Cheapness, like water, must sooner or later find its own level; and a great cheapener of production, like the LINOTYPE, is bound to find its way into every nook and corner ultimately. It is no figure of speech to predict that some day the LINOTYPE may, in newer adaptations, be in every office and every household. It can do much work that is common to the 'type-writer' in banks and large mercantile establishments. It is infinitely more preferable than all these gelatine 'multipliers' which the dearness and slowness of printing have brought into existence by thousands.

Its possibilities of development and adaptation to many branches of work hardly dreamt of now, are immeasurable.

Hundreds of authors, who hate the drudgery and cramp of writing or revising manuscripts, will economise their patience, time, and money by the entertaining pastime of playing out their thoughts, pianoforte fashion, on the LINOTYPE.

Those who have tried setting up and casting 'LINOTYPE' bars, like Mr. GLADSTONE, without any previous experience as compositors, have been delighted with the facility with which they could set up easy sentences within a few minutes. An Invention that is at once so simple, so efficacious, and so cheap, must necessarily have a great future before it, outside the limits even of newspaper and printing offices.

[. . .]

For, in truth, few men can really, even now, imagine what is likely to flow from that 'peaceful revolution', of which the LINOTYPE is destined to be the humble instrument. Well might Mr. Gladstone, when he came to examine and operate for himself the LINOTYPE Machine, last June, say he was '*staggered*'.

The great ex-Chancellor of the Exchequer, who charmed and electrified friends and foes alike by his magical, fiscal Budgets during the days of Lord Palmerston's Ministry, and who, in the year 1860, carried a Bill for the Repeal of the paper duty, saw with quick, penetrative instinct that whatever beneficent results were predicted by Milner Gibson, Richard Cobden, and others, as likely to ensue from the removal of the 'taxes on knowledge', they were doomed to be surpassed by the cheapening of printing by from 50 to 80 per cent.

We erect monuments and treasure up with feelings of almost tender sacredness every relic of Guthenburg, Caxton, and others, as if they had been second Messiahs.

But for every printed book that Caxton's press placed within the reach of the people of his day, the LINOTYPE will be the means of placing millions.

Advancing side by side as it will in future years, with every forward step in the educational machinery of the people – the spread of schools, technical universities, &c. – one will create a demand for the other. More people, and those containing a higher percentages of readers than before, will need more newspapers and books; more LINOTYPE Machines will be wanted to produce them, and more skilled operatives to work the Machines. Artizans will then be able to buy shilling books for perhaps threepence or fourpence, and will no longer care to borrow greasy volumes from the free libraries.

Macmillan and Co., by republishing Kingsley's 'Westward Ho!' at sixpence, shew even to-day what can be done by enterprise. The 'magic power of ownership will be shown' by each artizan being able to own a supply of good books. 'My Library' will be more than a boast. It will mean the elevation of the home.

This is not by any means an overdrawn picture.

Its truth will become more apparent as years go on; and instead of £1,000,000 (nominal) of Capital being considered sufficient to pay for and work so great an Invention, people will be amazed that it was bought so cheaply.

Mr. Edison, has been maturing and developing, the Phonograph, just as the Linotype was for many years matured and developed. But can it be said that the phonograph has yet attained the dignity or utility of a practically every-day serviceable commodity, saving money to mankind, like the LINOTYPE has proved to be capable of doing? Or will it ever effect the welfare of the millions of mankind, as cheapened printing will? Yet, notwithstanding this, the *Pall Mall Gazette*, of the 2nd October, 1889, announced on the occasion of Mr. Edison's visit to this country, that he was keeping back the phonograph, although he had been offered *five millions sterling* for it by English financiers! In the same journal, on October 2nd, 1889, alluding to the phonograph and graphophone, it was stated that six millions sterling had already been invested in them. Yet so far as compared with the LINOTYPE they are mere toys!

Mr. Marinoni, of Paris, is reputed to have 'cleared' over two millions sterling in profits by Rotary printing machines, which simply accelerate the rate of speed, or the number of copies of newspapers, &c., printed per hour. And, moreover, that machine by its great price is beyond the reach of nine out of ten printers who can afford to *hire* the LINOTYPE.

The nearest analogy to the LINOTYPE would probably be the Sewing Machine. If any one likes to exercise his mind by calculating what would have been a fair capitalised value for the Patents used in the Sewing Machine Industry alone, five years ago, and comparing it with the profits made in it to-day, he will readily see how moderate has been the capital price paid for the LINOTYPE.

Let him only think what the latter has *cost* since its birth up to now!

PART 5

Sound and vision

5.1

Stereoscope and stereoscopic photography

DOI: 10.4324/9781315400303-58

5.1 Stereoscope and stereoscopic photography

David Brewster, *The Stereoscope* [extract] (London: Murray, 1856), pp. 196–200.
John Henry Pepper, 'The Stereoscope' [extract], in *The Boy's Playbook of Science* (London: Routledge, 1866), pp. 320–323.

Victorian inventions and technological things changed the way that people saw the world – quite literally. As with the railway, rather than focusing broadly on the technologies of photography, the texts here emphasise the circulation of specific kinds of objects and technologies that offered the Victorians new visual experiences. Before his work with William Forthergill Cooke on the electric telegraph, Charles Wheatstone had invented the stereoscope, an optical device that created the illusion of three dimensionality from flat images. By presenting slightly different pictures to each of the viewer's eyes, the stereoscope both demonstrated and simulated the power of human binocular depth perception. Like several of the century's other new visual technologies, the stereoscope would go on to enjoy a multifaceted career as scientific discovery, educational toy and consumer entertainment medium.

David Brewster, a pioneer of optics and optical devices (he had invented the kaleidoscope), improved the stereoscope, adding lenses and creating a device small and light enough to be held in the hand. For Brewster, not only did the stereoscope supplement the knowledge from flat images in books but it also broadened access to knowledge by providing students and others with a kind of virtual reality experience. John Henry Pepper invented the Pepper's Ghost stage illusion, which uses an angled piece of glass to create a live, ghostly image. In *The Boy's Playbook of Science*, Pepper highlights the relationship between the 'spectral' images of the stereoscope and the visual effects created in the shows and spectacles he has produced. As the stereoscope became a popular format for viewing photographs, Victorian photographers offered thousands of series of stereographic images for popular consumption: images of national beauty, famous landmarks, exotic locales, celebrities and many other subjects.[1]

Note

1 For impressively comprehensive accounts of the stereoscope and stereographic images, see Paul Wing, *Stereoscopes: The First One Hundred Years* (Nashua, NH: Transition, 1996); William C. Darrah, *The World of Stereographs* (Gettysburg, PA: Darrah, 1977). Stereoscopic photography took its place alongside other new Victorian technologies of mass visuality, yet it also extended older traditions of the picturesque; see Rachel Teukolsky, *Picture World: Image, Aesthetics, and Victorian New Media* (Oxford: Oxford University Press, 2020). The suggestions for further reading in the following section include works that consider the stereoscope alongside other nineteenth-century optical toys and devices.

41

DAVID BREWSTER, *THE STEREOSCOPE* [EXTRACT]

(London: Murray, 1856), pp. 196–200

One of the most palpable advantages to be derived from the illustration of school-books by pictures in relief, is the communication of correct knowledge of the various objects of natural history. If, as we have already shewn, the naturalist derives important assistance in his studies from correct representations of animated nature, how much more valuable must they be to the scholar who never saw, and may never see the objects themselves. In the department of zoology, the picture might frequently be taken from the living animal, standing before the camera in vigorous life and transcendent beauty; or when this cannot be done, from the fine specimens of zoological forms which adorn our metropolitan and provincial museums. The trees and plants, too, of distant zones, whether naked in their osteology, or luxurious in their foliage, would shew themselves in full relief; – the banyan, clinging with its hundred roots to the ground, – the bread-fruit tree, with its beneficent burden, – the cow tree, with its wholesome beverage, – the caoutchouc tree, yielding its valuable juice, – or the deadly upas, preparing its poison for the arrow of the savage or the poniard of the assassin.

With no less interest will the schoolboy gaze on the forms of insect life, which will almost flutter before him, and on the tenants of the air and of the ocean, defective only in the colours which adorn them. The structures of the inorganic world will equally command his admiration. The minerals which have grown in the earth beneath his feet, and the crystals which chemistry has conjured into being, will display to him their geometric forms, infinite in variety, and interesting from their rarity and value. Painted by the very light which streamed from them, he will see, in their retiring and advancing facets, the Kohinoor and other diamonds, and the huge rubies, and sapphires, and emeralds, which have adorned the chaplet of beauty, or sparkled in the diadem of kings. The gigantic productions of the earth will appeal to him with equal power, – the colossal granites, which have travelled in chariots of ice, and the rounded boulders, which have been transported in torrents of mud; and while he admires, in their strong relief, the precipices of ancient lava – the Doric colonnades of basalt – the upheaved and contorted strata beside them, and the undisturbed beds which no internal convulsions have shaken, he will stand appalled before the fossil giants of the primeval world that trod the

DOI: 10.4324/9781315400303-59

earth during its preparation for man, and have been embalmed in stone to instruct and to humble him.

In acquiring a knowledge of physical geography, in which the grander aspects of nature arrest our attention, their stereoscopic representations will be particularly instructive. The mountain range, whether abrupt in its elevation, or retiring from our view, – whether scarred with peaks or undulating in outline, – the insulated mountain tipped with snow or glowing with fire, – the volcano ejecting its burning missiles, – the iceberg fixed in the shore, or floating on the deep, – the deafening cataract, – the glacier and its moraines, sinking gently to the plains, – and even the colossal wave with its foaming crest, will be portrayed in the binocular camera, and exhibited in all the grandeur and life of nature.

The works of human hands, – the structures of civilisation, will stand before the historian and the antiquary, as well as the student, in their pristine solidity, or in their ruined grandeur, – the monuments by which sovereigns and nations have sought to perpetuate their names, – the gorgeous palaces of kings, – the garish temples of superstition, – the humbler edifices of Christian faith, – the bastions and strongholds of war, will display themselves in the stereoscope as if the observer were placed at their base, and warmed by the very sun which shone upon their walls.

Although few of our village youth may become sculptors, yet the exhibition of ancient statues in their actual relief, and real apparent magnitude, cannot fail to give them salutary instruction and rational pleasure. To gaze upon the Apollo Belvidere, – the Venus de Medici, – the Laocoon, and the other masterpieces of ancient art, standing in the very halls which they now occupy; or to see the *chef d'œuvres* of Canova, Thorvaldsen, and Chantrey, or the productions of living artists in their own studio, with the sculptor himself standing by their side, will excite an interest of no ordinary kind.

From the works of the architect, the engineer, and the mechanist, as exhibited in full relief, the student, whether at our schools or colleges, will derive the most valuable instruction. The gigantic aqueducts of ancient and modern times, – the viaducts and bridges which span our valleys and our rivers, and the machinery in our arsenals, factories, and workshops, will be objects of deep interest to the general as well as the professional inquirer.

There is yet another application of the stereoscope to educational purposes, not less important than those which have been mentioned. In the production of diagrams representing instruments and apparatus, which cannot be understood from drawings of them on a plane, it will be of incalculable use to the teacher to have stereoscopic pictures of them. In every branch of physical science, diagrams of this kind are required. When they are intended to represent apparatus and instruments, either for illustrating known truths, or carrying on physical researches, binocular pictures can be easily obtained; but when the diagrams have not been taken from apparatus, but are merely combinations of lines, we can obtain binocular photographs of them only from models constructed on purpose. These models will give binocular representations in various azimuths, so that the true position of planes at different inclinations, and lines at various angles with each other, and at different distances from the eye, will be readily apprehended. Astronomical diagrams, in which orbits, &c., may be represented by wires, and optical figures, in which the rays may be formed by threads or wires, would be thus easily executed.

Among the binocular diagrams, consisting of white lines upon a black ground, which have been executed in Paris, there is one representing the apparatus in which a ray of light, polarized by reflexion from a glass plate, passes through a crystallized film perpendicular to the plane of the paper, and is subsequently analysed by reflexion from another plate at right angle to the following plate. This diagram, when placed in relief by the stereoscope, gives as correct an idea of the process as the apparatus itself.

42

JOHN HENRY PEPPER, 'THE STEREOSCOPE' [EXTRACT]

The Boy's Playbook of Science (London: Routledge, 1866), pp. 320–323

This instrument has now attained a popularity quite equal to, if it does not surpass, that formerly enjoyed by the kaleidoscope, and without entering upon the much-vexed question of priority of discovery, it is sufficient again to mention with the highest respect the names of Sir David Brewster and Professor Wheatstone as identified with the discovery and use of this most pleasing optical instrument.

The principle of the stereoscope (meaning, *solid I see*) is copied from nature: *i.e.*, when both eyes are employed in the examination of an object, two separate pictures, embracing dissimilar forms, are impressed upon the retinæ, and produce the effect of solidity; if the pictures formed at the back of the eyes could be examined by another person with a stereoscope, they would come together, and also produce the effect of solidity.

Stereoscopic pictures are obtained by exposing sensitized paper in the camera to the picture of an object taken in two positions, or two cameras are employed to obtain the same result. If the latter mode is adopted, the stereoscopic pictures must not be taken from positions too widely separated from each other; or else, when the two pictures are placed in the stereoscope, they will stand out with a relief that is quite unnatural, and the object will appear like a very reduced solid model, instead of having the natural appearance presented by pictures which have been taken at positions too distant from each other.

Sir David Brewster says, 'In order to obtain photographic pictures mathematically exact, we must construct a binocular camera which will take the pictures simultaneously, and of the same size; that is, by a camera with two lenses of the same aperture and focal length, placed at the same distance as the two eyes. As it is impossible to grind and polish two lenses, whether single or achromatic, of exactly the same focal lengths, even if we had the very same glass for each, I propose to bisect the lenses, and construct the instrument with semi-lenses, which will give us pictures of precisely the same size and definition. These lenses should be placed with their diameters of bisection parallel to one another, and at a distance of 2½ inches, *which is the average distance of the eyes in man;* and when fixed in a box of sufficient size, will form a binocular camera, which will give us

DOI: 10.4324/9781315400303-60

at the same instant, with the same lights and shadows, and of the same size, such dissimilar pictures of statues, buildings, landscapes, and living objects, as will reproduce them in relief in the stereoscope'. Thus with a single camera provided with semi-lenses, or two lenses of the same focal length, stereoscopic pictures can be obtained.

To bring the images of the two pictures together, and produce the effect of solidity; either of two instruments may be employed. The reflecting stereoscope is the invention of Professor Wheatstone. The refracting or lenticular stereoscope that of Sir David Brewster.

The former is constructed by placing two upright boards on a wooden stand at a moderate distance from each other; the stereoscopic pictures are attached to these boards, which may be made to move up or down, and if the pictures are held in grooves, they may be pulled right or left at pleasure, and thus four movements are secured – viz., upward, downward, right, or left. Between the two stereoscopic pictures are placed two looking-glasses, so adjusted that their backs form an angle of ninety degrees with each other.

The pictures are illuminated at night by a lamp or gas flame placed at the back of the mirrors, which, when fixed together, have the same shape as a prism; indeed, Professor Wheatstone substituted a prism for the mirrors, and thus paved the way for the invention of the lenticular stereoscope.

The stereoscopic effect is obtained by bringing the eyes close to the inclined mirrors, so that the two reflected images coincide at the intersection of the optic axis; the coincidence of the images is further secured by moving either picture a little to the right or left, and if the upright boards move bodily in grooves to or from the centre mirror, the greatest nicety of adjustment is procured.

During the last three years of the author's directorship of the Polytechnic – viz., in 1856, 1857, 1858 – nearly the whole of the pictures shown by the dissolving-view apparatus were coloured photographs from Mr. Hine's original pictures, painted two feet square in blue and white, and reduced on the glass to about six inches square. The collodion film being frequently thick and difficult to penetrate with light, was etched and scratched away where required, and filled in with colour, and when these pictures were looked at with *one* eye only, they appeared to be almost solid or stereoscopic on the disc.

The lenticular stereoscope consists of a box of a pyramidal shape, open at the base, and provided with grooves in which are placed the stereoscopic pictures; if the latter are taken on glass the base of the box is held directly against the light, but if they are daguerreotypes or paper pictures, then a side light is reflected upon them by means of a lid covered in the inside with tinfoil, which is raised or lowered at pleasure from the top part of the box. Two semi-lenses are now fitted into the narrow part of the box, and are placed at such a distance from each other that the centres of the semi-lenses correspond with the pupil of the eyes, and this distance has already been stated to amount to 2½ inches.

The centres of the two stereoscopic pictures [. . .] correspond with the centres of the lenses, and the rays of light *diverging* from [them] fall upon the semi-lenses, and being refracted nearly *parallel* are, by the prismatic form of the semi-lenses, deflected from their course, and leave the surfaces of the lenses in the same direction as if they actually emanated from [a single image between them]; and as all images of bodies appear to come in a straight line from the point whence they are seen, the two pictures are superimposed on each other, and together produce the appearance of solidity, so that a stereoscopic result is obtained when the *spectral images* of the two stereoscopic pictures are made to overlap each other. By taking one of the semi-lenses in each hand, and looking at the two pictures, the over-lapping of the *spectral images* becomes very apparent, so that the combined *spectral images*, and not the *pictures* themselves, are seen when we look into a stereoscope.

5.2

Zoetrope, phenakistiscope, thaumatrope

DOI: 10.4324/9781315400303-61

5.2 Zoetrope, phenakistiscope, thaumatrope

William B. Carpenter, 'On the Zoetrope and Its Antecedents' [extract], *The Student and Intellectual Observer of Science, Literature, and Art*, 2 (1869), pp. 25–27.

The Young Ladies' Treasure Book: A Complete Practical Cyclopedia of Practical Instruction and Direction for All Indoor and Outdoor Occupations and Amusements Suitable to Young Ladies [extract] (London: Ward, Lock, 1884), pp. 806–808.

The stereoscope was not the only new nineteenth-century visual medium that began as a kind of scientific toy, illuminated the properties of human vision, and also pointed the way to future modes of media consumption. Devices such as the phenakistiscope (sometimes spelled as 'phenakistoscope'), the zoetrope (or 'zootrope') and the thaumatrope also enlisted the physiology of the human eye and brain to create their illusions. Despite their unusual names, they actually worked according to simple but far-reaching principles. The phenakistiscope consisted of a disc mounted on a handle, with a sequence of slightly different drawings on the disk and small slits spaced evenly along it. A viewer placed the phenakistiscope facing a mirror, spun the disc, and then looked through the slits at the mirror to see the drawings animated into what looked like a continuously moving image. The zoetrope worked along similar lines. It was made of a spinning cylinder with a sequence of images mounted inside and vertical slits through which viewers would look into the cylinder and see the illusion of repeated motion. The thaumatrope, the simplest of these devices, was simply a flat disc with perforations for attaching it to two strings and complementary images on each side of the disc. The operator would use the strings to spin the disc rapidly around its horizontal axis, making the two images appear to merge into one.

Such optical toys could offer 'amusement' and scientific play (as the titles of some of the works excerpted here have it). Construction of the thaumatropes might even provide an easy rainy-day project for young ladies and gentlemen. But these simple devices also modeled important features of visual perception: the persistence of vision (the lingering of images in the eye because of the retina's response time) and the beta movement and phi phenomenon (how the brain creates the illusion of motion from rapid or flickering sequences of still images). Furthermore, they could be adapted as popular amusements for the lecture hall or the arcade alike. As visual diversions that depended on the optics of perception, Victorian optical toys connect the histories of illustration and illusion to the prehistory of cinema, a later medium based on a succession of still images that appear to flicker into movement, taking advantage of just these same properties of human vision. The brief films produced at the turn of the century, in the earliest years of motion pictures, have been called a 'cinema of attractions', which solicited viewers' attention to spectacular images rather than their absorption in a narrative – a further resemblance between early cinema and the optical toys and visual amusements discussed here.[1]

Note

1 Tom Gunning, 'The Cinema of Attractions: Early Film, Its Spectator, and the Avant Garde', in *Early Cinema: Space Frame Narrative*, ed. Thomas Elsaesser (London: British Film Institute, 1989), pp. 56–65.

For considerations of nineteenth-century optical toys and visual cultures, see Jonathan Crary, *Techniques of the Observer: On Vision and Modernity in the Nineteenth Century* (Cambridge, MA: MIT Press, 1990); Meredith A. Bak, *Playful Visions: Optical Toys and the Emergence of Children's Media Culture* (Cambridge, MA: MIT Press, 2020). On the long history of optical toys and media devices and their relationships to cinema and screen, see Crary as well as Laurent Mannoni, *Great Art of Light and Shadow: Archaeology of the Cinema*, trans. by Richard Crangle (Exeter: University of Exeter Press, 2000); Hermann Hecht, *Pre-Cinema History: An Encyclopaedia and Annotated Bibliography of the Moving Image Before 1896*, ed. Ann Hecht (London: Bowker Saur/British Film Institute, 1993); Barbara Maria Stafford and Frances Terpak, *Devices of Wonder: From the World in a Box to Images on a Screen* (Los Angeles: Getty Research Institute, 2001).

43

WILLIAM B. CARPENTER, 'ON THE ZOETROPE AND ITS ANTECEDENTS' [EXTRACT]

The Student and Intellectual Observer of Science, Literature, and Art, 2 (1869), pp. 25–27

All the devices by which motion is given to the spectra in the Phenakisticope and Stroboscope are constructed upon these two principles; movements of *translation*, forwards or backwards, being determined by a difference between the number of figures disposed in circular series and the number of slits through which they are viewed; and movements *in the parts of figures* being produced by varying the disposition of those parts, either gradationally or interruptedly, as the effect may require.

It is a very curious feature in all these illusions, that the effect produced upon the consciousness by the succession of gradationally varying images, is that of uninterrupted movement, except in cases in which the reverse is intended; the passage between each visual impression and the next being *smoothed over* (so to speak) *by the mind*, which itself completes the conception of continuous movement, that is only *suggested* by the succession of separate dissimilar impressions. This principle is admirably illustrated by a little apparatus lately shown to the writer by Sir Charles Wheatstone, who devised it for the purpose of exhibiting the effects produced by the Phenakisticope and Stroboscope in such a manner as to indicate their true *rationale*. It consists of a disk of card, near the circumference of which are painted at regular intervals a series of black figures representing a man with his limbs in different attitudes; each figure being intermediate in position between the figures on either side of it. This disk is made to revolve, by means of a cog-wheel acting on a 'snail', not continuously, but in a series of interrupted jerks; the movement being so arranged that by each jerk the disk is advanced very quickly through the interval between one figure and the next, whilst it remains stationary for an appreciable time between each translation. Hence, if the eyes be fixed, without any intermediate apparatus whatever, on some one part of the disk, and the wheel be made to revolve in the manner above described, each figure, as

DOI: 10.4324/9781315400303-62

it comes to a momentary stop, makes its own visual impression, which remains so distinct that the succession is scarcely impaired by the rapid intervening movement of translation; and thus if the figures were all similar, that succession would produce the mental image of the wheel with its circle of figures at absolute rest. But as the attitude of each figure which passes before the spot at which we are looking, differs from that of the figure which preceded it, we see on the spot at which we gaze, not a series of similar figures, but a succession of dissimilar figures; and thus, when the disk is made to revolve with a certain degree of rapidity, that spot seems to be occupied by a figure, of which the limbs are in continual movement. This movement, however, is not in a series of jerks, as might have been anticipated from the interruptedness of the sequence of the visual impressions on which the appearance depends, but seems to be as continuous as it would be in nature; and this apparent continuity can only be explained by attributing it to a *mental filling-up* of the intervals between the images actually received through the visual sense, converting (so to speak) a series of steps into a smooth incline.

This mental action becomes very perceptible, when we study the illusions exhibited by the *Zoetrope*, with·sufficient care to distinguish between the *actual impressions* which we receive through our sight, and the *notions* which those impressions suggest.

This instrument differs from its predecessors merely in this – that instead of looking at one revolving disk through slits in another, or looking through slits in a disk at its image reflected in a mirror, we look through slits in the side of a vertical revolving drum at the interior of the opposite side of that drum, which moves, of course, in a direction opposite to that of the side next the eye, and with precisely the same velocity. If, when we cause the drum to revolve with considerable quickness, we look *over its edge* at the slits on the opposite side, these appear so blended by the motion as to be indistinguishable; but if we look at them through any of the slits on the side next us, a spectrum of the opposite inner side is seen, with its slits very clearly defined and at perfect rest. This is precisely what might be anticipated from all that has gone before. And when one of the long strips covered with figures is placed in the lower part of the drum, and is viewed through the slits in its near side, the effect is exactly the same as that produced by looking through the slits near the margin of the disks of the Phenakisticope or Stroboscope, at the reflected images of the figures which are circularly disposed within. The Zoetrope has the double advantage of enabling a large number of spectators to witness its curious effects at the same time; and of serving for the ready exhibition of any number of different designs, which are printed on long strips of stiff paper (the length of each being adjusted to that of the internal circumference of the drum), so that one can be easily substituted for another.

Now, if these designs be examined, it will be found that the movements which they represent all depend upon two conditions – the movements of *translation*, in which the figures appear to pass onwards or backwards round the interior of the drum, being all due to the numerical relation between the *figures* and the *slits;* while the changes in the *positions* of the figures, which may or may not be combined with a movement of translation, depend upon the relations between the parts of those figures as we follow them from one end of the strip to the other, these relations being so adjusted in the drawing as to produce the effect either of continuous or of interrupted or reversed movement, as the subject may require.

44

THE YOUNG LADIES' TREASURE BOOK: A COMPLETE PRACTICAL CYCLOPEDIA OF PRACTICAL INSTRUCTION AND DIRECTION FOR ALL INDOOR AND OUTDOOR OCCUPATIONS AND AMUSEMENTS SUITABLE TO YOUNG LADIES [EXTRACT]

(London: Ward, Lock, 1884), pp. 806–808

The Thaumatrope

We are now going to mention several toys based on the illusions of vision and the persistence of impressions on the retina, and the Thaumatrope is the first of them. This is a plaything of very ancient origin. It consists of a cardboard disc, which we put in motion by pulling two cords. On one side of the disc a cage [. . .] is portrayed, on the other a bird [. . .]. When the little contrivance is turned round, the two designs are seen at the same time, and form but one image – that of the bird in its cage. It is of course hardly necessary to add that the designs may be varied.

The Phenakistoscope

The rotating toy [. . .] goes under this name [. . .]. Through the narrow slits we perceive in succession representations of different positions of a certain action. The persistence of the luminous impressions on the retina gives to the eye the sensation of a continuous image, which seems animated by the same movements as those portrayed in the different phases.

The Zootrope

This is a perfected specimen of the apparatus last mentioned. It is composed of a cylinder of cardboard, turning on a central axis. The cylinder is pierced with

DOI: 10.4324/9781315400303-63

vertical slits at regular intervals, through which the spectator can see the designs upon a band of paper adapted to the interior of the apparatus in rotation. The designs are so executed that they represent the different times of a movement between two extremes; and in consequence of the impressions upon the retina the successive phases are mingled, so the spectator believes he sees, without transition, the entire movement. The extremes of the movement are right and left; the intermediary figures make the transitions, and they are usually equal in number to the slits in the Zootrope. It is not difficult to construct such an instrument [. . .]. The earth might be represented turning in space, or a fire-engine pumping water could be given, and thus the Zootrope might be quite a vehicle of instruction as well as of amusement. This instrument is certainly one of the most curious in the range of optics, and never fails to excite interest. The ingenious contrivances which have up to the present time reproduced it, all consist in the employment of narrow slits, which, besides reducing the light to a great extent, and consequently the light and clearness of the object, require the instrument to be set in rapid rotation, which greatly exaggerates the rapidity of the movements represented, and without which the intermissions of the spectacle could not unite in a continuous sensation.

5.3

Aniline dye

DOI: 10.4324/9781315400303-64

5.3 Aniline dye

Thomas W. Salter, *Field's Chromatography; or, Treatise on Colours and Pigments As Used by Artists* [extract] (London: Winsor and Newton, 1869), pp. 161–163.

Even amid the smoke and steam, Victorian technological things could also point to a brighter, more colourful life. In 1856, a young London chemistry student named William Henry Perkin was trying to follow up a teacher's suggestion that it might be possible to derive the anti-malarial extract quinine from coal tar, when he inadvertently produced a new substance with a vivid purple colour. Perkin received a patent on the chemical and began to promote it as mauveine, the first commercial artificial dye, a new colour for the great British textile industry and an alternative to expensive natural dyes. The success of mauvine inspired the search for other new aniline dyes, which soon came to include brilliant magentas, blues, pinks, yellows, greens and other colours. Aniline dyes brought a range of vibrant hues to a variety of products, particularly women's dresses, and amounted to a revolution in textile production and fashion.

The Victorians marvelled over the fact that ugly coal tar, a waste product left over after the conversion of coal into industrial coke, could yield such colour and beauty. Field and Salter's *Chromatography* emphasises the wonder and romance of the aniline dyes that were being produced by the ton by this time. But aniline dyes did not simply attest to the wondrous power of chemistry to harvest a rainbow from pieces of rock. In the late nineteenth and twentieth centuries, these chemical innovations would continue to have dramatic implications not only for the textile industry and fashion but also for the burgeoning field of industrial chemistry more broadly. As it turned out, a wide array of chemical products could be synthesised from coal tar: paints, adhesives, detergents and even medicines (the antipyretic pain reliever paracetamol or acetaminophen is an aniline analgesic). But this innovation had a dark side, as well. It would also become clear that aniline dyes, their by-products, and the industry they initiated could present new chemical threats to the health of textile and chemical workers, the environment and, in some cases, even the wearers of those beautifully dyed clothes.[1]

Note

1 On the hazards of aniline dyes and of the textile industry more broadly, see Alison Matthews David, *Fashion Victims: The Dangers of Dress Past and Present* (London: Bloomsbury, 2015).

An engaging history of Perkins and aniline dyes is provided by Simon Garfield, *Mauve: How One Man Invented a Colour That Changed the World* (London: Faber and Faber, 2001). For a comprehensive history of the entire industry, see Fred Aftalion, *A History of the International Chemical Industry: From the 'Early Days' to 2000*, trans. by Otto Theodor Benfey, 2nd ed. (Philadelphia: Chemistry Heritage, 2001).

45

THOMAS W. SALTER, *FIELD'S CHROMATOGRAPHY; OR, TREATISE ON COLOURS AND PIGMENTS AS USED BY ARTISTS* [EXTRACT]

(London: Winsor and Newton, [1869]), pp. 161–164

Previous to the year 1856 the colouring matters derived from coal-tar were practically unknown. Until then, that black evil-smelling substance was looked upon as almost worthless; but gradually the unsightly grub emerged into a beautiful butterfly, clothed first in mauve and next in magenta. After its long winter of neglect, there sprung from coal-tar the most vivid and varied hues, like flowers from the earth at spring. At a touch of the fairy wand of science, the waste land became a garden of tropic tints, and colour succeeded colour, until the whole gamut had been gone through. Never was transformation more dazzling or more complete. The once despised refuse was now a valued commercial product – indeed a trade in itself. Perfectly fascinated by the study, chemists threw themselves heart and soul into coal-tar, and coal-tar colours were to be seen everywhere.

It were beside our purpose to enter into the various stages through which coal has to pass to become colour. Enough to state that to the introduction of gas-light we are indebted for the acquisition of coal-tar colours, the starting point for the production of mauve, magenta, &c., being the manufacture of coal-gas. From the destructive distillation of coal, coal-tar oil results; and from this are obtained the products which yield the colours in question. Among these products may be mentioned aniline, rosaniline, napthaline, chinoline, carbolic acid, picric acid, &c., with their derivatives.

Of the fifty-one compounds furnished by the distillation of coal, perhaps the most popularly associated with coal-tar colours is aniline, to which we will therefore confine ourselves. Discovered in 1826, this body was formerly prepared from indigo – in Spanish, *anil*, whence the name; but is now produced on a larger scale from benzol, a coal-tar product. As the source of mauve and magenta, aniline must be considered the parent of coal-tar colours generally. Little was known of it at one time except that on being mixed with a solution of

DOI: 10.4324/9781315400303-65

chloride of lime there was formed a splendid purple liquid, which immediately gave place to a dingy reddish precipitate. From the investigation of this simple fact, however, by Mr. W. Perkin, there was created a new and important branch of chemical industry – the manufacture of coal-tar colours. The violet mauve led the way, followed by the red magenta, the blue azuline, the yellow phosphine, the green emeraldine, the orange aurine, by purple, and brown, and black. Such were the hues, with many intermediate tints and shades, which one reaction brought forth. The world rubbed its eyes with astonishment; and truly it seemed almost as wonderful to produce the colours of the rainbow from a lump of coal, as to extract sunshine from cucumbers.

The history of these colours reads more like a romance than a sober story, but to the artist it is of slight practical interest. Sufficiently stable as dyes, though they be, coal-tar colours are not adapted to the palette. Mauve, magenta, with a few others, have been introduced as pigments and fairly tried, but a want of permanence has been fatal to their success. Mauve is more durable than magenta, and the rest vary in stability, but none of them have proved really fitted for artists' colours. Exposed to light and air, they all more or less fade, especially in thin washes; and they have mostly the objection of staining and permeating the paper or canvas on which they are employed. Used in body, some may be found eligible in portfolio illuminations and the like, where the brilliancy of their colours shows to advantage; but in landscapes and pictures of life, coal-tar pigments are best avoided.

5.4

Pianista

DOI: 10.4324/9781315400303-66

5.4 Pianista

'The Inventions Exhibition: The 'Miranda Pianista', *British Trade Journal* (1 May 1885), p. 297.

Inventions changed how people heard the world, as well as the things that they heard. The player piano or pianola was not the first automatic musical instrument. Barrel organs and music boxes date to the eighteenth century, and other instruments had been crafted even before then. But the mechanics of striking the keys of a piano made the creation of a self-playing piano somewhat more challenging. The pianola, which became the popular standard design for the player piano at the turn of the century, was played by running a scroll-like paper music roll across a pneumatic reader. Slits cut in the paper activated particular keys on the piano in a manner reminiscent of the punchcards first used in the Jacquard loom – a link between industrial production, entertainment media and the history of tabulation and computing.

A few years before the pianola, the 'miranda pianista' worked in a somewhat similar fashion. As the pianola would, the miranda pianista used punched paper to replay music, but rather than being a self-playing piano, it was actually a separate mechanism that fit over an existing instrument's keyboard and played the keys like a sort of mechanical pianist. The pianista brought together art, commerce and technology; it might be especially useful for dancing parties and in the colonies where musicians were hard to find, speculates the *British Trade Journal*. With their ability to mimic songs as played by human pianists and the ease with which one piece of music could be swapped out for others, automatic pianos, pianistas and their punched-paper medium represent a significant chapter in the history of recorded music, in the broadest sense.[1]

Note

1 For further reading on the history – and the sheer variety – of automatic musical instruments, see Q. David Bowers, *Encyclopedia of Automatic Musical Instruments* (Lanham, MD: Vestal, 1972); Arthur A. Reblitz, *The Golden Age of Automatic Musical Instruments* (Woodsville, NH: Mechanical Music, 2001); W. J. G. Ord-Hume, *Clockwork Music: An Illustrated History of Mechanical Musical Instruments from the Musical Box to the Pianola, from Automaton Lady Virginal Players to Orchestrion* (London: Allen and Unwin; New York: Crown, 1973).

46

'THE INVENTIONS EXHIBITION: THE MIRANDA PIANISTA'

British Trade Journal (1 May 1885), p. 297

In the musical section of the exhibition one of the most novel inventions is the 'Miranda Pianista'. It is an apparatus for the mechanical playing of all key-board instruments, such as the piano, organ, &c. The inventors are Messrs. Bishop & Down, and there is no doubt they have hit upon an idea which will be practically useful. It would be an interesting calculation for a member of the Statistical Society to determine how many pianos there are which are never played, simply because there is no one sufficiently skilful to produce good music from them. They become, in many households, simply articles of furniture. The purpose of the 'Miranda Pianista' is to remedy this state of things. It is a handsome case, about 3 feet high and 4 feet broad, from the back of which projects a number of fingers or levers corresponding to the keys of a piano or organ. This is placed in front of the instrument to be played, the levers resting upon the keys. Music in the form of perforated sheets of cardboard is then put into the pianista. On turning the handle, the levers are brought smartly down upon the keys in the same way as the fingers of the player would be, and the music-sheet gradually moves forward. In this way anyone entirely unskilled as a musician can play the piano or organ rather more efficiently than a great majority of those who have undergone several courses of music lessons. The expression of *piano* or *forte* is produced by moving a small lever with the left hand. The pedals of the pianoforte can also be extended, and carried through to the front of the pianista, so that they are also under the control of the player. The mechanical arrangement within the invention, by which the striking-levers are worked, is of greater simplicity than one would at first sight suppose. It consists chiefly of bellows and an air-reservoir. A pressure is exerted which, when certain points come under the perforation in the music-card, is released, and thus made to move the fingers. The music is supplied quite as cheaply as ordinary music, and is already in great variety. Among the special times when such an apparatus would be useful must be classed dancing parties and balls, where the trouble of playing would be relegated to the servant. In the colonies especially the invention should be favourably received. The class there with leisure to study and practise musical instruments is naturally smaller than at home, and such an invention as this, there is no doubt, would be heartily welcomed in many a colonist's home.

DOI: 10.4324/9781315400303-67

5.5

Phonograph

DOI: 10.4324/9781315400303-68

5.5 Phonograph

W. H. Preece, 'The Phonograph', *Journal of the Society of Arts* (10 May 1878), pp. 534–537.
'The New Phonograph', *Cassell's Family Magazine* (1888), pp. 315–317.
'Mr. Edison's Phonograph', *Times* (30 June 1888), p. 5.
'What Will Come of the Phonograph?' *Spectator* (30 June 1888), p. 9.

A pianola or pianista performed a preset sequence of notes on a piano, demonstrating that a machine could take the place of a living pianist. But another Victorian technological object created a wholesale revolution in the history of sound reproduction. In 1878, Thomas Edison patented the phonograph, which could record sound on a rotating cylinder and then play it back. Sound is a pattern of vibrations through a medium such as air; it unfolds in time and cannot stand still. Until Edison's breakthrough, a sound had been considered the model of evanescence, a unique event that even as it unfolds is on its way to vanishing forever. Shortly after Edison announced his invention, the electrical engineer William Henry Preece not only explained the new device but also placed it in the context of the mechanics of sound as well as among a chorus of recent acoustic inventions: the telephone, the microphone and the aerophone (a device that could amplify sound over distance).[1]

Yet the promise of the early phonograph to inscribe sound patterns onto a surface and save them for repeated future replay far outpaced the actual results. Edison's original phonograph was a marvel of science, but for its recording surface it used tin foil, which turned out to be too delicate for long-term recording and playback. In practice, the removal of a foil recording from a phonograph's cylinder instantly spoiled the recording, making the phonograph more of a lecture-hall curiosity than a potential consumer device. A decade later, Edison launched the 'Perfected Phonograph', which recorded sound on wax cylinders. The relaunch of the phonograph inspired a new round of prognostication in print about its potential use and significance. Although it was initially marketed as a business instrument, by the early 1890s, this 'new phonograph' was on its way to a long career in recorded entertainment. The phonograph with its recorded cylinders would eventually give way to the gramophone and its more familiar disc format, while the recording medium of wax would be superseded by shellac, celluloid and finally vinyl.[2]

Notes

1 Important explorations of the nineteenth-century history and culture of sound recording include Jonathan Sterne, *The Audible Past: Cultural Origins of Sound Reproduction* (Durham, NC: Duke University Press, 2003), and Lisa Gitelman, *Scripts, Grooves, and Writing Machines: Representing Technology in the Edison Era* (Stanford, CA: Stanford University Press, 1999).

2 The history of sound recording connects a number of topics: the technical design and properties of devices and their media, the businesses of marketing machines and of

preserving and selling sound, the history and aesthetics of recorded speech and music, and the relationships of all of these to the broader histories of modern cultures and media. For accounts of the phonograph and recorded sound that effectively bring together and address such topics, see Roland Gelatt, *The Fabulous Phonograph, 1877–1977*, 2nd ed. (London: Collier Macmillan, 1977); Walter L. Welch and Leah Brodbeck Stenzel Burt, *From Tinfoil to Stereo: The Acoustic Years of the Recording Industry, 1877–1929* (Gainesville, FL: University Press of Florida, 1994); A. J. Millard, *America on Record: A History of Recorded Sound*, 2nd ed. (Cambridge: Cambridge University Press, 2005); Richard Osborne, *Vinyl: A History of the Analogue Record* (Farnham, Surrey: Ashgate, 2012); Jason Camlot, *Phonopoetics: The Making of Early Literary Recordings* (Stanford, CA: Stanford University Press, 2019).

47

W. H. PREECE, 'THE PHONOGRAPH'

Journal of the Society of Arts (10 May 1878), pp. 534–538

The science of acoustics has taken most marvellous strides within the last few months. We have already had in this room a description of the telephone itself. We have, in addition to that, another instrument that has created a great deal of sensation, and which I shall have the pleasure of bringing before you to-night. But besides the telephone and the phonograph, there are other wonders in store. There is an instrument – which has not yet come from the other side of the Atlantic – called the aerophone. The aerophone is an instrument that enables the voice to be heard at a distance of four miles. On the other hand, we have within the last few days produced in England an instrument that will be brought before the Royal Society to-morrow night, which is called the microphone. The microphone is an instrument which acts towards the ear as the microscope does to the eye. It will render evident to us sounds that are otherwise absolutely inaudible. I have heard myself the tramp of a little fly across a box with a tread almost as loud as that of a horse across a wooden bridge. There was a remarkable sound that accompanied the tramp of Mr. Fly, and a facetious friend of mine told me he thought the noise was occasioned by the neighing of the proboscis of the fly. Between the microphone on the one side and the aerophone on the other, we have, occupying a middle position, the instrument I have to bring before you to-night. All these instruments depend upon the operation of that marvellous force, if we may so call it, which we call sound. If I ring a bell, blow a musical instrument, or strike anything, what is it that has happened, which passing from me to everybody's ear in this room has produced that sensation which we call sound? I know you are all anxious to see the phonograph in operation, but I think it is just as well to make you acquainted shortly with the principles on which the phonograph works, for if you comprehend the principles, you will, to an infinitely greater extent, admire the instrument itself. So let us ask ourselves, what is this thing which we call sound? Sound of any kind is reducible to motion. The motion of matter is necessary and essential for the production of sound, and the motion of the air, the air that surrounds us and which we breathe, that bathes everybody in this room, is essential for the production of that operation which is now taking place in my throat. I am rather sorry to find that it is still daylight to a certain extent, but I am in hopes if the gas is put down I shall be able to give you a little notion of what sonorous vibration is.

DOI: 10.4324/9781315400303-69

Our notion of waves is derived from what we see upon the sea shore; we see there a motion of ascent and descent, accompanied by a motion of translation, but in this room, although at the present moment while I am speaking to you the air is chased and engraved in the most exquisite manner by the undulations I am imparting to it, all this is invisible to us, and it must so remain. All that we can do is to give you a faint conception of how this air acts. If you could see a tube of air, for instance, coming from my mouth to any one of your ears, then that tube of air, by every sound that is uttered, is thrown into vibration. But it is not a vibration of ascent and descent like the waves of the ocean, but it is an excursion to and fro, and between me and the end of the room, for every sound I utter there is in every particle of air an excursion to and fro. Now, notes or sounds vary in three particular ways.

In the first place, we have the pitch of a note. The pitch of a note is that which determines whether it shall be A, B, or C, or any other note of music; and the pitch of a note is the number of vibrations that are made per second, or, in other words, the length of the wave. So that the first property connected with notes is that of their pitch, and their pitch depends upon the length of the sonorous wave.

The second property of sound is that of loudness. I can speak to you softly, I can speak to you loudly; you can hear the note of a piano gently played, you can press the pedal, and you can hear it loudly played. You can produce sounds that vary in intensity between great extremes, and the reason why one sound is greater than another is, that the amplitude of the excursion of particles of air are greater in one case than in the other; in other words, their velocity being different they hit the drum of the ear with greater force. In the same way, if you take a common smooth-bore gun which drives a ball with the initial velocity of a few feet, and you take an Armstrong gun, which drives the ball with a velocity of 1,500 feet, in the one case you have the ball making an indentation in a metal shield, while in the other case you have the ball sent right through the shield. So when you utter sounds softly, the tympanum of the ear is struck gently; and when you utter sounds loudly, the ear is struck with greater force. The loudness of sound is dependent upon the amplitude to and fro of the particles of air.

But there is a third property of sound, which is one of its principal properties, the one which distinguishes one voice from another, that distinguishes the note C on the violin from the same note on the piano; the cause of the difference between the sound of the drum and a cornet, and all the differences that occur between various sounds. All these differences are solely dependent upon the form in which the waves take their excursion to and fro. They may jerk to and fro, they may move gently forward and back again, with a high velocity or a low velocity, and so they may vary their mode of excursion to and fro in innumerable forms and produce various shades of intonation and articulation. So that we have, first of all, the pitch of a note which depends, as I told you, on the length of the wave; secondly, the loudness of a note, which depends on the amplitude of the excursion; and, thirdly, the quality of a note, which depends upon the form of the wave.

I will endeavour to give you an idea of what a sonorous wave is. On this screen you will see a little spot of light. I am not sure that the light is visible to the whole of the room, but that little spot of light is supposed to represent a particle of air now in a state of quiescence in some part of this room. If we move the slide up and down, you will see it takes a motion backward and forward, which represents very roughly the movement to and fro of the particles of air between me and the end of the room. The next slide shows a portion of the supposititious tube of air, including several of these particles, and in this I have endeavoured to illustrate to you what takes place to form a wave. A wave means a succession of lines of compression and of rarefaction. Since there is no up and down movement like the waves of the sea, there is an excursion to and fro, which excursion results in a series of compressions and rarefactions. Now, if we move that slide up and down, you will see passing over it a series of waves, and those waves are simply a series of condensations and rarefactions. They are very erratic, and rather crude, and I should be very sorry indeed for anybody to imagine that what you see on the screen is an actual representation of what takes place in nature. Nature in all her laws is beautiful, but in this poor attempt to illustrate her laws, we have nothing but what is crude and rough. It is, however, an attempt to bring before you what is taking place in this room. That shows what takes place in only one line between my mouth and any ear in this room. But there are millions upon millions of particles going through the same operations of condensation and rarefaction, which you see. When the mind attempts to fix itself upon what takes place in this air, when you endeavour to picture what is going on in nature, you become lost in the effort.

I am now going to show you how matter itself vibrates when you put it in a line of these moving particles. Here is another rough attempt to show you what really occurs, but this is not an effort to induce you to exercise your imagination, but to show you actually what takes place when one speaks at an elastic medium. Now, Mr. Stroh has in front of him an india-rubber diaphragm, upon which is fixed a mirror, and this mirror will reflect upon the screen a spot of light. You will see that, as he sounds a note, the diaphragm vibrates, giving evidence of its vibration by the motion of the spot of light. If, while he sounds the note, he moves backwards and forwards, the spot of light is thrown across the screen, and you find there is an illustration of what I told you, that the note is simply dependent upon the number of vibrations per second; for, if he sounds a low note and then a high note, the difference in vibrations will be apparent to you.

I do not know whether those experiments were sufficient to illustrate to you two facts – first, that sound is produced by the vibration of the particles of air; and, secondly, that objects placed in these paths of vibrating air can themselves be vibrated. It is said that Lablache could sound a note so loud and strong that he could crack a tumbler; and in the Midland Counties there is a serjeant-major of a volunteer corps who is often brought into the room after mess to crack a tumbler in this way. So far as regards the production of sound.

Now, one or two words about the transmission of sound, before we come to the phonograph, which, doubtless, you are all anxious to see. The transmission of sound is twofold; we can have the mechanical transmission, and we can have the reproduction by electrical means. In the earliest days of civilisation, the ancient Greeks acquired the art of transmitting sound, and there were actors who addressed the audience through speaking trumpets. With these they marched up and down the stage, directing their speeches by this means to the furthest end of the theatre. I do not think in the present day we could stand Mr. Henry Irving reciting 'To be, or not to be', through speaking trumpet.

Amongst the proposals to transmit sound, there is one very interesting record of that marvellous old gentleman, who lived some 200 years ago, Mr. Robert Hook, and invented what we know now as the toy telephone. He found that sounds could be transmitted round corners, and to a distance of a hundred yards, by means of diaphragms and wire. Wheatstone, within our memory, produced his [mechanical] telephone, which succeeded in transmitting from the lower to the upper regions – from the cellars of the Polytechnic to the galleries above – musical sounds with all their beauty and variety. We have all doubtless spent our shilling at the London Stereoscopic Company, in buying the toy telephone, which brings before us all the notions I have to bring before you.

The electrical transmission of sound was inaugurated in the year 1860 by a German of the name of Reiss, who showed how, by taking advantage of that vibrating disc, which Mr. Stroh just now showed you, to complete and make a circuit, you could make sounds be heard at a distance. Reiss succeeded in transmitting music, and Gray, of Chicago, succeeded in doing the same. The climax was gained when Professor Graham Bell produced his speaking telephone. About twelve months ago, or, perhaps, a little more than that, I do not believe there was a man in England who believed that it was possible to carry the voice a distance of 50, or even 20 miles. A little more than twelve months ago, I did not believe it myself. I went over to America in the early part of last year, especially to inquire into those advances in telegraphy which our friends on the other side of the Atlantic had made, and when I went there I fully expected I should have the pleasure of exposing the telephone. I had not been there long before I met Professor Bell. I saw his telephone, and I became a convert. I may mention that it was my special pleasure to be the first person to bring this instrument to England; I exhibited it at the meeting of the British Association at Plymouth, and gradually the fact has dawned upon every one, that it is possible to convey the human voice from one spot to another. Well, others have worked in this field. Edison has worked in the footsteps of Professor Bell, and as the outcome of it, he has produced the phonograph. Professor Hughes is the gentleman who has succeeded in making us hear the fly walk, and others are working in the same line. What I want you to clearly understand is this, that all these instruments, whether it be the microphone of Professor Hughes, the telephone of Professor Bell, the aerophone of Mr. Edison, or the interesting instrument behind me, the phonograph, they all depend on this one simple, wonderful fact, which, to my mind, is one of the greatest discoveries of this age, namely, that a mere vibrating diaphragm can give us all the articulation and all the variety and beauty of the human voice. I am sure there is scarcely a man in England who would have believed six months ago that it was possible for a diaphragm of this kind to reproduce the human voice. Certainly, men like Sir

Charles Wheatstone and others, who devoted the best part of their lives to perfecting the speaking instrument, would have thought us stark staring mad if we had told them that the whole beauty of the human voice would ever be reproduced by a plain, simple diaphragm.

Now, in some of the instruments which I have mentioned to you, I have referred to the use of electricity and the use of magnetism, but in the phonograph, to which I am coming, we have neither electricity nor magnetism; and I want at once to disabuse your minds of the idea that there is any electricity used with it, because one of the first questions which is usually asked me is, where is the magnet? There is nothing of the sort here; it is simply a mechanical contrivance. We have merely to insert a diaphragm in the paths of the sonorous vibrations emitted from our mouths, to produce motion. Philosophers have taken advantage of this motion to record sound, and to produce an instrument called the phonautograph.

Mr. William Henry Barlow, one of our most eminent engineers, produced what is termed the logograph, that being an instrument which recorded, not the sonorous vibrations properly of the mouth, but the variations of the air pressure in the immediate vicinity of the mouth. On the diagram to your right there is an enlarged representation, on Mr. Barlow's logograph, of the line, 'The minstrel boy to the war has gone – In the ranks of death you'll find him'. There you will see depicted in curves the different sounds uttered by the voice. They give you, in their amplitude, the loudness of the sound; in their length, the pitch of the sound; and in their form, the quality of the sound – the *timbre*, as the French call it. From this we spring at once to the phonograph, of which we have now all the elements before us. The phonograph was discovered, like many other things, by mere chance. Edison himself was experimenting with the telephone, trying all kinds of experiments, as all of us have been doing, to improve the telephone; in doing so, he pricked his finger, and, drawing it rapidly away, a line was made on his finger. This gave him the notion that if the diaphragm of a telephone could mark his finger, why should it not mark paper, and if it marked paper, why could the sound not be reproduced? So he took a piece of Morse paper and inserted the diaphragm of the telephone, where the ordinary style of the Morse instrument is, and there he found on the paper, when he uttered the words, 'Halloa! halloa!' distinct marks, varying dots and dashes, or a series of dots. Then he took this strip of paper and allowed it to pass back again. He simply reversed the process, and instead of making the diaphragm vibrate with his voice, by passing the paper back again in the reverse direction, he caused the paper to make the diaphragm vibrate, and the result was, he heard a faint 'Halloa! halloa!' come out of the diaphragm. This was a glorious triumph for Edison. It occurred on a Wednesday afternoon. He worked at it all the Wednesday, all Wednesday night, all Thursday, and Thursday night, all Friday, and Friday night incessantly, without eating, drinking, or sleeping, until on Saturday morning he produced his first phonograph. I have on this diagram a drawing of this first phonograph. His difficulty was, having secured the principle of the vibrating diaphragm, to procure some substance which would retain those marks. By a happy inspiration he almost at once lighted upon tinfoil. Tinfoil is in itself a highly inelastic substance, and is not only very inelastic, but is a very yielding substance. Any mark made on tinfoil remains impressed there, and will remain there for an indefinite period. He then made a cylinder of brass, which he covered with a sheet of tinfoil. The cylinder was centred on a screwed axis supported by bearings, and was rotated by a handle at the extreme end. A heavy fly-wheel was attached to it to secure uniform velocity, and there you have all the mechanical contrivances required to make a phonograph. The mode in which it moves is shown in this section on the lower part of the diagram, which is a section taken through the diaphragm of the cylinder. It shows here the section of a diaphragm with its point behind it, the rough end of the cylinder depicts the vibrations, and the forms that are marked on the tinfoil somewhat similar to the forms that are marked on Mr. Barlow's logograph. The great difficulty that persons at first have in following the description of the phonograph is this. We can all very readily see how the vibration of a diaphragm can make marks upon tinfoil, but it is not so easy to see how it is that when you reverse the process these marks on the tinfoil reproduce or repeat the same vibrations. We fancy that the effect of reversing this process, and passing the tinfoil under the diaphragm, would be not to make the diaphragm vibrate, but to rub out the marks on the tinfoil. But the marks are not rubbed out. It appears that the resistance which the diaphragm makes to the vibrations caused by the marks on the tinfoil is very slight, and the same piece of tinfoil can be used over and over again. I have used the same piece as many as 20 times, with a very slight difference in the intensity of sounds produced. The fact remains, that when you pass this marked tinfoil a second time beneath the point at the back of the diaphragm, it then causes the diaphragm to vibrate in exactly the same way as it vibrated under your voice, and the result is if you cause the diaphragm to vibrate in the same way that it vibrated under your voice, you get precisely the same notes, of the same pitch, and the same quality as were contributed to it by your voice. I do not know whether I have made myself clear, but if I have not the instrument shall speak for itself. Here we have the latest form of instrument. It is made by one of the first mechanicians in this country, Mr. Stroh, for the London Stereoscopic Company, who have secured the right of using the phonograph in England, and to whose courtesy and kindness we are indebted for its exhibition to-night. It differs considerably, as you see, from the instrument I have described to you, viz., Edison's first instrument, although it is essentially the same in principle. One great defect in the instrument shown on the diagram, is that you cannot ensure the same velocity of rotation in the cylinder when the sounds are repeated as it had when the sounds were given to it. It requires great delicacy, and a great deal of experience to rotate an instrument of the kind with uniform velocity by the hand, although aided by a fly-wheel. Here, by an exceedingly pretty contrivance, there is a falling weight, which, by an endless chain, and two or three wheels, imparts rotation to the cylinder, and it has this governor above it, these expanding wings, which, by their resistance to the air, give to the instrument what it wants, namely, uniform velocity. The result is, that when you speak into this instrument, you obtain very nearly a reproduction of the sounds emitted – very nearly, not quite. The instrument has not quite reached that perfection when the tones of a Patti, or the speeches of a Gladstone, or the sermons of a Liddon, can be faithfully repeated; in fact, to some extent it is a burlesque or parody of the human voice. You have heard me speak for so many minutes that you will be able to judge how far the instrument will reproduce my own voice. It gives off musical sounds admirably, but unfortunately I am not a musician. I am like the gentleman who only knew two songs, one of which was 'God save the Queen', and the other was not. I do not know the song that was not, so I will presently give you 'God save the Queen', but before we come to that, we will try some poetical quotation, or some learned aphorism, and see what the effect will be.

[Various experiments were made with the instrument, which reproduced some lines of a nursery rhyme, some remarks made by the Chairman, a verse of 'God save the Queen' sung as a duet, the notes of a bugle, some imitations of animals, &c.]

I dare say many of us have thought to ourselves, what uses can this instrument be put to. Now, it is quite evident to you that though the production of sound is very wonderful, it is not very perfect; in fact, there are some consonants that are wanting altogether. The *s* for instance at the beginning and end of a word is almost entirely lost – is entirely lost, although it is heard slightly in the middle of a word. The *d* and the *t* are exactly the same; and the same in *m* and *n, mane* and *name* are not distinguishable. Hence, it is extremely difficult to read what is said upon this instrument; if a person is put out of the room, and you speak into it, he can with difficulty translate what it says. Still, I read distinctly on the first instrument sent over from America to me, a message that was sent to me by its inventor, Mr. Edison. It said distinctly, 'How do you do? What do you think of my phonograph?' Those words were spoken into the instrument in New York, were carried across the Atlantic, and, more than a fortnight after they were uttered, I heard and translated them. But the principal purpose to which it was thought that it could be applied, viz.: to dispense with our friends the shorthand writers, is, I am afraid, still very far in the future. It has been proposed to fill libraries with speeches, with sermons, with plays recited by eminent actors, but the instrument has not yet reached that stage when such a thing is probable. It remains an extremely interesting scientific toy, a wonderful novelty. But it is only a chick. It is only three months old, and if it can do what you have heard to-night when three months old, what will it do when three years old? One of the purposes to which it is proposed to be applied is this. This is what Edison says: – 'I saw the President of the American Philological Society the other day, and he had a conversation with a Portuguese who was in the room through the phonograph. He wants one of my improved phonographs to preserve the accents of the Ormandagas and Tuscaroras, who are dying out. One old man speaks the language fluently and correctly, and he is afraid he will die. You see, one man goes amongst the Indians and represents the pronunciation of their words by English syllables; another represents the same words differently; there is nothing definite. The phonograph will preserve the exact pronunciation, and the President of the Philological Society means to travel with it amongst all the North American tribes'. And so if men in future ages want to know how our Chairman pronounced the English language, or how your lecturer sang, we have only to hand down to posterity this piece of tinfoil.

I do not think I can show you any more of the wonderful performance of this instrument collectively, but we will keep it going for your amusement for some time. I am much obliged to you for the attention you have bestowed, and I must say I have felt great pleasure in bringing the phonograph before the Society of Arts. The inventor of it was kind enough to send me the second instrument that was ever made, and it has been my privilege as well as my great pleasure to bring his wonderful invention before the British public.

48

'THE NEW PHONOGRAPH'

Cassell's Family Magazine (1888), pp. 315–317

Ten years ago Mr. Edison announced his invention of a machine for the storage and reproduction of speech, and the announcement was received at the time with a good deal of incredulity, notwithstanding the partial success of Faber and others in devising mechanical articulators. The simplicity of Edison's invention when it was seen and heard elicited much admiration; and though the novelty as then constructed did not answer all the expectations which a sanguine inventor had raised concerning it, it was nevertheless regarded as a remarkable instrument and the germ of something better. If the words spoken into the instrument were heard in the first place, the likeness of the reproduction was found to be unmistakable. Indeed, so close was the replica of sounds that a member of the French Academy of Sciences declined to believe there was no ventriloquism or other trickery in connection with it. It was evident, however, that before the phonograph could become the practical instrument it was claimed to be, further improvements in the nicety of its articulation were required. The introduction of the electric light diverted Mr. Edison's energies from the task of improving it, although he does not seem to have lost faith in his pet invention. During the past ten years he has accumulated a colossal fortune, and been the means of introducing both electric light and power to the world at large. Quite recently, however, he returned to his earlier love, and has at length, it appears, succeeded in perfecting it so as to redeem his past promises and fulfil his hopes regarding it.

The old instrument consisted, as is well known, of a vibrating tympan or drum, from the centre of which projected a steel point or stylus, in such a manner that on speaking to the tympan its vibrations would urge the stylus to dig into a sheet of tinfoil moving past its point. The foil was supported on a grooved barrel, so that the hollow of the groove behind it permitted the foil to give under the point of the stylus and cause it, instead of penetrating the foil, to indent it more or less according to the force of the vibrations of the tympan. The result was that along the spiral groove of the barrel the tinfoil was deformed with undulations corresponding to the vibrations of the speech. Thus recorded on a yielding but somewhat stiff material, these undulations could be preserved and at a future time made to deflect the point of a similar stylus, and set a corresponding diaphragm or tympan into vibration, so as to give out the original sounds, or an imitation of them.

DOI: 10.4324/9781315400303-70

Tinfoil, however, is not a very satisfactory material on which to receive the vibrations in the first place. It does not precisely respond to the movements of the marking stylus in taking the impression, and does not guide the receiving stylus sufficiently well in reproducing sounds. Mr. Edison, like Professor Bell, has therefore adopted wax in the new phonograph; and instead of tinfoil spread on a grooved support, he now employs a cylinder of wax to take the print of the vibrations. Moreover, he no longer uses the same kind of diaphragm to print and receive the sounds, but employs a more delicate one for receiving. The marking cylinder is now kept in motion by an electric motor, instead of by hand-turning as in the earlier instrument.

The new phonograph of Edison is about the size of an ordinary sewing machine and is of exquisite workmanship; the performance depending to a great extent on the perfection and fitness of the mechanism. It consists of a horizontal spindle [. . .], carrying at one end the wax cylinder [. . .], on which the sonorous vibrations are to be imprinted. Over the cylinder is supported a diaphragm or tympan [. . .] provided with a conical mouthpiece [. . .] for speaking into. Under the tympan there is a delicate needle or stylus, with its point projecting from the centre of the tympan downwards to the surface of the wax cylinder, so that when a person speaks into the mouthpiece, the voice vibrates the tympan and drives the point of the stylus down into the wax, making an imprint more or less deep in accordance with the vibrations of the voice. The cylinder is kept revolving in a spiral path, at a uniform speed, by means of an electric motor [. . .] fitted with a sensitive regulator and situated at the base of the machine. The result is that a delicate and ridgy trace is cut in the surface of wax along a spiral line. This is the sound record, and by substituting a finer tympan for the one used in producing it, the ridges and inequalities of the trace can be made to agitate a light stylus resting on them, and cause it to set the delicate tympan into vibrations corresponding very accurately to those of the original sounds. The tympan employed for receiving is made of gold-beater's skin – having a stud at its centre and a springy pointer of steel wire. The sounds emitted by this device are almost a whisper as compared to the original ones, but they are faithful in articulation, which is the main object, and they are conveyed to the ear by means of flexible hearing-tubes.

These tympans are interchangeable at will, and the arm which carries them is also provided with a turning tool for smoothing the wax cylinder prior to its receiving the print. The cylinders are made of different sizes, from 1 to 8 inches long and 4 inches in diameter. The former has a storage capacity of 200 words. The next in size has twice that, or 400 words, and so on. Mr. Edison states that four of the large 8-inch cylinders can record all 'Nicholas Nickleby', which could therefore be automatically read to a private invalid or to a number of patients in a hospital simultaneously, by means of a bunch of hearing-tubes. The cylinders can be readily posted like letters, and made to deliver their contents *vivâ voce* in a duplicate phonograph, every tone and expression of the writer being rendered with more or less fidelity. In addition to facilitating correspondence by dictation, Mr. Edison hopes that the new instrument will be useful in matters of law and the interests of justice; for example, in the detective service, as the photographic camera is now. It lends itself to type-setting by the reproduction of a dictated article in the ear of the compositor; and it may also be employed to copy music and to render it again. In fact, numerous applications of the instrument can be suggested, from recording animal sounds, foreign languages, and decaying dialects, to the preservation of oratorical and vocal specimens of great singers, orators, and statesmen, or the accents of friendly voices which will one day be stilled. It should be added that the electric motor [. . .] which drives the machine is actuated by two or three Leclanché cells, and that a special factory has been set apart by Edison for the manufacture of the apparatus.

49

'MR. EDISON'S PHONOGRAPH'

Times (30 June 1888), p. 5

(FROM A CORRESPONDENT.)

The Times published on Wednesday a letter from Colonel Gouraud, Mr. Edison's agent in this country, describing the arrival of the new phonograph which the great inventor has for some time past been engaged in completing, and giving an outline of the effects which the instrument had already produced. It will be remembered that the first phonograph, which was contrived by Mr. Edison many years ago, demonstrated the practicability of preserving records of vocal and other sounds and of reproducing them at pleasure; but the results then attained were not sufficiently accurate to be of any practical utility, or to do more than establish the correctness of the principle on which the instrument was based. This first phonograph contained a metal cylinder, over which was stretched a smooth sheet of tinfoil, and which could be made to revolve by turning a handle. The sounds were received by a mica diaphragm, from the centre of which projected a needle or style, with its free extremity resting upon the tinfoil. Sound waves impinging upon the diaphragm produced vibrations, which were communicated to the style, and caused it to make indentations in the tinfoil; and these indentations, by putting the cylinder into revolution while a forward movement was impressed upon the style, were extended into a continuous spiral line. In order to reproduce sounds, the process was reversed, the point of the style being brought back to the commencement of the spiral line which it had traced, and the cylinder being again made to revolve. Then, just as the style had been originally thrown into definite movements by the vibrations of the diaphragm, so the diaphragm in its turn was thrown into definite vibrations by the movements of the style, and the sounds which had in the first instance traced the line were again excited by its agency. The diaphragm was contained within a tube, into the mouth of which it was necessary to speak; and the reproduced voice, although accurate as far as the repetition of words was concerned, was not accurate in the reproduction of tones or other individual characteristics. The words were more or less 'bleated' and the original speaker could not in any case be identified with certainty. The tinfoil could not be removed without destroying the trace; so that a given sound could only be reproduced by the instrument which had received it, and only so long as the foil remained undisturbed and uninjured. The phonograph was used in order to

DOI: 10.4324/9781315400303-71

illustrate a principle, by popular lecturers on science; but was otherwise scarcely more than an ingenious toy.

Mr. Edison, although his attention was long diverted from the phonograph by the pressure of other demands upon him, appears always to have believed in its perfectibility, and in the wide range of its ultimate applications; and, for the last twelve months, he has devoted himself closely to the subject. In order to attain scientific perfection, it was necessary to replace the tinfoil by some substance which yielded more readily, and more accurately in minute particulars, to the varying pressure of the style, and which yet, either in its original form or after some simple process of hardening, should possess sufficient firmness to guide the style with absolute correctness for the reproduction of sound. It was also necessary to provide for identity of speed in the revolutions of the cylinder, whether this was receiving sound or transmitting it; and to secure the maintenance of this identity of speed in all the instruments which might be manufactured. For purposes of practical utility, it was further necessary to obtain a recording material which would bear transmission from place to place, or transference from one instrument to another, and which would admit of being accurately copied by electrotype or other processes, and, in this way, of being indefinitely multiplied. All these ends have now been completely or approximately attained; and the phonograph has acquired a form in which it promises shortly to be accessible to the public for a great variety of uses. The tracings of the style are received upon a material which is shaped into cylinders, and these cylinders can be slipped on or off the fixed spindle of the machine. They are of such a quality as to record and reproduce with great accuracy; they can be multiplied indefinitely; they can be transmitted from place to place, or transferred from one phonograph to another; and they will repeat for an indefinite number of times the words or other sounds which they have received. The words and messages mentioned by Colonel Gouraud, for example, were spoken in the first place to an instrument in Mr. Edison's laboratory, the cylinders which received them were removed, packed up, sent across the Atlantic, and finally placed upon another instrument at Norwood. As soon as this second instrument is set in motion, the words are repeated in voices which appear to be perfectly natural. I have never had the pleasure of hearing Mr. Edison speak at first hand, but I think I should be able to recognize his voice without difficulty; and, in a cylinder which recorded a dialogue between him and Colonel Gouraud, the individualities of the two voices were perfectly well marked. The phonograph now in England not only embodies the last improvements of the inventor, but is actually one of the first two which do so, and was finished very hurriedly for despatch by a particular steamer. It cannot be said to be perfectly finished in certain details, some contrivances which it contains are still unpatented, and its repeating style has not escaped quite uninjured from the voyage. For these reasons, and also because the best material for the recording cylinders has not yet been finally decided upon, the phonograph is not ready for public exhibition; but I have been kindly permitted by Colonel Gouraud to hear its performances. Among them was the repetition of a piano solo, of a duet between piano and cornet, and of a trio of piano, cornet, and violin. This particular phonograph requires to be closely addressed, and, when it is speaking, the sound emitted is feeble unless conducted into the ears of the listeners by tubes; but I am informed that Mr. Edison has also succeeded in a construction which will be capable of recording general conversation in a room, the evidence of witnesses in Courts of justice, the addresses of public speakers, the performances of an orchestra, or the notes of a *prima donna.* Mr. Edison, in the course of the message to which I have referred, twice cleared his throat in order to speak more plainly, and the sounds thus produced are as definite as those of his voice. The impressed cylinders, or phonograms, as it is proposed to call them, will be readily transmissible by post in boxes prepared for the purpose; and, when desirable, they can be multiplied at small cost in any number. The machine, as a whole, is portable, being little larger than a Remington type-writer; and arrangements have been made for its manufacture upon an enormous scale, with the view of supplying at a moderate cost a demand which is expected to be almost without limit. In the form now at Norwood the phonograph will be of great value as a substitute for letters on matters of business, as being, in fact, a species of telephone between points to and from which no wires have yet been carried. Many of Mr. Edison's friends were of opinion that the instruments might have been brought before the public two or three months ago; but he was not at that time entirely satisfied with them, and has spent the intervening period in providing against every difficulty which experience has brought to light. The phonograph, in its present form, may therefore be fairly described as an approach to the fulfilment of the desires and anticipations of the inventor.

It would be difficult, at first sight, to exhaust in imagination the possible applications of such an apparatus. The power of fixing and reproducing human speech will form an era in the history of civilization. It will enable our descendants to compare the oratory of this generation with that of generations yet to come, and will preserve the vocal tones and accents of all languages as they are now or may hereafter be spoken for the instruction of all time. It will probably, on many matters, supersede written communications; for there are numerous subjects on which we hesitate to write fully, but on which we should like to speak our thoughts, and to send them away in a form to admit of our speech being reproduced. It is likely to call into existence a new profession, the business of which will be to read to the phonograph, with perfect elocution, books of sufficient value and importance, in order that the impressed cylinders may be multiplied, and that those who desire to hear perfect reading may obtain cabinets of such cylinders, and may listen at will to the thoughts of favourite authors, rendered by the voices of accomplished readers. It will make it a profitable occupation for popular authors to read their own books, and may even enable the world in general to realize the extent to which Parliamentary oratory is indebted to the skilful pruning of the reporter, and to the omission of the repetitions and tricks of speech by which, in an artistic sense, most eloquence is more or less disfigured. It will afford to speakers an opportunity of hearing themselves as others hear them, and thus, perhaps, of correcting faults of style of which they were previously ignorant. In this way it should be of conspicuous utility to vocalists, actors, and aspiring politicians; and will afford a constant supply of correct models to any who desire to cultivate the art of mimicry. It will assist in the acquisition of the pronunciation of foreign languages, and will enable the learner constantly to compare his best efforts with the actual result at which he aims. It may be so employed as to prevent the possibility of any misrepresentation of what has passed in an otherwise private interview; and, if it had been in use three years ago, might have nipped in the bud the controversy between Lord Carnarvon and Mr. Parnell. Each of the participators in any similar conference would be clearly entitled to preserve a sealed record of what had been said on either side. To what extent a phonograph will necessarily be conspicuous time alone can show; but, if it can be brought into operation in places where its presence is not suspected, it will be in many respects a terror to evil doers, and a source of joy to novelists as an entirely new source of startling disclosures and of unexpected *dénouements*. Like all other great contrivances, it may have its evil or dangerous applications; but there can be no doubt that these will be enormously overbalanced by its utility, and, even if they were not, it would be impossible to withhold the tribute of admiration which is justly due to the genius and the industry of the inventor. It is safe to predict that Mr. Edison will hold the first place among those who, in the present century, have increased the comforts and conveniences of daily life by the practical applications of science, and who are likely to be held in grateful remembrance, as benefactors of the human race, when many who now strut more conspicuously upon the stage of affairs will have passed away into oblivion.

50

'WHAT WILL COME OF THE PHONOGRAPH?'

Spectator (30 June 1888), p. 9

When a child of seven can recognise distinctly in the phonograph the voice of a friend which he has not heard since he was five, we may feel pretty sure that that marvellous instrument has at last triumphantly solved the problem which Mr. Edison set himself. We are told that two distinct voices, as well as a great number of musical airs, have passed over the Atlantic and become audible again here after being silent for ten days, to the ears for which they were destined when they were committed to the phonograph in the United States. What are we to expect from this wonderful invention? Mainly, we fear, an immense storing up of sounds that it might be better not to store up, an immense accumulation of those winged words whose wings are best employed in carrying off into nothingness what deserves only temporary life. Men are becoming so vastly ingenious in finding the means of magnifying and embalming every little ripple of human energy, that we tremble for the consequences. The earth will soon be made a museum of odds and ends of form and speech; and unless man suddenly takes a great spring into a moral greatness worthy of all this careful storing, we may have future generations drowned beneath the accumulated scraps of ancestral voices and expressions. Only consider that this wonderful discovery will very likely furnish a future Madame Tussaud with the means of reproducing minutely a Parliamentary or Municipal debate, by depositing within the figure of every wax representative a phonogram of some speech which its original had made, and winding these off in turn in the order in which the actual speakers had addressed the assembly. It is quite conceivable that in the year 2000 there may be the means not only of hearing figures like Lord Salisbury or Mr. Gladstone pour forth in the actual tones of those orators speeches which were actually made by them in our own day, not only of hearing Lord Tennyson recite 'Maud' in the twentieth or thirtieth century with that rich and peculiar burr with which he pours it forth to his intimates, but of revivifying every little notoriety of our day, from Dr. Parker to Dr. Tanner, – bottling up their voices for the ears of our posterity, as well as making their forms visible to future generations, till 'earth is sick and Heaven is weary', as Wordsworth has it, of the hollow words which phonographs utter for the purpose of recalling a past that is not worth recalling. It will be something, no doubt, that the Colonies should be

 DOI: 10.4324/9781315400303-72

able to hear within a few weeks the very voice of the statesman or the Sovereign whose words have turned the balance as it was inclining to either war or peace; that Germans in Philadelphia should be able to hang on the accents of Prince Bismarck's declarations to the Reichstag on a critical conjuncture; or that the Australasians should hear with their own ears what Mr. Gladstone says on the Federation of the Empire, or what M. Goblet says of the intentions of the French with regard to New Caledonia or the New Hebrides. It will be a singular satisfaction to many an exile in India to take with him a number of assurances of regard from the voice he loves best, and listen to the reiteration of these assurances thousands of miles away, in days, perhaps, when they have long ceased to represent existing realities; and to the blind it may prove a constant delight to correspond with friends by an interchange of actual speech, when the speech has been bottled up in phonographs instead of committed to letters which the blind must trust other friends to read aloud to them. The number of small and great gratifications which the phonograph, like the photograph, will afford to those who hunger and thirst for living signs of those from whom land and seas separate them, is likely to be quite limitless. But, nevertheless, we cannot help fearing that all these rapidly multiplying agencies by which we are enabled to perpetuate the most trivial expressions, – whether visual or audible, – threaten to overwhelm coming generations with the superabundant vestiges and records of the past. Shall we not come to regard it as a singular virtue when men obliterate voluntarily traces of themselves which, instead of being useful to posterity, would only serve the purpose of the dust in which useful things are so often smothered? Are we not discovering a great deal too many means of defeating the benefits conferred by oblivion? Are we not likely to rescue from forgetfulness what it should be the first duty of human beings who do not wish to miss their way in the steadily accumulating piles of human rubbish, to forget? We cannot help being appalled at the shrinkage of character which seems to go on simultaneously with the growth of these manifold devices for erecting massive monuments to character. Are not men daily becoming less and less massive, – less and less impressive in proportion to the machinery for taking impressions of them, and recording delicately all the outcome of their much-fretted and subdivided and attenuated lives? We are often tempted to wish that human nature should be allowed time to overtake the scientific paraphernalia in which it is almost suffocated, before any more discoveries are made by which the pettiness of our lives may gain in artificial importance, the distractions of our posterity may be multiplied, and the complexity of their inherited memories increased.

As it is, we fear that the phonograph may add to the great picture-galleries of our great houses, voice-galleries almost more impressive, from the vivacity with which grandparents and great-grandparents may be made to address the descendants who never knew them, and that, too, in all sorts of contending strains. Imagine a man in the next century whose great-grandfather was a Gladstonian, whose grandfather was entrusted with a command in the war with Ireland to which Home-rule had led, and whose father had sided with the Irish in resisting the oppressions of the restored Government, – and imagine these ancestors addressing their descendant in all the different accents of political passion to which their different situations in life had given rise, while their portraits look severely down upon him, enforcing by their expression the earnestness of their political view, – would not such a man carry into life a consciousness even more hesitating and divided than even that which gives birth to our nineteenth-century vacillations? Or imagine a man in the same century whose great-grandmother was a vehement partisan of women's suffrage, whose grandmother was a lady-doctor who held that the nerves of the women of the day had been ruined by educational over-pressure, and whose mother, after carrying a law for embodying Amazon regiments and womanning a few ironclads, had emigrated to escape the consequences of the French conquest of our Southern Counties, – and imagine him listening to the most characteristic utterances of each of these ancestresses as they frowned upon him from the living canvas on his walls, – would not he too carry into life a very strange complexity of vivid associations such as might easily embarrass him with the singular conflict of their pathetic eloquence? We have a very strong belief that the scientific ingenuities of our day, acting under the imperious guidance of sensibilities which are as narrow as they are tender, will contrive to fill the world we leave behind us much too full of us for the free growth of our posterity; and that a time will come when it will be necessary to preach a sort of iconoclasm towards the pieties of ancestry in order to clear the way for anything like independent growth. One of the most effective of Arabian fairy-tales describes how the prince who is to break the spell of the wicked magician's enchantment, has to pass along a way where voices in the greatest confusion address him from every side, in every accent of scorn, or ridicule, or indignation, all appearing to come from the mere stocks and stones beside his path. Was this an unconscious anticipation of the phonograph? We much doubt whether Edison's wonderful and admirable discovery, and the extensions that must follow, will not tend to bewilder the world in which our children's children live, at least as much as the outcries of the bewitched valley of rocks bewildered the hero of that Eastern tale.

5.6

Wireless telegraphy and future media

DOI: 10.4324/9781315400303-73

5.6 Wireless telegraphy and future media

M. Griffith, 'An Electric Eye: The Marvellous Discovery of an Eastern Professor Which Distances the Röntgen Rays As They Distance Photography', *Pearson's Magazine* (December 1896), pp. 749–756.

James Knowles, 'Wireless Telegraphy and "Brain-waves"', *Nineteenth Century* (1899), pp. 857–864.

By the end of the nineteenth century, popular attention to the march of invention, along with the heady predictions that seemed to attend every new contraption that made a public splash, could help inspire even more expansive views of future technologies. Notwithstanding all of the astonishing inventions that already existed, late-Victorian writers now assumed that even more of them lay ahead. These possible future technological things might seem all the more exciting or troubling when they drew on forces beyond the realm of visibility. The German physicist Wilhelm Röntgen discovered the existence of the radiation he called 'x-rays' (the *x* signified their mystery) and created the first X-ray photographs in 1895, even as Guglielmo Marconi and others were experimenting with wireless telegraphy (the transmission of Morse code via radio waves, which laid the foundation for radio broadcast in the next century).

The Indian scientist Jagadish Chandra Bose contributed to the early study of radio by studying what are now called microwaves – both their properties and the possibility of detecting them. In the view of an interviewer from *Pearson's* magazine, Bose's experiments with the electromagnetic spectrum presaged technological invasions of privacy that went even beyond the recent discovery of 'Röntgen rays' that revealed the bones beneath the skin.[1] We should also pause to note the modernity of the events behind this magazine piece itself: a British woman journalist met with a non-Western scientist for the sake of that quintessentially modern print genre, the interview.

James Knowles viewed the extension of existing technologies in more mystical terms. For Knowles, who was both the editor of the journal *Nineteenth Century* and the founder of the Metaphysical Society (a discussion group that included Victorian intellectual men from the poet Alfred, Lord Tennyson, to the biologist and evolutionist Thomas Huxley among its members), Marconi's experiments in wireless communication supported Knowles's own earlier hypothesis that 'brain-waves' might be psychically transmitted or recorded across space and time, thereby providing a scientific explanation for phenomena such as telepathy, clairvoyance, and mesmerism.[2] Both of the articles here confirm that looking at Victorian discussions of imagined, hypothetical or occult technologies can help us understand the cultural significance of real ones.[3]

Notes

1 On the cultural as well as the medical repercussions of X-ray photography, see Bettyann Holtzmann Kevles, *Naked to the Bone: Medical Imaging in the Twentieth Century* (New Brunswick, NJ: Rutgers University Press, 1997).

2 For a consideration of telepathy itself as part of a great age of new tele-technologies, see Roger Luckhurst, *The Invention of Telepathy, 1870–1901* (Oxford: Oxford University Press, 2002).

3 Such a perspective accords with the loose-knit, twenty-first-century perspective on media known as 'media archaeology', which often emphasises failed, 'weird' and even imaginary or hypothetical technologies and media as part of its attempt to go beyond media history as a triumphant story of technologies advancing one after the other. See Jussi Parikka, *What Is Media Archaeology?* (Cambridge: Polity, 2012); Erkki Huhtamo and Jussi Parikka (eds.), *Media Archaeology: Approaches, Applications, and Implications* (Berkeley and Los Angeles: University of California Press, 2011).

51

M. GRIFFITH, 'AN ELECTRIC EYE: THE MARVELLOUS DISCOVERY OF AN EASTERN PROFESSOR WHICH DISTANCES THE RÖNTGEN RAYS AS THEY DISTANCE PHOTOGRAPHY'

Pearson's Magazine (December 1896), pp. 749–756

The nationality of great men – though often the cause of much argument and pen-warfare – is in itself a matter of no importance, for, in reality, they have neither nationality, individuality, nor age – they are citizens of the world. In the present instance, however, the 'Star' has risen in the East, in India, which we have hitherto regarded as a land of romance, of barbaric splendour and glitter, of dainty arts and crafts, as the home of mysticism and legendary lore, a luxurious lotus-eating country, where life can be happily spent in peaceful contemplation.

Her people we looked upon as highly imaginative, but devoid of thoroughness and practicability.

We seem to have forgotten the stately colleges of their long past ages, their great philosophers and learned men, the result of whose researches in astronomy, mathematics, and abstract thought has filtered down to us through the Arabs and Greeks. For many years the intellectual progress of India was hindered by foreign invasions and internal hostilities, but now, favoured with a period of peace and the advantages of education, mental activity is re-asserting itself.

Even in the domain of modern sciences, working under insuperable difficulties, an Indian professor has done remarkable work, and his paper on Electric Waves, read before the British Association, caused quite a sensation among the many distinguished European savants present.

Jagadis Chunder Bose, M.A. (Cantab.) and D.Sc. (London), Professor of Physical Science at the Presidency College at Calcutta, is a Hindu, and a native of Bengal. His father, Mr. Bhagaban Chunder Bose, was a great scholar, and a distinguished mathematician, but he died before his son achieved his present greatness.

DOI: 10.4324/9781315400303-74

Professor Bose, after taking his degree at the Calcutta University, went to Christ's College, Cambridge, where he was elected a Scholar, and after three years took his degree in the Natural Science Tripos. He at the same time took his degree of Bachelor of Science in the University of London.

He has recently, in recognition of important scientific researches, had conferred upon him by the University of London, the degree of Doctor of Science, the highest distinction within its gift, and that without his presenting himself for examination.

Dr. Bose is now in Europe, having been deputed by the Indian Government to lay before the British Association the results of his researches and also to visit the principal laboratories in Great Britain, France, Switzerland, and Germany, with a view to the equipment some day by the India Government of an efficient laboratory in connection with the Presidency College.

This Eastern scientist is in the first energies of manhood; he has a very winning personality, and is an enthusiast about his work, which he describes so simply, yet graphically, that the dry bones of science become fascinating, even to an outsider.

Surrounded by his instruments, which he designed, elaborated, and even had a hand in constructing, he is at home, both with his subject and guests, and will talk with the greatest animation. But to the interviewer he is like an oyster, the sight of a pencil and note book sends him at once into his shell. To know the man outside his work requires the subtlety of a Machiavelli, the wiliness of a serpent, and the endurance and patience of a Stoic. Even then, except in the disguise of a convert to the enthralments of his pet science, but little will be gained beyond that the Professor is an adept in giving doses of scientific information in the pleasantest manner possible, and unknowingly those who seek him become developed into amateur scientists, learned in waves, vibrations, 'electric' eyes and their wondrous properties.

Having given these few particulars of the life and personality of this illustrious Indian, I will turn to the wonderful researches in which he is engaged and to the far-reaching developments which they foreshadow.

I will first, as briefly and as simply as possible, indicate exactly what Professor Bose has already accomplished, then I will outline the deductions which have led him to concentrate his energies on one particular branch of science, and the means he has employed to follow out so successfully his arduous experiments; and finally I should like for a moment to draw aside the curtain and by a process of logical deduction reveal the mysteries which we may anticipate will be found behind the scenes.

Professor Bose has been working in the region of lights which are invisible to us, produced by electric waves in the ether, and he has discovered that these invisible lights have the power not only of penetrating the atmosphere and ordinarily transparent substances, but also such unpromising material as doors, brick walls, granite, rock, mounds of earth, and, above all, of retaining their active properties after the passage.

These waves falling on a suitable receiver produce signals, and it is thus possible to signal from one room to another, from one place to another, without any visible means of communication.

No known substances, with the exception of metallic plates of fair thickness, offer more than a trifling opposition to the passage of these ether waves. Pitch, coal tar, the human form, all of these are as transparent to the ether waves as glass is to light.

What a marvellous discovery!

The blackest of black substances gaining such a reputation for transparency! For the passage of the electric waves through coal tar or pitch, is even more easy than through wood, whilst a human being, though slightly less transparent than wood, so far as the electric waves are concerned, presents but trifling difficulties to this wondrous invisible force.

Professor Bose has elaborated a perfect instrument by which these forces are readily produced and their marvellous properties detected and examined, but, with one exception, the investigations are of too abstruse a character for explanation in an article which is not purely scientific and severely technical.

A word with regard to the exception. Everyone knows that if a penholder be held in a glass of water it appears to be bent beneath the surface. This is due to what is called the refractive power of water. Now every substance in nature is refractive, but up to the present the amount of refraction can only be investigated for bodies which are transparent to ordinary light.

But the electric waves can pass through many substances which are opaque to light, and the refraction produced by these substances can be measured very accurately by an ingenious method devised by Professor Bose.

Thus it is possible to determine the refractive power of wood, brick, and, in fact, of every material which is not metallic.

Now, no two substances have the same refractive power, so that given, say, a piece of granite, and another substance which looks like granite, it is possible to tell, by determining its refractive power, whether the latter material is really granite or not.

A similar method has long been employed in the detection of spurious gems. But of course, up to the present, it has only been possible to make the investigation in the case of substances transparent to light.

In the future we shall be able to tell infallibly whether our billiard balls are made of ivory or celluloid, however good the imitation, and whether the sideboard is really oak, or a dressed-up, cheaper wood. Again, if the waves are sent through a substance, say a piece of rock, which has a strain or twist inside, the wave will come out twisted. It is possible to measure this twist of the invisible wave, and thereby detect the strain inside a structure, which could not have been detected in any other way. A hundred other useful applications will occur to us.

Sufficient has, I think, now been said of the practical applications of these ether waves. We now proceed to say something about their nature.

'The idea of ether waves', explained the Doctor to me, 'will perhaps become familiar if we first picture to ourselves some form of visible waves. Have you ever watched the paddles of a steamer in motion? Every stroke gives rise to waves on the water. These wave motions are radiated in all directions, and perhaps a piece of floating cork at a distance is seen to move up and down with the waves. The rhythmic stroke of the paddles is the source of the disturbance, water is the medium which carries the motion to distant places, and the cork indicates the motion. So you see we have now three important factors – the source of disturbance, the medium, and an indicator or receiver which interprets.

'Again, if the string of a violin be struck the quivering wire gives up its motion to the air, which carries it to our ear, and the motion communicated to the brain produces the sensation of sound'.

'Then, Professor, light and sound are mere vibrations?'

'Yes. Sound is produced by the vibration of matter, and light is due to the vibration of ether. Just as there may be sounds that are inaudible, so there may be lights, *i.e.* ether-vibrations, which are invisible.

'The most curious thing which science has demonstrated is the fact that there are great gaps in our consciousness. We first begin to be aware of a sound note, when the air is quivering at a rate of about sixteen vibrations in a second. When the vibrating string which gives rise to sound is shortened, higher and higher notes are given out. In this way', the Professor continued, 'we pass from lower to higher octaves, and when the vibration reaches the rate of 32,000 beats in a second, the limit of audibility is reached.

'As we near the superior limit of audibility the notes become more shrill and attenuated, and finally, when the note is raised still higher, or in other words the rate of vibration exceeds 32,000 beats to the second, the ear fails to respond, and to the shrill tumult succeeds unbroken silence. There is thus a lower and an upper limit of hearing, owing to the imperfection of the ear. Very low-pitched or very high-pitched notes are beyond our power of hearing.

'To detect these inaudible sounds scientists construct an artificial ear, which consists of a slender jet of burning gas known as the sensitive flame, which responds to sound by fluttering.

'Just as vibration is produced in air by a mechanical disturbance, so may the impalpable ether be thrown into vibration by an electric disturbance. There may thus be produced ethereal notes, a few of which are detected by our sensation of touch as warmth, and a few others by the eye as light. Slower or quicker vibrations than these we cannot perceive. Do you understand?'

'Oh, yes', I replied, but I almost wished science had left us happy in our ignorance. It is not particularly comfortable to know that we are floating about in oceans of ether, with many things round us that we cannot see, all kinds of noises that we cannot hear, and substances in contact with us that we cannot feel.

The Professor, however, seemed perfectly unmoved, and went on to explain and quote figures that were perfectly brain-reeling, for instance – 'That vibrations of ether lying between two hundred and four hundred *billions* of vibrations in one second produce the sensation of warmth, and those between four hundred and eight hundred billions in a second excite the sensation of light. These', he continued, 'are comprised, to use a musical term, between two octaves – only a narrow fringe in the infinite range of possible vibrations. A lower or higher perceptible vibration would give us a new colour. The order in which we detect colours is first red, then yellow, green, blue, and violet, the exceeding quick vibration – invisible to the eye – includes the ultra-violet rays'.

'What of the rest? Do they exist?'

'Well, from analogies we are led to believe in the existence of an infinite variety of forces, which we cannot perceive – of other forms of light which we cannot see. These are the problems which are engaging the attention of the great scientists – the study of invisible lights and their properties. The great English scientist, Maxwell, made predictions about them. Hertz was the first to actually verify the existence of these electric waves, though two other eminent British physicists, Profs. Fitzgerald and Lodge, have made many important investigations with them.'

Thus we see the curious parallel which exists between sound waves and ether waves. The ether waves when making fewer than 200 billion vibrations a second are beyond our perception. We know that for vibrations between 200 and 400 billions to the second warmth is produced, and from 400 to 800 visible light. But beyond 800 billion vibrations in a second, mystery again surrounds us.

The theory has been propounded that the Röntgen Rays may exist in this unknown land of vibrations, working at the bewildering rate of more than 800 billions to the second, but at present this suggestion is only hypothetical.

The ether waves, to which Professor Bose has devoted his attention, are amongst those vibrating less often than 200 billion times to the second.

As regards the practical uses to which these investigations may lead, we gathered from the Professor that scientific men as a rule do not look at these things from a purely utilitarian point of view. They are more concerned in patiently unravelling the many mysteries by which we are surrounded – in detecting and measuring the properties of unknown forces. When that is done it is easy to turn the knowledge so acquired to many practical uses. In fact there is hardly a scientific discovery that has not been followed by practical applications of great importance. The observation of the twitching of a dead frog by Galvani heralded the present electric age.

The possibilities of sending signals through space with these electric waves has already been alluded to. In fact, several astounding experiments have been carried out, by which bells have been rung, and pistols fired by the action of the invisible electric waves, upsetting a delicately balanced electric current, the waves passing without difficulty through intervening walls.

With regard to the sending of signals to a great distance, Professor Bose's determinations of the refractive power of various substances, opaque to visible light, have been utilised.

Special lenses of pitch or ebonite have been constructed, and signals have thereby been sent to a distance of nearly a mile.

Doctor Bose here related how, on one occasion in India, in a popular lecture, he was trying the experiment of firing off a pistol in an adjoining room with a closed door between, when the Governor of Bengal, who was present at the lecture, and who takes a keen interest in science, placed himself in the way of the wave, and asked the Professor to start it.

The experimenter was naturally a little taken aback, as he had never before attempted such a thing. It was, however, done, the interposition of the Governor did not stop the wave which fired off the pistol in the next room. The same experiment has been accomplished through several intervening walls.

The great difficulty in these investigations was the detection of the invisible light. It was necessary to perfect an artificial 'electric eye' that could see the invisible. The ingenuity exhibited, and the trouble entailed in the elaboration of this additional organ of sense was very great.

The essential parts which co-operate in producing vision are (1) a sensitive surface known as the retina on which the image of the external objects is focussed by the eye-lens; (2) a conductive strand known as the optical nerve, which carries the visual impulse to the (3) brain. The twitching produced in the brain by this impulse gives rise to the sensation of sight.

The electrical eye is worked on somewhat similar principles to the real eye; there is a sensitive layer on which the invisible light falling gives rise to an electric impulse, which is carried by conducting wire and produces a twitching motion to a part corresponding to the brain. This movement is made manifest by the magnified motion of a spot of light reflected from the moving part. It is wonderful to watch the movement of this spot of light in response to the invisible light acting in the artificial eye. The electric eye is subject to fatigue just as our ordinary eyes, and has to be rubbed now and then to make it 'see' more clearly. Sometimes it gets dazed, and then a fresh eye is rapidly substituted. The exhausted eye recovers its sensibility after a period of rest.

Asked if the human eye had and continued to have the same range of power in detecting ether vibrations, the Professor said that possibly this power had increased, and that in the very early ages the range was not as great as at present. 'With regard to animals, they may have additional senses, which we do not possess. For you know', he continued, 'they are said to feel and show an uneasiness before an earthquake or other terrestrial disturbance long before any indications reach us; but you must understand that we possess no positive proof yet about these things'.

Each substance possesses selective power of absorption, and may therefore be opaque to one kind of light, but transparent to another. A solid wall, though opaque to visible light, is very transparent to the electric ray. Alum is transparent to ordinary light, but opaque to the heat rays. Muscles and bones are both opaque to the electric ray, but muscles are transparent to the Röntgen rays, while bones are relatively opaque to them.

We should see many wonderful things could we but 'develop' our eyes. For had the human eye been somewhat differently constructed, and the rods and cones in the retina been larger in size, it would have been easy to see through stone walls. On the other hand, if the elements in the retina had been somewhat smaller, and their surface sensitised with a solution of, say, Barium-Platino-Cyanide – we could have easily seen each other's insides. The necessity of such a proceeding has not hitherto been of great importance in the struggle for existence, and the human eye remains undeveloped, and therefore unresponsive to the Röntgen rays and the electric waves.

What a great deal we have to be thankful for!

'Do you never give your many eyes a change, Doctor? Surely they require something more occasionally than a rub and a rest'.

'Well, my "electric eyes" are quite satisfied with that, but I occasionally vary the monotony for the natural ones, by treating them to a course of Nature's beauties. My few holidays I spend in places where tourists are unknown, sometimes drifting in a house-boat on the Jhelum in the fair land of Kashmir'.

Until a few years ago, Professor Bose did not concentrate his energies on one specialised subject; he loved to follow the march of progress in the different sciences, till the fascination of physical research made him a specialist, and drew him to concentrate his attention to one subject. Although the investigations were rendered difficult in India from the want of facility for constructing suitable instruments, he ultimately succeeded in constructing for himself a complete apparatus, with which the numerous researches connected with the electric wave have been carried out.

It must be borne in mind that these new researches require the detection of forces which are beyond our perception, of effects extremely minute; the necessity of the construction of apparatus having the highest delicacy, becomes at once apparent. Considering the magnitude of the work, a well organised laboratory, with all the best appliances and materials, and the co-operation of a number of assistants seem essential necessaries for the continuation of these researches.

Some idea of the advantage of organisation may be obtained from the work accomplished in a single night at Mr. Edison's laboratory, when the distinguished inventor was attempting to find a fluorescent substance to make the Röntgen rays visible.

It is said that 700 different chemical compounds were examined in the course of a night. This shows what can be accomplished by time-saving arrangements in a well-equipped laboratory. It would have taken a very long time, had the investigations depended on the unassisted labour of a single individual.

We cannot help admiring the patience and the extraordinary ability of our Indian scientist when we remember that in the course of less than eighteen months he has brought to a successful conclusion six very important investigations on subjects the most difficult in electrical science. It is all the more remarkable that all this has been accomplished in odd hours snatched from his incessant duties as a Professor. He had to design the most elaborate apparatus out of the crudest material, and with only such help as could be rendered by an ordinary mechanic.

If he had the advantages that a European laboratory affords, and the appliances at his disposal, which every scientific man in England has, had he been surrounded by a scientific public and kindred workers, to take away the feeling of utter loneliness, we should have seen an extraordinary amount of successful activity.

But, as it is, the outlook from a scientific point of view, is one of splendid promise, although the ordinary individual may not view it with such equanimity. Professor Bose is undoubtedly on the edge of a very great discovery indeed – far greater than those which, as it is, will be associated with his name in future generations. We shall soon be nothing but transparent heaps of jelly to each other, and even the dignity imparted by robes of state, uniforms, or the chiffons that women delight in, will be ruthlessly dragged from us.

I look forward with doubtful pleasure to the time when I can sit by my own fireside and spy upon the doings of my friends and enemies in their homes two or three streets away, or it may be at the other end of London, knowing at the same time that a hundred pairs of eyes are watching me in whichever direction I may turn.

This may appear rather fanciful, but no more so at the present day than the wonders of telegraphy would have appeared to our forefathers. And what is more, such a state of affairs as I have portrayed follows logically from the discoveries already made. For if these ether waves can see through doors, partitions, brick walls, why should they not be able to tell us what will be found on the other side? Just as with our natural eyes we can *see* a transparent substance, such as glass, and can also distinguish objects beyond.

It is quite within the range of possibility that the editor in his town house will be able to communicate with his assistants at his office by means of a generator and an 'electric eye' at each end. A system of electric flashes, manipulated after the fashion of the Morse code of telegraphy, might be devised by which the messages could be sent.

Again, for signalling purposes at sea, these ether waves have a tremendous future before them. At present there is no light which is powerful enough to penetrate a thick fog on a stormy sea to any distance, but rig up an electric generator on the lighthouse which can flash the ether waves through the fog, as easily as the sun's rays can pierce a clear atmosphere, and we see the possibilities of electric waves.

Every ship must be provided with an electric eye, and as it comes within the sphere of influence of the ether waves from the electric light-house the 'eye' will 'see' the invisible light and the captain of the ship will realise his dangerous position. Such an apparatus, for instance, would have saved the *Eider*, which, it will be remembered, was lost by striking on the rocks of the light-house itself in a fog.

And then carrying ourselves a step further, what a vista opens itself before our bewildered imagination. Invisible eyes peeping at us from every corner, ready to note our every action, for ever tracking us down like sleuth hounds. An end to peace, rest, privacy, and all that makes home sacred. But my pen trembles at the thought.

Professor Bose's researches have met with the warmest appreciation from the scientific world. They have elicited the highest commendation from the greatest scientist of the age, Lord Kelvin. The Royal Society has published them, and has marked their importance by a grant from the Government Grant Fund for their continuation. In fact, Professor Bose has had a most flattering reception from the eminent scientific men of this country.

The one regret that may be felt by the reader of this article is the lack of adequate illustration. But it is obviously impossible to photograph the workings of an invisible force, and it would be equally foolish to transcend the bounds of actuality by employing an artist to make imaginary drawings from his own inner consciousness.

52

JAMES KNOWLES, 'WIRELESS TELEGRAPHY AND "BRAIN-WAVES"'

Nineteenth Century (1899), pp. 857–864

The wonderful discovery of wireless telegraphy tempts me to put forward again a theory which I ventured to publish thirty years ago, and to which Signor Marconi's new invention seems, in some ways, to lend an additional 'plausibility'. Its republication may be perhaps forgiven for the sake of the incidents in support of it contributed by Lord Tennyson, Mr. Browning, and Mr. Woolner, which are certainly worth preserving.

Signor Marconi has proved to the whole world that, by the use of his apparatus, messages can be passed through space, for great distances, from brain to brain in the entire absence of any known means of physical communication between two widely separated stations.

To explain, or even to express, the *modus operandi* of what occurs it is necessary, in the present state of science, to assume the existence of that 'ethereal medium' pervading space which has become for many reasons an indispensable scientific assumption, and also the existence of movements, tremors or waves of energy propagated through the ether, from the generating to the receiving station.

All that is in practice essentially requisite is, *in the first place*, an electric energy derived from the cells of an ordinary galvanic battery – an energy which is regulated into a code of signals under the superintendence of a human brain at a certain locality; and, *in the second place*, at another locality, a delicately contrived receiving apparatus which is sensitive to those signals and can repeat them to another human brain.

Now if a small electric battery can send out tremors or waves of energy which are propagated through space for thirty miles or more, and can then be caught and manifested by a sensitive mechanical receiver, why may not such a mechanism as the human brain – which is perpetually, while in action, decomposing its own material, and which is in this respect analogous to an electric battery – generate and emit tremors or waves of energy which such sensitive 'receivers' as other human brains might catch and feel, although not conveyed to them through the usual channels of sensation? Why might not such a battery as, say, the brain of Mr.

 DOI: 10.4324/9781315400303-75

Gladstone radiate into space, when in action, quasi-magnetic waves of influence which might affect other brains brought within the magnetic field of his great personality, much as the influence of a great magnet deflects a small compass needle? Many men (some perhaps of Mr. Gladstone's own colleagues) would admit their experience of such a quasi-magnetic force in his case, a predisposing and persuasive influence quite apart from and independent of the influence of spoken words.

The idea of 'brain-waves' as a possible explanation of the *modus operandi* of such and such-like influences occurred to me about the year 1851, when watching experiments in what was then called electro-biology. I saw men whom I had known long and intimately, and upon whose complete uprightness, straightforwardness, honesty, and intelligence I could absolutely rely, brought into a dazed and half-awake state by staring at a metal disc held in their hands, and who were then subjected to the will of an utter stranger, the operator, till they became his mere victims and tools and slavishly and maniacally obeyed whatever suggestion he put into their minds through their brains. They were as clay in the hands of the potter, and the operator's brain seemed to completely control and act as it were in lieu of their own, driving them into actions and antics utterly and hatefully foreign to their habits and ways. It was inexplicable except on the assumption that their brains were not under their own control at all, but under that of another quite external to theirs. When I came to find, as I did, that such control was sometimes exercised from a distance and without any visible or audible signal from the operator to his victim, the thought came to me which I embodied in the word Brain-waves. I discussed the theory with friends for many years, accumulating additional observations as time went on, and at length, when I came to know Lord (then Mr.) Tennyson, I talked it over with him, and asked him what he thought of my hypothesis. He said he thought there was a great deal very plausible in it; that I had at any rate made a good word in 'brain-waves', and a word which would live; and he encouraged me to publish the idea, as I accordingly did in the subjoined communication to the *Spectator* of the 30th of January, 1869.

JAMES KNOWLES.

Brain-waves. – a theory

[TO THE EDITOR OF THE *Spectator*]

SIR, – A collection of authenticated ghost stories relating to contemporary persons and events would not only be curious and interesting, but might serve to throw light on one of the darkest fields of science, a field, indeed, hardly yet claimed by science.

The mere collocation might bring out features suggestive of a law. If to such a collection were added so many of the 'manifestations' of mesmerists, spiritualists, electro-biologists, and clairvoyants as have a clear residuum of fact (and after a sweeping deduction of professional contributions), the indication of a common action of force through them all might probably become still more obvious.

Such statements as the following, coming as they do within the scope of a single person's observation, may, doubtless, be taken to stand for very many similar ones.

In giving them as sample narratives, I do so with two objects, firstly, to commence in your pages, if you are willing to open them for it, a veracious and authenticated catalogue of such experiences; and secondly, to venture on a crude hypothesis by way of explanation, which, of course, will be taken merely for what it is worth, but which has appeared plausible to some. It may, perhaps, at any rate serve as a temporary thread whereon to collect illustrative or contradictory instances.

Mr. Robert Browning, of whose keen study of the subject his poem of *Mr. Sludge the Medium* would be alone sufficient proof, tells me that when he was in Florence, some years since, an Italian nobleman (a Count Ginnasi, of Ravenna), visiting at Florence, was brought to his house, without previous introduction, by an intimate friend. The Count professed to have great mesmeric or clairvoyant faculties, and declared, in reply to Mr. Browning's avowed scepticism, that he would undertake to convince him somehow or other of his powers. He then asked Mr. Browning whether he had anything about him then and there which he could hand to him, and which was in any way a relic or memento. This, Mr. Browning thought, was perhaps because he habitually wore no sort of trinket or ornament, not even a watch-guard, and might, therefore, turn out to be a safe challenge. But it so happened that by a curious accident he was then wearing under his coat-sleeves some gold wrist-studs to his shirt, which he had quite recently taken into use, in the absence (by mistake of a sempstress) of his ordinary wrist-buttons. He had never before worn them in Florence or elsewhere, and had found them in some old drawer where they had lain forgotten for years. One of these gold studs he took out and handed to the Count, who held it in his hand awhile, looking earnestly in Mr. Browning's face, and then said, as if much impressed, 'C' è qualche cosa che mi grida nell' orecchio, "Uccisione, uccisione!"' ('There is something here which cries out in my ear, "Murder, murder!"')

> And truly [says Mr. Browning] those very studs were taken from the dead body of a great-uncle of mine, who was violently killed on his estate in St. Kitt's, nearly eighty years ago. These, with a gold watch and other personal objects of value, were produced in a court of justice as proof that robbery had not been the purpose of the slaughter which was effected by his own slaves. They were then transmitted to my grandfather, who had his initials engraved on them, and wore them all his life. They were taken out of the night-gown in which he died, and given to me, not my father. I may add, that I tried to get Count Ginnasi to use his *clairvoyance* on *this* termination of ownership also; and that he *nearly* hit upon something like the fact, mentioning a bed in a room; but he failed in attempting to describe the room – situation of the bed with respect to windows and door. The occurrence of my great-uncle's murder was known only to myself, of all men in Florence, as certainly was also my possession of the studs.

Mr. Woolner, the sculptor, tells me the following story of two young men – one of them a personal friend of his own, now living. These two men lived for very long as great friends, but ultimately quarrelled, shortly before the departure of one of them to New Zealand. The emigrant had been absent for many years, and his friend at home (Mr. Woolner's informant), never having kept up correspondence with him, had naturally almost lost the habit of thinking about him or his affairs. One day, however, as he sat in his rooms in a street near Oxford Street, the thought of his friend came suddenly upon him, accompanied by the most restless and indefinable discomfort. He could by no means account for it, but, finding the feeling grow more and more oppressive, tried to throw it off by change of occupation. Still the discomfort grew, till it amounted to a sort of strange horror. He thought he must be sickening for a bad illness, and at length, being unable to do anything else, went out of doors and walked up and down the busiest streets, hoping by the sight and sound of multitudes of men and ordinary things to dissipate his strange and mysterious misery. Not, however, till he had wandered to and fro in the most wretched state of feeling for nearly two hours, utterly unable to shake off an intolerable sort of vague consciousness of his friend, did the impression leave him and his usual frame of mind return. So greatly was he struck and puzzled by all this that he wrote down precisely the date of the day and hour of the occurrence, fully expecting to have news shortly of or from his old friend. And surely, when the next mail or the next but one arrived, there came the horrible news that at that very day and hour (*allowance being made for longitude*) his friend had been made prisoner by the natives of New Zealand, and put to a slow death with the most frightful tortures.

Of this same kind, though happily different in result, is a story of his own experience which Mr. Tennyson, the Poet Laureate, tells me, viz. that some years ago he was induced to try (successfully) the curative effect of mesmerism by passes of the hands upon a patient, who became so sensitive as to be aware on one occasion of his approach by railway two hours before he reached the house, and when his coming was entirely unannounced and unpremeditated. On another occasion, the same patient positively asserted to a third person that Mr. Tennyson had been there the day before, when Mr. Tennyson himself was equally positive to the contrary, till he afterwards remembered that he had come as far as the grounds of the house, and then changed his mind and turned back.

So far for authenticated sample narratives, to which, as I have said, many more may probably be added, with due care.

To come now to my crude hypothesis of a *Brain-wave* as explanatory of them and of kindred stories.

Let it be granted that whensoever any action takes place in the brain, a chemical change of its substance takes place also; or, in other words, an atomic movement occurs; for all chemical change involves – perhaps consists in – a change in the relative positions of the constituent particles of the substance changed.

[An electric manifestation is the likeliest outcome of any such chemical change, whatever other manifestations may also occur.]

Let it be also granted that there is, diffused throughout all known space, and permeating the interspaces of all bodies, solid, fluid, or gaseous, an universal, impalpable, elastic 'Ether', or material medium of surpassing and inconceivable tenuity.

[The undulations of this imponderable ether, if not of substances submerged in it, may probably prove to be light, magnetism, heat, &c.]

But if these two assumptions be granted – and the present condition of discovery seems to warrant them – should it not follow that no brain action can take place without creating a wave or undulation (whether electric or otherwise) in the ether; for the movement of any solid particle submerged in any such medium must create a wave?

If so, we should have as one result of brain action an undulation or wave in the circumambient, all-embracing ether – we should have what I will call Brain-waves proceeding from every brain when in action.

Each acting, thinking brain then would become a centre of undulations transmitted from it in all directions through space. Such undulations would vary in character and intensity in accordance with the varying nature and force of brain actions; *e.g.* the thoughts of love or hate, of life or death, of murder or rescue, of consent or refusal, would each have its corresponding tone or intensity of brain action, and consequently of brain-wave (just as each passion has its corresponding tone of voice).

Why might not such undulations, when meeting with and falling upon duly sensitive substances, as if upon the sensitised paper of the photographer, produce impressions, dim portraits of thoughts, as undulations of light produce portraits of objects?

The sound-wave passes on through myriads of bodies, and among a million makes but one thing shake, or sound to it; a sympathy of structure makes it sensitive, and it alone. A voice or tone may pass unnoticed by ten thousand ears, but strike and vibrate one into a madness of recollection.

In the same way the brain-wave of Damon passing through space, producing no perceptible effect, meets somewhere with the sensitised and sympathetic brain of Pythias, falls upon it, and thrills it with a familiar movement. The brain of Pythias is affected as by a tone, a perfume, a colour with which he has been used to associate his friend; he knows not how or why, but Damon comes into his thoughts, and the things concerning him by association live again. If the last brain-waves of life be frequently intensest – convulsive in their energy, as the firefly's dying flash is its brightest, and as oftentimes the 'lightening before death' would seem to show – we may perhaps seem to see how it is that apparitions at the hour of death are far more numerous and clear than any other ghost stories.[1]

Such oblique methods of communicating between brain and brain (if such there be) would probably but rarely take effect. The influences would be too minute and subtle to tell upon any brain already preoccupied by action of its own, or on any but brains of extreme, perhaps morbid, susceptibility. But if, indeed, there be radiating from living brains any such streams of vibratory movements (as surely there must be),[2] these may well have an effect, even without speech, and be, perhaps, the *modus operandi* of 'the little flash – the mystic hint', of the poet – of that dark and strange sphere of half-experiences which the world has never been without.

There surely are brains so susceptible, and so ready to move to the slightest sympathetic touch, that

> Thought leaps out to wed with Thought,
> Ere Thought could wed itself with speech.

Such exceptionally sensitive and susceptible brains – open to the minutest influences – would be the ghost-seers, the 'mediums' of all ages and countries. The wizards and magicians – true or false – the mesmerists and biologisers would be the men who have discovered that their brains can and do (sometimes even without speech) pre-dispose and compel the brains of these sensitive ones, so as to fill them with emotions and impressions more or less at will.

It will but be a vague, dim way, at the best, of communicating thought, or the sense of human presence, and proportionally so as the receiving brain is less and less highly sensitive. Yet, though it can never take the place of rudest articulation, it may have its own place and office other than and beyond speech. It may convey sympathies of feeling beyond all words to tell – groanings of the spirit which cannot be uttered, visions of influences and impressions not elsehow communicable, may carry one's living human presence to another by a more subtle and excellent way of sympathy.

> Star to star vibrates light: may soul to soul
> Strike thro' a finer element of her own?
> So, from afar, touch us at once?[3]

The application of such a theory to such narratives as I have given above is obvious.[4] In Mr. Browning's case, his brain, full of the murder-thought, and overflowing with its correspondent brainwave, floods the sensitive brain of the Count, who *feels* it directly. His attempt to read the second transfer of ownership is almost as illustrative as his closer success with the first. The death-bed thought and its correspondent brain-wave were sufficiently strong and striking in Mr. Browning's mind to have a character of their own; the rest of the complicated picture was too minute and ordinary, did not burn itself into or out of his brain with enough distinctness. The prominent notes of the music were alone caught by the listener.

In Mr. Woolner's case, the death-convulsion of the emigrant's brain and the correspondent brain-wave flooded space with the intensity and swiftness of a flash of actual light or magnetism, and wheresoever it happened to find the sympathetic substance, the substance accustomed to vibrate to it, and not too violently preoccupied with other action to be insensible to such fine impressions, shook it with the terrible vague subtle force of association described. The intervening space and matter need be no more an obstacle than the 3,000 miles of Atlantic wire are to the galvanic current, or the countless distances of its travel to the light from Sirius. A similar explanation holds good for Mr. Tennyson's story, in which the less distances seem somehow less staggering at first sight.

In such a manner, too, the answers given by the so-called 'spirit-rapping' (when not imposture) seem explicable. These are made by the spelling-out of words letter by letter, the questioner alone knowing the reply, and the letter which would be right to help it. The character of his thought, and consequent brain-wave, changes from denial to consent, when, letter after letter being pointed to in vain, the right letter is reached at last. That change of thought-state is reflected in a change of brain-action and wave-movement, which the sensitive medium *feels*, and at once acts upon.

Many ghost and dream stories seem to yield also to some such mode of interpretation, and much might be added in illustration and expansion of it, as touching rumours, presentiments, panics, revivals, epidemic-manias, and so forth; but I have said enough to put the suggestion before better minds, whether for correction or disproof.

I am, Sir, &c.
J. T. K.

Notes

1 The experience of Admiral Beaufort when drowning (confirmed by other similar accounts) points to an extreme and marvellously intense action of the brain just before death. Some years since a ghost club existed at Cambridge which sifted all the stories it could find, and concluded that those only bore the test of searching inquiry which concerned apparitions at the hour of death.

2 No doubt atomic movements, causing waves in space, must start from other parts of the body as well as from the brain, and, indeed, from the fluctuations of all material bodies (whence Hitchcock's ingenious fancy of the 'Universal Telegraph'). But the question here is simply limited to how *brains* are affected by the movements of other brains. Just as the question of how one pendulum will make other pendulums swing with it is a fair mechanical inquiry by itself, though, doubtless, other questions would remain as to how the movement of the pendulum would affect all other material bodies, as well as pendulums in the same room with it.

3 *Aylmer's Field.*

4 I need hardly say that I alone am responsible for such an attempt at explanation of these narratives, and not their authors.

PART 6

Daily life – and death

6.1

Sewing machine

DOI: 10.4324/9781315400303-77

6.1 Sewing machine

'Sewing Machines', *All the Year Round* (27 March 1869), pp. 394–397.

The development of a widespread culture of invention meant that innovation and technology could come to affect any number of human pursuits. The technological things represented in this section have been included for their intrinsic interest, their diversity, and their connections to broader issues in Victorian culture, from health and nutrition to industry and imperialism.

Sewing was both a major form of paid labour and an unpaid household task for women of all classes. Indeed, it was so universal for Victorian women that it was often simply referred to as 'work', although the kind of sewing that particular women undertook (everyday 'plain work' versus decorative 'fancy work') varied according to their skills and acquirements, as well as their household needs and their class status. The creation of complex machines to make sewing faster and easier dates to the eighteenth century, but in the second half of the nineteenth century, the previous work of many decades was brought together with new breakthroughs in design and production to create a modern consumer device – a familiar pattern for Victorian technologies. But in the case of the new sewing machine, these breakthroughs were not only technical but also legal and commercial. In America, the 'Sewing Machine War' of the 1850s ended with the unprecedented negotiation of a patent pool among rival inventors, which proved to be the start of an international industry as notable for its marketing as for its machines.[1]

The sewing machine became a sensationally popular home appliance, a revolution in domestic 'work' as well as a new device for industrial production. As the columnist in Dickens' *All the Year Round* frets, the machine might also worsen the lives and health of poor women who used them to sew for a living. Still, perhaps the invention might help to solve the problems that it has engendered: the writer proposes not regulation or reform but the supersession of the treadle sewing machine, which was powered by the workwoman herself, by new machines equipped with small electric motors. The writer notes an additional benefit of the plan that should give us pause: feeding electricity to small motors costs less than feeding extra food to working-class women who have to spend their workdays pumping treadles. The labouring woman herself figures here as something like another technological object.[2]

Notes

1 On the history and significance of the Sewing Machine War for the patent system, see Adam Mossoff, 'The Rise and Fall of the First American Patent Thicket: The Sewing Machine War of the 1850s', *Arizona Law Review* 53 (2011), pp. 165–211.

2 Notable histories of the sewing machine include Grace Rogers Cooper, *The Sewing Machine: Its Invention and Development*, 2nd ed. (Washington, DC: Smithsonian Institution, 1976); Ruth Brandon, *Singer and the Sewing Machine: A Capitalist Romance* (London: Barrie and Jenkins, 1977); and Frank P. Godfrey, *An International History of the Sewing Machine* (London: Hale, 1982).

53

'SEWING MACHINES'

(27 March 1869), pp. 394–397

We could fill a whole number of *All the Year Round* with the claims of the French to *every* modern scientific discovery. The last claim, put forth by M. Henri de Parville, on behalf of their invention of the sewing machine, we should scarcely have noticed here, but for the important remarks of that able writer on the imperfection of the implement as it stands.

First, in respect to the invention: It appears that, about 1825, there lived at Saint Etienne (a manufacturing town to the southwest of Lyons) a poor wretch of a tailor noted for his thriftlessness and eccentricity. So far from his customers increasing, the few he had dropped off one by one; which seemed to trouble him very little. He was rarely to be found at home on his board, and still more rarely did he call for orders. In 1827 he was held to have a bee in his bonnet, and in 1829 he went for downright crazy. This reputed madman, Barthélemy Thimonnier, the son of a Lyons dyer, was born at Arbreste (Department of the Rhône) in 1793. He learnt tailoring, and worked at the trade first at Amplepuis and then at Saint Etienne. The manufacturers of Tarare get a great deal of crochet embroidery done in the mountains of the Lyonnais. Thimonnier, while watching the young women at work, conceived the first idea of the sewing machine. He brooded over it and worked incessantly at it for four long years, losing his credit, ruining himself, but triumphantly resolving the problem. In 1830 he took out a patent for an apparatus executing chain-stitch by mechanical means.

An inspector-general of mines, M. Beaunier, then residing at Saint Etienne, saw the machine, and at a glance comprehended its importance. He took the inventor to Paris. Thimonnier, one Ferrand, Germain Petit and Company of Paris, entered into partnership for working the apparatus. In 1831, there was to be seen in the Rue de Sèvres, a factory in which eighty wooden sewing machines were at work: they made soldiers' clothing by machinery. Now, machinery suppresses manual labour, and the workman looks no further than that; the plain fact strikes him, and he will hear no more. Thimonnier's sewing machines were broken in 1831, exactly as the first threshing machines were destroyed in England by riotous agricultural labourers.

DOI: 10.4324/9781315400303-78

Thimonnier ran away. A few months afterwards, M. Beaunier's death broke up the partnership with Germain Petit and Company. In 1834, Thimonnier returned to Paris, and used his machine to do tailoring work, at the same time trying to improve it. In 1836, reduced to utter poverty, he returned to his native town. He travelled on foot, says one of his biographers (M. Meyssin, of Lyons) with his machine on his back, and kept soul and body together by exhibiting its performance as a curiosity. Retiring to Amplepuis, he constructed several machines, and sold them with very great difficulty. In 1845, the original contrivance already made two hundred stitches a minute. At that period, an intelligent manufacturer, M. Magnin, of Villefranche, offered his co-operation, which was accepted; the partners sold machines at fifty francs (two pounds) each. In 1848, as testified by a patent, Thimonnier's machine executed three hundred stitches per minute; it embroidered, and sewed not only muslin but cloth, and even leather.

The revolution of February, 1848, checked the invention, just as it was gaining ground. Thimonnier sold his patent for England to a company at Manchester, and sent an improved specimen to the London Exhibition of 1851. The machine was delayed on the road, and did not reach its destination until after the jury had given their awards. After thirty years of struggle, toil, and want, Thimonnier died in poverty at Amplepuis, on the fifth of August, 1857, at the age of sixty-four. He shared the fate of many inventors. In 1832, in his eighty-first year, there expired at the Invalides, forgotten by all, the Marquis Claude Jouffroy d'Albans, the inventor of steamboats. On the tenth of August, 1807, the banks of the Hudson had rung with shouts in acclamation of Fulton's triumph. France, says M. de Parville, had sown; America reaped. It was not till ten years after America and England that France possessed her first steamer, the Elise, which for a while ran regularly between Rouen and Elbeuf. The sewing machine also, like the steamboat, after having been invented in France, returned thither from America. M. de Parville naturally regrets that the circumstance should be so frequently forgotten.

While Thimonnier was struggling with poverty, his machine was being improved across the Ocean. In 1845, an American, Elias Howe, took out a patent for a sewing machine with two threads, needle, and shuttle. In 1851 the jury at the Crystal Palace were registering Elias Howe's improvement, whilst Thimonnier's machine was lingering on the way. Soon, nothing was talked of but the American machines, and from 1855 the Continent was inundated with them. We now possess excellent English, French, and German models; the old world has taken her revenge. Well-made in general, simple, giving marvellous results of speed, sewing machines have found their way everywhere; into factories, work-rooms, drawing-rooms. They have brought about a complete revolution in the process of sewing. A good seamstress could make her twenty-five or thirty stitches per minute; a sewing machine will now do eight hundred. It is an increase of speed unparalleled in industrial history. The economical results immediately showed themselves by a general drop in the price of the most essential articles of clothing. We have all reaped the benefit of the invention; and how many have ever heard of Thimonnier's name?

And now for the physical and moral effects. The commercial results are palpable, immense; the hygienic consequences are the reverse of advantageous. For, the sewing machine is a tool, and so is the needle. But the needle is so light, so essentially feminine; the machine so heavy, so fatiguing to work! It illustrates the mechanical axiom, 'What you gain in speed, you expend in strength'. You get on wonderfully faster than with the needle, but you must employ quite a different degree of force to work this charming little implement. Has the idea ever struck anybody at any time or place?

One would hardly think it, to see poor girls fixed to their sewing machine as no other motive power ever was before. Riding-school horses are changed every three hours; omnibus horses every two hours; but here is no change. For ten or twelve hours a day, and sometimes more, the feet have to press alternately on the pedals, and the frame has to be shaken by the same continuous and regular movements.

The object of all machinery ought to be to replace manual labour by mechanical labour; but sewing by machinery leads to the very reverse. It compels women to exert muscular efforts, to a degree never before required of them. It is an absolute contradiction to common sense. Instead of advancing in respect to hygienic considerations, we have actually gone backward. It has been seen that the implement beats the needle in speed, but by a greater expenditure of muscular power. Now, who supplies this muscular power? Who, except the workwoman? And do we fancy that muscular power is to be had gratuitously, without something to sustain it? Nothing in this world comes of nothing. Our bodies are machines, consuming fuel, quite as much as steam engines are. There is a close connection between the work turned off by the human machine, and the alimentary substances with which it is fed. If you increase the work, and do not wish exhaustion and death to be the consequence, you must also augment the daily allowance of food. If the labour required be excessive, overtaxing the supply of strength which the organisation is able to furnish, a morbid condition of the frame is speedily induced.

To the increased production which we so much admire, there corresponds, in fact, an increased expenditure of the workwoman's strength, which she must meet by a fuller and more generous diet. If the fatigue be more than *that* can resist, there ensues a derangement of health and a decay of the natural powers. We can only transform or transmit force; we cannot *create* the strength to lift a feather. Every mode of exercise we take, costs some grains of alimentary substance, and we cannot lift our hand to our head without an expenditure of the provision laid in at breakfast or dinner.

These facts are confirmed by experiment. In 1866, Dr. Guibout gave the alarm in a report to the Hospital Medical Society. While attending the Hospital Saint Louis, he had to prescribe for several workwomen, whose weakness and exhaustion were more than suspicious: these evils were evinced in pale and hollow cheeks, bowed backs, epigastric pains, &c. Afterwards, the same symptoms were noticed in the provinces as well as in Paris. Consumption even was a possible consequence. It cannot be denied that the sewing machine may threaten permanent danger to the workwoman's health and morality. She *must* be better fed than ordinary workwomen; if her earnings do not supply the means, great cities offer only too many other resources. Female prisoners who worked at sewing machines, have not been able to stand the fatigue with the ordinary prison diet. They were obliged to be allowed supplementary rations; broth and boiled beef every day, roast meat twice a week.

The danger is greatly diminished when the machine is only employed temporarily or occasionally. Still, there ought to be limits for delicate young persons. By the way, similar symptoms have been observed in young ladies who regularly practise the piano for several consecutive hours per day. With sewing machines, having ascertained the exact cause of evil, the remedy becomes easier to indicate. We must consider the sewing machine as a simple implement; and, like all implements rapid in their action, we must make it work by means of a motor.

In large work-rooms, like those of M. Godillot, where five hundred sewing machines are at work at once, the motive power employed is steam. Each workwoman, by means of a pedal pressing on the communicator of motion, can regulate the velocity of her machine, or stop it altogether. But in small establishments steam is inapplicable, still less in chamber work. What is wanted to make the sewing machine uninjurious to health, is to couple with it a motive power inconsiderable in size, to be set going or stopped at will, a supplier of artificial muscular power, dispensing with that of the workwoman. We want a sewing machine capable of setting itself agoing. The desideratum is now realised to such an extent that it is quite possible for everybody to have their automaton or self-acting sewing machine.

A French engineer, Monsieur H. Cazal, has invented a little electric motor which, by its combination with the sewing machine, resolves the problem. On touching a button, the machinery turns, exactly as if an invisible workwoman were treading the pedals. Electricity does the work, and the woman superintends it. A pile stuck in a corner, or concealed in a footstool, supplies the motive force required.

The workwoman, to work, must be liberally fed: the electric motor, too, must be supplied with victuals, and luckily its digestion is never out of order, while its appetite is considerable. The pile is its stomach, which assimilates zinc, exactly as the steam engine consumes coal. Electric work costs about thirty times as much as steam work; notwithstanding which, its expense is low enough to allow of its employment in domestic industry.

M. Cazal, by attaching his little motor directly to the implement, suppresses the ordinary modes of transmitting force by which much power is unavoidably lost. He also thus diminishes the first effort which has to be made to set the thing a going. Four Bunsen's elements, for instance, suffice to put the motor in action. Now each one of these consumes about the fifth of a pennyworth of zinc per hour, making the expense for a day about sevenpence halfpenny or eightpence. For those who want to work only several hours per day, a few pence cover the cost. Now if the workwoman, or her employer, remembers that she must spend more than that on extra diet to keep up her strength, it will be found that there is a manifest advantage in employing the electric motive power, not to mention the question of health. Moreover, there are times when mothers of families cannot without danger work at a sewing machine. At such periods, a self-acting machine will afford invaluable assistance. The machines, besides, are furnished with pedals, so that they can be set in action either by electricity or by human strength. Finally, the electro-motor is so ingeniously contrived, that it will probably be found applicable to other things besides sewing machines.

6.2

Refrigeration and frozen food

DOI: 10.4324/9781315400303-79

6.2 Refrigeration and frozen food

James Harrison, 'Food Committee' [extract], *Journal of the Society of Arts*, 22 (28 Nov. 1873), pp. 24–28.
'Refrigeration and Preservation', *Cassell's Family Magazine* (1879), p. 189.

In the second half of the nineteenth century, to write about very different kinds of inventions was to participate in similar modes of prophecy and imaginative problem-solving. The Scottish-Australian editor and inventor James Harrison was a pioneer of mechanical refrigeration and ice-making. Harrison's vision of large-scale commercial refrigeration emphasised the freezing of food for long-distance shipping, especially the possibility of exporting frozen meat from the Australian colonies to Great Britain. Refrigeration promised a future of global food sourcing, year-round food availability, climate-controlled spaces and bountiful frozen meat. Harrison's inaugural shipment from the Antipodes to Great Britain proved inauspicious, however. Rather than constructing an onboard refrigeration apparatus, Harrison had packed 20 tonnes of carefully pre-frozen meat in at least as much ice, using special insulated tanks installed in the ship's hold. During the three-month journey from Melbourne via Cape Horn to London, the tanks proved defective and the 20 tonnes of meat rotted.[1]

Note

1 W. R. (Roy) Lang, *James Harrison, Pioneering Genius* (Newtown, Victoria: Neptune, 1982), pp. 91–94.

For a wider view of the history of refrigerated food, from meat and milk to fruit and vegetables, see Susanne Freidberg, *Fresh: A Perishable History* (Cambridge, MA: Harvard University Press, 2009). An entertaining, compressed account of the long history of refrigeration is provided by Tom Jackson, *Chilled: How Refrigeration Changed the World, and Might Do So Again* (London: Bloomsbury Sigma, 2015); see also Alan J. Cooper, *The World Below Zero: A History of Refrigeration in the UK* (Aylesbury: ACR Today and Battlepress, 1997).

54

JAMES HARRISON, 'FOOD COMMITTEE' [EXTRACT]

Journal of the Society of Arts, 22 (28 Nov. 1873), pp. 24–28

The Committee met on Friday, November 21st. Present: – Benjamin Shaw, Esq., in the chair, Lord Alfred S. Churchill, Sir Daniel Cooper, Bart., Dr. Blakiston, Messrs. F. A. Abel, F.R.S., W. H. Michael, Seymour Teulon, and E. Wilson. This meeting was specially summoned to receive a report from Mr. James Harrison, of Melbourne, with reference to his experiment in the conveyance of frozen meat on board the ship *Norfolk*, from Australia to England. Members generally were invited to it, as well as other gentlemen specially interested in the subject.

Mr. Harrison read the following paper: –

It would have been more pleasant to me, and gratifying to you, if I had come forward to announce a success instead of having to account for a failure; but it is some satisfaction to know that the work in which I have been engaged was a success before it was a failure – a fact which renders the present temporary disappointment the more easily borne. My task is indeed twofold – to describe a success and to record a mischance. The success was that of a principle and a process; the failure was that of the workmen who were entrusted with the construction of the requisite mechanical appliances. But in saying so, I do not seek to shield myself from a fair share of blame. It was my duty to see that the appliances were sufficient, and my only excuse is that I could not recall the time wasted by others. I had allowed myself a week for supervision, but even on the last day the work was not finished, and it was then too late even to abandon the experiment. But I am anticipating. I merely throw out these remarks at the outset to bespeak a favourable hearing; not that I have any reason to fear the contrary, for it is my greatest consolation to find that, despite this failure, I have been cheered by assurances, both from acquaintances and strangers, that there is a very general confidence in my ultimate success – a confidence which I will endeavour to justify.

Descending from generalities to particulars, I may be allowed to say that, from my previous habits of thought and experience, I felt myself well qualified to grapple with the problem I have attempted to solve. On the occasion of my last visit to England, 17 years ago, I introduced my process of ice-making by the evaporation

DOI: 10.4324/9781315400303-80

and condensation of ether – a process which, as is known to many of you, became at once a pronounced success.[1] The very first machine I had constructed was as good as any that has been made since; and this success was achieved by careful forethought and minute attention to details. For many years, however, I had ceased to take any interest in that invention, and it was not until the great food question – the problem how best to convey the superabundance of one-half of the world to satisfy the wants of the other half – became urgent, that I felt called upon to resume my old studies. I took my time, and went over the matter carefully. The conclusions I arrived at, and my reasons for them, I will now briefly recount. The various plans for producing cold on board ship by means of machinery and apparatus requiring fuel are open to many and serious objections. The use of ether is undesirable, on account of the inflammability of the material. Ammonia is a powerful refrigerant, but the pressure under which it would have to be used when within the tropics is so enormous that it is questionable whether vessels which could be relied upon for containing it can be made. This pressure may be diminished, but with corresponding loss of efficiency. The use of air condensed and expanded by machinery is the most plausible, and I may say, fascinating, of these devices, but it is also the most expensive. All these schemes are open to the objections that considerable space is required for the apparatus as well as for fuel, and that their success depends upon the efficiency of complicated machinery, which would have to be erected in duplicate. It appeared to me that the expense of these processes would be too great to permit of their adoption. No doubt, with meat at a penny per pound in Australia and a shilling in England, there is a margin broad enough apparently to warrant any outlay. But the very essence of the problem is here overlooked. The object should be to assimilate as nearly as possible the prices at the port of supply and at the port of debarcation. It is not how to buy meat at a penny and sell it at twelve pennies, but how to raise it to fourpence at one end and lower it to sixpence at the other. The process of meat-preserving, to be satisfactory, must be inexpensive as well as effectual. The use of ice alone is, within certain limits, sufficient, but is not generally reliable. If not entirely surrounded by ice, the temperature of the meat will be some degrees above freezing, while its juices remain fluid some degrees below that point, and while fluid they are liable to chemical as well as organic change. The presence of moisture where there is ice is not easily preventible [sic]. Something more than ice is wanted. Even if it be not requisite to freeze the meat (and on this point there is room for much discussion), it is certainly desirable to have the control of a very low temperature. This is requisite, even though the desired average should be above 32°[F], just as it is requisite to have a good fire to boil a kettle of water; it would be slow work if the fire were no warmer than the steam. In my search for a cheap refrigerant, I, of course, could not but take cognisance of the oldest of all freezing mixtures, ice and salt. Everybody knows how this mixture is made to do daily service in the production of ice-creams, but the received idea of it is that it is rapid and transient in its action, and there is at first something startling, if not ridiculous, in the proposition to take a shipment of ice and salt through the tropics. It did not appear very promising at first sight, but, after careful consideration and a few experiments, I arrived at the law which governed the conduct of this and other freezing mixtures when partially isolated from surrounding influences. I found, in fact, that a mixture of ice and salt melts no faster than would the ice itself under an equivalent difference of temperature. If we take an ice-chamber at 32°[F], with the outside atmosphere at 82°[F], the difference of temperature is 50°[F]. If, again, we take a mixture of ice and salt at zero [degrees Fahrenheit], with the external air at 50°[F], the difference is the same; and we will find that the freezing mixture and the ice alone melt at the same rate. But if the atmosphere be at 82°[F] in both cases, we shall then have the melting of the ice and salt and of the ice alone in the ratio of 82°[F] to 50°[F]; or if we adopt a time measure, the ratio is inverse, the mixture melting in 50 hours or days, and the ice melting in 82 hours or days. But we do not want so low a temperature as zero, and I then had to consider how it could be regulated. Ice and salt are usually mixed together with a great expenditure of animal heat and sweat, but it occurred to me that a more certain result could be attained with little labour, by directing a stream of brine among the ice, the strength of the brine being regulated so as to produce the required degree of cold. This, on experiment, was found to answer well, and the law by which the temperature was effected was found to be very simple. It requires just one per cent. of salt in the water for each degree below 32°[F]. Five per cent., or half-a-pound of salt in the gallon, reduces the temperature to 27°[F], a very convenient point for meat freezing. The melting of ice subjected to this process as compared with ice alone, is in the ratio within the tropics of 55 to 56. In other words, in order to attain the control of 5 degrees [Fahrenheit] below the freezing point, it is only requisite to ship one ton of ice for every ten tons that would be requisite to maintain a temperature of 32°[F]. Of course, I assume that the actual freezing of the meat has been accomplished before starting. The importance of establishing these two points, the law of the melting of freezing mixtures and the proportion of brine required to produce definite results, will be at once seen. They do not deserve the name of discoveries, but they are, so far as comes within my knowledge, inferences drawn and demonstrated for the first time, and as such I submit them. They will be of value to all who turn their attention to this subject.

I next investigated the best means of employing the brine thus artificially cooled to the preservation of the meat. There was no difficulty about that. To allow it to circulate in tubes round the enclosed chamber was the most obvious plan, but tubes are expensive, and must have many joints. I preferred to make the meat tank double, and to allow the brine to circulate in the interspace. To remove pressure, and to diminish the risk of leakage, I filled the space with sheets of coarse blanketing, hanging loosely, so that the brine should keep them continually wet, and yet not run away too fast. The surplus I pumped up occasionally to be used over again. This pumping, for which the labour of one man for two or three hours a day suffices, is all the work attached to the process.

There was one other matter which I had to make the subject of research and experiment before my plans were complete. I had to ascertain the relative properties of the heat-resisting materials available for forming the protecting envelope of the meat and ice chambers, and to ascertain the rate of melting under different conditions. The relative merits of sawdust, charcoal, wool, tallow, and analogous substances are but indifferently known, and they are usually applied as regards their thickness and distribution according to no recognised rule. It is correctly laid down in the textbooks that heat is conducted through any substance in the inverse ratio of its thickness, or, in other words, that heat is obstructed in its passage through a given substance in direct proportion to the thickness of that substance, each kind of material having its special coefficient of conductivity. But, in the practical application of this law to enclosed spaces, a difficulty arises. At first, it would seem that if one foot of thickness gave a certain amount of protection, two feet would afford twice as much; but it is not so. The inner or cold surface is necessarily less than the outer or warm surface, and with every additional layer the disproportion increases. The results will be equally erroneous, whether the inner or the outer surfaces be taken as the basis of calculation, and what is true of a small enclosure will not be true when applied to a larger. It occurred to me that, to ensure accuracy, it would be requisite to ascertain the position and extent of an intermediate neutral surface, or line of mean temperature. There are difficulties in the way of ascertaining this by experiment, but I have ascertained with, I think, sufficient exactness for practical purposes, the approximate law by which this line is to be found. The warm moiety of the envelope is to the cold moiety as the outer is to the inner surface. If, for instance, the outer surface is of double the extent of the inner, the neutral line will be found at a distance of one-third of the thickness from the inner surface and two-thirds from the outer. Even this is only true when the enclosure is spherical. If it be a cube the masses of envelope at the angles will exercise a disturbing influence and carry the neutral line nearer to the inner surface than at the sides. If the masses at the angles were absolute non-conductors, then the neutral line would be found equidistant between the inner and outer surfaces at the sides; but if of the same material as the sides, then the neutral line will be a curve of variable radii, the cold moiety of the envelope being thickest at the centre of each side, and thinnest at each angle. It is not requisite to go into the mathematics of the problem to see the great importance of fortifying the angles by the employment of the best heat-resisting material in the construction of the envelope at these points, while it would be thrown away if used in the centre of the sides. It is with a heat-resisting envelope as with a fortress – its strength is that of its most vulnerable point.

With respect to the relative value of heat-resisting substances, my experiments were limited to those which I found practically available in the colony. The properties of sawdust are well known, and I adopted that as the standard of comparison for tallow and bark, the articles of produce best available for shipment. Tallow I found to be inferior to sawdust in the proportion of three to two, that is, the ice surrounded by tallow lasted only two-thirds of the time it lasted when packed with sawdust. Bark, roughly ground or finely chopped, was as good as sawdust, and when finely ground was even better. It is also superior to sawdust, inasmuch as it is not so liable to heat when damp. This was exceedingly satisfactory, wattle bark being a staple export for which there is always a market in England. I therefore used it, packing it in bags, and filling up the interstices with sawdust. Charcoal was not obtainable in quantity on short notice, but I tried pounded gas coke, and found it, contrary to expectation, far inferior to sawdust, and no better than tallow. Wool I did not try, as it is a material too valuable and delicate to employ as mere dunnage.

My experiments on the waste of ice, and of ice immersed in brine, were made on three several occasions at different times of the year. The temperature of the air and the waste of ice were noted daily, and the results posted up on the outside of the enclosure in the Exhibition building, so that they might be tested at any time. From the data thus obtained I shipped on board the *Norfolk* a quantity which should have lasted 120 days. That there was no error on this score I am confident. But it was not until the fourteenth day that I discovered that there was a strong current of air passing downwards among the ice, and escaping, of course, at a lower point into the hold. The fittings were, indeed, defective at the very points where I was most solicitous about their efficiency. When my back was turned, the carpenters, who were not quite sober, covered up their scamped work, and the stevedores had it banked up with cargo before it could be inspected. It was not until the greater part of the meat was thrown overboard that I could secure the remnant of ice from rapid waste. During the first thirty-seven days, in the coldest part of the run, I lost 20 tons of ice, and I carried the remaining 5 tons for thirty-nine days, including the run through the tropics. This of itself is collateral evidence of the correctness of my estimate, and of the abnormal waste of ice caused by defective fittings.

Throughout my experiments I attended to the desiccation of the air of the meat-chamber, so as, in fact, to keep up a slow but constant evaporation from the surfaces of the meat. In experiments on a small scale, I found it sufficient to place in one corner a wide-mouthed bottle containing fragments of chloride of calcium; but on board ship I placed the chloride in a separate compartment, with tubes leading to and from it in such a position as would ensure a continuous circulation of the air of the meat-chamber. This arrangement was, however, rendered nugatory by leakage into the meat tanks, from one of which three, and from the other seven, bucketsful of brine were taken after the meat was removed. But I do not care to go much into these details. To me they are simply sickening. The greatest loss was that of the brine, which leaked away, instead of doing the work allotted to it. This loss I reported to the captain of the vessel within seven days after sailing, and on the eighth day the chief officer called my attention to the discolouration of the bilge-water brought up by the ship's pumps, attributable, as he thought, to the admixture of my brine after percolating through the bottom tier of wattle bark. There could be no doubt of it. The bark and the brine, impregnated with iron from the tanks, formed a kind of ink which recorded its own history.

I have said that the process was a success before it was involved in failure. Happily, on this point I am not called upon to give my own testimony. The process was subjected to the severest of tests in a crowded exhibition, surrounded with flaring gas, in the hottest month of the year; and I more than once left it to itself, not going near the meat-chamber for a week at a stretch, and when I did go it was merely to see that the brine was of the requisite strength. In the *Times* there has already appeared the account of a public luncheon which was given to me prior to my leaving the colony, the principal dishes on the table being beef and mutton which had been frozen for eighty-five days. Many of you have, no doubt, seen the letter I refer to. Strange to say I have not seen it myself, so I cannot quote from it. But I have in my hand an official report supplied to the Department of Lands and Agriculture in Victoria, the author of the report being the Rev. Dr. Bleasdale, well known in scientific circles as a reliable authority. With your permission I will read an extract or two, and will then leave the report on the table for those who wish to examine it more particularly.

The first extract relates to the meat which was preserved in the Exhibition building, and for which I was awarded the medal: –

> I had a piece of beef 14 or 15 lbs. weight cut off the next lump that was taken out. The whole might have weighed 60 or 70 lbs. It was all that an experimenter could desire, being from between the loin and rump, and from the size of the piece presented a more than average surface to the air, and not too much fat. I caused this piece, and a corresponding lump, fresh from the butcher, to be hung up in a corridor close to my office in the Exhibition buildings, with a thermometer midway between them. During the whole period of the first experiment it ranged from 63 degrees to 68 degrees Fahrenheit. Other portions of this beef were thawed in the orthodox way, in cold water, and cooked in the oven, and found quite equal to newly-killed beef, of good quality, full of gravy, and rather tough, as new meat usually is.
>
> At the expiration of twenty-four hours (11 a.m. Christmas morning) I called the officer in charge of that division of Exhibition work, a very intelligent man, and he took down the meat and reported the thermometer at 67 degrees [Fahrenheit]. Not without some misgivings, I cut off a steak of about 24 ozs., and ordered it to be cooked in the ordinary way for breakfast.
>
> While the cooking was in progress, it occurred to me to try the then temperature of the lump, and, having some good thermometers at hand, I inserted one in the lump and left another in contact with its outer surface. Even then they both indicated what I should have expected if the meat had been ice, certainly not what I then anticipated. The inserted one indicated the temperature of ordinary ice, and the one on the outer surface that of ice passing into thaw, rather lower than the other.
>
> Now for the first time I began to hit upon the difference between Mr. Harrison's work and the American practice.
>
> The meat was cooked, and the officer and I made an excellent Christmas breakfast off it. The lump was suspended again in the same place,

and the fresh meat examined; but, beyond the slight bleaching of the fat and blackening of the lean, there was nothing worthy of remark.

About 10 p.m. of Christmas day, when this lump had been thirty-five hours out of the ice, it was re-examined in presence of several ladies and gentlemen, and found to be not only perfectly sweet, but assuming the ordinary characteristics of kept meat. But the fresh butcher-meat, hanging not six feet from it, had turned sour, and was beginning to show signs of greenness, and, in order that it might not be lost, was given to the housekeeper to cook.

I then began to think there was no further use in following up the investigation, for if meat would keep in a temperature of 68 degrees [Fahrenheit], it would, on arriving at a British port, have a fairer chance than that newly killed. So thenceforth the remainder of the piece was let hang, and every six or seven hours re-examined, to see if it had become tainted. But what was my utter astonishment when the remnant, say about 5 lbs., was directed to be cooked, and found when served up to be excellent. Dr. McCrea, the Chief Medical Officer, Dr. Gilbee, and myself partook of it. The Chief Medical Officer dined off it, Dr. Gilbee lunched off it, and I carved it, and tasted both the meat and the gravy. Now this was at least seventy-five hours after I first hung it up.

. . . .

On the fortieth day after the meat had been first placed in the preserving-room, Mr. Harrison directed the remainder, a number of very large pieces, some of 40 lbs. or 50 lbs. weight, to be cooked, and, on successive days, given in the refreshment-room to any one who might think well to lunch off it. The further prosecution of this most interesting and valuable demonstration is in the hands of squatters, stockowners, and merchants.

The next extract relates to an experiment tried about three months afterwards: –

On this occasion Mr. J. Cosmo Newberry, scientific superintendant of the Technological Museum, was associated with me, and we both were made privy to all the details of the process. I entered on this second study of the frozen meat with the more pleasure because it would enable me, in company with Mr. Newbery, to control my former experiments, even if he added nothing new to the facts already ascertained.

On the 28th May, when the meat had lain four and a half weeks in the keeping chamber, it was opened at 11 a.m. in the presence of Lieut.-Colonel Stephens, Messrs. Hughes, Wilson, myself, several other gentlemen and representatives of the press. The principal reasons for opening the chamber at the end of thirty-two days were, firstly, to check the results obtained by watching the daily amount of water thawed by the weight of the remaining unthawed ice; secondly, suppose that from any cause it should be necessary on the long voyage to open the chamber, what would be the effect – the loss in ice – under such a possible occurrence; thirdly, what became of the aqueous vapour admitted into the chamber in the process of its ventilation. As I had conducted the first course of inspection and examination, as recorded above, I was naturally enough asked to carry out the second.

In regard to the first, 480 lbs. remained unthawed, and nearly corresponded with the calculations of the quantity that ought to be found.

At this moment (27th June) there is no reply to the second, because the chamber has not been re-opened; but this may be said, that during the first thirty-two days 720 lbs. were thawed, and that with substantially the same quantity of meat to keep. The next thirty days have not consumed 480 lbs., the weather being all the time of about the same average temperature. The reply to the third reason is most satisfactory. The towels laid over and around the meat were perfectly dry – not frozen – but actually dry; and we found the aqueous vapour of ventilation deposited like fine snow, and adhering to the under side of the lid cover of the chamber – a strong plate of iron. The chamber was left open more than four hours, and then closed, and the remainder of the ice replaced as before.

One of the reasons was that mentioned already – that I might repeat my former examination and check the results then obtained, as recorded in the first portion of this essay.

As soon as it was opened Mr. Harrison selected a large saddle of mutton (24 lbs.) that lay on the top of the stack, and a 19 lbs. piece of the thick rib of beef (a roasting joint) from the very bottom of the chamber. Two exactly corresponding pieces (a saddle and ribs) were obtained from the butchers who supplied the pieces frozen. This meat had been killed about thirty hours, and of course was quite fresh. I caused them to be hung in my office, not as before in a corridor, because I thought the air inside would more nearly resemble that of a butcher's cellar or a gentleman's larder. I rigged saucers under the frozen pieces to catch any drip falling either during or after the thawing. Thermometers in the room registered 59.21 degrees [Fahrenheit].

. . . .

At 11 a.m. on the 29th May, twenty-four hours after the meat had been exposed to the air, we found the temperature in the room 56.5 degrees [Fahrenheit]. On examining the saucers we found hardly one-eighth of a fluid ounce of drip from the beef, and about half-ounce from the mutton, and this consisted mostly of blood. This seemed to have dripped down from the region of the kidneys, which, however, had been removed previous to the meat having been frozen. Both pieces smelled quite sweet. On taking the actual temperature of all the meat, we found that of the unfrozen beef to be 54 degrees [Fahrenheit]; ditto mutton 53 degrees [Fahrenheit]. Frozen beef 50 degrees [Fahrenheit], at a depth of four inches in the thickest part; frozen mutton 52 degrees [Fahrenheit] – the thaw was nearly complete.

. . . .

30th May. – At 12 noon to-day, twenty-five hours more, on entering I found several large blow-flies in the room, and noticed one on the frozen saddle of mutton; and fearing lest it should have blown the meat, I removed a few small bits from the place, and then had all the pieces enclosed in muslin bags, to keep off flies for the future. Temperature of the room nearly 60 degrees [Fahrenheit]. Yesterday, and still more today, the weather was close, warm, and damp. Wind N.E. to E. All the pieces were perfectly good; but the frozen beef was firmer to the touch than the unfrozen, and no sign of mildew or sourness. Much grey mildew on the unfrozen piece, both on the thick and thin parts exposed.

There was nothing to remark about the mutton to-day, except that there was a single drop of reddish fluid hanging on the end of the spine bone of the frozen piece; and after removing the bits where the fly had been seen, both the frozen and unfrozen pieces were dusted with flour. Both pieces were perfectly sweet, and in the opinion of an experienced housekeeper, every way likely for keeping yet two or three days more, even in this very unfavourable weather. There was no mildew on either joint of mutton. As the weather became worse, I deemed it right to watch the meat very carefully. So at 4 p.m. I found the temperature of the room 60 degrees [Fahrenheit]. Rain was falling, and I closed the windows completely. Again at 7.20 I examined the thermometers, and found the temperature rising – 60.5 degrees [Fahrenheit]. This was fifty-six and a half hours after the meat was taken out of the freezing-chamber. Nothing fresh to remark.

31st May. – At 11 a.m., thermometer in the office 59 degrees [Fahrenheit]. We found all the meat quite sweet; it was now seventy-three hours out of the chamber. I caused the frozen saddle to be cut down the spine, and sent one-half to be roasted for luncheon at 1:15 p.m. At the same time I had a large steak cut from each of the pieces of beef to be served up at the same hour.

I invited several gentlemen, not directly concerned in pastoral pursuits, of known repute, and competent judges, to partake of these meats, who met at the appointed hour. I append the note made on the occasion, merely remarking that it was only by guessing that any one could say which pieces had been frozen and which had not.

The portions not used were ordered to be examined again next day, to see if the cold meat would prove as good in proportion as when fresh roasted.

June 1st. – 1:20 p.m., thermometer in office registered 62 degrees, with wind north-westerly, very light, weather cloudy and muggy. Mr. Newbery and I examined the meat, in company with Lieut-Colonel Stevens and Mr. and Mrs. Shaw.

After being ninety-nine hours out of the ice-chamber, the frozen beef was found to be quite sound and sweet; but in one or two places, where thermometers had been thrust into the thin parts near the bone, it showed signs of approaching change. I dissected the meat from the bone, but found no evidence of change but that just noted. Yet, for safety sake, it was put into a hot oven for ten minutes, and ordered to be cooked for luncheon next day. This meat was sour where the steak had been cut off, and much covered with grey mildew. The half of the saddle was looking wonderfully good, and devoid of any smell but mutton, even under the kidney fat and the flaps. It was ordered to remain until to-morrow.

It is but fair to remark that the beef was much handled and breathed upon by visitors anxious to satisfy their curiosity to the utmost. We observed another matter of interest to ourselves: – viz., when the frozen beef was first hung up the whole of the fat visible was quite white; it remained so until after the thawing was complete, and only after forty-eight hours did it resume fully its original yellow-brown colour. It was then wholly undistinguishable from the unfrozen as far as the colour of the fat was concerned.

To-day we tasted the cold mutton from yesterday and found it excellent. Some of it was made into a hash, and much relished by the gentlemen who had been invited. Mr. Harrison himself was present on this as on most of the previous occasions at luncheon.

2nd June. – We inspected the half saddle of mutton at 11:30 a. m., and found it perfectly sweet, even where the thermometers had been inserted. This was one hundred and twenty-three hours after being removed from the freezing chamber. The unfrozen mutton was also quite sweet. This morning our thermometers registered 58.34 degrees [Fahrenheit]. It seemed hardly worth while to watch the keeping longer, since one hundred hours would be ample to allow it for sale and distribution in England, and place it, under equal conditions of temperature, &c., on a level, at least, with any fresh butcher-meat.

John I. Bleasdale, D.D.

Memorandum

Public Library, Museums, &c., Melbourne,

2nd June, 1873.

We, the undersigned, having partaken of a saddle of mutton and ribs of beef, preserved by Mr. Harrison's freezing process, desire to state that we have found the meat in admirable condition, not only palatable, but absolutely indistinguishable from fresh meat.

We are of opinion that if meat can be landed in England in the same condition as that eaten by us, the English purchaser can partake of a joint of mutton or beef absolutely as good in every way as the best of freshly-killed meat procurable from his own butcher.

(Signed)

HENRY AMSINCK, Capt. R.N.,

WILLIAM GIILBEE, Surgeon-Major, V.V.,

GEORGE HARRISON, Capt., R.N., Melbourne Club,

J. COSMO NEWBERRY, Superintendent Technological Museum,

MARCUS CLARKE, Secretary to the Trustees of the Public Libraries, Museums, &c., Melbourne,

W. F. STEPHENS, Lieut.-Colonel,

JOHN I. BLEASDALE, D.D., F.G.S., Honorary Member of the Medical Society of Victoria, &c., &c.

The report from which I have just read was not published until after I left the colony; but I have some information still more recent to afford, and it is news even to myself. When I came away I left some pieces of meat in the chamber which was still standing in the Exhibition building. I had left the meat to take its chance, as I had more important business in hand. I merely left instructions that it should be removed before the ice had melted. Dr. Bleasdale, in his anxiety to make his investigation as complete as possible, intercepted some of the meat when in course of removal, and subjected it to experiment, in order to ascertain if the frozen meat was available for being salted. In a letter to the newspapers he records the result: –

While there had been obtained abundance of evidence upon the safeness of the process as a preservative one, and also that on arrival in Great Britain or India there would be more than sufficient time for its distribution or transmission by railway to outlying towns or stations, there yet remained one point unsettled, and by no means the least important, viz., would the flesh when thawed take salt? It is obvious that if it could be salted the wholesale purchaser would be secured against ultimate waste, as there is always a market for salt meat. In the study of other circumstances this one was overlooked to the very last, and it was only after Mr. Harrison had sailed for England with his large experiment that it occurred to me to think of salting. I succeeded in obtaining all I required for this purpose from the person to whom Mr. Harrison had entrusted the removal and disposal of the meat remaining at the Exhibition buildings. It should in all fairness be stated that during the fortnight preceding the sailing of the ship *Norfolk*, Mr. Harrison had wholly neglected the preserving chamber, so that the meat was hardly protected at all, yet it was found to be sound after having been opened twice during the ninety-two days that had elapsed since it was first frozen. I took for the purpose of this investigation a large rib of beef and a leg of mutton that had been cut into in several places some days before, and caused them to be put in salt without saltpetre. It was left in salt seven clear days, and took it most perfectly, the beef even more severely than the mutton. On the 31st July, the undermentioned gentlemen partook of it, and have left the subjoined expression of their opinions as to the success of this last stage of the study and investigation.

JOHN I. BLEASDALE, D.D.

The Public Library, 31st July, 1873.

We, the undersigned, having this day partaken of a portion of a leg of mutton and ribs of beef, salted, preserved by Mr. Harrison's freezing process, wish to state that we found the meat palatable, wholesome, and in no way inferior to that of an animal killed and salted by a butcher in the ordinary course of his trade. The meat of which we partook has been preserved, frozen, and then thawed eighty-five days, and had then been subsequently seven full days in salt without saltpetre – in all ninety-two days. If therefore Mr. Harrison can, with profit to himself, supply meat to the tables of English buyers in the same condition as that which we have now tasted, there can be, in our opinion, no doubt whatever of the commercial success of his invention.

(Signed)
ROBERT SIMSON.
CHARLES RYAN.
A. R. WALLIS.
MARCUS CLARKE.
JOHN J. SHILLINGLAW.
J. COSMO NEWBERY.
JNO. B. HUGHES.
W. F. STEPHENS, LT.-COL.
JOHN I. BLEASDALE, D.D.

In conclusion, it has been suggested to me that I should make some experiments, either in the preservation of meat in England, or in bringing meat from Texas, Brazil, or the Black Sea before my departure for Australia. I can only say that I shall be happy to cooperate in any experiments that may be suggested. I do not require to make any experiment for my own satisfaction; but, of course, I have not encountered adversity, in the shape of an apparent failure, without learning some precious lessons, and I shall be very glad to put them to the proof. I do not, however, propose to give any exposition of further improvements; my object in reading this paper being merely to point out what has been done; and with respect to what may yet be done I will pay regard to Mr. Anthony Trollope's advice to Australians generally, and Victorians particularly – 'Don't blow'.

Note

1 In support of his claim to be considered well-fitted to investigate the subject, Mr. Harrison read the following note from Professor Tyndall, which he had just received: – 'Mr. Harrison. Dear Sir, – I clearly remember accompanying Professor Faraday on a visit of inspection to your ice machine; and I have an equal recollection of the pleasure we both experienced in witnessing the performance of the machine. I afterwards experimented with the machine myself; and from first to last was impressed with the honesty and the thoroughness with which you had worked out your problem. That the machine has many useful applications as regards the preservation of meat I do not for a moment doubt. In expressing this opinion I believe myself to be aiding a worthy man and a worthy invention. – Yours truly, JOHN TYNDALL'.

55

'REFRIGERATION AND PRESERVATION'

Cassell's Family Magazine (1879), p. 189

Refrigeration and preservation

A new process of refrigeration has been invented, by the application of which animal food, fruit, and vegetables may be imported and preserved for a considerable time without injury or decay. To produce in any given substance a great heat by artificial means has never been a serious matter, but to reduce temperature downwards to any considerable or useful degree has always been a process attended with much difficulty. Nevertheless, there have existed urgent demands for such a process in the pursuit of various industries, and although many systems were in use, none were found to answer all requirements. A well-known firm of importers of American meat have during the last three months, by their system of refrigeration, imported no less than eight millions of pounds of animal food from America. Their plan was to fix up the chamber of dead meat with ice, and cause a fan-blast, driven by a small steam-engine, to maintain a constant circulation of air over and through the ice, which supplied a uniformly low temperature throughout the whole compartment. But this method, admirable though it is, was not all that could be desired, for the air thus blown over the ice was so necessarily laden with moisture that most of the meat became damp, and consequently unsaleable. The inventors have, therefore, patented in Great Britain, United States, Canada, Germany, and France the refrigerating apparatus shown in the accompanying engraving. This apparatus consists of two horizontal steam cylinders, with their pistons connected by the usual connecting rods to cranks upon a shaft at right angles to each other. The piston-rods of the air cylinders are also carried through the cylinder-ends, and are connected to a double-acting air-pump. There are two air-expansion cylinders fitted upon the same sole-plate, and between the air-pump and steam cylinder, and the piston-rods are attached to the same crank-shaft as the steam piston, and have cranks set at different angles. The piston-rods of the air cylinders are also carried through the cylinder-ends, each having a double-action of the same capacity as those driven by the steam cylinders attached to it. With two cold-water pumps these comprise the working part of the whole apparatus. When working, the machine extracts air out of the meat chamber by the aid of its air-pumps, and in them it is compressed, in contact with a small injection of cold

 DOI: 10.4324/9781315400303-81

water, to about 30 lbs. per square inch. From a communication we have received from one of the patentees, we gather that the Anchor Line steamers are already being fitted with this apparatus, and that several practical tests have been made, which have resulted in proving the invention to be perfect in every way. No alterations have been found requisite, and in making the tests no single hitch occurred, which proves that both theoretically and practically the invention is a success. May we not, therefore, expect in the future, by the aid of this system of preservation, fruits, animal food, vegetables, and other produce of the earth placed on our tables whenever they may be required, whether in or out of season, and also expect to see the same apparatus extended to the further use of ventilating and cooling our concert-halls and various other public buildings?

6.3

Roller skate

6.3 Roller skate

'Skating Rinks and Rinkomania', *Cassell's Family Magazine* (1875), pp. 304–306.
J. A. Harwood, *Rinks and Rollers* [extract] (London: Routledge, [1876]), pp. 13–20.

The earliest roller skates date to the eighteenth century. But the Victorians continued to improve skates. In 1863, the American James Leonard Plimpton patented the quad-wheel skate, and over the next decade the first toe stops appeared on roller skates, while British skate-makers helped to create the modern wheel design. Moreover, in the same decade, Victorian Britain built the first roller skating rinks and experienced what the press called 'rinkomania', a sudden fad for roller rinks and skates. Like the bicycle, roller skates promised health and leisure, especially to the young and the physically bold. Young people might also take advantage of a roller rink's potential for unchaperoned sociability – another explanation for the rinkomania of the era. Perhaps, also like the bicycle, roller skates would someday provide efficient personal transport, suggests the writer of 'Skating Rinks and Rinkomania' in *Cassell's Family Magazine*, at least once the government stepped in to create skateable paths everywhere.[1]

Note

1 The most thorough account of roller skating as sport and pastime is by James Turner and Michael Zaidman, *The History of Roller Skating* (Lincoln, NE: National Museum of Roller Skating, 1997).

56

'SKATING RINKS AND RINKOMANIA'

Cassell's Family Magazine (1875), pp. 304–306

When Winter nowadays 'comes to rule the varied year', he must be somewhat surprised to find that skaters, whom he has hitherto patronised, can do without him. Skating is now altogether independent of weather: it can be enjoyed in the merry month of May, or under the harvest-moon, quite as well as in the keen air of January. All we need is a properly constructed skating-rink and a pair of roller-skates.

The term 'rink', by the way, has a curious history. It has for ages been applied in Scotland by curlers to the piece of ice swept clear of snow on which they practise their roaring game. From Scotland, the word was exported to Canada, where it is given to the sheets of smooth ice, under cover, on which our fellow-subjects practise, in their long and windless frosts, such skating feats as are seldom seen in this country. Then 'rink' travelled all over the United States, from New York to San Francisco, as the best possible term for the courts with flooring that looked just like ice touched with hoar-frost, where the new pastime of skating on wheels was enjoyed. It crossed the sea again, and now in England is in everybody's mouth.

The origin of almost all popular amusements is hid in obscurity, and we are unable to lay our finger on the benefactor of his race who first thought of roller-skating. The most we can discover is that about forty years since the public had a wheeled skate offered to them by one Tyers, of Piccadilly. It had five little wheels all in a row, that of the largest diameter being in the middle, and the others diminishing slightly towards the heel and toe. By means of this invention, it was said, 'persons may rapidly glide over any level surface'. The 'drawing-room' skate of modern days appears to be based on the same principle.

The next we hear of wheel-skating is at Dresden, where skating waitresses were introduced at a café. Then, about twenty-five years ago, the famous 'Pas des Patineurs' of *Le Prophète* was brought before the public. But in Meyerbeer's opera moving on wheels seemed at least as difficult as walking on stilts; not unfrequently one of the dancers lost control of her skates, and was carried forward almost into the orchestra.

It is only within the last few years that the pastime of roller-skating has become popular. The credit of its present position is due in a great measure to Mr. Plimpton,

DOI: 10.4324/9781315400303-83

of New York, who has invented a 'Circular Running Roller Skate', of ingenious mechanical construction, by which a new era has been opened up for skaters.

The skate consists of four wheels about two inches in diameter, and three-quarters of an inch in width, two parallel wheels being at the toe and the other two at the heel. These wheels are so hung on pivots that their axles are moved out of parallel by the transverse rocking of the skater's foot, the wheels setting squarely on the surface, whether the skater be upright or 'canted'. In this way, to whatever angle the skater may incline, the wheels will 'cramp' or turn so as to describe the curve consistent with his inclination.

Everything that can be done with the ordinary ice-skates can be accomplished with the Plimpton skates. Both allow of 'twelve fundamental movements', and consequently of nearly five hundred million 'combination movements'. When one has mastered the balance, he may betake himself at the rink to practising all the mysteries of outside edges and cross rolls, backwards and forwards, threes and double threes, serpentine lines and grape-vines, continuous eights, spread eagles, and what not. Nothing in the beautiful art of figure-skating need be set down as impossible.

The exertion of skating with roller-skates is trifling. 'Compared with ordinary skating on ice', says one authority, 'one would have thought that the friction of four wheels on an unslippery surface would have demanded much extra exertion; whereas the fact is that on a wooden floor the roller-skates save nearly a quarter of the expenditure of physical strength, and on a concrete floor one-tenth'.

Roller-skates were first patented by Mr. Plimpton in 1863: subsequently he secured rights in every country in which patent laws exist. We are informed that it took him fifteen years to perfect his invention. One of his great difficulties was to settle what the wheels were to be made of. Woods and metals of all sorts, bone, ivory, and a host of other substances were tried. Box-wood was at last chosen, it being found that it best suited both wooden and other artificial ice-flooring. As is the case with all good things, Mr. Plimpton's success has conjured up a host of imitators. Before his patent there were only nine patents in England, France, and America for roller-skates; there are now at least fifty-five.

Every rink has its own flooring, and the question is not yet settled as to what sort is absolutely the best. It is said that Mr. Plimpton prefers wood. The skating-rink at Paris is made by first laying down a layer of concrete, and on that two layers of asphalte, so that the rink is nearly a foot in thickness. The largest skating-rink in London, that of the Royal Avenue, Chelsea, is composed of Portland cement and concrete, laid down to the depth of ten inches, and over this is placed a hard firm substance, which forms the skating surface. Mixtures of crystallised salts have been tried for rink-floorings, but with little success; metal surfaces have fared no better.

The skating-rink presents a very different scene to the frozen loch with its real ice and wintry surroundings. There is no sitting down on a rock by the water-side to put on one's skates; no rapid motion through the frosty air; and there are no blue, chill, starved-looking spectators, blowing their fingers to keep them warm.

But the artificial ice of the rink is as good, for all practical purposes, as if it were the result of a long and steady frost, whilst skaters are spared anxiety about either a thaw or a fall of snow. There is also no danger at a skating-rink of their being drowned.

Every one knows the sharp sound that rises from a loch covered with skaters. The noise of the rink is not like that. It resembles nothing so much as a thousand easy chairs all being wheeled at once to the fireside. Perhaps a poetical imagination might liken it to the noise of a brook flowing over a bed of pebbles – a sound 'resounding long in listening Fancy's ear'. But a fig for sentiment!

One admirable feature possessed by rink-skating is, that it is as suitable for girls as for men. The former do not learn so fast as the latter, but when they have learned the result is pleasing. A fine, graceful skater of a girl is more worth looking at than a man any day.

The rule appears to be that skaters pursue their way alone and with an awful earnestness. To the enthusiast, skating must ever be, more or less, a solitary amusement: his attention is too much engrossed for him to be playing the part of the cavalier. To the beginner it is of necessity solitary: when he is not gliding over the rink, he is engaged in solving the problem as to the softest way to fall. But flirting, or practising, or learning, no doubt the skating hour is a happy hour with everybody. As some one says, 'The care to maintain one's perpendicular drives away all other care!'

Skating on asphalte is easy to learn, even for those who are not expert at skating on ice. On one of the London rinks, a late Minister of the Crown may be seen practising this new amusement with considerable skill. At an advanced age he has become proficient after only a week or two of instruction. The art of figure-skating, of course, is not to be acquired thoroughly without considerable perseverance. But it is worth taking trouble about.

There has been much outcry in some quarters about the dangers of skating-rinks. We have been told of sprained ankles, twisted shoulders, and not a few broken arms. One skater falls on the back of his head, and not only sees stars, but disorders his intellect; another falls on his face, and breaks his nose. A statistically-minded man was said, some time ago, to have calculated that skating on wheels was twice as dangerous as steeplechasing, and ten times as much so as fox-hunting.

But it is easier to invent rumours than roller-skates. All the talk about the dangers of the rink is highly exaggerated. Of course there is a risk, but so there is in every game worth playing at. 'With care, and a little more provision for teaching', says a well-known medical contemporary, 'the risk is very slight for any persons adapted to the exercise'. That rink-skating is favourable to health when pursued under proper conditions, cannot be denied. One has but to look at the glowing faces and graceful figures of many of the skaters to rest satisfied on this head.

At the same time, people cannot be too careful in their selection of a rink. One can readily understand that there is a strong objection to places, the only passport to which is the payment of a certain fee. A higher principle of selection is absolutely necessary in order to secure the young of either sex from coming within the pernicious influences that otherwise may creep in – unwise companionships too readily formed, and other evils which need not be mentioned here. The only safeguard against these contingencies is a rink formed on the club principle, where the character of every member is guaranteed by a committee, which shall be responsible to the members for every person admitted.

No doubt the recreation is still only in its infancy. There is great room for development. In time we shall have the rinks handsomely decorated, maybe in character, with pines, and holly, and artificial snow: the bands – for a band seems to be a necessary accompaniment to a skating-rink – will always play in tune, which they do not always at present: and fancy dress fêtes, rink-balls, illuminated entertainments, and suchlike gatherings, will then be of common occurrence. And at last, when all members of the community have become proficient in the art, a paternal Government will lay the footwalks in cities and every country road with asphalte [sic], and we shall go skating about our daily business.

57

J. A. HARWOOD, *RINKS AND ROLLERS* [EXTRACT]

(London: Routledge, [1876]), pp. 13–20

Too little attention is paid in these days to the cultivation of the body. A degenerate age looks too much to the culture of the brain and the acquirement of money – both very excellent things, no doubt, but vastly overestimated. The Greeks were wiser, and knew that by exercising both mind and body both are stronger than if either were fostered at the other's expense. It is a great wonder that they did not anticipate Mr. Plimpton's patent. They knew most things, but they were unacquainted even with the practice of skating upon ice. What grand attitudes might we not have had for our imitation at Prince's had Praxiteles sculptured Phryne on wheels, or Apelles painted her so! Would not the Cnidian Venus and the Anadyomene have been improved? And it would have been invaluable to have had such models on which to base our position for the outside edge. But no! It was reserved for Dutch painters – for Teniers and Jan Steen, with their innate sense of ugliness, to hold the mirror up to Nature. And we have no skating statue on the outside edge for the simple reason that no statue could be worthy of its name, that is, be 'made to stand' in that position without an iron rod to support it, which would rather detract from the effect of the figure. But the Greeks attained the height of bodily excellence, taking but little heed of casualties on the march; and though we can never reach their pitch of perfection, we may perhaps get a stride nearer to it on the rink. We shall be at least thereby assisted greatly towards that enviable state of health – the *mens sana in corpore sano*.

Not only to young ladies, who have time enough for other exercises and amusement, but to hard-worked professional men daily exercise on the rink would prove of great benefit. Their time is to them money, and they are unable to take long walks, as Charles Dickens used, to counterbalance their mental toil. He, it is true, overdid it; but within bounds some such relaxation is essential to all who have a great amount of intellectual strain. Riding is frequently prescribed by doctors in such cases, but it is an expensive prescription to get made up, and rinking would sometimes supply the want at a much cheaper rate, and with far less trouble. The cost of such exercise would be about a twentieth part of that on horseback. And even in the short space of a quarter of an hour, if that were all that could be spared, an amount of exertion might be undergone which would not be without a

DOI: 10.4324/9781315400303-84

beneficial effect. Half-a-dozen 'double threes', a succession of 'Canadian eights', and a 'spread eagle' would afford as much exercise and more interest than could be gained by a walk of two miles, and in half the time that would be taken by the walk. Even paterfamilias, who sits at home and grumbles over his port, 'You are all rink-mad!' would be benefited by a little plain-sailing skating, undertaken with due precautions to avoid dangerous consequences arising from the impact of a heavy body against a hard substance. But 'there is no fool like an old one', and probably if he were to trip it on the swift erratic skate, he would exceed the bounds of due discretion, and aim at things unattempted yet on ice or wheels, to the great delight of his undutiful and expectant relations. It would, in fact, suit them 'down to the ground'. Whereupon the unfortunate sire could go home and parody Tom Ingoldsby's last lines somewhat in this manner: –

As I went a-rynkynge, a-rynkynge, a-rynkynge,
Merrie played the bande a tune from 'Giroflé';
There came a youthful wyghte,
With Brown's buckles shynynge bryghte,
And his gallant heart was lyghte,
Free and gaye;
As I went a-rynkynge, he runk upon his waye.

As I went a-rynkynge, a-rynkynge, a-rynkynge,
Badly played the band a Sankeyan melodie.
There was a heavy blowe,
And the gallant youth lay low,
For his skates would faster goe
Far than he;
As I went a-rynkynge, most pitiful to see.

As I went a-rynkynge, a-rynkynge, a-rynkynge,
Merrie played the bande the old Danube 'schön und blau';
A lovely mayde glode bye,
And a gentil swayne was nyghe,
And he breathed many a syghe
And a vowe;
As I went a-rynkynge, her heart was gladsome now.

As I went a-rynkynge, a-rynkynge, a-rynkynge,
Gladly played the bande a most outlandish jygge;
The swayne in his despaire
Caughte hold of her back haire,
Which came off! I declare
'Twas a wygge!
But she went on a-rynkynge, she cared not a fygge.

As I went a-rynkynge, a-rynkynge, a-rynkynge,
Feebly played the bande (they only played for hire);
There came a horrid childe,
With skating weak and wilde,
Yet joyously he smiled
On his sire;
As I went a-rynkynge, him no one did admire.

But I went a-rynkynge, a-rynkynge, a-rynkynge,
And madly played the bande (on that same hire intent);
That joyous smile was gone,
And with faces white and wan,
We both lay the floor upon,
Or cement;
As I went a-rynkynge, in my head there was a dent.

As I laye a-thynkynge, the folks around me rynkynge,
O heavie was my head as it sunk upon my breast,
And before my throbbing eyes
Gleam'd kaleidoscopic skies
And bright stars that seem'd to rise
In the west.

As I laye a-thynkynge, my thynkynge I exprest: –
'Oh, take my skates away!
It boots not to delay,
I am weary of to-day;
I want rest.'

There is another aspect in which to regard this pastime, and that a most important one – namely, the social aspect. People meet at the rink in a way in which they meet nowhere else – I do not mean in collision. They meet others whom they may or may not wish to see, and form acquaintances or cement friendships that may or may not be desirable. Parents frequently frown with cause at the idea of their daughters having any knowledge of the odd folks to whom somehow or other they get introduced while skating; parents also object to the facilities afforded by the rink for meeting unauthorized or forbidden friends and lovers. Now and then, too, the family circle is startled by a young lady not returning home after her morning's exercise, and learns some days afterwards that she went and got married instead on the morning in question. So that it is not surprising that there is a general outcry against the immorality of the thing. Prince's must be put down. The flirtation-ground must be abolished. This cry is of course swelled by those who have been black-balled for the club, and by those who never had any chance of being proposed. These would, it is true, give their ears to belong to it, but as they can't get in, no one else ought to go there.

Alas! There is a little truth in these aspersions. Young people have an imprudent knack of choosing their own partners for life if they get the chance. As a rule girls do not get the chance. But here an opportunity springs up, and they embrace it. They had much better leave the selection of their husbands to other people who know so much more about it, but they will not. Small wonder, then, if parents are furious at seeing one of their most cherished privileges in danger of being wrested from them. Perhaps if they would listen they would hear their offspring reply somewhat to this effect: – that it is better that they who have to live with their husbands should choose them; that if they prefer to be less rich and more happy it is their business; that they cannot form an accurate judgment of a man by dancing with him twice at two balls; that they can do so better by meeting him daily at the rink under sometimes rather trying circumstances; that they are able to converse there more freely than in the crush-room at the Opera, at a dinner-party, or even in the Park; and much more nonsense of that kind.

With regard to the objection that undesirable acquaintances may be formed, it is evident that there is no more reason for speaking to people you meet on the rink than for speaking to people you meet in the street. It is a public place, and the liberty of cutting people you do not intend to know, and of ignoring those you never saw before, is preserved in all its integrity. If all else fails to secure this privilege, you can skate elsewhere. Here is the proper province of chaperons – by tact and watchfulness to avoid unpleasant rencontres, or to neutralize their effect. So much for the objections that may be imported socially into this question.

6.4

Maxim gun

DOI: 10.4324/9781315400303-85

6.4 Maxim gun

'The Maxim Machine Gun', *Chambers's Journal*, 64 (1887), pp. 190–191.
C. H. W. Donovan, *With Wilson in Matabeleland, or Sport and War in Zambesia* [extract] (London: Henry, 1894), pp. 181–184.
'News of the Week' [extract], *The Spectator* (2 Oct. 1897), p. 1.

Writing about inventions and technological things often conveys and promotes a sense of exhilaration in the power of modern ingenuity and progress – even when it comes to the most monstrous sides of Victorian life. After noting the millions of lives lost to the past century of war in 'civilised' countries, a writer for *Chambers's Journal* moves on from 'sentimental' considerations to consider the wonders of the Maxim gun, which had won a gold medal at the 1885 International Inventions Exhibition in South Kensington. Invented by the American-born Briton Hiram Maxwell, this weapon was cleverly designed to use its own recoil to eject each spent bullet cartridge and load the next one – a major advance over previous hand-cranked weaponry such as the Gatling gun. In nineteenth-century military thought, machine guns were generally considered to be too murderous and unsportsmanlike for use against armies of white soldiers. But beginning with the First Matabele War in what is now Zimbabwe (1893–1894), British forces used them to kill and especially to terrify native forces who resisted imperial dominion, as these readings indicate. Indeed, machine guns soon became both instruments and symbols of turn-of-the-century imperialism. Maxim himself was knighted for his services to the empire.

The final source in this section is a report on the Tirah campaign (1897–1898), which aimed to subdue a revolt by the Afridi tribal people near the Khyber Pass in modern day Pakistan. The *Spectator* piece celebrates the use of the Maxim to 'shatter' the enemy forces, but it decries another, older Victorian technology: the 'over-detailed telegrams' that circulated on the imperial telegraph lines, messages that supposedly muddled official orders and alarmed the public by providing too much information. As a result of this now mundane technology of communication, it claims, London quickly hears the details of every far-off skirmish and the name of every British soldier killed or wounded, and this excessive level of detail from a remote imperial outpost undermines military 'audacity'. This information overload in Great Britain offers a remarkable but unremarked contrast to the indiscriminate use of the Maxim gun to kill nameless, numberless, indigenous fighters across the British Empire.[1]

Note

1 On the invention, history and impact of machine guns, see John Ellis, *The Social History of the Machine Gun* (Baltimore, MD: Johns Hopkins University Press, 1986[1975]); Anthony Smith, *Machine Gun: The Story of the Men and the Weapon That Changed the Face of War* (London: Piatkus, 2002). An exhaustive and well-illustrated history of the machine guns used by the British military is provided by John Hutchins, *Death Rattle: The British Soldier's Machine Gun 1870 to 2015* (Woking, Surrey: Tommy Atkins Media, 2016).

58

'THE MAXIM MACHINE GUN'

Chambers's Journal, 64 (1887), pp. 190–191

Statisticians inform us that the entire loss of life in wars between so-called civilised countries from the year 1793 down to 1877 has reached the enormous amount of four million four hundred and seventy thousand. To many persons these figures convey a sad and salutary lesson. On the other hand, there are many who act as if they heeded or knew them not. Readers will differ as to whether it is laudable or otherwise to invent any means by which the above figures might possibly be increased; but, leaving the sentimental part of the subject aside, all will readily unite in admiring the wonderful mechanism which makes the Maxim Machine Gun an engine of terrible destructiveness. Particular interest attaches to it at the present time owing to the fact that the great African explorer, Stanley, provided himself with this formidable weapon, to be used defensively in the expedition on which he recently started for the relief of Emin Bey. Moreover, it obtained a gold medal at the Inventions Exhibition, and has been approved of, if not actually adopted, by many governments, the Chinese government being particularly mentioned as one of the largest purchasers.

Its rate of firing – six hundred rounds a minute – is at least three times as rapid as that of any other machine gun. It has only a single barrel, which, when the shot is fired, recoils a distance of three-quarters of an inch on the other parts of the gun. This recoil sets moving the machinery which automatically keeps up a continuous fire at the extraordinary rate of ten rounds a second. Each recoil of the barrel has therefore to perform the necessary functions of extracting and ejecting the empty cartridge, of bringing up the next full one and placing it in its proper position in the barrel, of cocking the hammer and pulling the trigger. As long as the firing continues, these functions are repeated round after round in succession. The barrel is provided with a water jacket, to prevent excessive heating; and is so mounted that it can be raised or lowered or set at any angle, or turned horizontally to the left or to the right. The bore is adapted to the present size of cartridges; and the maximum range is eighteen hundred yards. The gun can therefore be made to sweep a circle upwards of a mile in radius.

Nor is the gun excessively heavy, its total weight being only one hundred and six pounds, made up thus: Tripod, fifty pounds; pivot (on which the gun turns and by which it is attached to the tripod), sixteen pounds; gun and firing mechanism,

DOI: 10.4324/9781315400303-86

forty pounds. The parts can be easily detached and conveniently folded for carriage, and may be put together again so quickly that if the belt containing the cartridges is in position, the first shot can be delivered within ten seconds. It would therefore be extremely serviceable in preventing disaster through a body of troops being surprised. Reconnoitring parties, too, would deem it prudent to pay greater deference to an enemy's lonely sentry on advanced outpost duty, if the latter were provided with this new Machine Gun, instead of the ordinary rifle.

Immediately below the barrel of the gun, a box is placed, containing the belt which carries the cartridges. The belts vary in length. Those commonly used are seven feet long, and capable of holding three hundred and thirty-three cartridges; shorter ones hold one hundred and twenty cartridges; but the several pieces can be joined together for continuous firing. Single shots can be fired at any time whether the belt is in position or not – in the former case by pressing a button, which prevents the recoil; in the latter, by hand-loading in the ordinary way. To start firing, one end of the belt is inserted in the gun, the trigger is pulled by the hand once, after which the movement becomes continuous and automatic as long as the supply of cartridges lasts. At each recoil of the barrel, the belt is pushed sufficiently onward to bring the next cartridge into position; the mechanism grasps this cartridge, draws it from the belt, and passes it on to the barrel. Should a faulty or an empty cartridge find its way in, and the gun does not go off in consequence, there is of course no recoil to keep up the repeating action, and the mechanism ceases to work until the obstruction is removed.

So long as nations continue to vie with each other for superiority in these engines of destruction, so long will the skilled mechanic be found willing to employ his inventive faculties, and exchange the fruits thereof for the princely rewards that await him. This latest invention is probably unsurpassable in rapidity of fire, and apparently leaves nothing to be desired; but of course its real value can only be determined in actual warfare. To devise and adjust the necessary parts of the machine with such precision that each part performs its proper function at the exact moment pre-arranged for it – to do all this while the gun fires at the enormous rate of six hundred rounds a minute, must have cost an immensity of thought, of labour, and of time.

Mr Maxim, the inventor, is well known in the electrical world for his useful additions to the carefully adjusted machinery required for electric lighting and kindred purposes.

59

C. H. W. DONOVAN, *WITH WILSON IN MATABELELAND, OR SPORT AND WAR IN ZAMBESIA* [EXTRACT]

(London: Henry, 1894), pp. 181–184

The most important part of the preparations for war was the drilling of men to use and manage the Maxim guns, which we knew we were to have the honour of being the first to put to a practical test. They had been tried before on several occasions with varying success; but in this case we were staking our lives on their power and efficiency. It has been calculated that each gun is worth two hundred men; but surely it is worth more, for it does not require two hundred horses to transport it – six are sufficient. Nor is there the necessity of providing rations for two hundred men and the same number of horses, together with the wagons for carrying these rations, and animals, which must also be fed, for drawing the wagons. It must be remembered that each additional wagon extra to those absolutely required for forming the laager is only an encumbrance to the column; and of course the more numerous the wagons, the longer it takes to form the laager, and consequently the greater the advantage to the enemy, if he attacks.

The great drawback to the Maxim is the quantity of ammunition it requires to keep it properly fed during a lengthy engagement; the transport of the vast quantities of ammunition both for machine guns and magazine rifles will be a serious consideration in all future wars. It seems to me that the chief concern of commanders will be to keep the firing line supplied with fuel in the shape of cartridges; and when the ammunition-wagons have unloaded, the 'returned empties' will be a source of inconvenience, though I am sure that the Transport branch of the Army Service Corps will grapple successfully with the difficulty when the time comes. For all these reasons, it is fortunate that the cartridges for the new Magazine Rifle are so small and light.

Captain Lendy was careful to instruct all his men not only in the theory of the Maxim, but also in the use of the various parts of its terribly complicated Chinese-puzzle of a lock; and this to such an extent that not only was each man able to take a lock to pieces, but he could also put it together again in a very few minutes. He thoughtfully provided each gun with a spare lock, so that if anything went wrong,

DOI: 10.4324/9781315400303-87

the original lock could be taken out, and the spare one used during its repair, and thus prevent the gun being out of action for any length of time. He also arranged for the supply of several spare main-springs and other parts most liable to get out of order or damaged.

Each gun was mounted on its own carriage, and carried its tripod. And we had a couple of pack-saddles to put them on, for easier and more speedy transport, in case we should have to go where wheels could not travel.

60

'NEWS OF THE WEEK' [EXTRACT]

The Spectator (2 Oct. 1897), p. 1

The accounts from the Indian frontier are encouraging both in general and in detail. The general result is that with the new big guns, the fire of shrapnel and the Maxims, and the new use of cavalry in pursuit, the British are much better armed for mountain warfare than they ever were before. The clansmen suffer heavily in all attacks on our troops, and their sangars, or stone stockades, are no longer tenable, so that we waste ammunition instead of lives in carrying them. This great change of itself is fatal to the mountaineers, who obviously after each brush lose heart, and offer terms, often inadequate, but still terms. On September 22nd General Westmacott's brigade carried the Bedmanai Pass, as General Elles telegraphed, 'beautifully', storming the hills, upon which the enemy, as they retreated, were shattered by the fire of the Maxims. The two most prominent Moollahs, the Mad Moollah and the White Moollah, were present, and fled, like their followers, in dismay, and it is believed that the total result will be the submission of the Northern tribes. Fragments of them are coming in, but they resist the order to disarm, and the Government so distrusts them that the victorious brigade which was to have gone south to join Sir William Lockhart has been ordered to remain. The Afridis in their hills south-east of Peshawur have still to be subdued, but Sir William Lockhart, with a more than adequate force, will commence his attack on October 3rd. The Afridis must fight or be dishonoured, but the new artillery will be too much for them, and we expect before the end of October a general, though sullen, submission. They must, of course, accept the building of forts to command their valleys, and must aid actively in the making of roads.

The improved artillery is our strong point, but some weak points come out in the over-detailed telegrams. The clansmen are better armed than they were, and whenever they have an advantage, follow it up very boldly. The orders from Simla change every day with unusual indecision, as if the central authority were badly informed or yielded now to this opinion and then to that, and the number of men employed is everywhere large beyond precedent. That may be wise, but it points to a hesitation unusual in Indian history, and will, of course, greatly increase the cost of the campaign. With Sir William Lockhart in the field, however, hesitation will disappear, and he will probably not only defeat, but subjugate, the Afridis, who are already disheartened, and have applied for aid to the Ameer, which was

DOI: 10.4324/9781315400303-88

curtly refused. Abdurrahman Khan sees how things are going, and is while we triumph heartily on our side. It must not be forgotten that the daily telegrams with the lists of killed and wounded greatly increase the apparent importance of very small engagements. Formerly officers and men were expended like shells, and only results were recorded, but today London is looking as through a spy-glass at each operation. That change increases carefulness, but it also decreases the old audacity. The Generals will risk anything except London comments on a reverse.

INDEX